MILTON STUDIES

XXIV

MILTON STUDIES

XXIV ❧ Edited by

James D. Simmonds

UNIVERSITY OF PITTSBURGH PRESS

MILTON STUDIES

is published annually by the University of Pittsburgh Press as a forum for Milton scholarship and criticism. Articles submitted for publication may be biographical; they may interpret some aspect of Milton's writings; or they may define literary, intellectual, or historical contexts — by studying the work of his contemporaries, the traditions which affected his thought and art, contemporary political and religious movements, his influence on other writers, or the history of critical response to his work.

Manuscripts should be upwards of 3,000 words in length and should conform to the *MLA Style Sheet*. Manuscripts and editorial correspondence should be addressed to James D. Simmonds, Department of English, University of Pittsburgh, Pittsburgh, Pa. 15260.

Milton Studies does not review books.

Within the United States, *Milton Studies* may be ordered from the University of Pittsburgh Press, Pittsburgh, Pa. 15260.

Overseas orders should be addressed to Feffer and Simons, Inc., 100 Park Avenue, New York, N.Y. 10017, U.S.A.

Library of Congress Catalog Card Number 69-12335

ISBN 0-8229-3591-0

US ISSN 0076-8820

Published by the University of Pittsburgh Press, Pittsburgh, Pa. 15260

Copyright © 1989, University of Pittsburgh Press

Feffer & Simons, Inc., London

Manufactured in the United States of America

CONTENTS

MILTON STUDIES

XXIV

YOUNG MILTON'S EQUIPMENT FOR LIVING: *L'ALLEGRO* AND *IL PENSEROSO*

Greg W. Zacharias

MILTON'S CRITICS have differed about the poet's motive for writing *L'Allegro* and *Il Penseroso*. Formal criticism of the poems has produced a great deal of valuable scholarship which helps us understand Milton's use of the poetic elements. By explaining the elements that make up the poems, these critics enrich our understanding of the meanings of those elements, then of the poems. Yet because criticism of the poems' formal elements forces the critic to consider his own poetic element, excised from the poem, to be significant, the formal critic tends to confuse his motif for Milton's motive. One formal critic who studies the light and dark images in the twin poems concludes that the poems are "about" Day and Night.[1] The serial critics reason that since Milton worked deliberately over the course of his career to complete the Virgilian *rota*, and that because the general movement of these two poems seems to parallel in light, dark, and other images, that progress of poetic living, then Milton's motive for writing the poems was to represent a plan for his career as an epic poet. The serialist approach to the poems moves closer to touching Milton's motive because these critics are willing to use biographical evidence in order to help them explain the poetry.[2] But the serial conception of the poems necessarily subordinates *L'Allegro* to *Il Penseroso* morally as well as poetically. This subordination forces Milton to make an unfair and unlikely choice between two ways of living. By giving moral value to the intellectual and isolated Il Penseroso, the serial view of the poems debases the sensuous and social L'Allegro. Evidence in Milton's writing outside the two poems, especially *Early Prolusion*, the *Sixth Prolusion*, a letter to Diodati, *The Reason of Church-Government*, *Of Education*, *Tetrachordon*, and Book IV of *Paradise Regained*, suggests that Milton himself believed in the complementarity of leisure to work, sense to intellect, and society to contemplation rather than in the subordination of one to the other.[3]

Kenneth Burke's "language as symbolic action" provides a critical strategy that is especially suited to the demands and problems of investigating the poet's motive for *L'Allegro* and *Il Penseroso*. A "dramatis-

3

tic" (Burke's term) way of reading them respects their nature as dramatic lyrics through personae which take poetic form from Milton's own drama of living. Because Burke's method rests on an investigation of the poet's relation to his poem, it enables us to test provisional dramatistic readings of the poems by comparing patterns of action and gesture within *L'Allegro* and *Il Penseroso* to analogous patterns of action and gesture, often expressed more explicitly, in the poet's writing elsewhere. Burke's technique applies well to Milton because the poet's habit of putting himself into his work allows us to test the validity of hypotheses drawn from a Burkean reading of the poems against Milton's words elsewhere concerning that hypothetical subject. The hypothetical subjects dramatized through the symbolic action of *L'Allegro* and *Il Penseroso* are leisure and work, the senses and the intellect, and their proper relation. Burke's language as symbolic action is a critical strategy that could help interpret *L'Allegro* and *Il Penseroso* by emphasizing the relation of the poet's motive — what the poems are "about" — to dramatic performance rather than formal poetic elements. Burke writes: "As far as possible, one should not treat a play [or a poem] as "about" religion or fate, and such (in the sense of being contributions to theology, science, history, and the like), but as *using* religion, or fate or revolt and such for the production of poetic effects."[4] The consequence of Burke's statement for *L'Allegro* and *Il Penseroso* is that we should not study the formal elements of the poems if our purpose is to investigate Milton's motivation to write the poems. If we want to examine Milton's motivation, we ought to investigate the way Milton uses formal elements in the poems to express symbolically his way of responding to situations in life which involve concerns analogous to the dramatic action of *L'Allegro* and *Il Penseroso*.

Burke develops his method from the following assumption: "If man is characteristically the symbol-using animal, then he should take pleasure in the use of his powers as a symbolizer, just as a bird presumably likes to fly or a fish to swim."[5] He explores the relation of the symbol used to the motive of the symbol user:

However, complications arise secondarily. Even if you would write a drama, for instance, simply for the satisfaction of writing a drama, you must write your drama about *something*. . . . These subjects involve tensions, or problems — and since you can't make a drama without the use of some situation marked by *conflict*, even though you hypothetically began through a sheer love of dramatic exercise, in the course of so exercising you tend to use as your subject matter such tensions or problems as exercise yourself, or your potential audience, or mankind in general.[6]

The area of connection Burke points out between biography and symbolic action marks the area of investigation I will examine between Milton's strategy for living and his twin poems.

The "new historicist" criticism is broadly similar in conception to that of Burke. Both methods share an interest in self-critical methodology, biography, history, sociology, and patterns of poetic tension in order to interpret the work of a poet. Both methods employ the vocabulary of drama and performance.[7] But where the historicist interprets the patterns of expression in the work of a poet by means of the work's cultural-historical-literary context, the Burkean method seeks to explain patterns of symbolic action in the narrower context of the poet's other work. In the case of Milton's *L'Allegro* and *Il Penseroso*, a Burkean approach provides a better tool for explaining what the poems are about because so much of Milton's own poetry and prose is available as symbolic context for the language of these individual poems.

In "Literature as Equipment for Living," Burke concentrates on the "active nature" of all literature.[8] He advances his argument through a discussion of the way proverbs, and by extension poetry, help us cope with the problems and pleasures of daily life: "People have often commented on the fact that there are contrary *proverbs*. But I believe that the above approach to proverbs suggests a necessary modification of that comment. The apparent contradictions depend upon differences in *attitude*, involving a correspondingly different choice of strategy."[9] Discussing definitions of "strategy" as a military word and relating the definitions to his approach to proverbs, Burke continues: "One seeks to 'direct the larger movements and operations' in one's campaign of living. One 'maneuvers,' and the maneuvering is an 'art.'"[10] The artful strategy for living that I read as young Milton's primary motive in the twin poems is one he developed to cope with all kinds of experience in order to direct, at an especially vulnerable time in his life, the movement of his career. In addition, Milton supplies a strategy for living from which his readers could profit. Whether soft or severe, didacticism is a usual characteristic of Milton's writing. According to the "active nature" of poetic language, Milton's twin poems operate as proverbs and make themselves available for a Burkean analysis. Such a reading would not be biographical in the narrow sense. It sees the twin poems as an emerging product of a young poet's developing vision of living.

Closest to my reading of *L'Allegro* and *Il Penseroso* is Thomas M. Greene's "The Meeting Soul in Milton's Companion Poems." Greene finds complementarity between *L'Allegro* and *Il Penseroso* through a common pattern of action which he calls "retrospective internalization."[11] Also in common with the Burkean method, Greene examines the patterns of action of each speaker as a way to understand Milton's meaning in the poems. Greene remarks: "Both poems seem intermittently to want to pull away from the alert wakefulness of daylit humanity, as though their speakers envied 'the immortal mind that hath forsook / Her mansion in this fleshly nook' (P 91–92)."[12] Greene identifies behind the poems "an invisible third presence who is tempted by each but committed to neither."[13] But where the Burkean method actively pursues the relation of the poet to the poem's meaning, Greene probes lightly. Burke's approach comes equipped with a critical method that enables us to make reasoned speculations on the meaning of the poems through the poet Milton, the significant "third presence" behind L'Allegro and Il Penseroso.

As soon as we recognize Milton's habit of putting himself into his work, and if we are willing to use Milton's other writing to help us explain the patterns of movement and gesture in the twin poems, the stage is set for a dramatistic reading and exploration of L'Allegro and Il Penseroso in terms of this motive: that in L'Allegro and Il Penseroso the young Milton is writing about his struggle to maintain a special internal order that would nourish both mind and body in order to support what the poet articulates later as the "whole man."[14] The Burkean method gives us a critical tool we may use to learn how Milton thought about the relation of the intellect to the senses and contemplative isolation to society in other texts which then operate as Miltonic reference points to explain the dramatistic expression in L'Allegro and Il Penseroso.

The differences between L'Allegro and Il Penseroso have been well documented and discussed.[15] Yet the similarities between the two speakers' patterns of action, which a Burkean reading allows us to recognize, have not been treated as completely as the differences. The similarities between the two speakers' patterns of action underline the complementarity of the poems and their subjects, provide a way of finding Milton's role behind the poems, and help us interpret Milton's motive for writing L'Allegro and Il Penseroso.

Milton demonstrates throughout his works the important circular relation and chain of mutual dependence of nature to feelings to imagination to contemplation of ideas (ideals) to morality and full humanness to art to God and back to nature. As the narrator in Paradise Regained comments, "Nature taught Art."[16] In this system each element of the nature-art cycle contributes to the vitality of the entire circuit and to the rich wholeness of human life. Milton expresses that circuit through symbolic language in L'Allegro and Il Penseroso.

A dramatistic reading of *L'Allegro* and *Il Penseroso* shows us that both speakers desire to free their minds from anything that would interfere with the goal at hand. This reading adds to the criticism of the poems that from Dr. Johnson to Thomas M. Greene has noted similarities between the attitudes of the two speakers. The reading also shows us that as the structure of images of both poems constitutes a circuit of light and dark and of action and intellection, so the artful attitudes expressed by each speaker through the poetic elements of his poem work together to complete a circuit of symbolic action which casts light on the poet's motive.

The mirthful and the melancholic speaker each attempts to determine his own state of mind. At dawn a contemplative L'Allegro banishes melancholy in order to feel more intensely with an unburdened mind nature's impressions. What is interesting and significant in the first ten lines of *L'Allegro* is that the mirthful man orders Melancholy to get away from him and into an "uncouth" or unfamiliar cell. One inference I draw from the command is that the cell from which L'Allegro banishes Melancholy at the outset of the poem is a usual or at least regular haunt of the loathed one. In the evening an active Il Penseroso banishes spontaneous L'Allegran responses and attraction to nature and society in order to give fully his disciplined attention to the intellectual world. The efforts of both speakers are most apparent in the first ten lines of their poems. There they prepare themselves to assume their characteristic attitudes by redirecting their imaginative powers. Both speakers display skillful self-control which allows each of them to determine his own attitude and attain most efficiently the pleasure he desires. L'Allegro shows us how he relaxes in order to experience the world through his five senses, assisted by his imagination. Il Penseroso shows us how he gathers, intensifies, and concentrates his mind in order to pierce the barrier of the printed page and enter imaginatively into it.

Dr. Johnson points out that evening links the poems because at that time of the poem's day we see most clearly the melancholy in L'Allegro's mirth.[17] Seeing the poems as a circuit of dramatic action establishes dawn, in addition to evening, as a second temporal link between *L'Allegro* and *Il Penseroso* and allows us to recognize that as L'Allegro displays melancholy at evening, so at morning does Il Penseroso seek mildly sensual L'Allegran pleasures before he sleeps. When Il Penseroso tires, he treats Morpheus's "train" differently than he did in the opening lines when he was preparing to "outwatch the *Bear*" (87). At morning Il Penseroso acts to release himself from the burden of study just as L'Allegro, during his morning, seeks relief from "loathed Melancholy."

As daylight breaks after Il Penseroso's thoughtful night of study, we return to that time of day at which *L'Allegro* opened. Il Penseroso's attention at morning, like his counterpart's, turns from his cramped room to the outdoor world: "To arched walks of twilight groves, / And shadows brown that *Sylvan* loves / Of Pine, or monumental Oake" (CM I, p. 44, 133–35). The speaker in *Il Penseroso* shows us by his mention of Melancholy's conception in "secret shades / Of woody *Ida's* inmost grove" (23–30), of the "twilight groves" (133), of "the Bee with Honied thie" (142), and of the brook's "Waters murmuring" (144) that he too notices and cares about what surrounds him in the physical world—as long as he is not engaged in concentrated intellectual activity. When the melancholic speaker concludes his period of study and seeks "dewy-feather'd Sleep" (146), he allows himself to ask his "sad Virgin" for an uncharacteristically undefined and unrestricted dream "Of lively portrature" (149), curiously like L'Allegro's dream of "Towred Cities" and "busie humm of men" (117–18). From the combination of sense and imagination which Il Penseroso uses to describe his life in his last twenty lines, we learn that the pensive man does not want to exclude either sensuous or intellectual pleasure from his life any more than L'Allegro excludes certain qualities of the pensive man from his own dramatic lyric. Il Penseroso will achieve the "Prophetic strain" by experiencing heavenly ecstasies through intellectual contact with books as well as through the sensuous delights in his world.

Seeing *L'Allegro* and *Il Penseroso* as a poetic drama as well as a structure of discrete words, images, phrases, and lines of poetry helps us see that each speaker focuses all his effort to control the state of his mind and that each speaker exhibits qualities usually associated with the other speaker. Full control of the mental faculties would greatly increase the likelihood that each speaker would achieve his desired goal, either to run free and unburdened through the countryside or to study hard through the night.

The efforts of L'Allegro are, somewhat unexpectedly, primarily intellectual, marking an important realm of common activity with Il Penseroso. L'Allegro follows the physical activity of the opening lines with intense mental activity. This pattern of action must be so because after he directs Mirth to bring to him "The Mountain Nymph, sweet Liberty" (36), L'Allegro does not perform the action of the poem; he imagines it. As L'Allegro imagines what living with Mirth and sweet Liberty would be like, his physical world merges with the one borne in his imagination. At the moment he requests Liberty, he is enabled to go beyond simply thinking about Mirth and Liberty to a kind of imaginative habitation with them. The appearance of the lark at his window is the poetic cue to the convergence of L'Allegro's physical and imaginative worlds because the lark, which exists in the physical world of the poem, also becomes part of the imaginary world of Mirth and Liberty. He imagines what it would be like "To hear the Lark begin his flight" (41). The infinitive "to hear" parallels the previous one, "to live," and we find that while the speaker is able "to live" imaginatively with Mirth, he can actually hear the lark's song and see it on his window sill.

While there is no evidence that the speaker could not see the barnyard, the rising sun, the rural workers, the pleasing landscape, the castle towers, the tufted trees, or the cottage, he would not have the physical capability to see into the cottage. He could only see through the cottage walls by means of a mental act. He places inside the picturesque cottage the typical pair from pastoral literature, Corydon and Thyrsis, animates these figures to action, and allows himself the intellectual pleasure of inventing a history for them. In this early section of the poem, L'Allegro may be said to allow the power of his imagination to act on whatever sights his eyes catch.

In the last section of the poem L'Allegro resumes, in more moderate language, the petition that he has suspended for a hundred lines for Mirth to immerse him in "soft *Lydian* Aires" (136). The result of that apparent digression is to enable him, perhaps like the warbling playwright Shakespeare who had appeared earlier in his dream, to produce "immortal verse" (137) by learning to control his mind and mood and to gather, build, and release by will the poetic force within him in a way that would impress even Orpheus.

Burke's concept of language as symbolic action allows us to see the poems as symbolic, strategic responses to problems in Milton's life. The critical method facilitates an investigation into Milton's motive for writing *L'Allegro* and *Il Penseroso* by giving us an apparatus to map and compare patterns of symbolic action in these poems with patterns in his other poetry and prose.

Milton's motivation to write *L'Allegro* and *Il Penseroso*, like the attitudes of his two speakers, was both serious and pleasurable. There can be no substantial argument against Milton's ultimate seriousness as a poet. A more difficult problem is the relation of Allegran leisure (different from excessive or slothful idleness) to the serious career of a scholar/poet as Milton dramatizes it in the serious speaker of *Il Penseroso*. Milton's words on this relation, in a variety of contexts, are consistent with a dramatistic view of *L'Allegro* and *Il Penseroso* as circular and complementary. Milton's writing on leisure and work outside the twin poems helps us see that *L'Allegro* and *Il Penseroso* could contribute to a single effect, rather than indicating Milton's preference for the experience of Il Penseroso at the expense of that enjoyed by L'Allegro, as a linear or serial, rather than circular and complementary, conception of the poems implies. Milton demonstrates symbolically in his poetry and states directly in his prose that his method of living best requires the individual to control his attitude, either pleasurable or serious, in order to achieve a better life.

In *Early Prolusion*, young Milton relates rather than separates the power of feeling to the power of thinking when he writes that morning is the best time of day both for experiencing the sensuous delights of nature and for study, because in the morning, "'You have wit in readiness'" (CM XII, p. 289). One implication of "readiness" is that Milton recognized early in life the importance of the proper preparation of one's mood or attitude in order to obtain the most one could from both the sensuous delights of nature and the intellectual pleasures of study through books.

In his *Sixth Prolusion*, describing his plan to devote his summer holiday to "scholarly leisure," Milton comments on work and leisure. It is significant that both the contemplative and mirthful attitudes, named in the passage "labor and pleasure," were utilized by the poet in "alternation" for the best living:

When I came back hither recently, fellow students, from that city which is the capital of cities, stuffed, I might almost say, to corpulence with all the pleasures in which that place overflows beyond measure, I hoped I might have again hereafter that literary leisure, a kind of life in which I believe the heavenly spirits rejoice; and there was deeply in my mind a desire now at last to bury myself in literature and to besiege by day and by night most gracious Philosophy: thus always the alternation of labor and pleasure is wont to banish the weariness of satiety and to bring it to pass that things neglected for a while are taken up again most eagerly. (CM XII, p. 205)

To Diodati, Milton distinguishes their different habits of working and, implicitly, their habits of living. Burke's method points out that poets use symbolic language in personal letters and public prose, as well as in their poetry, to "'direct the larger movements and operations' in one's campaign of living."[18] In the following passage Milton expresses the importance of directing the larger movements and operations of one's attitude: "It makes also for my favour that I know your method of studying to be so arranged that you frequently take breath in the middle, visit your friends, write much, sometimes make a journey, whereas my genius is such that no delay, no rest, no care or thought almost of anything, holds me aside until I reach the end I am making for, and round off, as it were, some great period of my studies" (CM XII, p. 19). It is clear from this letter that an essential element in Milton's drive to learn was to take "breaths." But unlike Diodati, Milton could control his breathing by allowing nature and society to inspire him, and then, by "exhaling" that vital breath into bookish ideas, animate them for his ultimate gain as well as our own. If we read the poem dramatistically, we recognize that Il Penseroso, by breathing in this way, is able to "unsphear / The spirit of *Plato* to unfold / What Worlds, or what vast Regions hold" (CM I, p. 43, 88–90).

Tracing Milton's point of view concerning the relation of work and play to one's life after the time he probably wrote our two poems (1631–32) helps us to establish a wider context for the symbolic action the poet expresses in *L'Allegro* and *Il Penseroso*. In *The Reason of Church-Government* (1642), Milton states that the best way to educate the young is through both "recreation & instruction" (CM III, p. 240). Two years later, in *Of Education*, he is more specific. In the section of the pamphlet titled "Their Exercise," after noting that he is following an educational model of the Greeks which "bred up such a number of renowned Philosophers, Orators, Historians, Poets, and Princes," Milton continues:

But to return to our own institute, besides these constant exercises at home, there is another opportunity of gaining experience to be won from pleasure itself abroad; In those vernal seasons of the year, when the air is calm and pleasant, it were an injury and sullenness against nature not to go out and see her riches and partake in her rejoycing with Heaven and Earth. (CM IV, p. 290)

Milton unites "Heaven and Earth" in his composition of a key sentence in the passage, as a Burkean reading of the patterns of action in *L'Allegro* and *Il Penseroso* suggest Milton does in the symbolic action of his circular and complementary poems. The following excerpts from the *Tetrachordon* (1645) function as glosses on the special relationship of leisure to a full development of human faculties and a virtuous life dramatized in *L'Allegro* and *Il Penseroso*:

No mortall nature can endure either in the actions of Religion, or study of wisdome, without sometime slackning the cords of intense thought and labour. . . . *I was*, saith the eternall wisdome, *dayly his delight, playing alwayes before him.* And to him indeed wisdom is as a high towr of pleasure. . . . We cannot therefore always be contemplative or pragmaticall abroad, but have need of som delightfull intermissions, wherein the enlarg'd soul may leav off a while her severe schooling; and like a glad youth in wandring vacancy, may keep her hollidaies to joy and harmless pastime. (CM IV, pp. 85–86)

Finally, in Book IV of *Paradise Regained*, Milton expresses an attitude similar to the one we discover when we read *L'Allegro* as a complement to *Il Penseroso*. Milton's Christ "sagely" addresses his tempter:

> However many books
> Wise men have said are wearisom; who reads
> Incessantly, and to his reading brings not
> A spirit and judgment equal or superior,
> (And what he brings, what needs he elsewhere seek)
> Uncertain and unsettl'd still remains,
> Deep verst in books and shallow in himself,
> Crude or intoxicate, collecting toys,
> And trifles for choice matters, worth a spunge;
> As children gathering pibles on the shore.
>
> (CM II, pp. 470–71, 321–30)

Made over the course of Milton's life, these statements regarding leisure and study — often taken to be the "subjects" or "motifs" (read "motives") of *L'Allegro* and *Il Penseroso* — help us in our reading of the symbolic language of the poems by relating a pattern of experience in the poems with a similar pattern in Milton's life. Burke's method allows us to do this comparison because of its attention to the symbolic nature of language and language's relation to motive. In his writing outside the twin poems Milton not only asserts his belief that together the sensuous and intellectual would contribute to a fuller life for everyone, but, through the symbolic action of his poems, Milton implies that this way of living is fundamental for the epic poet. He demonstrates an effort to expose himself to nature and to deep study. In addition, Milton indicates his commitment to work to control that cycle of exposure in order to convert fully the energy and vitality which he draws from a primary relation with nature into fuel for his poetic imagination. Having gained that special inspiration from nature, the poet can then direct and focus the excitement of imagination and feeling, which *L'Allegro* shows, into his hours of study in order to maintain his enthusiastic concentration and animate those essentially dead ideas he finds in books. *Il Penseroso* does not study Hermes and Plato as an archaeologist studies a past civilization. Like Milton, the pensive man enjoys them as living and life-giving ideas. As Milton has Christ say to Satan in *Paradise Regained*: "he who reigns within himself, and rules / Passions, Desires, and Fears, is more a King; / Which every wise and vertuous man attains" (*PR* II, 466–68). Low writes that "Milton can delight in leisure because he has worked for it, because he is content to seek it not as a permanent state but as a well-earned respite from labor."[19]

Typically arranged, *L'Allegro* precedes *Il Penseroso*. But if we can argue that the poems form a circular, complementary pattern, then we can as well say that *L'Allegro* follows and contributes to *Il Penseroso*. If the attitude of *L'Allegro* contributes to the success of *Il Penseroso*, if feeling excites the pensive man's sympathetic imagination and enables him to project it into what he studies, then the knowledge he gains during his flights of study would help him enter into closer sympathy with nature and society. This is how the attitude of *Il Penseroso* contributes to the success of learned *L'Allegro* and how Milton outlined a successful life. The speaker of *L'Allegro*, after a night of concentrated study like the one depicted in *Il Penseroso*, "rounds-off" that period at dawn instead of ceaselessly projecting his powerful and disciplined mind into his books after the sun begins to rise. *L'Allegro* realizes his control over his imagination and, using his disciplined ability to control and release the focus of his mind, frees it from the narrow range of eye to page and projects it past the vines on his window, past the lark on his ledge, and allows it to explode out of his cell and run freely in the open air. The mental training involved in learning enables him to redirect his imagination as if by force of will and assists his spontaneous mind in the sensuous experience of the outdoor world, not only as a close observer of God's nature, but even through the eyes of the characters he dreams and imagines. Last, while *L'Allegro* never restricts the direction of his imagination until the end of his poem, he gains his greatest freedom by using his mind's eye and learned imagination to help him feel nature more deeply by giving life to and even "living with" those traditional pastoral characters that he must have met first in his reading. As Il Penseroso gives life to Plato by a self-disciplined imagination fired by feelings, so does L'Allegro bring imaginative life to nature by a self-liberated imagination fired and polished by learning.

Together, then, the poems can be read as Milton's attempt as he begins his poetic career to express symbolically his strategy to control the full range of experience, from the sensuousness our parents enjoyed in Eden to the arduous task of trying to recover that individual Paradise which he, and we, take up daily.

New York University

NOTES

I would like to express my gratitude to Dustin Griffin and Anthony Low for the helpful suggestions which they made during the revisions of this essay.

1. E.M.W. Tillyard, "*L'Allegro* and *Il Penseroso*," in *The Miltonic Setting Past and Present* (New York, 1966), pp. 1–28. In addition, Rosemond Tuve, "Structural Figures of *L'Allegro* and *Il Penseroso*," in *Milton: Modern Essays in Criticism*, ed. Arthur E. Barker (New York, 1965), pp. 58–76, improving the work of the "critic of images" (p. 59), sees the poems as structures of images with which Milton intended to convey two kinds of pleasure. J. B. Leishman, "*L'Allegro* and *Il Penseroso* in Their Relation to Seventeenth Century Poetry," in *Milton's Minor Poems*, ed. Geoffrey Tillotson (Pittsburgh, 1969), pp. 120–59, studies the poems in the context of seventeenth-century poetry. He concludes a discussion of the poems by saying that although the poems are not original, they improve the existing "craft" of poetry of Milton's day. Michael Fixler, "The Orphic Technique of *L'Allegro* and *Il Penseroso*," *ELR* I (1971), 165–77, concentrating on genre, sees the poems as a "deliberate exercise" (165) in which technique carries meaning.

2. Of the serial critics, Donald C. Dorian, "The Question of Autobiographical Significance in *L'Allegro* and *Il Penseroso*," *MP* XXXI (1933), 175–82, comes close to my strategy with these poems, but views them as compensatory. Dorian believes that while Milton wrote the poems "under the veil of artistic or artificial objectivity, these poems also 'cover uncertainty and debate' as to a genuine personal problem" (182). Don Cameron Allen, "The Search for the Prophetic Strain: *L'Allegro* and *Il Penseroso*," in *The Harmonious Vision* (Baltimore, 1954), pp. 3–23, sees the poems as a process of Milton's "proposed course of life which he would employ to find and explain God" (p. 4). Eleanor Tate, "Milton's *L'Allegro* and *Il Penseroso* — Balance, Progression, or Dichotomy?" *MLN* LXXVI (1961), 585–90, looks at the two poems as one statement on the role of the poet as Milton saw it, a progression of the poetic ideal from fame to an "inspired poet-prophet" (589). George C. Geckle, "Miltonic Idealism: *L'Allegro* and *Il Penseroso*," *TSLL* IX (1968), 455–73, views the poems dramatically, as a "simple dichotomy" of the life of the body and the life of the mind (457). Gary Stringer, "The Unity of *L'Allegro* and *Il Penseroso*," *TSLL* XII (1970), 221–29, argues "that '*L'Allegro*' portrays a young man who loves Mirth and that '*Il Penseroso*' concerns an older man who has come to prefer Melancholy" (221). For Gerard H. Cox, "Unbinding 'The Hidden Soul of Harmony': *L'Allegro* and *Il Penseroso* and the Hermetic Tradition," in *Milton Studies*, vol. XVIII, ed. James D. Simmonds (Pittsburgh, 1983), pp. 45–62, the pivotal concept is that of harmony between the poems, achieved by Milton through "like and unlike correspondences" (p. 45) of poetic elements. Cox derives this concept of harmony "from a sophisticated and self-conscious hermetic tradition" (p. 47). Cox's concentration on *Il Penseroso* from the perspective of the hermetic tradition privileges the pensive man's experience and speech over the mirthful man's. In this way, Cox's perspective is a version of the serial criticism of the poems which sees moral and poetic progress in the attitude of *Il Penseroso* over that of *L'Allegro*. In addition, see articles by Leslie Brisman, "'All Before Them Where to Choose': 'L'Allegro' and 'Il Penseroso,'" *JEGP* LXXI (1972), 226–40, and Thomas J. Embry, "Sensuality and Chastity in *L'Allegro* and *Il Penseroso*," *JEGP* LXXVII (1978), 504–29.

3. For extensive discussion of Milton's writing on work and leisure, see Anthony Low, *The Georgic Revolution* (Princeton, 1985), pp. 296–352, especially pp. 296, 318, 340–52. Nan C. Carpenter, "The Place of Music in *L'Allegro* and *Il Penseroso*," *UTQ* XXII (1953), 354–67, and Marilyn C. Williamson, "The Myth of Orpheus in 'L'Allegro' and 'Il Penseroso,'" *MLQ* XXXII (1971), 377–86, both see the poems as a single unit, though not necessarily as complements. Other critics who have raised or implied the importance of the autobiographical component of work and leisure and the potential for their complementarity in *L'Allegro* and *Il Penseroso* include: W. V. Moody, "L'Allegro and Il Penseroso: Introduction," in *The Complete Poetical Works of John Milton* (Boston, 1924),

pp. 23–26; James Holly Hanford, "The Youth of Milton: An Interpretation of His Early Literary Development," in *Studies in Shakespeare, Milton and Donne* (New York, 1925), 87–163 (esp. pp. 131–33); Cleanth Brooks, "The Light Symbolism in *L'Allegro* and *Il Penseroso*," in *The Well Wrought Urn* (New York, 1947), pp. 50–66.

4. Kenneth Burke, *Language as Symbolic Action* (Berkeley and Los Angeles, 1966), p. 297.

5. Ibid., p. 29.

6. Ibid., p. 29.

7. See, for example, Stephen J. Greenblatt, *Renaissance Self-Fashioning* (Chicago, 1980); Richard Helgerson, *Elizabethan Prodigals* (Berkeley and Los Angeles, 1976); *Self-Crowned Laureates* (Berkeley and Los Angeles, 1983); Stephen Orgel, *Patronage in the Renaissance* (Princeton, 1981); Jonathan Goldberg, ed., *James I and the Politics of Literature* (Baltimore, 1983); and Frank Whigham, *Ambition and Privilege* (Berkeley and Los Angeles, 1984).

8. Kenneth Burke, "Literature as Equipment for Living," in *The Philosophy of Literary Form*, 3rd ed. (Berkeley and Los Angeles, 1973), p. 296.

9. Ibid., p. 297.

10. Ibid., p. 298.

11. Thomas M. Greene, "The Meeting Soul in Milton's Companion Poems," *ELR* XIV (1984), 164.

12. Ibid., p. 169.

13. Ibid., p. 174.

14. Norman T. Burns, *Christian Mortalism From Tyndale to Milton* (Cambridge, 1972), p. 175. Burns also writes that: "Milton and Overton both believe in the thnetopsychist variety of mortalism. . . . According to Milton, God breathed into the body of Adam a 'measure of the divine virtue or influence,' just as 'every living thing receives animation from one and the same source of life and breath.' . . . and that the whole man is soul, and the soul man, that is to say, a body or substance individual, animated, sensitive, and rational" (pp. 174, 175).

15. See Douglas Bush's fine summary of the critical history of *L'Allegro* and *Il Penseroso* in A.S.P. Woodhouse and Douglas Bush, eds., *A Variorum Commentary on the Poems of John Milton*, gen. ed. Merritt Y. Hughes (New York, 1972), II, iii, 241–69.

16. John Milton, *Paradise Regained*, II, 295, in *The Works of John Milton*, 18 vols., ed. Frank Allen Patterson et al. (New York, 1931–38), vol. II, p. 434. All quotations from Milton's prose and poetry are from this edition, and subsequent references will appear in the text as CM.

17. Bush, *A Variorum*, p. 242.

18. Burke, "Literature as Equipment for Living," p. 298.

19. Anthony Low, *The Georgic Revolution* (Princeton, 1985), pp. 313–14.

HISTORY AND REFORM IN MILTON'S
READIE AND EASIE WAY

Kevin Gilmartin

I F B Y 1660 Milton's left hand had slipped from the political pulse of the nation, its polemical skill was undiminished. *The Readie and Easie Way* is a stirring attempt to revive England's revolutionary expectations in the face of a rising tide of royalist sentiment. Setting aside the difficult and divisive issues of the moment, Milton begins his pamphlet with a backward glance, hoping to alert his readers to the "bad principles and fals apprehensions"[1] currently in circulation by celebrating past accomplishments:

> The Parliament of England, assisted by a great number of the people who appeerd and stuck to them faithfullest in defence of religion and thir civil liberties, judging kingship by long experience a government unnecessarie, burdensom and dangerous, justly and magnanimously abolishd it; turning regal bondage into a free Commonwealth, to the admiration and terrour of our emulous neighbors. (YP VII, p. 409)

This defense of the parliamentary cause, which continues for several pages, forms the opening salvo of Milton's argument in *The Readie and Easie Way*. In it, he struggles to reaffirm for himself and for England the revolutionary principles which he had advocated since the episcopal controversy of the early 1640s.

The historical nature of Milton's argument, its recourse to past events in order to justify some future course, points to an internal tension which seems to me central to an understanding of the *The Readie and Easie Way*. By 1660, the Revolution which Milton had earlier conceived in progressive and apocalyptic terms had become for him a matter of tradition. Confronted with a hopelessly complex present, and a future dominated by the specter of restoration, Milton lodged his political hopes in the immediate past. *The Readie and Easie Way* is his attempt to consolidate and firmly institute that past, and preserve it for all time. This is evident later, when he outlines the mechanisms of a "free Commonwealth" which will resist historical change and suppress political activity. However, the seeds of Milton's reaction to contemporary trends are

17

contained in the historical retrospective that initiates the tract; it is here that Milton first records the effects of a disintegration of "the good Old Cause" on his political thinking.

I

The rehearsal of past events is for Milton a return to earlier principles. He had long held that freedom is an essential precondition for ethical and political activity. This passage from *Areopagitica* is typical:

If it be desir'd to know the immediat cause of all this free writing and free speaking, there cannot be assign'd a truer then your own mild, and free, and human government; it is the liberty, Lords and Commons, which your own valorous and happy counsels have purchast us, liberty which is the nurse of all great wits; this is that which hath rarify'd and enlightn'd our spirits like the influence of heav'n; this is that which hath enfranchis'd, enlarg'd, and lifted up our apprehensions degrees above themselves. (YP II, p. 559)

The Readie and Easie Way agrees. The members of Parliament have effectively transformed a nation's political life by freeing themselves from inherited restraints:

They knew the people of England to be a free people, themselves the representers of that freedom; & although many were excluded, & as many fled (so they pretended) from tumults to Oxford, yet they were left a sufficient number to act in Parlament; therefor not bound by any statute of preceding Parlaments, but by the law of nature only, which is the only law of laws truly and properly to all mankinde fundamental; the beginning and the end of all Government; to which no Parlament or people that will throughly reforme, but may and must have recourse; as they had and must yet have in church reformation (if they throughly intend it) to evangelic rules; not to ecclesiastical canons, though never so ancient, so ratifi'd and established in the land by Statutes, which for the most part are meer positive laws, neither natural nor moral, & so by any Parlament for just and serious considerations, without scruple to be at any time repeal'd. (YP VII, pp. 411–13)

A condition of human liberty mandates free recourse, "at any time," from political and ecclesiastical tradition ("meer positive laws") to a more essential "natural and moral" law. Reform has liberated England from "the old encroachments" on its liberties (YP VII, p. 423), and appears for Milton to have released the nation entirely from the burden of its history.

Throughout this account of the revolutionary decades, Milton rejects historical (and therefore merely accidental) standards of conduct in favor of such absolutes as "vertue," "wisdom," "justice," and "righteousness in the sight of God" (YP VII, pp. 409, 415–16, 419). The undaunted members of Parliament "made not thir covnant concerning [Charles] with no difference between a king and a god," but instead recognized that "we could not serve two contrary maisters, God and the king, or the king and that more supreme law, . . . our safetie and our libertie" (p. 411). If humanity is restricted by any "natural and moral law," liberty is one of its essential mandates. Once Milton has securely bound his defense of freedom to the divine and the ideal, he shows some willingness to discover precedents for his cause. However, historical argument is for him most often an appeal to principle rather than mere antiquity: there is "a spirit in this nation no less noble and well fitted to the liberty of a Commonwealth, then in the ancient Greeks or Romans" (p. 420).

The threatening political conditions which account for the retrospective emphasis in *The Readie and Easie Way* thrust this historical dimension of Milton's thinking into an unusual prominence, transforming the iconoclast into a traditionalist.[2] "Our liberty and religion" have already been "prosperously fought for, gaind and many years possessd," and we "are never like to attain thus far as we are now advanc'd to the recoverie of our freedom, never to have it in possession as we now have it" (YP VIII, pp. 421–23). Milton implores his reader to preserve the legacy of "so many thousand faithfull and valiant English men, who left us in this libertie" (pp. 423–24), and to leave "posteritie" something more than an infamous example of failed rebellion (p. 449). Revolutionary energies have sedimented as received traditions, and freedom has become a capacity to be preserved, rather than exercised in the interest of reform. Though Milton defends the English Revolution as a past achievement, he issues this anguished and hardly iconoclastic response to the present crisis: "Shall we never grow old anough to be wise to make seasonable use of gravest autorities, experiences, examples?" (p. 448). By the final paragraph of *The Readie and Easie Way*, the writer has been reduced to a desperate and embattled proponent of "the good Old Cause" (p. 463).

History had, of course, figured in Milton's understanding of reform before *The Readie and Easie Way*. As *Areopagitica* so forcefully argues, absolute standards such as truth and virtue can be realized on earth only through an unfolding historical process. With the Restoration looming on the forward horizon, though, Milton's political vision, and his conception of historical activity, become almost exclusively retrospective. He prefers a project of preservation and consolidation to one of reform. The account of the Revolution contains some remnants of an earlier progressivism: England is "a glorious rising Commonwealth," "more & more unbound" from its ancient fetters through the "constancie and fortitude" of Parliament (YP VII, pp. 409, 420–21). However, progress is threatened when Milton confronts those royalists who wish "to fall back or rather to creep back . . . to thir once abjur'd and detested thraldom of Kingship" (p. 422):

If we returne to Kingship, and soon repent, as undoubtedly we shall, when we begin to finde the old encroachments coming on by little and little upon our consciences, which must necessarily proceed from king and bishop united inseparably in one interest, we may be forc'd perhaps to fight over again all that we have fought, and spend over again all that we have spent, but are never like to attain thus far as we are now advanc'd to the recoverie of our freedom, never to have it in possession as we now have it, never to be voutsaf'd heerafter the like mercies and signal assistances from heaven in our cause, if by our ingratefull backsliding we make these fruitless; flying now to regal concessions from his divine condescensions and gratious answers to our once importuning praiers against the tyrannie which we then groand under . . . losing by a strange after game of folly all the battels we have wonn . . . [and] treading back again with lost labour all our happie steps in the progress of reformation. (Pp. 423–24)

The conceptual framework is a progressive timeline, but the "zealous backsliders" (p. 452) have reversed the direction of movement, retracing "all our happie steps in the progress of reformation." Under this threat, Milton comes to view reform as an activity that has already reached its culmination; history is thus a thing of the past rather than an unfolding process.

It is true that Milton had engaged the phenomenon of regression before. In the early attacks on episcopacy, there was a "dangerous earnest of sliding back to Rome" (YP I, p. 527); later, "Malignant backsliders" (YP III, p. 222) abandoned the cause of the regicides and threatened to "slide back into neutrality" (YP III, p. 600). However, regressive tendencies had never before so dominated the contemporary scene and so obscured Milton's political vision. The city of London, singled out in *Areopagitica* as "the mansion house of liberty" (YP II, pp. 553–54), was by 1660 leading the cry for "a full and free parliament" and king; for the first time in years the royalists were openly championing their cause in the press and in the pulpit.[3] As a result, the future figures in *The Readie and Easie Way* as a field of loss rather than promise: "we may be forc'd perhaps to fight over again all that we have fought, and spend over again all that we have spent." The tract is punctuated throughout by visions of "a strange degenerate contagion suddenly spread among us (YP VII, p. 422), and by fears of "the diabolical forerunning libells" which are "the harbingers of those that are in expectation to raign over us" (YP VII, p. 452). It concludes with a plea that the reader "exhort this torrent . . . of the people not to be so impetuos, but to keep thir due channel; and . . . stay these ruinous proceedings" (YP VII, p. 463), vivid metaphorical evidence of the writer's antagonism to contemporary political trends. As Milton negotiates the difficult transition from the introductory retrospective to future remedies, the restrictive effects upon his writing of a threatening political climate are increasingly evident.

II

The first significant consequence for Milton's political proposals of a retreat from the promise of time is his desire for an immediate, inflexible settlement. The "Readie and Easie" of the tract's title, rather than the "Way," bears the emphasis throughout. Though Milton criticizes the people for their "impatience" (YP VII, pp. 430–31, 463), his own call for "a speedie and immediat settlement" (p. 421) is a symptom of the same fault. The idea of immediate, unobstructed social transformation had attracted Milton before, particularly in the attacks on episcopacy, where he envisions "a compleate Reform" (YP I, p. 529) of the church, and argues that if change "be from worse to better, certainly wee ought to hie us from evill like a torrent" (p. 602). However, the impatience of these early writings is tempered by an enthusiasm for the "opposition" that is "the triall of an unfained goodnesse and magnanimity" (p. 795), and by a commitment to the necessary process of "searching, trying, [and] examining all things" (p. 566); "exact Reformation is not perfited at the first push" (p. 536). In *Areopagitica*, Milton's progressive view of history is more fully developed. The Christian life involves "the triall of vertue, and the exercise of truth" (YP II, p. 528). Milton unflinchingly engages the obstacles of this world:

I cannot praise a fugitive and cloister'd vertue, unexercis'd & unbreath'd, that never sallies out and sees her adversary, but slinks out of the race, where that immortall garland is to be run for, not without dust and heat. Assuredly we bring not innocence into the world, we bring impurity much rather: that which purifies us is triall, and triall is by what is contrary. (YP II, p. 515)

The idea of an active struggle for improvement is supplanted in *The Readie and Easie Way* by the satisfaction with present achievement that marks the retrospective introduction. Any worldly opposition to an immediate realization of Milton's political expectations dissolves before the sure promise of "instant fruition" (YP VII, p. 424): "I say again, this way lies free and smooth before us; is not tangl'd with inconveniencies; invents no new incumbrances; requires no perilous, no injurious alteration or circumscription of mens lands and proprieties" (p. 445). Only a willful blindness to current conditions could lead anyone to insist in 1660 that the way was "Readie and Easie."[4] Indeed, we should grant Milton a more advanced political understanding than these arguments suggest; his overt denial of political resistance is undermined by a sophisticated rhetorical strategy, which repeatedly anticipates and accommodates objections which his opponents might advance.

If "instant fruition" is a truncated version of progressive reform, the political system which such a process realizes involves an even more thorough rejection of unfolding historical activity. Horrified by a people "who past reason and recoverie are devoted to kingship" (YP VII, p. 455), the weary reformer demands that England select once and for all the "able and worthie men" (p. 449) who will oppose monarchy, and install them in a perpetual Grand Council. A static institution replaces progress and reform as the means of England's political salvation. Milton's dual concern for instant achievement and perpetual fulfillment produces some unusual juxtapositions:

Now . . . nothing remains, but in all reason the certain hopes of a speedie and immediat settlement for ever in a firm and free Commonwealth. (YP VII, p. 421)

Now is the opportunitie, now the very season wherein we may obtain a free Commonwealth and establish it for ever in the land, without difficulty or much delay. (YP VII, p. 430)

The Grand Council is offered as a means of confronting the immediate difficulties of an unstable world: political demands are "oft times urgent; the opportunitie of affairs gaind or lost in a moment" (YP VII, p. 433). However, its perpetual tenure marks it as an institutional mechanism for resisting temporal change and transcending politics altogether. As always, Milton's political imagery is revealing. In earlier tracts, "the tall and goodly Vessell of the Common-wealth" had to pass through "all the gusts and tides of the Worlds mutability" (YP I, p. 601), and various "winds and flaws" tested "the floting vessell of our faith whether it be stanch and sayl well" (p. 794). By 1660 Milton has tired of the uncertainty which these oceangoing metaphors suggest, and argues that the institutions of a commonwealth are threatened less by the exigencies of this world than by the slightest internal disturbance: "The ship of the Commonwealth is alwais under sail: they [members of the Grand Council] sit at the stern; and if they stear well, what need is ther to change them; it being rather dangerous?" (YP VII, pp. 433–34). The tendency toward a static conception of politics is confirmed as this image of the ship "always under sail" immediately gives way to the tract's prevailing metaphor of a firm foundation: "Add to this, that the Grand Councel is both foundation and main pillar of the whole State" (p. 434).

So powerful is Milton's antagonism to a historical condition that he even seeks to overcome human mortality. It seems to him "safest . . . and of least hazard or interruption to affairs, that none of the Grand Councel be mov'd, unless by death" (YP VII, p. 435), and even this threat recedes when his perfect institution is viewed from a distance:

Kingship it self is . . . counted the more safe and durable [form of government], because the king and, for the most part, his councel, is not chang'd during his life: but a Commonwealth is held immortal; and therin firmest, safest and most above fortune: for the death of a king, causeth ofttimes many dangerous alterations; but the death now and then of a Senator is not felt; the main bodie of them still continuing permanent in greatest and noblest Commonwealths, and as it were eternal. (P. 436)

By collecting the best individuals in the enduring body of a council, we escape the degenerative effects of time, and make humanity "as it were eternal." This ideal of a collective, institutional stability that neutralizes history controls much of Milton's political agenda: rotation introduces "successive and transitorie Parlaments" which have "too much affinitie with the wheel of fortune"; popular assemblies "cannot but be troublesom and chargeable, both in thir motion and thir session"; inherited monarchy commits "the summ of [the people's] welbeing, the whole state of thir safetie to fortune" (YP VII, pp. 434–35, 441, 448). In each case, Milton rejects an unstable political form in favor of a transcendental permanence.

The utopian desire for a condition unthreatened by mortality is closely linked to Milton's attempt to overcome the civil strife that marked the previous decades, and reached a peak after the death of Oliver Cromwell in 1658. Freedom from historical change in a commonwealth is accompanied by freedom from political and social disorder. The English are criticized for having fallen "into a wors confusion, not of tongues, but of factions, then those at the tower of Babel" (YP VII, p. 423), and the familiar alternatives to Milton's own proposal are each rejected on the grounds of their destabilizing effects. Successive parliaments "are much likelier continually to unsettle rather then to settle a free government; to breed commotions, changes, novelties and uncertainties" (p. 434), and a popular assembly is "emulous and always jarring with the other Senat" (p. 441). As England has well learned, if a monarch proves intolerable, he is "not to be remov'd, not to be controul'd, much less accus'd or brought to punishment, without danger of a common ruin, without the shaking and almost subversion of the whole land" (p. 426). In a free commonwealth, on the other hand, "any governor or chief counselor offending, may be remov'd and punishd without the least commotion" (pp. 426–27). Milton contends that England can only be transported "past fear of commotions or mutations" (p. 430) if his own proposals are put into effect: "Till this be don, I am in doubt whether our State will be ever certainly and throughly setl'd; never likely till then to see an end of our troubles and continual changes or at least never the true settlement and assurance of our libertie" (p. 444). Michael Fixler suggests that the promise of order is an appeal to a nation weary of political instability.[5] If this is true, it should not obscure the fact that Milton shares the sentiments of his audience. In *A Letter to a Friend* (20 October 1659), he laments the "dangerous ruptures of the common wealth" (YP VII, p. 324); there is a note of topical urgency in his fear of "approaching ruine," brought on by an unruly army and the lack of any "counselling & governing power" (p. 329). If by April of 1660 the prospect of a restoration reassured much of England, it signalled for Milton the final disaster, and we can safely assume that his response — an appeal from uncertainty to inflexible order — is a sincere political desire.

III

The novelty for Milton of the view that human political institutions might achieve an immutability approaching perfection can only be gauged through a detailed consideration of his earlier writings. The rejection of monarchy in *The Readie and Easie Way* rests on the claim that any individual is inadequate to such high office. "We need depend on none but God and our own counsels"; to "devolve all on a single person," who will then "display . . . his regal splendor . . . supereminently above other mortal men" (YP VII, pp. 427, 429) is surely an act of collective madness. *The Tenure of Kings and Magistrates* musters similar principles in defense of the regicides. The king is merely "a mortal Magistrate," whose claims of divine election and superiority to the law "arrogate . . . unreasonably above the human condition" (YP III, p. 204). The arguments of the two tracts coincide exactly in a rejection of "those pagan Caesars that deifi'd themselves" (YP III, p. 204), and a disgust at the spectacle of a king "ador'd like a Demigod" (YP VII, p. 425), his subjects reduced to a servile idolatry. However, the passage of ten years finds Milton drawing on the same principles for very different political ends. The defender of regicide is by 1660 struggling to reconstruct the political order, and he adjusts his political principles accordingly.

Sovereignty in *The Tenure* "is nothing else, but what is only derivative, transferr'd and committed to [kings and magistrates] in trust from the People . . . in whom the power yet remains fundamentally" (YP III, p. 202). Beyond the free individual, power can be traced only to

God, or to a sphere of ideals: "Justice is the onely true sovran and supreme Majesty upon earth" (p. 237). In Milton's version of the social contract, individuals yield to institutions provisionally, as an unfortunate consequence of the fall:

No man who knows ought, can be so stupid to deny that all men naturally were borne free, being the image and resemblance of God himself, and were by privilege above all the creatures, born to command and not to obey: and that they liv'd so. Till from the root of Adams transgression, falling among themselves to doe wrong and violence, and foreseeing that such courses must needs tend to the destruction of them all, they agreed by common league to bind each other from mutual injury, and joyntly to defend themselves against any that gave disturbance or opposition to such agreement. Hence came Citties, Townes and Commonwealths. (Pp. 198–99)

Kings and magistrates soon follow, but nations have secured their political destiny by transcending merely human rule. They "invent Laws . . . that should confine and limit the autority of whom they chose to govern them: that so man, of whose failing they had proof, might no more rule over them, but law and reason abstracted as much as might be from personal errors and frailties" (pp. 199–200).

The commonwealth of *The Readie and Easie Way* also seeks to overcome the uncertainty of personal government. However, Milton discards the suspicion of institutions that permeates *The Tenure*, and his commitment to the sovereignty of the individual seems to fade as well. Far from being a badge of human impairment, the Grand Council becomes a means to social perfection. This collection of individuals, rather than abstract "law and reason," is the final arbiter of political affairs: "The ground and basis of every just and free government . . . is a general councel of ablest men" (YP VII, p. 432). The aggregate quality of the council seems enough to make Milton forget the "personal errors and frailty" of its human components. Councillors will themselves realize the ideals which in *The Tenure* were exercised from above, or were the exclusive province of each individual. "In a full and free Councel . . . no single person, but reason only swaies" (p. 427). Milton cannot find superlatives enough for the virtue of his government:

A free Commonwealth [is] not only held by wisest men in all ages the noblest, the manliest, the equallest, the justest government, the most agreeable to all due libertie, and proportiond equalitie, both human, civil, and Christian, most cherishing to vertue and true religion, but also (I may say with greatest probabilitie) planely commended, or rather enjoind by our Saviour himself, to all Christians. (P. 424).

Milton's sense of the limits of human institutions, so prominent in his violent attacks on monarchy, yields to an enthusiasm for a lasting political settlement. The anxious claim for divine sanction is an indication of Milton's desperate position. Earlier tracts are more skeptical about the gospel's political content: "Christ . . . declares professedly his judicature to be spiritual, abstract from Civil managements, and therfore leaves all Nations to thir own particular Lawes, and way of Government" (YP III, p. 587).

The effort to construct, on earth and out of merely human parts, a secure and permanent depository for such ideals as reason and justice is the most striking evidence of Milton's retreat from historical change as the way to perfection. In its defense of the trial and execution of a king, *The Tenure* had argued the essential instability of political systems:

Since the King or Magistrate holds his autoritie of the people . . . then may the people as oft as they shall judge it for the best, either choose him or reject him, retaine or depose him though no Tyrant, meerly by the liberty and right of free born Men, to be govern'd as seems to them best. (YP III, p. 206)

And surely they that shall boast, as we doe, to be a free Nation, and not have in themselves the power to remove, or to abolish any governour supreme, or subordinat, with the government it self upon urgent causes, may please thir fancy with a ridiculous and painted freedom, fit to coz'n babies; but are indeed under tyranny and servitude; as wanting that power, which is the root and sourse of all liberty, to dispose and oeconomize in the Land which God hath giv'n them. (YP III, pp. 236–37)

This free exercise of individual sovereignty extends even to the removal of a government "not illegal, or intolerable" (YP III, p. 237), leading Perez Zagorin to call *The Tenure* "a bold and uncompromising assertion of the right of revolution."[6] Nothing could be further from the equally "uncompromising" perpetual tenure of the Grand Council. The claim in *The Readie and Easie Way* that power is "not transferrd, but delegated only, and as it were deposited" in the council (YP VII, p. 432) resembles a key formula in *The Tenure:* "The power of Kings and Magistrates is nothing else, but what is only derivative, transferr'd and committed to them in trust from the People" (YP III, p. 202). However, the willingness in the later tract to equate sovereignty "transferrd" and sovereignty "deposited" confirms Milton's new commitment to inflexible, sedimented civil forms. The main provision for dissent from the perpetual rule of the Grand Council is the removal of individual members found unfit. In *Proposalls of Certaine Expedients* (October–December 1659), even this exception "is not urged, lest it be misinterpreted" (YP VII, p. 338) as a concession to political change.

Until the period of *The Readie and Easie Way* Milton had generally resisted the temptation of assigning historical progress any terminus short of the millennium. His support for sustained reform in earlier tracts is expressed in terms of the metaphorical opposition of dynamic activity and stagnant restraint. The licensing order of 1643 restricts the "streaming fountain" of progressive enlightenment, returning "the freedom of learning . . . to her old fetters"; as a result, England will be "starched" into "a stanch and solid peece of frame-work, as any January could freeze together" (YP II, pp. 541–45). Though most striking in *Areopagitica*, this metaphorical pattern runs throughout the prose. It achieves lyrical expression in *The Reason of Church-Government*, as Milton ridicules the claim that episcopacy suppresses schism:

The Winter might as well vaunt it selfe against the Spring, I destroy all noysome and rank weeds, I keepe downe all pestilent vapours. Yes and all wholesome herbs, and all fresh dews, by your violent & hidebound frost; but when the gentle west winds shall open the fruitfull bosome of the earth thus over-girded by your imprisonment, then the flowers put forth and spring, and then the Sunne shall scatter the mists, and the manuring hand of the Tiller shall root up all that burdens the soile without thank to your bondage. (YP I, p. 785)

Restraint under the bishops is indeed "farre worse then any frozen captivity"; the early Milton prefers the alternative promise of revolutionary rebirth brought about by vigorous activity.

Milton appears unembarrassed by his own inflexible proposals in *The Readie and Easie Way*, and actually invokes the same metaphorical pattern in his attack on alternative political forms. A restored monarchy will return England to "thraldom" or "bondage,"[7] while Harrington's "exotic models" will "manacle the native liberty of mankinde; turning all vertue into prescription, servitude, and necessitie, to the great impairing and frustrating of Christian libertie" (YP VII, p. 445). We should recall that Harringtonian rotation is elsewhere condemned as flexible to the point of instability, and that the same monarchy which would constrain England earlier threatens "the shaking . . . of the whole land" (p. 426). Milton resolves any contradiction in his appeal for both stability and freedom by introducing the idea of a "foundation," and further complicating his metaphorical system. The Grand Council is a stable political base, the "foundation and main pillar of the whole State" (p. 434). It represses disorder without restricting liberty, leaving England on the fortunate ground between bondage and instability — "*secure* from the exasperated regal power, and out of *snares*" (p. 420, my emphasis).[8]

The metaphor of foundation is central to Milton's argument in *The Readie and Easie Way*, and provides a revealing index of his retreat from the revolutionary process that has "more and more unbound us." The demand that England get "at least the foundation firmly laid of a free Commonwealth, and good part also erected of the main structure" (YP VII, p. 432) suggests a continuing effort; this makes sense, since the Grand Council is only "the ground and basis" (p. 432) of good government, not its entire form. However, Milton's architectural language comes to prefer a completed political edifice to any unfolding process of construction. If the English restore monarchy, they will leave a revolutionary project unfinished, "which will render us a scorn and derision to all our neighbours": "And what will they at best say of us and of the whole English name, but scoffingly as of that foolish builder, mentiond by our Saviour, who began to build a tower, and was not able to finish it. Where is this goodly tower of a Commonwealth, which the English boasted they would build to overshaddow kings, and be another Rome in the west?" (pp. 422–23). Yielding to a fear that present accomplishments may be lost, Milton abandons his earlier progressivism. The attack on Harringtonian rotation cited earlier indicates the extent to which the idea of a foundation involves an investment in unchanging political forms:

The Grand Councel is both foundation and main pillar of the whole State; and to move pillars and foundations, not faultie, cannot be safe for the building. I see not therefor, how we can be advantag'd by successive and transitorie Parlaments; but that they are much likelier continually to unsettle rather then to settle a free government; to breed commotions, changes, novelties, and uncertainties. (P. 434)

Rotation produces a "floating foundation," no solution at all to "the fluxible fault . . . of our watry situation" as "Ilanders" (pp. 436–37). Only static "pillars" can effectively overcome the instability of this world, and raise England above the chaos of its history.

Milton's readiness to ascribe to the Grand Council a structure "not faultie" registers the effect of the disintegration of "the good Old Cause" on his political conceptions. Even the optimistic antiepiscopal tracts concede that absolute perfection is not of this world, particularly in political forms:

And because things simply pure are inconsistent in the masse of nature, nor are the elements or humors in Mans Body exactly homogeneall, and hence the best founded Common-wealths, and least barbarous have aym'd at a certaine mixture and temperament, partaking the severall vertues of each other State, that each part drawing to it selfe may keep up a steddy, and eev'n uprightnesse in common. (YP I, p. 599)

Given the inconsistency of nature, the best humanity can expect of its political institutions is the "steddy, and eev'n uprightnesse" offered by "mixture and temperament." England's own mixed government is not perfect, but only "more divinely and harmoniously tun'd, more equally ballanc'd" than others (p. 599). It has nothing like the purity and monolithic stability of Milton's later Grand Council.

Areopagitica is as always furthest from Milton's position in 1660. In that tract Milton frankly concedes the improbability of any uniform human construction. A time may come when the world's diverse seekers "joyn, and unite into one general and brotherly search after Truth" (YP II, p. 554), but life remains to the end an active effort with imperfect results:

There must be many schisms and many dissections made in the quarry and in the timber, ere the house of God can be built. And when every stone is laid artfully together, it cannot be united into a continuity, it can be but contiguous in this world; neither can every peece of the building be of one form; nay rather the perfection consists in this, that out of many moderat varieties and brotherly dissimilitudes that are not vastly disproportionall arises the goodly and the gracefull symmetry that commends the whole pile and structure. (YP II, p. 555)

Human achievement is limited to the "graceful symmetry" of parts "not vastly disproportionall." Absolute perfection is a transcendental quality: "It is not possible for man to sever the wheat from the tares, the good fish from the other frie; that must be the Angels Ministry at the end of mortall things" (YP VII, pp. 564–65). In *The Readie and Easie Way*, Milton usurps this "Angels ministry." His elaborate electoral system selects "the worthiest" and "ablest men" through successive "sifting and refining of exactest choice" (pp. 432, 443); these men achieve an "end to mortall things" by forming an institution which is "as it were eternal." A piece of writing rooted in a recognition of "this wavering condition of our affairs" (p. 441) thus yields to a desire to transcend that condition. Milton's own well-known attack on escapist utopias serves as an effective critique of the achievement of *The Readie and Easie Way*: "To sequester out of the world into Atlantick and Eutopian polities, which never can be drawn into use, will not mend our condition; but to ordain wisely as in this world of evill, in the midd'st whereof God hath plac't us unavoidably" (YP II, p. 526).

IV

Throughout Milton's prose, historical progress is fulfilled, and human perfection achieved, upon the return of Christ. Since the Grand Council signals a retrenchment of Milton's expectations for humanity, and marks a premature end to historical progress, Milton's understanding of the millennial process in *The Readie and Easie Way* is seriously deformed. His earlier tracts reveal an affiliation with radical puritanism through their aggressive pursuit of a politically charged millennium. In *Of Reformation*, such "former Deliverances" as the Reformation and the destruction of the Spanish Armada prefigure the "greatest happinesse to come" (YP I, p. 615). The Last Judgment involves a realignment of earthly powers favorable to the English:

This great and Warlike Nation, instructed and inur'd to the fervent and continuall practice of Truth and Righteousnesse, and casting farre from her the rags of her old vices may presse on hard to that high and happy emulation to be found the soberest, wisest, and most Christian People, at that day when thou the Eternall and shortly-expected King shalt open the Clouds to judge the severall Kingdomes of the World, and distributing Nationall Honours and Rewards to Religious and just Common-wealths, shalt put an end to all Earthly Tyrannies, proclaiming thy universal and milde Monarchy through Heaven and Earth. (YP I, p. 616)[9]

The millennial visions of *Areopagitica* are less spectacular, but the human role in preparing for Christ's return is further elaborated. Under a providential view of history, humanity does not actually "cause" the millennium, but our realization of a capacity for self-improvement is at the very least a sign that the kingdom is at hand. "In these latter ages," Milton sees England "casting off the old and wrincl'd skin of corruption" (YP II, p. 557), sustaining an effort first undertaken in the Reformation. He demands an active and unfolding millennial process, and resists the complacency fostered by visions of static fulfillment:

He who thinks we are to pitch our tent here, and have attain'd the utmost prospect of reformation, that the mortall glasse wherein we contemplate, can shew us, till we come to beatific vision, that man by this very opinion declares, that he is yet farre short of Truth. . . . The light which we have gain'd, was giv'n us, not to be ever staring on, but by it to discover onward things more remote from our knowledge. (YP II, p. 549–50)

Ernest Tuveson has applied the excellent phrase "apocalyptic progressivism" to this coalescence of human activity and millennial fulfillment in *Areopagitica*.[10] God's chosen people "continue seeking," never discouraged by the fact that on earth truth is only gradually approximated, and must await full expression at "her Masters second comming" (YP II, p. 549).

The *Readie and Easie Way* is consistent with Milton's earlier thinking in its postponement of Christ's kingdom. In the first edition, Milton ridicules any "pretending to a fifth monarchie of the saints" as a contemporary political solution (YP VII, p. 380); the second edition agrees that "the kingdom of Christ our common King and Lord, is hid to this world" (p. 429). However, the millennium is here deferred in the interest of present settlement, rather than further activity. Michael Fixler has pointed out that despite an expressed hostility to the Fifth Monarchists, Milton himself "suffuse[s] something of a millenarian aura about his proposal,"[11] appealing for scriptural sanction, and offering his reader "the hopes of a glorious rising Commonwealth" (p. 420). The familiar link between politics and the return of Christ is activated, but its force is greatly weakened:

The Grand Councel being thus firmly constituted to perpetuitie, and still, upon the death or default of any member, suppli'd and kept in full number, ther can be no cause alleag'd why peace, justice, plentifull trade and all prosperitie should not thereupon ensue throughout the whole land; with as much assurance as can be of human things, that they shall so continue (if God favour us, and our wilfull sins provoke him not) even to the coming of our true and rightfull and only to be expected King, only worthie as he is our only Saviour, the Messiah, the Christ, the only heir of his eternal father, the only by him anointed and ordained since the work of our redemption finishd, Universal Lord of all mankinde. (Pp. 444–45)

Milton had formerly conceived dynamic and even violent human activity as the necessary prologue to Christ's return. Such events as the Reformation and the execution of Charles were the first stirrings of the imminent renovation of heaven and earth, and immediate historical experience was thus infused with apocalyptic significance. The God who sanctions a free commonwealth in *The Readie and Easie Way* is a less venturesome deity, preferring stability and prosperity to revolutionary convulsions. The active, vital connection Milton had once drawn between politics and the millennium is reduced to mere contiguity: a stable commonwealth may precede Christ's return, but is in no way engaged in the process that brings it about. A passage cut from the second edition of the tract suggests the effect of a desire for order and settlement on Milton's apocalyptic visions. Any subjection of Parliament to a restored monarchy will, he argues, "leave the contest endless between prerogative and petition of right, till only dooms-day end it" (p. 366). The millennium figures not as the glorious fulfillment of human progress, but rather as sheer relief from disorder and futile political activity.

V

Despite his desire for a settlement that suppresses political instability, Milton's characteristic interest in individual liberty does survive in *The Readie and Easie Way*. The attack on monarchy turns upon this issue.

A king demands that his subjects "renounce their own freedom" (YP VII, p. 428), and seeks "to make the people . . . softest, basest, vitiousest, servilest, easiest to be kept under" (p. 460), whereas a commonwealth "aims most to make the people flourishing, vertuous, noble and high spirited" (p. 460). The distinction between enslaved subject and free citizen appears to revive Milton's enthusiasm for reform. A nation ruled by a monarch wastes its potentially progressive energy in degrading activities; the ruling classes in particular are "debas'd with court opinions, contrarie to all vertue and reformation": "[The king] will have little els to do, but to bestow the eating and drinking of excessive dainties, to set a pompous face upon the superficial actings of State, to pageant himself up and down in progress among the perpetual bowings and cringings of an abject people, on either side deifying and adoring him for nothing don that can deserve it" (p. 426). Solomon's proverb of the industrious ant confirms that "lawless anarchie" is not the only alternative to futile monarchy: "these diligent creatures . . . are set the examples to imprudent and ungovernd men, of a frugal and self-governing democratie or Commonwealth; safer and more thriving in the joint providence and counsel of many industrious equals, then under the single domination of one imperious Lord" (p. 427).

Unfortunately, the promise of a "flourishing, vertuous, noble and high spirited" republican population bears little fruit. A utopian condition achieved via "The Readie and Easie Way" proves an unsatisfying alternative to the strenuous pursuit of perfection. Milton resorts to vague and ultimately hollow assurances that there is vitality in his conception of a perfect society: "The Grand Councel being thus firmly constituted to perpetuitie . . . ther can be no cause alleag'd why peace, justice, plentifull trade and all prosperitie should not thereupon ensue throughout the whole land" (YP VII, p. 444). His strident claims that a free commonwealth will provide "all the freedom, peace, justice, [and] plentie that we can desire" (pp. 455–56), and that "we shall live the cleerest and absolutest free nation in the world" (p. 446), convey the almost comic force of an intense desire for immediate fulfillment. Having spent his rhetorical energies on the unchanging foundations of the commonwealth, Milton has little of interest to say about its superstructure. Indeed, I would argue that the Grand Council itself, rather than society at large, is the locus of Milton's utopianism in *The Readie and Easie Way*. The principles which animate his earlier sense of human perfectibility— reasoned activity, vital Christian community, and the penetration of this world by transcendent ideals—are relocated in the council, and thus spared destruction at the hands of English history. This alternative utopian space holds the promise of immediate achievement because it is insulated from the worldly imperfections and obstructions which inspire Milton's earlier progressivism. The price of this vision of instant gratification is a severe narrowing of Milton's expectations, and a degradation of his cherished ideals to their merely institutional form.

If there is little interest in society in *The Readie and Easie Way*, politics receives more attention. Milton's elaborate provisions for local political activity seem, at first glance, to undermine my claim that the exercise of liberty has been forgotten. However, close attention to these proposals shows that they fail to relieve the tract's prevailing atmosphere of restraint. Despite a passing reference to the virtue of "a frugal and self-governing democratie or Commonwealth" (YP VII, p. 427), Milton's supposed enthusiasm for the principle of representative government is undermined by his hostility to any "licentious and unbridl'd democratie" (p. 438). The force behind the Restoration was, after all, "this torrent . . . of the people" (p. 463). Milton prefers a political order constructed upon absolute standards, "there being in number little vertue, but by weight and measure wisdom working all things" (pp. 415–16). The royalists "have both in reason and the trial of just battel, lost the right of their election what the government shall be," and power therefore devolves on the righteous few:

They who seek nothing but thir own just libertie, have alwais the right to winn it and to keep it, when ever they have the power, be the voices never so numerous that oppose it. And how much we above others are concernd to defend it from kingship, and from them who in pursuance therof so perniciously would betray us and themselves to most certain miserie and thraldom, will be needless to repeat. (P. 455)

Liberty, initially conceived in *The Readie and Easie Way* as the precondition of revolutionary change, is now a threatened condition which Milton jealously struggles "to keep" and "defend."[12]

However, the idea that truth outweighs the voice of the majority, and that the unworthy must be excluded from power, is not new for Milton. Its appearance in his political thinking can be traced back at least as far as *The Tenure*, where the judgment of tyranny is left "to Magistrates, at least to the uprighter sort of them, and of the people, though in number less by many, in whom faction least hath prevaild above the Law of nature and right reason" (YP III, p. 197).[13] In this sense, the exclusive political order of *The Readie and Easie Way* — its preference for the "well-affected" (YP VII, p. 435), and for a government directed by "the nobilitie and chief gentry" (pp. 458–59); its distaste for "the noise and shouting of a rude multitude" (p. 442) — represents the formalization of tendencies long present in Milton's political thinking. What is new here is a distinction Milton makes *within* the "worthy" political nation, a distinction which can be perceived as a split between the real power of the Grand Council and the largely redundant energies of the elite as a whole. In 1660, Milton felt that stability was among the highest virtues of good government. The practices familiar to England's political classes seemed to him to contain the threat of disorder, but he could not expect his proposals to receive a favorable reception without making some allowance for them. The result is the provincial assemblies of *The Readie and Easie Way*. Sovereignty is firmly located in the Grand Council; elsewhere, citizens express their political aspirations in activities which have little to do with real power.

Milton does not hide his impatience with those political forces which threaten the serenity of the Grand Council. Harringtonian rotation is reluctantly accepted, not without a bitter jab at "the ambition of such as think themselves injur'd that they also partake not of the government, and are impatient till they be chosen, cannot brook the perpetuitie of others chosen before them" (YP VII, p. 434). Similarly, Milton cannot veil his essential skepticism about the virtue of representative government. The system by which "every countie in the land were made a kinde of subordinate Commonaltie or Commonwealth" (p. 458) does not originate in a faith in provincial judgment, or in a fear of centralization. Instead, Milton wants to protect his perpetual council from popular suspicion, and to contain political energy at the local level:

But to prevent all mistrust, the people then will have thir several ordinarie assemblies . . . in the chief towns of every countie, without the trouble, charge, or time lost of summoning and assembling from far in so great a number, and so long residing from thir own houses, or removing of thir families, to do as much at home in thir several shires, entire or subdivided, toward the securing of thir libertie, as a numerous assembly of them all formd and conven'd on purpose with the wariest rotation. (Pp. 443–444)

In the *Proposalls*, Milton frankly admits that his appeal to a (supposedly) representative Parliament is the result of political realism rather than principle: "In regard that no government is like to continue unlesse founded upon the publick autority & consent of the people which is the parlament the only probable way in all appearance can be, & the only prevention of this civill war now at point to ensue, that the parlament be again treated with to sitt on these following condicions" (p. 336). He goes on to argue that the members of a Grand Council "shall rid their hands of much trouble & businesse not appertai[n]ing to them," and enjoy "great ease & health," if such troublesome details as religion and "the execution of lawes" are relegated to the local level (p. 338). The highest political aim, it seems, is that "our continuall changes" and "distracted anarchy" be suppressed, and that "great peace and quietnesse" be once again established (pp. 336, 338).

The judicial system proposed in *The Readie and Easie Way* most clearly reveals Milton's motivation in providing for local political organization. He assumes for a moment the popular guise of a judicial reformer:

The nobilitie and cheif gentry . . . [may] make thir own judicial laws, or use these that are, and execute them by thir own elected judicatures and judges without appeal, in all things of civil government between man and man. so they shall have justice in thir own hands, law executed fully and finally in thir own counties and precincts, long wishd, and spoken of, but never obtaind; they shall have none then to blame but themselves, if it be not well administered; and fewer laws to expect or fear from the supreme autoritie. (YP VII, pp. 458–59)

The essential indifference to legal change here cannot be ignored — new laws and old laws are all the same to Milton. Even more disturbing (considering the importance of the term *justice* in Milton's polemical arsenal) is the lack of concern for the equitable administration of the law. A local judiciary will be so completely independent that the right of appeal is sacrificed; if justice miscarry, Milton spitefully suggests that those who once complained of central interference "shall have none to blame but themselves," or as the *Proposalls* put it, "shall have no cause to clamour against the supreame Councell, nor can hope for more equall Justice in any other place" (p. 338). His aim is once again to buffer the central government from the disturbing but inescapable circumstances of political life.[14]

The interest in local government in *The Readie and Easie Way* does not mean that the provinces eclipse the power of the Grand Council. On this point Milton is unequivocal:

Nothing can be more essential to the freedom of a people, then to have the administration of justice and all public ornaments in thir own election and within thir own bounds, without long travelling or depending on remote places to obtain thir right or any civil accomplishment; so it be not supreme, but subordinate to the general power and union of the whole Republic. (YP VII, pp. 460–61)

An excess of local authority in the United Provinces works "oft times to the great disadvantage of that union" (VII, 459); England ought to prefer the stability offered by "one united and entrusted Sovrantie" (p. 461).

This principle can serve as a guide through the often tortuous polemics of *The Readie and Easie Way*. Milton's other statements about the dispersal of power in a free commonwealth are often confusing and contradictory. The assurance that sovereignty is "not transferrd" to the members of the Council, "but delegated only," comes "with this caution":

They must have the forces by sea and land committed to them for preservation of the common peace and libertie; must raise and manage the public revenue, at least with som inspectors deputed for the satisfaction of the people, how it is imploid; must make or propose . . . civil laws; treat of commerce, peace or warr with forein nations, and for the carrying on som particular affairs with more secrecie and expedition, must elect, as they have alreadie out of thir own number and others, a Councel of State. (Pp. 432–33)

A formidable body indeed, whose powers are in the *Proposalls* said to be "in a manner the same with that of parlaments" (p. 337). Later in *The Readie and Easie Way*, however, Milton assures his readers that "they shall not . . . need to be much mistrustfull of thir chosen Patriots in the Grand Councel; who will be then rightly call'd the true keepers of our libertie, though the most of thir business will be in forein affairs" (p. 443). Crucial legislative and fiscal responsibilities are glossed over.

　　Christopher Hill is undoubtedly correct when he locates sovereignty in this commonwealth firmly at the center: the Grand Council proposed by Milton "was not merely a piece of balancing machinery: it was itself to be the government."[15] This concentration of power is only obscured by the rhetorical sleight of hand with which Milton presents his system to a nation wary of the centralizing tendencies of the revolution:

When we have our forces by sea and land, either of a faithful Armie or a setl'd Militia, in our own hands to the firm establishing of a free Commonwealth, publick accounts under our own inspection, general laws and taxes with thir causes in our own domestic suffrages, judicial laws, offices and ornaments at home in our own ordering and administration . . . what can a perpetual senat have then wherin to grow corrupt, wherin to encroach upon us or usurp; or if they do, wherin to be formidable? (YP VII, p. 461)

If the scope of the Grand Council if indeed so limited, we might ask why it forms the heart of Milton's proposals, and why in the second edition of *The Readie and Easie Way* he enlarges "especially that part which argues for a perpetual Senat" (p. 409). More to the point, we might wonder how an institution so constrained, or as Milton puts it in another tract, "with so little matter in thir Hands" (p. 394), could possibly represent a nation's political salvation.

　　The stress on education as a means of popular improvement is the one detail of *The Readie and Easie Way* which seems unequivocally to reaffirm Milton's earlier sense of the revolutionary potential of human action in history. Several critics perceive a revived optimism in Milton's demand for improvements "not in grammar only, but in all liberal arts and exercises" (YP VII, p. 459). Austin Woolrych calls this "the most attractive of Milton's proposals," and Arthur E. Barker detects a continued faith "not only in the power but in the progress of truth."[16] However, the promise of growth and development which education extends is clearly incompatible with Milton's static political settlement. Improved instruction may spread "the natural heat of government and culture more distributively to all extreme parts, which now lie numm and neglected" (YP VII, p. 460), but under Milton's political settlement this "natural heat" is relegated exclusively to the provinces, so that the Grand Council can preserve its splendid and frozen isolation. Though he defends the "advancements of every person according to his merit" (p. 458), Milton rejects a system of rotation that would empower "inexpert and novice counselors" (p. 437): "For it appeers not how this [rotation] can be don, without danger and mischance of putting out a great number of the best and ablest: in whose stead new elections may bring in as many raw, unexperienc'd and otherwise affected, to the weakning and much altering for the wors of public transactions" (p. 435). Any active process of training or education threatens the fundamental principles of Milton's government. He suggests that younger statesmen "exercise and fit themselves" in local politics, "till thir lot fall to be chosen into the Grand Councel" (p. 459), but stifles such aspirations with a political system that provides real opportunity only on the rare occasion of the death or corruption of an individual councillor. The rebuke issued in *Eikonoklastes* to those who would establish as law "the wisdom and pietie of former Parlaments" and "the ancient and universall practise of Christian Churches" (YP III, p. 464) suggests, I think, the frustration with which an aspiring politician (and perhaps the earlier Milton) would confront the oppressive and inflexible political forms of *The Readie and Easie Way:*

As if they who come with full autority to redress public greevances, which ofttimes are Laws themselves, were to have thir hands bound by Laws in force, or the supposition of more pietie and wisdom in thir Ancestors, or the practise of Churches heertofore, whose Fathers, notwithstanding all these pretences, made as vast alterations to free themselves from ancient Popery. (YP III, p. 464)

Ultimately, the idea of education comes to serve rather than invigorate Milton's commonwealth. An educated populace is rendered eminently governable:

To make the people fittest to chuse, and the chosen fittest to govern, will be to mend our corrupt and faulty education, to teach the people faith not without vertue, temperance, modestie, sobrietie, parsimonie, justice; not to admire wealth or honour; to hate turbulence and ambition; to place every one his privat welfare and happiness in the public peace, libertie, and safetie. (YP VII, p. 443)

Particularly in the final clause, where individual interest yields to collective "peace" and "safetie," we sense that this is not precisely the "flourishing, vertuous, noble, and high spirited" citizenry elsewhere promised. If the inhabitants of Milton's free commonwealth are more than the obedient slaves of a king, they are something less than *Areopagitica*'s vigorous seekers after truth, and *The Tenure*'s sovereign, revolutionary individuals.

Milton's free commonwealth cannot, I think, be defended by attempts to discover the flexibility and vitality of his earlier thinking beneath its restrictive surfaces. Instead, *The Readie and Easie Way* should be assessed as a response (however unfortunate) to extraordinary political conditions. By proposing a firm, unrepresentative government that might stem the royalist tide, Milton resists what now appears an inevitable historical development. This accounts for critical praise of the tract as a heroic last stand, "the product of an idealism which refuses to be quenched even in the hour of defeat."[17] However, Milton's loyalty to "the good Old Cause" has deeper roots than this stalwart opposition to a particular historical trend. As the introductory retrospective of *The Readie and Easie Way* indicates, Milton felt that he was engaging an enemy intent on sacrificing England's revolutionary heritage; the royalists were rejecting a bold future for the comfortable past, "treading back again with lost labour all our happie steps in the progress of reformation" (YP VII, p. 424). Paradoxically, Milton's very commitment to the revolutionary promise of human activity produces his violent reaction to history, which surfaces in *The Readie and Easie Way* as a repression of instability and change. There is more at stake here than the form of government under which the writer will live out his days, since Milton had long argued that the events of the English Revolution represented God's own historical design. What is unfortunate is that by 1660 Milton proves incapable of casting a vote for reform through some daring new departure of his own, and thus seems to confirm the bankruptcy of "the good Old Cause." He trades in some of his most cherished convictions about the progressive dimension of human social and political experience, and strives to arrest English history at what must have seemed to him its furthest point of advancement.

This is not Milton's final statement on the revolutionary potential of history. Instead, *The Readie and Easie Way* marks one important moment in the development of his thinking about history and reform. In this tract, the final disintegration of the parliamentary cause has brought about a sobering recognition that the course of human history is uncertain, and has forced Milton to abandon his confident "apocalyptic progressivism." At the same time, a desperate hope that the triumph of royalism is not yet inevitable, and that the remnants of a revolutionary heritage can be preserved, forestalls the appearance of his later conviction that improvement will come (and may even involve human effort), but that it must wait upon the will of God. Once the tide had indeed turned and the Restoration was an accomplished fact, Milton could once again embrace historical change, and look forward to revolutionary accomplishment in the fullness of time (represented in the abstract in *Paradise Regained* and *Samson Agonistes*). This deferral is undoubtedly a loss when viewed from the heady perspective of *Areopagitica*, where the hand of God is everywhere, and where any moment is potentially improving, but it is hardly a surprising development for a writer who had experienced the collapse of his own high expectations. Milton to the end refused to rest content with mere "beatific vision," and his renunciation of historical change in *The Readie and Easie Way* was short-lived: the revolutionary promise of time finally receded into the future, but it did not disappear.

University of Chicago

NOTES

1. *Complete Prose Works of John Milton*, 8 vols., ed. Don M. Wolfe et al. (New Haven, 1953–82), vol. VII, p. 408. All further references to Milton's prose are from this edition, and are included in the text as YP; dates for the texts are those provided in this edition. References to *The Readie and Easie Way* are to the second edition, except where otherwise noted.

2. Although Milton's fondness for the immediate past in *The Readie and Easie Way* is unprecedented, earlier tracts do engage in a historical polemic. *Areopagitica*, for example, examines the "pedigree" of licensing in order to show that the "best and wisest Commonwealths through all ages, and occasions have forborne to use it, and falsest seducers, and oppressors of men were the first who tooke it up" (YP II, p. 507); *The Tenure* defends the the execution of Charles "by autorities and reasons, not learnt in corners among Scisms and Heresies . . . but fetch'd out of the midst of choicest and most authentic learning" (YP III, p. 198). As these passages indicate, the appeal is again to principle rather than mere antiquity—"the best and the wisest," the "choicest and most authentic." Milton's arguments from history are often accompanied by a disclaimer which suggests an

unwillingness to bind the judgment of a regenerate Christian to even the purest of historical authorities. *Of Reformation* only turns to history after deriding "the votarists of Antiquity" (YP I, p. 541; *The Tenure* attacks those who would rather rely on tradition than exercise their own judgment. In *The Ready and Easy Way*, a historical polemic is not treated scornfully, and has more than a functional interest for Milton: the value of the revolutionary heritage is central to his argument.

3. The historical context of *The Readie and Easie Way* is thoroughly recounted in Austin Woolrych's "Introduction" to YP VII. On the resurgence of royalism, see especially pp. 109, 160–61, 195–98.

4. Milton's claim that there are no obstructions to the foundation of his commonwealth is certainly a rhetorical appeal to those who believed that monarchy offered the only sure escape from political instability; this should not, however, obscure his own intense commitment to an unproblematic solution. The rejection of "inconveniences" and "incumbrances" which I quote is, after all, probably directed at the proposals of another republican, James Harrington (YP VII, p. 445, n. 161). Whatever the faults of Harrington's *Oceana*, the author accepts a difficult political situation and attempts to meet it with fundamental revisionary mechanisms.

5. Michael Fixler, *Milton and the Kingdoms of God* (Evanston, Ill., 1964), p. 206.

6. Perez Zagorin, *A History of Political Thought in the English Revolution* (London, 1954), p. 114.

7. The image is pervasive; see for example YP VII, pp. 407, 409, 410, 422, 455.

8. While a metaphor of foundation is not new for Milton, other tracts tend to ascribe foundational stability to ideals rather than to human institutions. In *Of Reformation*, the king's "towring, and stedfast heighth rests upon the unmovable foundations of Justice, and Heroick vertue" (YP I, p. 582); in church reform, "tis not the common Law, nor the civil, but piety, and justice, that are our foundresses" (YP I, p. 605). Elsewhere, Christ is said to have "put our political freedom on a firm foundation" (YP IV, i, p. 375), and scripture is called the "main foundation" and "common ground" of the Protestant religion (YP VII, p. 242). In *The Readie and Easie Way*, "the ground and basis" of good government lies not in an ideal order, but rather in "a general councel of ablest men, chosen by the people" (YP VII, p. 432).

9. Michael Fixler, in his discussion of this closing prayer, comments that "Milton was talking . . . about spiritual beatitude, but in a historical setting with apparent political and social ramifications" (*Milton and the Kingdoms*, pp. 89–90).

10. Ernest Tuveson, *Millennium and Utopia: A Study in the Background of the Idea of Progress* (Berkeley and Los Angeles, 1949), p. 92.

11. Fixler, *Milton and the Kingdoms*, p. 206.

12. Arthur E. Barker, *Milton and the Puritan Dilemma* (Toronto, 1942), p. 272, detects in this passage "the frustration of a great idealism," and characterizes the argument as "an appeal, not quite to naked force, but to force and a justice recognized by few of Milton's countrymen." Although *The Readie and Easie Way* focuses on politics, there are suggestions of this same defensive attitude toward religious freedom. There is "no government more inclinable not to favor only but to protect [it], then a free Commonwealth" (YP VII, p. 456). Milton's aim is to "retain" (p. 420) religious freedom, rather than exercise it in the interest of continuing reform or enlightenment.

13. Perez Zagorin, *A History of a Political Thought*, pp. 111–19, has persuasively argued that an "aristocratic idealism," which would limit political participation to a virtuous elite, is the controlling principle in Milton's political thinking: "Even the idea of liberty, important as it is for Milton, had its claims determined at all times by his aristo-

cratic principle." As Zagorin points out, Milton's system of local government in *The Readie and Easie Way* is more oligarchic than democratic.

14. This attempt to construct a political structure which protects the central power from local activity can be usefully compared with an earlier proposal for ecclesiastical administration in *The Reason of Church-Government*. Milton prefers a presbyterian kind of church council, with a dynamic relationship between the center and its extremities, to the static "pyramidal figure" of episcopacy. His appeal for a reforming crusade manages to integrate activity and stability: "Of such a councell as this every parochiall Consistory is a right homogeneous and constituting part being in it selfe as it were a little Synod, and towards a generall assembly moving upon her own basis in an even and firme progression, as those smaller squares in battell unite in one great cube, the main phalanx, an embleme of truth and stedfastnesse" (YP I, p. 789).

15. Christopher Hill, *Milton and the English Revolution* (New York, 1979), p. 200. Woolrych, YP VII, p. 187, agrees, commenting that Milton's "noble celebration of the virtues of responsible self-government" is undercut by "the pitiably meagre participation that [*The Readie and Easie Way*] actually allows to the people in the shaping of their political destiny. The powers committed to the Grand Council are so very large, and its accountability to public opinion so very small."

16. Woolrych, YP VII, p. 186; Barker, *Milton and the Puritan Dilemma*, p. 276.

17. Barker, *Milton and the Puritan Dilemma*, p. 264.

MILTON'S CHIEF RABBI

Jason P. Rosenblatt

ALTHOUGH THE first systematic analyses of Milton's debt to Jewish exegesis appeared in the 1920s in the work of Denis Saurat, Harris Fletcher, and E. C. Baldwin, the first hint of such a debt appears in 1683, in Matthew Poole's *Annotations Upon the Holy Bible*.[1] In his commentary on the third chapter of Genesis, the author of *Synopsis criticorum*, whose eclecticism generally extends to those authorized patristic, scholastic, and reformation sources one expects to find in the most exhaustive scriptural commentaries of that century, considers the question "How the Serpent could speak, and what the Woman conceived of his speech, and why she was not affrighted, but continued the discourse with it":

> A late ingenious and learned Writer represents the matter thus, in which there is nothing absurd or incredible: The Serpent makes his address to the Woman with a short speech, and salutes her as the Empress of the World, &c. She is not affrighted, because there was as yet no cause of fear, no sin, and therefore no danger, but wonders and enquires what this meant, and whether he was not a brute Creature, and how he came to have speech, and understanding? The Serpent replies, that he was no better than a brute, and did indeed want both these gifts, but by eating of a certain fruit in this Garden he got both. She asked what Fruit and Tree that was? Which when he shewed her, she replied, This, no doubt, is an excellent fruit, and likely to make the eater of it wise; but God hath forbidden us this Fruit: To which the Serpent replies, as it here follows in the Text. It is true, this discourse is not in the Text; but it is confessed by Jewish, and other Expositors, that these words, *Yea, hath God said, & c.* are a short and abrupt sentence, and that they were but the close of a foregoing discourse; which might well enough be either this now mentioned, or some other of a like nature. And that expression which follows[,] *v. 6 When the Woman saw, i.e.* understood, *that it was a Tree to be desired to make one wise,* may seem to imply, both that the Serpent told her, and that she believed, that the speech and understanding of the Serpent was the effect of the eating of that Fruit; and therefore that if it raised him from a brute Beast to the degree of a reasonable Creature, it would elevate her from the humane to a kind of divine nature or condition. (Poole, *Annotations*, sig. B3r)

Of interest both here and in the rest of Poole's extensive annotations on this crucial chapter is the characterization of Milton as "ingenious and

43

learned" expositor rather than poet and, implicitly, of Books IX and X of *Paradise Lost* as biblical exegesis rather than epic. In this excerpt, as elsewhere in the annotations on Genesis, chapter iii, Poole appears to have Milton's great argument at his elbow, next to the Bible itself. He begins with the serpent's "short speech" (*PL* IX, 532–48) and subsequent salutation to the "Empress of this fair World, resplendent *Eve*" (IX, 568), and ends by paraphrasing the serpent's argument of proportional elevation ("I of brute human, yee of human Gods," IX, 712), which he regards as a gloss of "When the woman saw" (Genesis iii, 6).[2]

Less interesting, perhaps, to readers of Milton in general, but more relevant to the topic of this essay, Milton's use of extrabiblical Hebraica, is Poole's view of the long dialogue between Satan and Eve as a sort of midrash on Genesis iii, 1, for which he appeals to "Jewish, and other Expositors." Poole needed to look no further than Rashi's *Commentary* on this verse for the interpretation of the serpent's question as merely "the close of a foregoing discourse": "although he [the serpent] saw them [Adam and Eve] eating from other fruits yet he entered into a long conversation with her so that she should answer him, and so that he might then have an opportunity to talk about that *particular* tree."[3]

From the seventeenth through the nineteenth centuries, Milton's biographers assumed his familiarity with Hebrew, though, unlike Poole, they would have limited his use of it to the Old Testament. John Aubrey notes: "He was an early riser. Yea, after he lost his sight. He had a man read to him: the first thing he read was the Hebrew bible."[4] David Masson, unsurprisingly, discusses in tandem Milton's competence in Hebrew and Greek and concludes circumspectly: "there is evidence of his acquaintance with Greek authors, and of his having more than ventured on Hebrew."[5] Masson's magisterial study established Milton as a dogmatic Puritan, the sort who would have applied his Hebrew learning to the study of Scripture alone.

Poole's early invocation of Jewish expositors in connection with Milton is not unique. Another Bible scholar, Richard Laurence, in his 1819 edition of the apocryphal *Ascension of Isaiah,* mentioned Milton's debt to rabbinical literature, including the midrash *Pirke de-Rabbi Eliezer.*[6] Still, such invocations are rare, and they are echoed only in the twentieth century, when literary scholars belatedly develop the hints given by biblical scholars. As if making up for lost time, these scholars tend to exaggerate Milton's linguistic competence. Their extravagant claims are by now familiar to Miltonists: Denis Saurat's sweeping assertion that, except for his materialism and mortalism, "the whole of Milton's philosophy is found in the Kabbalah";[7] E. C. Baldwin's citations of midrashic sources for some of Milton's ideas in *Paradise Lost;* and Harris Fletcher's book-length argument that Milton read Buxtorf's edition of the *Biblia rabbinica* with the commentaries of Rashi, Ibn Ezra, Levi ben Gerson, and David Kimchi.

That these studies were at the time of publication (between 1925 and 1930) regarded as more or less persuasive may have something to do with the anti-Puritan climate of opinion in the 1920s. The program to create a new conception of the poet as the last great exemplar of Renaissance humanism rather than as merely a Puritan extended into the area of Milton's Hebrew readings. Emphasis was now placed not on the Bible but on arcane rabbinic materials that would demonstrate the poet's breadth of learning, daring originality, and unorthodoxy. Of course, Milton's general reputation for broad learning has in the past lent credibility to theories assuming his familiarity with all manner of obscure material. Exhibiting the range of his learning through allusion, borrowed image, or outright namedropping, Milton remains among the most compliant of all major English poets for a source study.

Inevitably, reaction set in, and more recent evaluations of these studies of Milton and Hebraica contain accusations of bad faith. Saurat was said to have relied on a faulty translation of the Zohar; Baldwin never considered the problem of the inaccessibility to Milton of the many extrabiblical sources he cited, and Baldwin himself relied not on the original sources but rather on Louis Ginzberg's compilation *The Legends of the Jews;* finally, Fletcher lacked the proficiency required to handle the Buxtorf Bible.[8] This sort of corrective scholarship goes far toward replacing Milton on his sectarian perch, but at least it stops short of accusing Milton himself of bad faith.

Such an accusation is strongly implicit in the most recent studies of Milton's use of the extrabiblical Hebraic sources he cites in his prose. Milton excoriates lazy scholars who, ignoring direct sources, rely instead on "an English concordance and a *topic folio*, the gatherings and savings of a sober graduatship, a *Harmony* and a *Catena* . . . not to reck'n up the infinit helps of interlinearies, breviaries, *synopses*, and other loitering gear."[9] Yet if there is at present a consensus on the subject of Milton's rabbinic learning, it is the skeptical one that Milton took his information from concordances, lexicons, and phrase books — in short, from seventeenth-century versions of Cliff's Notes.[10] The scholar who refers approvingly in *Doctrine and Discipline of Divorce* to medieval Hebrew commentaries on the Bible and to Maimonides's *Guide for the Perplexed;* who in *Tetrachordon* indicates his awareness of the controversy between Hillel and Shammai regarding divorce at will at the end of the talmudic

Tractate Gittin; and who cites Tractate Sanhedrin a number of times in his first *Defence of the People of England* is now accused of having "employed . . . dubious scholarship."[11]

In this essay I shall argue for an intermediate position on the question of Milton's Hebrew learning. I still maintain that Milton's competence in biblical Hebrew would have enabled him to read Rashi's *Commentary*, which appeared in more editions of the Hebrew Bible than any other.[12] Rashi's lucidity, the simplicity of his diction, his analytic approach to Scripture, which allies him to a tradition of literal exposition originating in the Middle Ages and culminating in the great exegetical works of the Reformation—all would have made him Milton's most accessible primary rabbinic source. Yet of course Rashi's *Commentary*, despite its likely influence on *Paradise Lost*, cannot account for other rabbinic presences in Milton's prose and poetry, such as the Talmud, Midrash, and Maimonides.

I should like to suggest that John Selden (1584–1654), the most learned person in England in the seventeenth century and the author of a half dozen immense rabbinical works, is the principal source of Milton's Jewish learning. In a Latin tortuous enough to discourage casual readers, Selden explores thoroughly the Jewish position on natural law, marriage and divorce, the division of authority between clergy and laity, the limitations of royal power, and manifold other topics that concerned Milton. To read Selden is to become something of an expert in Jewish learning. This means that while Milton may indeed have lacked the linguistic competence to tackle the Talmud directly, his knowledge of rabbinic sources would nonetheless have been extensive.

Scholars celebrated for their own broad and deep learning gladly conceded Selden's superiority and conferred titles on him. For Ben Jonson, who praised his "unweary'd paine / Of Gathering" and his "Bountie in pouring out againe," Selden was "Monarch in Letters"; for Grotius, he was the "glory of the English nation"; and for John Lightfoot, he was "the great Mr. Selden, the Learnedst man upon the earth."[13] One of the founders of English legal history, he was also an expert in antiquarian studies and oriental languages. According to the *Dictionary of National Biography*, most of "Selden's work as an orientalist consisted in the exposition of Jewish, or rather rabbinical, law. . . . The acquaintance with the original of the Old Testament and the ancient versions and commentaries which all these works display is very great. Their author's familiarity with rabbinical literature was such as has been acquired by few non-Israelite scholars." It is certain that Selden relied not merely on secondary materials, such as those of Johannes Buxtorf, both father and son, but read both the Babylonian and Jerusalem Talmud as well as the varied works of post-talmudic rabbinical literature that crowded his library.[14] And Maimonides's *Code* was his favorite source.

Milton shows himself to be familiar with Selden's *History of Tithes* (1617) in *The Likeliest Means to Remove Hirelings*, and *De dis Syriis* (1617) may have provided some of the names of pagan deities in the Nativity ode,[15] but three other works contribute a great deal more to the Hebraic factor in his prose and poetry. The first, *De jure naturali et gentium, Juxta disciplinam Ebraeorum* (London, 1640, 847 folio pages), treats from a rabbinic perspective universal and particular law — that is, those commandments given by pre-Mosaic revelation to the whole of the human race and those specifically given to Israel and binding only upon them. Among other things, this comprehensive and minutely detailed work provided Milton with the principal rabbinic comparisons of Edenic, natural, and Mosaic laws and thus helped to shape the polity of paradise in his great epic. Moreover, in a prefatory statement explaining his method in *De jure*, Selden typically appeals to precedent for publishing opposed and disagreeing views as a means of distinguishing more readily between truth and falsehood. In the *Areopagitica*, addressing Parliament, Milton also employs this firmly established usage and points to Selden, M.P. for the University of Oxford, to authorize it:

Wherof what better witnes can ye expect I should produce, then one of your own now sitting in Parlament, the chief of learned men reputed in this Land, Mr. *Selden*, whose volume of naturall & national laws proves, not only by great autorities brought together, but by exquisite reasons and theorems, almost mathematically demonstrative, that all opinions, yea errors, known, read, and collated, are of main service & assistance toward the speedy attainment of what is truest. (YP II, p. 513)

The final argument of Milton's *Doctrine and Discipline of Divorce* is that divorce should not be restrained by law, "*it being against the Law of nature and of Nations. The larger proof wherof referr'd to Mr.* Seldens *Book* De jure naturali & gentium" (YP II, p. 350). In the most Hebraic of Milton's prose works, the Mosaic law rather than the Son incarnates deity:

The hidden wayes of [God's] providence we adore & search not; but the law is his reveled will, his complete, his evident, and certain will; herein he appears to us as it were in human shape, enters into cov'nant with us, swears to keep it, binds himself like a just lawgiver to his own prescriptions, gives himself to be understood by men, judges and is judg'd, measures and is commensurat to right reason. (YP II, p. 292)

It is not surprising that in such a work Milton should recommend Selden to his reader: "let him hast'n to be acquainted with that noble volume written by our learned *Selden, Of the law of nature & of Nations,* a work more useful and more worthy to be perus'd, whosoever studies to be a great man in wisdom, equity, and justice, then all those *decretals,* and *sumles sums,* which the *Pontificial Clerks* have doted on" (YP II, pp. 350–51).

Regarding marriage and divorce, the rabbinical work by Selden of greatest influence on Milton is the *Uxor Ebraica, seu de nuptiis & divortiis ex iure civili, id est, divino & Talmudico, veterum Ebraeorum* (London, 1646, 630 quarto pages), an exhaustive summary of the Jewish law of marriage and divorce and of the status of the married woman under Jewish law. Five times in *De jure* Selden indicates that *Uxor Ebraica* is ready for the press, and Eivion Owen has already argued persuasively that Milton had access to the manuscript before writing *Tetrachordon.* Masson believes that in 1643 or 1644, when Milton had paid Selden the compliments quoted above, he "first made Selden's personal acquaintance."[16]

Milton praises the *Uxor Ebraica* whenever he names it, and he names it often, in contexts that indicate its importance to him. The man who married Katherine Woodcock in a civil ceremony performed by an alderman and a justice of the peace[17] appeals to "Selden . . . in his Uxor Heb. Book 2. c[hapter] 28, all of it, and [chapter] 29" for evidence "[t]hat the ministers of the Church had no right, among the earliest Christians, to share in the celebration of either contracts or nuptials."[18] In a striking passage of "The Likeliest Means to Remove Hirelings," composed a year after Katherine's death, he expands upon this point:

As for marriages that ministers should meddle with them, as not sanctifi'd or legitimat without their celebration, I finde no ground in scripture either of precept or example. Likeliest it is (which our *Selden* hath well observd, *1. 2, c. 28, ux. Eb.*) that in imitation of heathen priests who were wont at nuptials to use many rites and ceremonies, and especially, judging it would be profitable, and the increase of thir autoritie, not to be spectators only in busines of such concernment to the life of man, they insinuated that marriage was not holy without their benediction, and for the better colour, made it a sacrament; being of it self a civil ordinance, a household contract, a thing indifferent and free to the whole race of mankinde, not as religious, but as men: best, indeed, undertaken to religious ends. . . . Yet not therefor invalid or unholy without a minister and his pretended necessary hallowing, more then any other act, enterprise or contract of civil life, which ought all to be don also in the Lord and to his glorie. (YP VII, p. 299)

A section of the *Uxor* of capital importance to Milton is the account of the schools of Hillel and Shammai, which Selden compares with the Proculian and Sabinian schools of Roman law. This appears in a discussion that attempts to reconcile the talmudic-rabbinic view of divorce with Christ's statements in the New Testament. Milton refers to this section in places where the acknowledged presence of an external authority is rare, in *De doctrina Christiana*, where Scripture, in conjunction with the author's spirit, generally claims exclusive interpretative rights (YP VI, p. 378), and in the autobiographical section of the *Defensio secunda*, an itemized, retrospective account of his own prose production (YP IV, pp. 624–25).

The third rabbinical work, which may have influenced Milton almost as much as the other two though it has never been mentioned in connection with him, is *De synedriis et praefecturis juridicis veterum Ebraeorum* (London, 1650, 1653, 1655), published in three quarto books and occupying 1,132 huge folio columns in the *Opera omnia*.[19] *De synedriis*, a work of stupendous erudition, deals primarily with the constitution of Jewish ecclesiastical courts, drawing attention to relevant parallels with the constitution of the church as regards the division of authority between clergy and lay persons. Like the other two works that influenced Milton, *De synedriis* cites primary rabbinic sources in their original Hebrew and Aramaic and then translates them into Latin. Organized like the Talmud itself, in a style that is not so much digressive as voluminous, it begins by exploring a single topic's ramifications and ends by drawing those now interrelated topics into its plenum of discourse. There is no index in the edition of *De synedriis* that Milton used (nor is there any in the editions of the other two rabbinical works discussed here that were published in Milton's lifetime), and he could not have predicted where he might find the topic he was looking for, whether it was the seven Noachide commandments, pre-Mosaic courts of justice, capital punishment, the penalty of excommunication beginning with Adam, ordination of judges, the Christian doctrine of the Trinity and the Kabbalah, the seventy elders endowed with the divine spirit who formed the great Sanhedrin or Supreme Court in Israel, or limitations on royal authority.

I stress the inconvenience of using Selden, the talmudic thoroughness of his arguments, and the length of his rabbinical works in order to counter the implicit charge of bad faith brought against Milton recently by scholars investigating his knowledge and use of rabbinic materials. A close look at the most recent essays on this subject, one by Leonard Mendelsohn and two by Golda Werman,[20] should reveal that Milton's familiarity with extrabiblical Hebraica is less casual than they acknowledge and should strengthen the possibility of a connection between Milton and Selden. These skeptical scholars are more persuasive

than Fletcher and others, in part because they are more familiar with
the primary sources; moreover, they are both correct in their general
opinion that Milton relied on some intermediate Latin sources for most
of his rabbinic citations. Yet it may be unfair to conclude from this that
Milton's scholarship is "dubious"; that though he chides Salmasius for
turning over phrase books, lexicons, and glossaries he is guilty of the same
practice; that his understanding of the rabbinic material in the prose
tracts is "superficial"; and that he derived his material "by way of casual
gleanings . . . rather than from a deep study of the sources."[21]

In order to prove that Milton could not read the Talmud, Mendelsohn concentrates exclusively on the references to Tractate Sanhedrin in
the *Defence of the People of England*. Mendelsohn does not attempt to
supply the identity of Milton's sources; his purpose is rather to demonstrate in detail Milton's interpretative inadequacies. Here is Milton responding to Salmasius, who has attempted to elicit Talmudic support
for virtually unlimited royal prerogative:

in yet another ill-omened undertaking, you begin to give lessons on the Talmud.
In a desire to prove that a king is not judged you show from the Codex of Sanhedrin
that "the king neither judges nor is judged," but this conflicts with the request of
that people who sought a king for the very reason that he might judge them. You
try in vain to cover this over, and tell us indeed that it should be understood of
kings who ruled after the captivity; but listen to Maimonides, who gives this definition of the difference between the kings of Israel and Judah: "the descendants
of David judge and are judged," but says neither is true of the Israelites. (YP IV,
p. 354)

In *De synedriis*, which refers many hundreds of times to Tractate
Sanhedrin, Selden reconciles different opinions on whether that court
had the power to pass judgment on the king's person. He treats in a number of different contexts the topic "Rex Israelis non judicabat, nec judicabatur, Rex Judae & judicabat & judicabatur." Many times he cites both
the crucial discussion in the Talmud as well as Maimonides in the *Mish-
neh Torah* to prove that the distinction between the kings of Israel and
Judah is based on the haughtiness or violence of the former and the humility of the latter. Thus, Rabbi Joseph (in Sanhedrin 19a) holds that
the kings of Israel, violent and disobedient to the Torah, are kept from
judging and being judged;[22] and Maimonides concurs:

Reges familiae Davidicae & judicabant & judicabantur: Etiam testimonium ad-
versus eos praebere licuit. At vero de regibus Israel decrevere sapientes, eos nec
judicare nec judicari, nec testimonium praebere nec in ipsos praeberi testimonium,

quoniam corda eorum superba fuere, nec aliud inde manaret praeter scandalum
atque abolitionem institutorum legis. [marginal note: Maimonid. Halach. *Mela-
cim*, cap. 3. & *Sanhedrin*, cap. 2] (*Opera omnia*, I, ii, 1674–75)

[The kings of the House of David both judged and were judged, and it was lawful to give testimony against them. About the kings of Israel, however, the rabbis [*sapientes*] decreed that they should neither judge nor be judged, and that they
should not offer testimony nor testimony be offered against them, since their hearts
were proud, lest nothing spring therefrom except scandal and the abrogation of
the institutes of the law.]

In his essay, Mendelsohn, who has so far been cited with approval
by Miltonists, takes a proprietary attitude toward the Talmud: "It is not
the diction, but the style, grammar, and most of all, the system of approach to a problem which render the Talmud impenetrable for the un-
initiated" (p. 129, n.14.). Were Mendelsohn familiar with Selden, he
would recognize him as an initiate, capable of satisfying all the criteria
Mendelsohn himself has set down, such as understanding the Talmud's
"peculiar terminology, its abundant abbreviated and contracted words,
and its host of other stylistic peculiarities" (p. 129). Thus, for example,
regarding kings of the House of Israel neither judging nor being judged,
Selden quotes the following narrative evidence from Tractate Sanhedrin,
which in the original is indeed as elliptical as Mendelsohn would claim
it is. When the slave of King Alexander Jannaeus killed a man, Simeon
ben Shetah, leader of the Sanhedrin, required his presence at court. The
two leaders fell into an argument over whether the king should stand
or be seated, Jannaeus maintaining that he would respect the wishes of
the whole court in the matter:

He [Simeon ben Shetah] turned to his right, and they [the judges] bent their faces
down to the ground [as a result of fear and said nothing]; also when he turned to
his left, they looked down to the ground. Then Simeon ben Shetah said to them,
"Are you masters of thought? [You are calculating according to your own interests and thus remain silent.] Let the Master of Thoughts come and call you to account." Immediately, Gabriel came and struck them down to the ground, and they
died. At that moment [when the rabbis saw that the Sanhedrin lacked the power
to control the king], it was declared that a king [not of the House of David] may
neither judge nor be judged, testify nor testify against [because of the danger in
the matter].[23]

Selden cites the original text, then translates into Latin, consistently
filling in gaps and identifying the antecedents of pronouns, as in this
excerpt:

Simeon Ben Shatach *princeps synedrii* monuit collegas ut rem animadverterent atque in judicium vocarent. . . . Conversus *princeps synedrii* in dextram, vidit omnes oculos in solum defixisse. Idem, in sinistram conversus, vidit. . . . Confestim Gabriel advenit, & eos humi afflixit, adeo ut omnes morerentur. (Selden's italics; *Opera omnia*, I, ii, 1525)

[Simeon ben Shetah, the leader of the Sanhedrin, pointed out to his colleagues that they should consider the matter and bring it before the court. . . . When he turned to the right, the leader of the Sanhedrin saw all eyes fastened on the ground. Likewise, when he turned to the left, he saw [the same thing]. . . . Immediately Gabriel appeared and dashed them down to the ground so that all would die.]

In the *First Defence*, Milton derides this story, which after all supports his opponent Salmasius's contention that kings are exempt from judgment, though the tone seems to indicate that this exemption derives from a collective failure of nerve. The text is problematic, and Gabriel's smiting has also been interpreted (without the brackets provided in the English translation) as punishment for daring to require a king of Israel to stand. Milton is ungracious, but his comment does indicate an understanding of the literal account:

You say on my behalf that Aristobulus first and then Jannaeus surnamed Alexander did not receive that royal right [not to be judged] from the Sanhedrin which is the guardian and interpreter of rights, but rather by a gradual usurpation on their own account against the opposition of the council. To please these kings that fine tale about "Gabriel smiting" the leaders of the Sanhedrin was made up, and this great right of the king not to be judged, on which you seem to depend so much, was by your own confession derived from that old wives' tale or even worse, being but a rabbinical fable. (YP IV, p. 355)

Mendelsohn (p. 133) criticizes Milton for assuming that Gabriel smote the leaders of the Sanhedrin:

Whoever it was who consulted the Talmud directly was . . . misled by the indefinite pronoun references "them" and "they." Actually these pronouns refer not to the principal men, but to everyone else. All present, *except the principal men*, were slain. If Milton did confront this passage in the original, he was confused by the pronoun reference, though such confusion would argue against familiarity with Talmudic style. . . . it is much more probable that he never encountered this passage either in the original or in an accurate translation. (My emphasis)

One might argue that Milton's reading of the story is as valid as Mendelsohn's (the text does not indicate that the principal men were spared) and that the peremptory tone of the latter's essay unfairly diminishes Milton. Another talmudic passage less susceptible to definitive interpretation than Mendelsohn concedes deals with a basic point of difference regarding royal power: "R. Jose said: 'Whatever is enumerated in the chapter of the king, the king is permitted to do.' R. Judah said: 'This chapter was intended only to put fear into them [the people, so that they should receive the king's rule with fear]" (Sanhedrin, 20b).

In replying to Salmasius, Milton identifies "the chapter of the king" as Deuteronomy, chapter xvii, which deals with royal responsibility as well as privilege, rather than 1 Samuel, chapter viii, which deals exclusively with privilege:

You then turn to the rabbis and cite two of them with no better luck than you had before, for it is obvious that the chapter about the king which Rabbi Joses spoke of as containing the rights of kings is in Deuteronomy and not in Samuel; and Rabbi Judas declared quite correctly, contradicting you, that the passage in Samuel concerns only his putting fear into the people. (YP IV, p. 353)

Mendelsohn finds Milton's reading of this passage to be "inept"; for him it is "obvious" that R. Jose's "chapter about the king" is 1 Samuel, chapter viii, and any "doubt as to the source would be resolved by Rashi, who summarizes all the evidence for assigning the passage to Samuel" (Mendelsohn, pp. 129–30). Moreover, he continues, Milton might have consulted Kimchi on 1 Samuel viii, 9, in the Buxtorf Bible that Fletcher claims he knew, for a full explanation of the disagreement between R. Jose and R. Judah. Mendelsohn is overstating the case when he asserts that the talmudic text only appears to be ambiguous and that there is no rabbinic warrant for identifying R. Jose's chapter about the king as Deuteronomy, chapter xvii. Rav Meir Abulafia, the most renowned Spanish rabbi of the first half of the thirteenth century, in his commentary on Sanhedrin, *Yad ramah*, holds that the chapter on the king is not 1 Samuel, chapter viii, but (as Milton would have it) Deuteronomy, chapter xvii. According to this minority opinion, even the chapter in Deuteronomy does not deal with kingship as a positive commandment but rather threatens the people so that if they set a king over themselves his awe will be upon them. This view interprets the similar phrasing in both chapters, reflecting a desire for a king "like as all the nations that are about me" (Deut. xvii, 14; 1 Sam. viii, 5), to suggest that both intend to put fear into the people. The point here is that a rabbinic opinion unacknowledged by Mendelsohn but hardly inept interprets Deuteronomy, chapter xvii, as permitting rather than commanding the appointment of a king.

When Mendelsohn claims that Deuteronomy, chapter xvii, lists only limitations on a king's power and not privileges, he is ignoring the exten-

sive discussion in tractate Sanhedrin, in exactly the same textual neigh-
borhood he is visiting, of the privileges of kingship implicit in that chapter (Sanhedrin, 21a–22a). Finally, it is disingenuous to attack Milton
for not inferring the full positions of R. Jose and R. Judah from either
Rashi's brief comment or Kimchi's elliptical one.[24]

In her recent learned essay, "Milton's Use of Rabbinic Material,"
Golda Werman never resorts to verbal overkill, though she too assumes
that Milton's exclusive reliance on translation makes his understanding
of rabbinic material superficial. Yet if Milton read, say, Selden's comprehensive survey of opinion on whether the king was subject to stripes
from the Sanhedrin — ranging from Maimonides to contemporaries such
as Grotius, Petit, and Casaubon — then there are reserves of knowledge
behind even the following reproach to Salmasius: "That Hebrew kings
can be judged and even condemned to the lash is shown at length by
Sichard from the rabbinical writings; and it is to him that you owe all
this matter, though you are not ashamed to howl against him" (YP IV,
p. 355). Werman reads this not as an accusation of intellectual dishon-
esty but only of ingratitude toward the translator, upon whose compen-
dium Milton as well as Salmasius relied for this information (pp. 40–41).
Yet, even setting aside this reproach's similarity in spirit to earlier attacks on sciolism, Milton's well-placed confidence in his own proficiency
in Hebrew,[25] and a tone suggesting that the author has himself consulted
a more reliable source, Milton would have found in Selden's *De synedriis* both the information itself and evidence that Salmasius drew upon
Schickhard.

Against Grotius, who supposes that by stripes the rabbinic authorities meant only some symbolic or voluntary penance undergone by the
king for his sins, Selden quotes Maimonides, who clearly states that flogging is the punishment for violating the Deuteronomic prohibition against
the abuse of royal power. His note following the quotation refers to "Maimonid. Hal. *Melakim*, cap. 3, section 4 . . . & videsis Guil. Shickardum
in Jure Regio, cap. 2. theorem 7. pag. 60" (*De synedriis*, col. 1437). In
fact, Selden, who seems to have read all sources primary and secondary,
cites Schickhard on other talmudic passages that Salmasius uses. More
important, Selden also quotes at length from Salmasius's "In defensione
regia, cap. 2" on the question of flogging the king (*De synedriis*, cols.
1524–25, 1676).

Between Salmasius's *Defensio regia* (1649) and Milton's response to
it, *Pro populo defensio* (1651), comes Selden's *De synedriis* (Book I, 1650).
Just as Milton drew upon the manuscript of *Uxor Ebraica* in *Tetrachor-*

don, so does he draw here upon the manuscript of the other two books of *De synedriis* as well as upon the printed book, whose rhetorical contours one can trace in *The First Defence.* Thus, for example, Milton accuses Salmasius of twisting David's words in Psalm xvii ("let my sentence come forth from thy presence"):

> therefore, so Barnachmani has it, "none but God judges a king." But rather it seems more likely that David wrote these words when he was being harassed by Saul and, though already anointed of God, did not refuse even the judgment of Jonathan. . . . Now comes that old argument which is the masterpiece of our courtiers: "Against thee only have I sinned." (YP IV, p. 361)

Selden cites the same texts in the same order: "Hebraei Barnachmoni sententia exstat in dictis Rabbinorum, titulo de judicibus, nulla creatura judicat regem, sed Deus benedictus"; Psalm liv ("tibi soli peccavit"); and, in the same column, Salmasius's "*In defensione regia,* cap. 2."[26]

In March 1649, Milton was ordered to answer the *Eikon basilike,* and it has been suggested that Cromwell had earlier invited Selden to answer it, but that he refused.[27] A similar statement was made about Selden and a reply to Salmasius. In May 1650, Gui Patin wrote from Paris to Dr. Charles Spon that Selden had written a reply to Salmasius but that it was suppressed while being printed.[28] If any of this is true, one might conjecture that *De synedriis* contains a great deal of the material necessary for a response to Salmasius and that Selden might have allowed Milton to make use of it in *The First Defence.* With Selden at his elbow during the composition of *The First Defence,* Milton would have enjoyed the tactical advantage of reading and evaluating Salmasius's opinion on a given topic in the broad context of other arguments, ancient and contemporary.

The problem of how and why Milton used a source bears upon Professor Werman's second essay in which, taking a hint from a note by D. C. Allen, she argues that a Latin translation by Willem Vorstius of the midrashic *Pirke de-Rabbi Eliezer* is a source of material in *Paradise Lost.* Some difficulties that must be overcome if her study is to be successful include convincing the reader that Milton would have been drawn to this source; demonstrating that an idea in the source actually appears in the epic; and proving that the material in question does not also appear in a more accessible source. Werman's scholarship is unusually sound; nevertheless, these difficulties are not always overcome.[29]

The most striking image not of Christian provenance found by both Werman and Allen in the *Pirke* and the epic is that of the nuptial bower:

> it was a place
> Chos'n by the sovran Planter, when he fram'd
> All things to man's delightful use; the roof
> Of thickest covert was inwoven shade
> Laurel and Myrtle, and what higher grew
> Of firm and fragrant leaf; on either side
> *Acanthus*, and each odorous bushy shrub
> Fenc'd up the verdant wall; each beauteous flow'r,
> *Iris* all hues, Roses, and Jessamin
> Rear'd high thir flourisht heads between, and wrought Mosaic.
>
> (*PL* IV, 690–700)

The *Pirke* speaks of "ten wedding canopies" made by God for Adam from precious stones, pearls, and gold, and Vorstius renders *huppah* (canopy) as *thalamus*, which can mean a bride's room or marriage bed. Almost as if to concede tacitly that the union between the Pirke's *huppah* and the Edenic bower needs bolstering, Werman cites a talmudic text in which *huppah* unequivocally means a wedding chamber, though she doesn't indicate how Milton would have known that text (Werman, "Midrash," pp. 155, 170 n.14).

Milton would have found in Selden's writings numerous discussions of *huppah*, including but not limited to the text in *Pirke* as well as the talmudic text cited by Werman. An entire chapter of *Uxor Ebraica* discusses entry into the *huppah* ("introductionem in chuppam, id est, in thalamum nuptialem") and rehearses at length the rabbinic argument that entering into the bower rather than matrimonial blessings effects matrimony: "Non benedictio sponsorum facit seu perficit nuptias, sed deductio in thalamum."[30] "To the Nuptial Bow'r / I led her blushing like the Morn" (*PL* VIII, 510–11), Adam recounts, and perhaps this silent act solemnized his marriage to his blushing bride.

The bower is, in fact, the principal emblem of the wedding:

> Here in close recess
> With Flowers, Garlands, and sweet-smelling Herbs
> Espoused *Eve* deckt first her Nuptial Bed,
> And heav'nly Choirs the Hymenaean sung,
> What day the genial Angel to our Sire
> Brought her in naked beauty.   (*PL* IV, 708–13)

In books by Selden that Milton praised, one finds extensive rabbinic commentary on the bower itself and on nuptial garlands.[31] The most convincing sections of Professor Werman's essay on the *Pirke de-Rabbi Eliezer*'s influence on *Paradise Lost* deal with domestic matters (marriage in the garden, work in Eden), and Selden refers often to this midrash when he discusses marriage.[32]

According to the law of economy of means, Milton found midrashic commentary on the nuptial bower not in a separate volume of the *Pirke* but rather in works by Selden, who cites in addition to this midrash all the major rabbinic sources to which Milton refers or alludes — other *midrashim*, the Talmud, the commentaries of the *Biblia rabbinica*, Maimonides, even the Zohar. This does not necessarily mean that Milton was a one-stop shopper in Selden's supermarket of Hebraic materials. In the *Doctrine and Discipline of Divorce* alone, for example, he refers favorably to Buxtorf's translation of Maimonides's *Guide for the Perplexed* and to specifically rabbinic elements in works by Paulus Fagius and Hugo Grotius.[33] But the presence of rabbinic materials cited by Milton — including hundreds of references to Maimonides and a great many to Grotius as well — in the work of a scholar he singles out for praise does mean that Selden should be recognized as a major Miltonic source. The existence of Selden's work casts doubt on some recent conclusions reached by two Miltonists genuinely familiar with rabbinic learning; had it been noticed, as perhaps it should have been, when the topic of Milton's Hebraica was broached, then the claims of Saurat, Fletcher, and others, checked against the materials gathered by Selden, might have proved to have been more permanently persuasive.

Anyone who wants to enlarge even by one title the already vast wilderness of Miltonic sources should refer first to Selden and then perhaps to Grotius, Fagius, and the other Latin compendia of Hebraic scholarship cited by Milton. Unlike those other compendia, either indexed or at least organized by scriptural chapter and verse, Selden's work is difficult to plunder. One can glance at a work that is amenable to use as a dictionary of rabbinic ideas or as a repository of specific sources; but the reader drawn to Selden must be patient. And the reward of that long, slow gaze is to penetrate beyond such details as this essay has concerned itself with so far, to the heart of Selden's thought.

II

The subject of Milton's Hebraism and even that of John Selden's contribution to it require more than an essay's scope, but before concluding I should like to examine two important examples of rabbinic influence mediated by Selden: Milton's interpretation of the Deuteronomic divorce law in accord with ancient Jewish theory and practice, and his opinion that the polity of the Edenic books of *Paradise Lost* consists of both natural law and an originally benign, embryonic Mosaic law.

William Haller and Arthur Barker, two of this century's finest Miltonists, examine Milton's argument on the subject of divorce within a Puritan context narrowly conceived and thus fail to consider its radically Hebraic ethos.[34] Indeed, Barker actually traces Milton's formulation of the doctrine of Christian liberty, with its corollary of freedom from the bondage of the Mosaic law, to the second edition of *Doctrine and Discipline of Divorce*, which in fact emphasizes on almost every page the perfection and contemporary applicability of that law. The title-page rhetoric of the second edition, asserting that the true doctrine has been "Restor'd" "from . . . bondage," might seem at first to be that of a document of Christian liberty; as it turns out, however, each of Milton's title page changes — including a reference to "that which the Law of God allowes" and the addition of a verse from the Hebrew Bible (Proverbs xviii, 13) — underscores the harmony of law and gospel. In this tract the unabrogated Mosaic law restores freedom to those formerly under the bondage of canon law.

Certainly Milton's enemies attacked the *Doctrine and Discipline of Divorce* for presenting a specifically Jewish theory and practice. Of the relation between Christ's words and the Mosaic law, Milton had insisted: "If we examine over all [Christ's] sayings, we shall find him not so much interpreting the Law with his words, as referring his owne words to be interpreted by the Law" (YP II, p. 301). Henry Hammond might well be remembering this reversal of typology when he refers to the tract as the first in "these licentious times" to plead for divorce: "and the *special* artifice made use of, was that, of bringing back *Christ* unto *Moses*, of interpreting the restraint laid on this matter in the *New Testament*, by *analogie* with the *Judaical permission* in the Old."[35] Alexander Ross, an antitolerationist who would later oppose the readmission of the Jews into England, dismissed succinctly Milton's argument "that a man may put away his Wife, though not for adultery; so taught the Jews."[36]

As chastity in *Comus* incorporates all virtues, and as the single dietary prohibition in the Edenic books of *Paradise Lost* contains all laws, so does the brief Mosaic pronouncement on divorce (Deut. xxiv, 1–2) in Milton's first tract on that subject represent the entire Torah. Most interpreters of the New Testament hold that on one occasion only Jesus dissociated himself directly from a regulation of the Torah: when, in defiance of pharisaic interrogation (Matt. xix, 3–9), he rejected explicitly and categorically the Deuteronomic right of divorce. But in *Doctrine and Discipline of Divorce* Milton forces Christ's words into compliance with that Deuteronomic right and thus becomes in effect a defender of the entire Mosaic law.

When Milton refers on the title page to restoring the doctrine and discipline of divorce from bondage and to recovering the "long-lost meaning" of scriptural passages, "Seasonable to be now thought on in the Reformation intended," he hints at the persona he will be adopting in the body of the tract: that of a new Josiah. Like "good Josiah" (*PL* I, 418), whose discovery and consequent implementation of the "book of the law of the Lord given by Moses" (2 Chron. xxxiv, 2 Kings xxii), after years of idolatrous neglect, made him an obvious symbolic figure to Protestant Reformers, Milton sees himself as a moral archaeologist, picking up shards of truth buried for years in custom and error: "Bringing in my hands an ancient and most necessary, most charitable, and yet most injur'd Statute of *Moses* . . . thrown aside with much inconsiderat neglect, under the rubbish of Canonicall ignorance: as once the whole law was by some such like conveyance in *Josiahs* time (YP II, p. 224).

Milton keeps Josiah's reformative activities in mind when he refers to himself as "the sole advocate of a discount'nanc't truth" (YP II, p. 224); and later, in the *Areopagitica*, his figure stands as a conspicuous exception to the lament that "revolutions of ages do not oft recover the losse of a rejected truth, for the want of which whole Nations fare the worse" (p. 493). Of capital importance for Milton was the belief that the book of the law discovered and defended by Josiah was Deuteronomy, which made their missions identical.[37]

Since Milton's mission is to recover the true scriptural meaning, he values contemporary scholars such as Selden, Grotius, and Fagius only for their familiarity with ancient texts—including the Targum, the Talmud, and medieval rabbinica—and with ancient languages, including Hebrew and Aramaic. The original ideas of Beza, Paraeus, Perkins, and Rivetus he generally answers or corrects. Ultimately, as Robert W. Ayers has noted, the principal nonbiblical authorities upon whom Milton appears to rely in *Doctrine and Discipline of Divorce* are not Puritan, or indeed Christian, but Jewish. And the three principal positions advanced—availability of divorce with right of remarriage for both husband and wife, broadening of grounds to include incompatibility, and removal of divorce from public to private jurisdiction—all accord precisely with Jewish divorce law.[38]

Beginning in *Doctrine and Discipline of Divorce*, continuing in *Tetrachordon*, and concluding in *De doctrina Christiana*, Milton's Hebraic argument for divorce becomes increasingly more rabbinic in nature. This development coincides with his increasing reliance on the rabbinic authorities cited by Selden, first in *De jure naturali* and then in *Uxor Ebraica*. It is tempting to continue the method followed in the first part of this paper, by citing parallel passages: Milton's and Selden's specific references to the very same rabbinic commentaries on Judges who assert that the Hebrew word *zonah* need not refer to a prostitute; and their appeal to both Malachi ii, 16 and Maimonides for the argument that divorce can restore household peace.[39] Instead, I should like to identify as exclusively rabbinic the central argument in all of Milton's discussions of divorce, that Christ's pronouncement on divorce can be accommodated to the Deuteronomic permission.

The Mosaic law authorizes a husband to write a bill of divorce if, through "some uncleanness" (*ervat davar*), his wife should fail to find favor in his eyes (Deut. xxiv, 1); while Christ, speaking to the Pharisees, appears to reject this law and to grant divorce only "for fornication" (Matt. xix, 9). As we shall see, rabbinic discussions of these two key phrases, which appear at first to restrict the grounds of divorce to unchastity and sexual offense, widen their meaning to include any kind of obnoxious behavior.

In *Uxor Ebraica*, Selden quotes the entire talmudic dispute over the meaning of the Deuteronomic phrase *ervat davar*, which led to a fundamental break in the religious schools of Palestine in the first century B.C.E. The School of Shammai, emphasizing *ervah* (shame, nakedness, unchastity), permitted divorce when fornication occurred, because it made the continuation of marriage impossible. The School of Hillel, emphasizing *davar* (a thing), argued that divorce should be granted for any *thing*—that is, for any sort of cause. Selden, who reads Matthew, chapter xix, in the light of this talmudic text (Gittin 90a), demonstrates the consistency of Christ's position with that of an advocate of the School of Shammai. He also points out that the Pharisees whom Christ reproved in this chapter belonged to the School of Hillel.[40]

But then, extending his argument much further, Selden proves through exhaustive citation and analysis that "fornication" (Matt. xix, 9, and xv, 19) is the translation of the Hebrew word *zenut* that both the Old Testament and rabbinic sources apply generically to any form of turpitude (*Uxor*, pp. 479–500). Selden thus identifies the Gospel's ground of divorce, "fornication," with that of the Mosaic law, "some uncleanness," finding in both terms a vastly inclusive meaning. The practical result of narrowing considerably the gap between Hillel's most permissive and Christ's only apparently most restrictive interpretations is that divorce can be granted for virtually any cause at variance with marital harmony.

One can trace this two-pronged argument for reconciling Christ and Moses in all of Milton's major discussions of divorce, though it becomes progressively more explicit:

The cause of divorce mention'd in the Law is translated *some uncleannesse;* but in the Hebrew it sounds *nakednes of ought,* or *any reall nakednes:* which by all the learned interpreters is refer'd to the mind as well as the body. (*Doctrine and Discipline of Divorce,* YP II, p. 244)

For the language of Scripture signifies by fornication . . . not only the trespas of body . . . but signifies also any notable disobedience, or intractable cariage of the wife to the husband. . . . [Fornication] signifies the apparent alienation of mind . . . to any point of will worship, though to the true God; some times it notes the love of earthly things, or worldly pleasures though in a right beleever, some times the least suspicion of unwitting idolatry. As *Num.* 15.39. willfull disobedience to any the least of Gods commandements is call'd fornication. *Psal.* 73.26, 27. a distrust only in God, and withdrawing from the neernes of zeal and confidence which ought to be, is call'd fornication. (*Tetrachordon,* YP II, pp. 672–73)

as Selden demonstrated particularly well in his *Uxor Hebraea,* with the help of numerous Rabbinical texts, the word *fornication,* if it is considered in the light of the idiom of oriental languages, does not mean only adultery. It can mean also either what is called *some shameful thing* (i.e., the lack of some quality which might reasonably be required in a wife), Deut. xxiv. 1, or it can signify anything which is found to be persistently at variance with love, fidelity, help and society. . . . I have proved this elsewhere . . . and Selden has demonstrated the same thing. It would be almost laughable to tell the Pharisees, when they asked whether it was lawful to send away one's wife for every cause, that it was not lawful except in the case of adultery. Because everyone already knew that it was not merely lawful but one's duty to send away an adulteress, and not simply to divorce her but to send her to her death. So the word *fornication* must be interpreted in a much broader sense than that of adultery. (*De doctrina Christiana,* YP VI, p. 378)

In this last excerpt Milton relies on the two-pronged argument which interprets "some shameful thing" broadly, in the light of tractate Gittin 90a, and which then identifies it with "fornication," also broadly interpreted. The critical biblical argument for divorce thus depends ultimately on rabbinic interpretations of two key phrases, one in Hebrew, and the other, as Milton asserts, not Attic but Hebraic, a word which "the Evangelist heer *Hebraizes*" (*Tetrachordon,* YP II, p. 671).

Turning now from the divorce tracts to *Paradise Lost,* we should remember the importance of *Doctrine and Discipline of Divorce* not only in presenting in a favorable light the Mosaic law that Milton will apply to Edenic polity but also in providing a model of that law as easy, charitable, and permissive—more charitable, in fact, than the contemporary Christian interpretation of the law of divorce. In this tract, as in the Edenic books of his great epic, Milton asserts the perfect correspondence between God's will, incarnate in the Mosaic law, and natural law. Here, as in Eden before the Fall, "God and Nature bid the same" (*PL* VI, 176), and Milton speaks of "the fundamentall law book of nature; which *Moses* never thwarts but reverences" (YP II, p. 272):

mariage, unlesse it mean a fit and tolerable mariage, is not inseparable neither by nature nor institution. Not by nature, for then those Mosaick divorces had bin against nature, if separable and inseparable be not contraries, as who doubts they be: and what is against nature is against Law, if soundest Philosophy abuse us not: by this reckning *Moses* should be most unmosaick, that is, most illegal, not to say most unnaturall. (YP II, p. 310)[41]

In the remainder of this essay, I shall argue that in his great epic Milton places Adam and Eve under both natural law and an originally benign, embryonic Mosaic law. The source of Milton's natural law thinking is Selden's *De jure naturali et gentium;* and in that work Selden relies almost exclusively on rabbinic tradition based ultimately on the Talmud. Selden's idea that the prohibition formula in Genesis constitutes an embryonic Mosaic law is more or less commonplace. Absolutely original, however, is his belief, based on the Talmud, that natural law consists not merely of innate rational principles that are intuitively obvious but also of specific divine pronouncements uttered at a point in historical time.

In the chapter of *De doctrina Christiana* that deals with Edenic polity, we see that the prohibition formula in Eden (Gen. ii, 16–17) constitutes an unwritten, embryonic Mosaic law: "SIN, as defined by the apostle, is . . . the breaking of the law, 1 John iii.4. Here the word *law* means primarily that law which is innate and implanted in man's mind; and secondly it means the law which proceeded from the mouth of God; Gen. ii.17: *do not eat of this:* for the law written down by Moses is of a much later date" (YP VI, p. 382).

As Milton sees it, then, the first letter of John defines sin as the transgression of both natural law ("innate and implanted in man's mind") and of an external, oral law ("the law which proceeded from the mouth of God") that precedes the written Mosaic code. Under the latter, Adam and Eve are convicted of sin. Earlier in *De doctrina*, Milton cites the Edenic prohibition formula as part of a demonstration that the divine decree of predestination is conditional. He conflates the Old Testament and prelapsarian dispensations, and distinguishes them from salvation under the gospel, by identifying them as based on obedience: "scripture . . . offers salvation and eternal life to all equally, on condition of obedience to the Old Testament and faith in the New. . . . [t]he decree, as it was made public, is everywhere conditional: Gen.ii.17:

do not eat of this, for on the day you eat it you will die" (YP VI, pp. 177–78).

A survey of sources should indicate not only the commonplace nature of Milton's idea that the prohibition in Eden (Genesis ii, 17) constitutes an embryonic Mosaic law but also its adaptability to various points of view. Tertullian exploits this idea for an anti-Jewish purpose: to prove that the Jews are not God's chosen people and that the Gentiles are admissible to God's law:

God . . . gave to all nations the selfsame law. . . . For in the beginning of the world He gave to Adam himself and Eve a law, that they were not to eat of the fruit of the tree planted in the midst of paradise; but that, if they did contrariwise, by death they were to die. Which law had continued enough for them, had it been kept. For in this law given to Adam we recognize in embryo all the precepts which after-wards sprouted forth when given through Moses. . . . For the primordial law was given to Adam and Eve in paradise, as the womb of all the precepts of God. In short, if they had loved the Lord their God, they would not have contravened his precept; if they had habitually loved their neighbour — that is, themselves — they would not have believed the persuasion of the serpent, and thus would not have committed murder upon themselves, by falling from immortality, by contravening God's precept; from theft also they would have abstained, if they had not stealthily tasted of the fruit of the tree . . . nor would they have been made partners with the falsehood-asseverating devil, by believing him that they would be "like God"; and thus they would not have offended God either, as their Father, who had fashioned them from clay of the earth, as out of the womb of a mother. . . . Therefore, in this general and primordial law of God, the observance of which, in the case of the tree's fruit, He had sanctioned, we recognize enclosed all the precepts specially of the posterior Law, which germinated when disclosed at their proper times. . . . God's law was anterior even to Moses, and was not first given in Horeb, or in Sinai and in the desert, but was more ancient; existing first in paradise, subsequently re-formed for the patriarchs, and so again for the Jews, at definite periods.[42]

For Tertullian, as for Milton, the white light of the original prohibition in Eden has been broken up into countless refractive prohibitions of every color, a spectrum of offenses. Milton hints at the decalogic nature of the prohibition when, just after the Fall, Adam tells Eve: "if such pleasure be / In things to us forbidden, it might be wish'd, / For this one Tree had been forbidden ten" (*PL* IX, 1024–26). After violating the easy terms of the single prohibition, Adam and Eve, in the narrator's words, are "manifold in sin" (1024–26). Similarly, the serpent tempting Eve in Joseph Beaumont's *Psyche*, berating her for faint-heartedness, declares:

> For my part, did ten thousand Mandates grow
> Thick in my way, to barre me from this Tree,
> Through all I'd break, and so would you, if once
> Your Heart were fir'd by my Experience.[43]

John Salkeld, in his *Treatise of Paradise*, comments on Genesis ii, 17: "this commandment was given to *Adam*, as the first principall foundation and ground from whence all other lawes were derived, and in which all the ten Commandments be virtually included: so that as *Adam* was the first beginning of mankinde, so this was the first ground of all other lawes."[44]

The virtual inclusion of the decalogue in the Edenic prohibition permits Milton in *Paradise Lost* to extend Eden's temporal reach as far as Sinai, an advantage for a poet whose paradise is uniquely dynamic and whose principal characters enjoy a longer than average tenure in the state of perfection.

The most thoroughgoing analysis of Edenic polity in the seventeenth century occurs in Selden's *De jure naturali et gentium*, which sets forth "for the first time" the rabbinic position on the subject of natural law. Selden accepts the rabbinic identification of natural law with the Adamic and Noachide laws, considered by rabbinic tradition as the minimal moral duties enjoined by the Bible on all mankind. Besides citing Maimonides's *Code* and numerous other sources, he quotes in its entirety the *locus classicus* in Tractate Sanhedrin (56a–b), which includes the traditional enumeration of the Noachide laws: the prohibitions of idolatry, blasphemy, bloodshed, sexual sins, theft, and eating from a living animal, as well as the injunction to establish a legal system.

Selden includes R. Johanan's elaborate inference of these precepts from seven key words in Genesis ii, 16. The entire discussion, which at times conflates Edenic polity with laws pronounced to the sons of Noah, with the ten precepts given to the Israelites at Marah, and with the Decalogue, relies on the mode of talmudic interpretation known as *gezerah shawah*. This permits one to infer a rule from the use of a common scriptural expression in two verses; thus, R. Johanan infers from the similar use of the word "the Lord" in the original Edenic commandment (Gen. ii, 16) and in the later verse "he that blasphemeth the name of the Lord . . . shall surely be put to death" (Lev. xxiv, 16), a primordial prohibition against blasphemy (*De jure naturali*, p. 124).

Unlike Tertullian's argument, designed to disenfranchise the Jews, the thrust of Selden's rabbinic discussion is universalist. Selden blurs distinctions between the Edenic, Mosaic, and natural laws. All of these laws oblige because they are God's command, and because he will punish us for disobedience. To conflate these laws is to recognize that moral progress is the privilege and obligation of all mankind. Selden identifies the rabbinic Adamic and Noachide laws with natural law and asserts that this law is coeval with the beginning of mankind and that God's "most holy voice" pronounced it.[45]

Although Selden spoke of a faculty, the *intellectus agens*, by which mankind could perceive the principles of natural law, his belief that God pronounced this law at the beginning of time derives in large part from his skepticism regarding the power of unaided human reason. He puts the matter cogently in his *Table Talk:*

I cannot fancy to myself what the law of nature means, but the law of God. How should I know I ought not to steal, I ought not to commit adultery, unless some body had told me so? Surely 'tis because I have been told so. 'Tis not because I think I ought not to do them, nor because you think I ought not; if so, our minds might change: Whence then comes the restraint? From a higher power, nothing else can bind. I cannot bind myself, for I may untie myself again; nor an equal cannot bind me, for we may untie one another. It must be a superior power, even God Almighty.[46]

It would be difficult to exaggerate Selden's influence on the middle books of *Paradise Lost*, where the Mosaic law is the principal source of Edenic polity and where Milton conflates the Edenic, Mosaic, and natural laws. Like Selden, Milton infers many laws from the original Edenic commandment. The famous paragraph in *De doctrina Christiana* (YP VI, pp. 383–84) that lists the many sins contained in Adam and Eve's first act of disobedience (faithlessness, ingratitude, greed, uxoriousness, theft, murder, sacrilege, etc.) concludes with a neglected, explanatory scriptural verse: *"whoever keeps the whole law, and yet offends in one point, is guilty of all."* Like Paul, an ex-Pharisee and of the strictest school, Milton believes in the absolute indissolubility of the law. For Paul, the Mosaic law is a seamless garment which, once rent, can never be made whole again. In the Edenic books Milton exploits the obverse of this belief. If the Mosaic law is a single, indivisible entity, then Adam and Eve can keep the entire law by keeping one law, obeying the easy terms of the single prohibition. The Mosaic law is originally benign rather than impossible to keep. Only after the Fall will it become "a minister of death and condemnation."

Why haven't some of Milton's best readers acknowledged fully the Hebraic element in his work? Haller and Barker want to reconcile his opinions with those of Puritan divines; and the Yale editors of the divorce tracts, by citing contemporary parallels of Milton's statements, naturally emphasize the traditional and neglect the radical and iconoclastic. But the most important reason can be found in Milton's own dramatic *volte face* in *De doctrina Christiana* and the last books of *Paradise Lost*. Where John Selden's reliance on rabbinic tradition increased during his lifetime, John Milton's did not. In the divorce tracts, Milton accepted as part of God's eternal and unchanging moral law a section of the Pentateuch (Deut. xxiv, 1–4) interpreted by most Reformers as part of the now obsolete civil law of the Jews.[47] Arguing that an unfit mate drives her spouse from religious faith, he proclaims: "therefore by all the united force of the *Decalogue* she ought to be disbanded" (YP II, p. 260). In *De doctrina*, of course, Milton flirts with antinomianism by rejecting even the moral law, including the decalogue (YP VI, pp. 521–41).

At times the spirit of the Edenic books of *Paradise Lost* is not only biblically Hebraic but also nonbiblically rabbinic. The symbolic mode of these books is nontypological; when the divine voice first speaks to Eve, who has not yet seen Adam, the first epithet it uses for Adam is "no shadow": "I will bring thee where no shadow stays / Thy coming, and thy soft embraces" (*PL* IV, 470–71). In the last two books of the epic, however, Christian typology devalues peremptorily the Hebraic ethos of the middle books.

To conclude the essay, we might note that the chapters in *De doctrina Christiana* on the Mosaic law (YP VI, I.26) and Christian liberty (YP VI, I.27), the angel Michael's severe antitheses of law and gospel (*PL* XII, 287–314), and his Pauline rejection of the Jews by distinguishing between children of one's loins and children of faith (*PL* XII, 446–50; Rom. ix, 6–8) — all address the standard topics of Christian anti-Jewish polemic: the emancipation of Christians from the Mosaic law, or the annulment of the dispensation of law altogether; the repudiation of the Jewish people by God for their rejection of Christ; and the succession of the Church, the true Israel, the people of God, to all the prerogatives and promises once given to the Jews.[48] To whom, then, does Milton address his polemic? To himself, of course — that is, to the Milton of *Doctrine and Discipline of Divorce*, *Tetrachordon*, the *Areopagitica*, and the Edenic books of *Paradise Lost*. Milton's rejection and devaluation of Eden represent in mythic terms the rejection of his own Hebraism. This essay has attempted to demonstrate that a major source of that Hebraism was the work of Milton's chief rabbi, "the chief of learned men reputed in this Land, Mr. *Selden*" (*Areopagitica*, YP II, 513).

Georgetown University

NOTES

*Penn R. Szittya, a dear friend and Georgetown colleague, helped me with the Latin translations.

1. The pioneering work in this area includes: Denis Saurat, *Milton: Man and Thinker* (London, 1925); Harris F. Fletcher, *Milton's Semitic Studies and Some Manifestations of Them in His Poetry* (Chicago, 1926) and *Milton's Rabbinical Readings* (Urbana, 1930); and E. C. Baldwin, "Some Extra-Biblical Semitic Influences Upon Milton's Story of the Fall of Man," *JEGP* XXVIII (1929), 366–401. The first edition of Thomas Poole's *Annotations Upon the Holy Bible* (London) appeared in 1683; the Folger Library owns the third edition, published in London by Thomas Parkhurst in 1696.

2. *John Milton: Complete Poems and Major Prose*, ed. Merritt Y. Hughes (New York, 1957), p. 391. Unless otherwise indicated, parenthetic book and line references to Milton's poetry are to this edition.

3. *Pentateuch With Rashi's Commentary*, ed. and trans. M. Rosenbaum and A. M. Silbermann (London, 1946), p. 13.

4. John Aubrey, "Minutes of the Life of Mr. John Milton," ca. 1681, in *The Early Lives of Milton*, ed. Helen Darbishire (London, 1932), p. 6.

5. David Masson, *The Life of John Milton* (Cambridge and London, 1859–94), vol. I, p. 200.

6. Richard Laurence, *Ascensio Isaiae vatis* (Oxford, 1819), cited by Don Cameron Allen in "Milton and Rabbi Eliezer," *MLN* LXIII (1948), 262.

7. Denis Saurat, *Milton: Man and Thinker* (New York, 1925), p. 280.

8. R. J. Z. Werblowsky, "Milton and the Conjectura Cabbalistica," *Journal of the Warburg and Courtald Institutes* XVIII (1955), 90–113; Golda Werman, "Milton's Use of Rabbinic Material," in *Milton Studies*, vol. XXI, ed. James D. Simmonds (Pittsburgh, 1985), pp. 35–47; and Samuel S. Stollman, "Milton's Rabbinical Readings and Fletcher," in *Milton Studies*, vol. IV, ed. James D. Simmonds (Pittsburgh, 1972), pp. 195–215.

9. John Milton, "Areopagitica," in *The Complete Prose Works of John Milton*, ed. Don M. Wolfe et al. (New Haven, 1953–82), vol. II, p. 546. Further references to Milton's prose will be cited in the text as YP.

10. George Newton Conklin, *Biblical Criticism and Heresy in Milton* (New York, 1949), pp. 54–61; Robert M. Adams, *Ikon: John Milton and the Modern Critics* (Ithaca, 1955), pp. 133–47; Stollman, "Milton's Rabbinical Readings and Fletcher," pp. 195–215; Leonard R. Mendelsohn, "Milton and the Rabbis: A Later Inquiry," *SEL* XVIII (1978), 125–35. Invariably, these critics begin by discrediting Fletcher and others and end by discrediting Milton himself, though this devaluation of his scholarship is sometimes merely a byproduct of their critical procedure. Thus, for example, Conklin and Adams want to stress Milton's originality as a thinker and argue that he invented most of the material attributed to Jewish sources. The numerous rabbinic figures to whom Milton refers explicitly then become inconveniences, consigned to lexicons where, deprived of the persuasive intensity that only context can provide, they are powerless to violate his mind with the force of an idea.

11. Mendelsohn, "Milton and the Rabbis," 134–35.

12. This is the argument of my 1969 Brown University dissertation, "A Revaluation of Milton's Indebtedness to Hebraica"; see also Harold Fisch, "Hebraic Styles and Motifs in *Paradise Lost*," in *Language and Style in Milton*, ed. R. D. Emma and J. T. Shawcross (New York, 1967), pp. 34–35.

13. Ben Jonson, "An Epistle to Master John Selden," in *The Complete Poetry of Ben Jonson*, ed. William B. Hunter, Jr. (New York, 1963), pp. 144–47; Grotius cited in Sir Eric Fletcher, *John Selden* (London, 1969), p. 15; John Lightfoot, *The Harmony, Chronicle and Order of the Old Testament* (London, 1647), sig. B3r. What Gibbon said of Lightfoot could be said of Selden as well, that he, "by constant reading of the rabbis, became almost a rabbi himself."

14. Rawlinson MS 27837, Bodleian Library, Oxford, "A Catalogue of the books given by Mr Seldens Executors [in 1659] to the Library of the University of Oxford"; MS Selden 3473, Bodleian Library, "Catalogus librorum Orientalium [impressorum] Seldenianorum" [1660]; and see Falconer Madan, *A Summary Catalogue of Western Manuscripts in the Bodleian Library at Oxford* (Oxford, 1922), II, i, 594–654 (Selden MSS., 1659).

15. See YP VII, pp. 77, 233, 284, 288, 290–92, 301, and A.S.P. Woodhouse and Douglas Bush, eds., *A Variorum Commentary on the Poems of John Milton*, gen. ed. Merritt Y. Hughes (New York, 1972), I, ii, 101. See also *An Index to the Columbia Edition of the Works of John Milton*, ed. Frank Allen Patterson and French Rowe Fogle (New York, 1940), vol. II, p. 1765.

16. Eivion Owen, "Milton and Selden on Divorce," *SP* XLIII (1946), 233–57; Masson, *The Life of John Milton*, vol. III, p. 68.

17. Masson, vol. V, p. 281; William Riley Parker, *Milton: A Biography* (Oxford, 1968), vol. I, p. 480; vol. II, pp. 1052–53.

18. *Commonplace Book*, YP I, p. 402.

19. I have had access to *De synedriis* only in Selden's *Opera omnia*, ed. David Wilkins (London, 1726), I, ii, cols. 761–1892.

20. Mendelsohn, "Milton and the Rabbis," 125–35; Werman, "Milton's Use of Rabbinic Material," pp. 35–47; and Golda Werman, "Midrash in *Paradise Lost: Capitula Rabbi Elieser*," in *Milton Studies*, vol. XVIII, ed. James D. Simmonds (Pittsburgh, 1983), pp. 145–71.

21. The first two conclusions are from Mendelsohn, "Milton and the Rabbis," pp. 134–35; the last two from Werman, "Milton's Use of Rabbinic Material," p. 44.

22. Selden, *De synedriis*, in *Opera omnia*, I, ii, col. 1,524. Typically, Selden quotes first in Hebrew and then in Latin the Mishnah in question ("Rex non judicabat, nec judicabant alii ipsum; nec testimonium dabat forense, nec in ipsum testimonium dicebatur"); then cites his sources, which include both the Babylonian and Jerusalem Talmud, in the margin ("Gemar. Hierosolymit. ad tit. *Sanhedrin*, cap. 2, fol. 20 col. 1. Gemar. Babylon. ad tit. *Sanhedrin*, cap. 2, fol. 19); and then quotes at some length Rabbi Joseph's explanation of the Mishnah ("Dixit Rab Joseph, non recipi hoc nisi de regibus Israel; [id est, regibus qui non ex stirpe Davidica; velut Hasmonaeis, qui ex tribu Levitica; nec enim de cunctis regibus Israel illud capiendum satis ostendunt alia quae e Talmudicis sequuntur de judiciis etiam regum Israel] sed reges domus Judae & judicabant ipsi, & judicabant ipsi, & judicabant alii ipsos"). He follows this with a marginal reference to "Maimonides Halach. Melakin Wemalchemoth, cap. 3 [sect.] 7. alii passim."

23. Sanhedrin, 19a. My translations from Sanhedrin are based on the text of the Vilna edition of the Talmud (1908), which belonged to my late father, Rabbi M.D. Rosenblatt, and on the Hebrew translation by Adin Steinsaltz (Jerusalem, 1974). This elliptical narrative poses many problems: since the litigants in a case are seated, why did Simeon ben Shetah ask Jannaeus to stand? Perhaps he was angered because Jannaeus did not wait for an invitation to sit, or the text may be speaking of the moment when the verdict is pronounced and everyone is required to stand. Or Simeon erred in this matter, and other colleagues on the court were in fact empowered to allow Jannaeus to stand.

Indeed, if the court, out of respect for the Torah, can seat a scholar, then this applies all the more to a king. The RaN (on Sanhedrin 19a, in the Vilna edition of the Talmud), R. Jonah (cited by Steinsaltz, p. 83), and the Rashbah (in *Hiddushei Aggadot ha-Shas* [Tel Aviv, 1966]) consider these and many more problems in their commentaries on the narrative.

24. Rashi's commentary on *Parshath melech*, which Mendelsohn (p. 130) claims would have resolved all doubt for Milton, consists simply of a seven-word reference to 1 Samuel, chapter viii. Here in its entirety is Kimchi's commentary on verse 9 of that chapter, which Mendelsohn (pp. 129–30) claims Milton ought to have known if he could read the Buxtorf Bible: "R'Y [Rav Jose, though my dictionary of abbreviations, *Ozar rashe tevot*, lists twenty-three other possibilities as well] says that a king is permitted to do all that is listed in the chapter of the king, while R. Judah says that this chapter intends only to frighten and alarm the people." Kimchi, commenting on a verse in 1 Samuel, doesn't discuss the possibility that the chapter of the king may be in Deuteronomy, nor does he mention that the discussion he is summarizing can be found in Sanhedrin.

25. See for example *Colasterion*, YP II, p. 724, where Milton taxes his anonymous detractor with "bearing us in hand as if hee knew both Greek and Ebrew, and is not able to spell it." In *The First Defence*, YP IV, p. 349, the dispute between Milton and Salmasius over royal privilege can be reduced to the single word *mishpat* in 1 Samuel viii, 11, which in context means manner, the customary behavior of an oriental despot, rather than lawful procedure, the right of a king, as Salmasius would have it. In correcting Salmasius, Milton appeals to 1 Samuel ii, 13, where the word *mishpat* can only mean manner or custom. The attitude of the editor of *The Defence* toward Milton's Hebrew learning is consistently grudging, and he inexplicably sides with Salmasius here (p. 349 n.30).

26. *De synedriis*, col. 1676. What complicates matters here is that the order of this argument (Psalm xvii, Barnachmani, Psalm li) in both Salmasius and Selden may derive ultimately from Grotius's *"De jure belli ad pacis*, lib. 1, cap. 3, section 20," scrupulously acknowledged by Selden, who always observes the scholarly courtesies. Perhaps more striking are the identical texts used by Selden and Milton regarding cases in which the Sanhedrin had a power of judging and the king had not: *De synedriis*, cols. 1670–71; YP IV, p. 408. See also column 1677, where Selden quotes Josephus's commentary on Deuteronomy chapter xvii, which Milton cites in *The First Defence* (YP IV, p. 344).

27. This suggestion was made by David Wilkins, in *Opera omnia*, I, xliv. See also *The Life Records of John Milton*, ed. J. Milton French (New Brunswick, 1949–58), vol. II, p. 237.

28. *Regii sanguinis clamor* (The Hague, 1652), p. 8; *Lettres de Gui Patin*, (1846), vol. II, pp. 17–18, cited in Parker, *Milton: A Biography*, vol. II, pp. 962–63.

29. Werman, "Midrash in *Paradise Lost*," pp. 145–71. Don Cameron Allen, "Milton and Rabbi Eliezer," 262–63. Vorstius's edition is called *Capitula R. Elieser* (Leiden, 1644). Among Professor Werman's principal reasons for regarding the *Pirke* as an apt candidate for a source of the epic are the inherent interest of the Genesis material, the Arminianism of the translator, and the absence of anti-Christian polemic. Regarding the agreement of source and epic, Werman compares the unapproachability of the *Shekhinah* (Divine Presence) in the *Pirke* with that of the "Begotten Son, Divine Similitude, / In whose conspicuous count'nance, without cloud / Made visible, th' Almighty Father shines, / Whom else no creature can behold" (*PL* III, 384–87; Werman, "Midrash," p. 149). Yet this actually states — admittedly, in confusing syntax — not that the Son cannot be beheld but rather that only the Son can behold the Father. The notion that God laughs mockingly

at his enemies, attributed to the *Pirke* (Werman, "Midrash," p. 151), can of course also be found in Psalm ii, 4: "The Lord shall have them in derision."

30. *Uxor Ebraica*, II, xii, 182–II, xiii, 189. On this point alone Selden cites "Maimonides, *Halach Ishoth*, cap. 10," "*Shulcan Aruch lib. Aben haaezer*, cap. 54. section 2. vide Gem. Babylon. ad tit. *Cethuboth*, cap. 5. fol. 56.a." The related point that matrimony is effected from the moment the couple enters the bower elicits comments from, among others, "Maimonid. & autor *Shulcan Aruch*, loc. citat. & vide Magid Misna ad Maimonid. ibid. fol. 243.b. & Mos. Mikotzi Pracept. Affirm. 48."

31. See the lengthy discussion of *aperion, lectum conjugalem, fructificandi locum*, or *huppah*, in *De jure naturali*, V, iii, 545–51. Multiple rabbinic references here include "Gem. Bab. ad tit. *Sota*, cap. 1, fol. 12a & *Baal Aruch* in *aperion*. . . . J. Buxtorf. pater ad epist. Hebraic. lib. 2, ep. 7. Usurpatur *aperion* pro *huppah* seu *Thalamo* (sed templum innuitur) Cantic. Salom. 3.9." The nuptial bower is also discussed in *Uxor Ebraica*, II, xv, 192–98. See also the chapter heading, "De Sponsorum coronis, myrto ac palmarum ramis praeferendis," *Uxor Ebraica*, II, xv, 192.

32. See, for example, *Uxor Ebraica*, II, xiii, 184–86. But Selden's many references to specific chapters of "R. Eliaezer in *Pirke*" also appear in discussions of Adam and Eden (for example, *De jure*, III, xiii, 351n; *De synedriis*, col. 1025). In fact, in the first volume alone of Selden's *Opera omnia*, there are thirty-five references to *Pirke de-Rabbi Eliezer*, including both the Hebrew text and the translation by Vorstius.

33. For Maimonides, see *YP*, II, 257; on 238–39, Milton cites Fagius's *Thargum, Hoc Est, Paraphrasis Onkeli Chaldaica in Sacra Biblia* (Strassburg, 1546) and Hugo Grotius's *Annotationes in Libros Evangeliorum* (Amsterdam, 1641).

34. William Haller, "Hail Wedded Love," *ELH* XIII (1946), 79–97; William and Malleville Haller, "The Puritan Art of Love," *Huntington Library Quarterly* V (1942), 235–72; Arthur E. Barker, *Milton and the Puritan Dilemma, 1641–1660* (Toronto, 1942), pp. 98–120, and, on Christian liberty in particular, pp. 105–07.

35. Henry Hammond, *A Letter of Resolution to Six Quaeres, of Present Use in the Church of England* (London, 1653), p. 123.

36. Alexander Ross, *Pansebeia: or, A View of all Religions in the World, from the Creation, to These Times* (London, 1653), p. 400.

37. The discovery of the Book of Deuteronomy during repairs of the Temple transformed Judaism from a religion of cult to one of prayer and book. According to the editor of the Soncino edition of 2 Chronicles (London, 1952), p. 329, the modern scholarly view is that chapters v–xxviii or only xii–xxvi were discovered; these still would have included the crucial verses on divorce.

38. I owe this observation to an unpublished paper by Robert W. Ayers on *Doctrine and Discipline of Divorce* and ancient Jewish divorce law.

39. Milton, YP II, p. 335; Selden, *De jure naturali*, pp. 514–16, 530–34, 551–57, 615, 845; *Uxor Ebraica*, pp. 434ff. Milton, YP II, p. 257; Selden, *Uxor Ebraica*, pp. 439–43. See also Selden's *De successione in pontificatum Ebraeorum* (London, 1636), pp. 15–17.

40. *Uxor Ebraica*, pp. 432–33, 428–70. In addition to quoting in full the central talmudic text on the phrase *ervat davar*, Selden relies on additional biblical and rabbinic texts that emphasize its ambiguity. He explores the various meanings of *turpitudo rei, re turpitudinis, turpitudine in re*, and *turpitudine*.

41. This point about the conjunction of the natural and Mosaic laws is reiterated constantly in this tract, most emphatically in YP II, pp. 237, 297–98, 328, 330, 343, 346.

42. Tertullian, "An Answer to the Jews," in *The Writings of Quintus Sept. Flor. Tertullianus*, trans. S. Thelwall (Edinburgh, 1870), pp. 203–05.

Milton's Chief Rabbi

43. Joseph Beaumont, *Psyche, or Love's Mystery* (London, 1648), p. 93, canto VI, stanza 246.

44. John Salkeld, *A Treatise of Paradise* (London, 1617), p. 148. See also Vavasor Powell's *Christ and Moses Excellency, or Sion and Sinai's Glory* (London, 1650), p. 186, which identifies "that prohibition to Adam (that hee should not eate of the forbidden fruit)" with "all the Morall Law, or Ten Commandements, afterwards given to Moses."

45. *De Jure Naturali*, p. 109; "Aut scilicet intelligere eos ejusdem Juris capita tum in ipsis rebus initiis tum in ea quae fuit post diluvium instauratione Humano generi, ipsa Sanctissima Numinis Voce, fuisse imperata atque ad posteros per Traditionem solum inde manasse." See also p. 85: "Jus illud Naturale atque Universale, maxime quod sibi perpetuo constans est et numquam non obligat, petendum est." On the rabbinic discussion of Adamic laws promulgated in Eden, see p. 119.

46. *Opera omnia*, III, 2041. For Selden on natural law, see Richard Tuck, *Natural Rights Theories: Their Origin and Development* (Cambridge, 1979), pp. 82–100; and J. P. Sommerville, "John Selden, the Law of Nature, and the Origins of Government," *The Historical Journal* XXVII (1984), 437–47. In the course of a uniformly excellent survey of the topic, Sommerville corrects Tuck by pointing out that for Selden the "Noachide" laws go back not merely to a point after the Flood but in fact all the way back to Eden.

47. See, for example, William Perkins, cited in YP II, p. 244 n.9, who maintains that the Deuteronomic divorce law "was not morall, but civill, or politicke, for the good ordering of the commonwealth."

48. George Foot Moore, "Christian Writers on Judaism," *The Harvard Theological Review* XIV (1921), 197–254.

A SENSE OF THE SACRED:
RICHARD BENTLEY'S READING OF
PARADISE LOST AS "DIVINE NARRATIVE"

Robert E. Bourdette, Jr.

To raise Sense from mere Nonsense is much easier and surer of Acceptance, than to raise still Better Sense from Good or Tolerable.
— Richard Bentley, on *Paradise Lost* I, 259

Our acts of divination — for the acts that determine undetected latent sense are properly so called — our divinations are made necessary by the fact of our occupying, inescapably, a position in history which is not the position of the text we cultivate, and not a position of which we have much objective understanding, though it helps to constitute the complex of prejudices we bring to the task of discovering a sense, for us, in the text we value (another element of prejudice).
— Frank Kermode, *The Genesis of Secrecy:*
On the Interpretation of Narrative

O NE OF the more provocative acts of divination in *Milton's Paradise Lost: A New Edition, By Richard Bentley, D. D.* occurs in the first emendation as the "mighty Scholiast" begins his controversial task of discovering the sense in Milton's epic.[1] Having first made plain in his preface that "*all the Conjectures, that attempt a Restoration of the Genuine* Milton, [are] *cast into the Margin, and explain'd in the Notes. So that every Reader has his free Choice, whether he will accept or reject*" (p. a1v), Bentley strikes his finger on line six of Book I and conjectures that for "on the *secret* top / Of *Horeb* or of *Sinai*," Milton dictated "*sacred* top" (p. 1). With that same vigorous prose, wide-ranging erudition, and bold confidence in his divinatory genius by which he had wrested sense from the corrupted texts of the ancients and imposed it upon the texts of those moderns Edmond Halley and Isaac Newton, Bentley draws upon classical literature, English poetry, natural history and geography, aesthetics, Scripture, and the poet's own words elsewhere to confirm his *divinatio.*

From a firm aesthetics, he argues: "If therefore (which the best Poets have adjudg'd) a Proper Epithet is always preferable to a General one, and if *Secret* and *Sacred* are of a near Sound in Pronunciation; I have such an Esteem for our Poet; that which of the two Words is the better, That, I say, was dictated by *Milton*" (p. 1). This is his imperious summation; leading up to this choice of the "better Word," Bentley cites the literary tradition from which, for this poet, he assumes it must derive: from Milton's sage and serious "*Spenser*, in *Fairy Queen*, I. 10. 54 ['Or like that sacred hill, whose head full hie, / Adornd with fruitfull Oliues all arownd, / Is, as it were for endlesse memory / Of that deare Lord, who oft thereon was fownd, / For euer with a flowing girlond crownd']; and as frequently in the Classic Writers, *Mons Sacer,* ἱερὸν ὄρος." He provides, too, a brief essay on the reasonableness of his emendation, bringing into accord reason, science, and the Scriptures: "Some perhaps may prefer the present Reading, *Secret* top," he grants,

because in most Countries the high Mountains have against rainy Weather their Heads surrounded with Mists. True; but yet it's questionable, whether in the wide and dry Desert of *Arabia,* Mount *Horeb* has such a cloudy Cap. I have in my Youth read several Itineraries, where the Travellers went up to the Top of *Horeb;* and I remember not, that they take notice of its Cloudiness. And a just Presumption lies against it from Holy Writ, *Exod.* xvii; where the *Israelites,* encamp'd at the foot of *Horeb,* could find no Water; which was provided miraculously, when *Moses* smote the Rock with his sacred Rod: for all Natural History informs us, and Reason vouches it, That a Mountain, whose Head is cloudy, has always running Springs at its Foot. (P. 1)

Finally, as the final sentence here exemplifies, Bentley grounds his emendation in Holy Writ, citing Exodus iii, 1; iii, 5; xvii, 5–6; and 1 Kings xix, 8, and confirming this scriptural evidence by quoting *Paradise Lost* itself: "V. 619. VI. 25. *Sacred Hill*" (p. 1).

What are we to make of this farraginous defense for the change of a word that is, for us, so poetically, scripturally, and textually sound? That most of Bentley's critics — then and now — have thought it was *his* head that was cloudy in making this and the some eight hundred emendations that follow is a critical commonplace. However circumspect Bentley's marginal placement of the suggested changes and his prefatory assurance that "*not* ONE *Word*" of the received text had been altered (p. a1v), this high-handed "*Restoration of the Genuine* Milton" has seemed an excess of arrogance that, for many, was already too pronounced in his other restorations, whether of Horace's language, Homer's digamma, or Cambridge's Trinity College, where he ruled as Master for forty-two tumultuous years. "It has been often told me by Persons of Sense and Candour," Bentley reported in 1710,

that when I left them I might say of the College, what *Augustus* said of *Rome, Lateririum inveni, marmoreum reliqui.* The College-Chappel, from a decay'd antiquated Model, made one of the noblest in *England;* the College-Hall, from a dirty, sooty Place, restor'd to its Original Beauty. . . . In a word, every Garret of the House well repair'd and inhabited, many of which were wast[e] and empty before my coming.[2]

Such confident — and valid — claims reverberate not only in the Horace (1711), in which the poet's language was restored by Bentley's divining tact and inspiration, but in his reported words to a former student and family friend, John Byrom: he had made, Bentley said on 2 January 1726, "emendations upon Milton which he had given to [John] Heylin; that the English verses were hollow."[3] In both classical and Milton scholarship, however, these changes in Milton's privileged text are, with the notable exception of William Empson's polemical essay,[4] the *loci classici* of an astoundingly misused talent. Bentley's conjectures, in such a view, make up an edition that (to quote the judgment of just one historian of classical studies), "few reputations except his own could have survived" and one that (to quote only one version of the verdict by a Miltonist), "has remained for more than two centuries a monument of scholarly narrow-mindedness and critical presumption."[5]

The initial "sacred" is not the most common example by which Bentley's presumption and apparent poetic insensitivity have been illustrated; indeed, Bishop Newton wrote of having "met several people who have approved of Dr. Bentley's emendation," and, later in the century, one of Bentley's earliest biographers singled it out as at least one "improvement."[6] With these few exceptions, however, the Bentleian "sacred" has been routinely dismissed. *The Grub-street Journal* mocked it and several other rumored emendations even before the edition appeared; "Semicolon" and Zachary Pearce, perhaps one and the same, defended Milton's adjective against Bentley's tendentious assault by quoting Scripture.[7] And Jacob Tonson, long the publisher of Milton editions, rose to its provocation:

As for his notes the first is enlarged from y^t in his Specimen & his opinion not soe positive as to ye alteration of Sacred to Secret. Pray look on Milton in Addisons notes page 285. I think this makes for Secret. I desire any one to read Psalm the 19th, verses 9, 10, 11, 12 & psalm 97th, verse ye 2nd.

In the 18th psalm, verse ye I Ith I think makes for *Secret* before sacred, I suppose yᵉ Dʳ is himself of that opinion, but backward to own he coud or can possibly be mistaken.[8]

Such attacks have not been confined to Bentley's hostile contemporaries. The classicist W. B. Stanford has recently used this first emendation as prima facie evidence of Bentley's enmity to poetry, arguing that Bentley "knew better than most, *secretus* in Latin meant 'lonely, solitary, set apart'" and that "on a factualistic level, it is obvious that a remote and lonely mountain peak would be an excellent place for conveying esoteric illumination. [Finally], 'sacred' spoils the assonance with 'seed' in the next line and reduces the phrase to a platitude."[9]

Such judgments are hardly without foundation. The prefatory premises upon which Bentley constructed his edition were discredited in his own time and have not been rehabilitated since: he claimed he was advancing "*the present Text, which challenges to be the Truest and Correctest that has yet appeared*" (p. a1v); that, in addition to Milton's "*own Slips and Inadvertencies*" (p. a2v), *Paradise Lost* had been corrupted from the first moments of its transmission, first by an inept amanuensis, then by an intruding "*suppos'd Friend (call'd in these Notes the Editor)*" with poetic designs of his own (p. a2r), and by wretched printers. More audaciously, he asserted that there was no manuscript to consult so that it was only by his own "*Sagacity, and happy Conjecture*" that the "*Poet's own Words*" could be retrieved (p. a2v). To these discredited — and discrediting — claims have been added the bemused or outraged speculations of why and when Bentley conceived of an endeavor for which his critics have argued he was so unequal and one that, to the delight of his enemies and the despair of his friends, fulfilled the truth of his own maxim that "no man was ever written out of reputation but by himself."[10]

These audacious premises and their conclusive rejection, the unresolved debate about Bentley's motives, and the seemingly obtuse readings themselves have had an inevitable but damaging effect on our understanding of the edition's place in the history of early modern criticism. All these have divorced Bentley's Milton from its instructive continuity with his other prestigious, if ever controversial, criticism and — more crucially — from its essential context in contemporaneous textual and religious controversies. Whatever Bentley's motives — motives that this essay will explore — Bentley's edition shows us the greatest scholar of his age reading its most venerated poem, and that reading should not be devalued. Bentley, as Kermode would say, occupied a position in history very different from the text he cultivated; his edition is not a view of Milton's mind but of Bentley's own and of the "complex of prejudices" that he brought to that reading. That mind and that reading were formed during an extraordinary intellectual career that included Bentley's iconoclastic classical criticism, his influential eight sermons in the first series of the Boyle lectures (1692), which sought to harmonize Newton's *Principia* and Christian belief; his forceful arguments two decades later in the freethinking controversy (1713); and his sacred criticism that resulted in the *Proposals for Printing* (1720) of a new edition of the Greek New Testament, a plan that established him as "the chief founder, the πρῶτος εὑρετης, of the science of historical criticism."[11]

Recognizing the weight of opinion against Bentley's reading of *Paradise Lost*, I hazard the argument that Bentley was a far more astute reader of the poem than has been acknowledged; that, indeed, Bentley was exactly that "fit audience" capable of reason and choice whom Milton would have valued in debate. More specifically, Bentley's "sacred" gives us at the outset of the edition a proleptic clue to the "sense" of his reading, one that connects his interpretation to his other criticism and to the contemporary debate concerning two sacred texts — the Scriptures and *Paradise Lost*.

1. From "Secret" to "Sacred": The Value of a Superfluous Conjecture

Discussing those much-maligned eighteenth-century adapters of Shakespeare, Norman Rabkin has argued that what they wanted to simplify tells us something useful about the meaning of their undertaking, and Paul Maas has stated the value in textual criticism of the "superfluous" conjecture: "Whether the author of such a conjecture thought 'the writer *must* have written this' or 'he *ought* to have written this' is relatively unimportant; the conjecture stimulates enquiry and often decidedly advances it, and this in the briefest possible way."[12] So it proves with the superfluous "sacred." Bentley's learned daring and intuitive skill in spotting a textual crux were the distinction of his scholarship. A. E. Housman, one of the few modern classicists to be compared to Bentley, speaks of halting at some perplexity of a reading in a classical text and then turning to "Bentley the Great": He "strike[s] his finger on the place and say[s] '*thou ailest here, and here.*'"[13] Housman emphatically did not transfer such praise to Bentley's Milton, but Empson did: Bentley "may only produce a trivial piece of nagging, but he has a flair for choosing an important place to do it."[14] Nowhere in the edition is that flair less trivial, more stimulating to enquiry, or more indicative of the meaning of Bentley's reading than here at Book I, line 6.

Perceptive with the benefits of three centuries' worth of readings, scholarship, and concordances, we recognize that Milton's "secret" is one of his more potent words. In the Nativity ode, for instance, the poet's voice is to be made inspired by the hallowed fire from the Lord's "secret Altar" (28); in *Paradise Regain'd*, Milton summons the inspiring Spirit so that he may "tell of deeds / Above Heroic, though in secret done" (*PR* I, 14–15). Samson speaks of having "divulg'd the secret gift of God" (*SA*, 201) and in *Considerations Touching the Likeliest Means to Remove Hirelings*, Milton writes of Melchisdec, who brought bread and wine to Abraham, "incited to do so, first by the secret providence of God" (p. 861). In *Paradise Lost*, however — as with so many of its key terms — "secret" contains "knowledge of good and evil." It is used twice only pertaining to God. At Book I, line 6, the heavenly Muse, "on the *secret* top," inspires Moses, the type for the poet whose adventurous song — by that same providential inspiration — will tell of things secret: "*Of things* invisible to mortal sight" (III, 55); in Book X, "secret" describes the divine source that enables Moses to reveal "how the Heav'ns and Earth / Rose out of *Chaos*" (I, 9–10), the poet to reveal how "th' upright heart and pure" (18) may rise from the chaos of the Fall, and the angels to know "How all befel" (X, 28): "When the most High / Eternal Father from his secret cloud / Amidst in Thunder utter'd thus his voice" (X, 31–33).

All the other uses of "secret" are associated not with God but with our first parents' "secret foe" (IV, 7). Satan engenders Death upon Sin in "secret" (II, 766) and solipsistically projects a like secrecy upon God's plan to create mankind (II, 838); in "secret" he wishes to gaze upon that creation (III, 672), and "in secret" he plots the war in heaven (V, 672), a plot that materializes in the "secret" creation of gunpowder (VI, 522). The fallen angels sit "in close recess and secret conclave" (I, 795); the "Night-Hag" comes "when call'd / In secret" (II, 662–63). By the "secret amity" that links them, Sin intuits the success of Satan's corrupting mission (X, 248), and when she again encounters Satan, Sin speaks of her "Heart, which by a secret harmony / Still moves with thine" (X, 358–59). This satanic secrecy infects the human experience: after eating the forbidden fruit, Eve praises her new-found "Experience" that allows her to open "Wisdom's way / . . . though secret she retire" (IX, 809–10) and, immediately after, says, "I perhaps am secret" (811).

Bentley certainly overlooks the subliminal tension created by Milton's conflicting uses of the word, but it may be pointed out as partial defense of his reading that nowhere is "secret" used in Books VII to VIII and XI to XII, where God's providential ways are revealed to the human pair. Moreover, as discoverer of the secrets of corrupted texts and as theo-

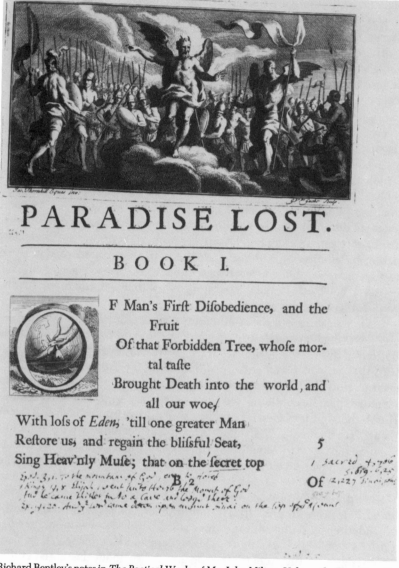

PARADISE LOST.

BOOK I.

F Man's Firſt Diſobedience, and the
    Fruit
    Of that Forbidden Tree, whoſe mor-
    tal taſte
    Brought Death into the world, and
    all our woe,
With loſs of *Eden*, 'till one greater Man
Reſtore us, and regain the bliſsful Seat,   5
Sing Heav'nly Muſe; that on the ſecret top

Richard Bentley's notes in *The Poetical Works of Mr. John Milton: Volume the First [Paradise Lost]* (London, 1720), p. 1. By permission of the Syndics of Cambridge University Library

logian, Bentley actively resists the concept of secrecy and "secret providence." In "A Sermon upon Popery," he argues against secrecy in the
liturgy that makes it like "the ἱερὰ γράμματα, the sacred and secret
writings to the Egyptian priests, or the Sibylline oracles to the Roman
pontifices, which no body else was to know,"[15] and in the Boyle Lectures
he insists that Providence is not secret but manifest in "The Origin and
Frame of the World" (*W* III, pp. 119–200). It is, however, Bentley's
solution to the apparent textual crux — the substitution of "sacred" for
"secret" — that suggests its latent sense. Some hint of this is declared in
the printed annotation: not the least evidence there assembled is biblical
text. The weight of just such biblical authority in reading *Paradise Lost*
is indicated by Tonson's letter, quoted above, in which he chooses to use
biblical text to *refute* Bentley's "sacred," rather than pointing to the
manuscript of Book I, which he had at hand and was using, in the same
letter, to discredit Bentley's claim that there was no manuscript of *Paradise Lost* to consult. And Bentley further supports Scripture and his emendation by citation of *Paradise Lost* itself. In the printed version these
two sacred texts, though clearly preeminent, are just two arguments for
revision; however, in the preparatory notes that Bentley made for his
edition this emphasis is absolute.[16]

After slashing out the comma after "woe," Bentley underlines "secret," writing his emendatory "/sacred" in the right-hand margin. At the
bottom of this first page of his working text, Bentley records the biblical
texts that support his emendation: "Exod. 3,i, To the mountain of God,
even to Horeb." Underneath this line he writes (perhaps quoting from
memory since he conflates two verses), "1 Kings 19, 8 Elijah went unto
Horeb the Mount of God [/] And he came thither into a Cave and lodgd
thear." He then notes "Ex. 19,20. And yᵉ Lord came down upon mount
Sinai on the top of yᵉ Mount." At the very bottom of the right-hand corner of the page, he cites "Exod. 3,5," the full text of which is carried
over into the edition: "*Moses came to the mountain of God, Horeb. And
God said, Put off thy shoes from off thy feet; for the place whereon thou
standest is* HOLY *ground*" (p. 1). Bentley confirms his scripturally based
emendation by citing Milton's own words from elsewhere in *Paradise
Lost*: "4, 706" ["*In shady Bowr / More sacred and sequester'd*"]; "5, 619"
["That day . . . they spent / In song and dance about the sacred Hill"];
"6,25" ["On to the sacred Hill / They led him high applauded"]; and "12,
227," which Bentley writes out: "Sinai, whose [/] gray top."[17]

Given *Paradise Lost*'s sacred subject, it is scarcely surprising that
it should be compared to and justified by the Scriptures or that the poem
itself should be equated to Holy Writ. "S.B.'s" encomium prefixed to the

second edition (1674) – the Latin of which Bentley also corrected in the 1720 edition – had asked "quid nisi cuncta legis? / Res cunctus, & cunctarum primordia rerum, / Et fata, & fines continet iste liber" ["What do you read but the story of all things and the first beginning of things"] (2–4; Hughes, p. 208), and Andrew Marvell in his prefatory poem in the same edition speaks of his anticipatory fears that Milton "would ruin . . . / The sacred Truths" (7–8; Hughes, p. 209) when, in fact, Milton triumphantly succeeded in presenting "things divine" (33). The title page of P[atrick?] H[ume?]'s commentary (1695) announces immediately its primary purpose: "ANNOTATIONS ON MILTON'S Paradise Lost. WHEREIN the Texts of Sacred Writ relating to the POEM are Quoted." Yet, when Richard Bentley begins to compare the Scriptures with *Paradise Lost* something other than a conventional pairing is at issue.

In 1713, Francis Hare published an open letter to the pseudonymous author of the *Remarks on a Late Discourse of Free-Thinking*, revealing Bentley's thin disguise and publicly thanking him for the rout of Anthony Collins's deistical arguments in his *Discourse* (1713). In praising Bentley, Hare notes that: "Men of Learning . . . would be very glad so great a Master would turn his Labours to the Scriptures; and if not a new Edition of the Testament, that he would give us at least a *Critice Sacra* on it, which from so able a Hand, would, on many accounts, be infinitely valuable." Hare concludes his request with just one note of caution: "that greater Modesty, Diffidence, and Caution should be us'd in changing the receiv'd Text in these, than has commonly been done in other Books; that Emendation from Conjecture should be confin'd to the Notes, and the Text very seldom or never alter'd, without the Authority of Manuscripts."[18] Bentley did turn his considerable skills to a new edition of the Greek New Testament, assuming the mantle of those like Richard Simon, whose *Critical History of the Old Testament* had proposed the correction of errors, corruptions, accretions, and mistranslations.[19] And Bentley's daring project became even more bitterly controversial than his other provoking criticism. Many of his contemporaries, including one of his harshest satirists and one of his strongest advocates, distrusted such critical tampering with the Scriptures: "[I do not] think," Jonathan Swift wrote, "it any part of *Prudence*, to perplex, the Minds of well-disposed People with Doubts," and John Evelyn, who had helped select Bentley for the first Boyle lectureship, warned against the "great danger and fatal consequence of [Simon's] 'Historie Critique'" because its purpose was not only "to unsettle but destroy" the "canon and rule of faith."[20]

The year after encouraging Bentley to undertake a "*Critice Sacra*" if not a new edition, Hare wrote presciently:

You see a present Example in the great *Bently* [sic]: What a Reputation has he acquir'd by the noble Edition he has given us of *Horace?* How are his Abilities confess'd and admir'd by all? But had the same Genius, the same Sagacity and Labour, been applied to the Study of the *Scriptures;* to Settle the Text in doubtful Places, to Mend corrupted ones, and to Trace ou[t] the literal Sense where it can be done; should he, I say, have attempted a Work of this Kind; instead of Thanks and Applause, 'tis more than probable he would have been treated as a rash Man, of no Judgment, of little Learning, and less Religion; and if his Works had been sentenced to the Flames, a Majority would have been for throwing him in after them.[21]

In dramatizing the thanklessness of the task, Hare glides over the fact that from the outset of Bentley's scholarly career, he had prepared for and engaged in the "Study of the *Scriptures.*" In Bentley's *Full Answer* to the attack on his *Proposals for Printing,* he recounts in detail his early textual work on the Bible (W III, p. 528); in his *Epistola ad Joannem Millium* (1691), he notes and emends a corrupted passage in Galatians (II, pp. 363–65). The opening sentence of his first Boyle Lecture refers to the textual problem posed by the fact that Psalm xiv, from which he takes his text, is repeated with little variation as Psalm liii (III, p. 1). And he added his voice to those of Milton and Newton in the heated debate over the textual authority of the "Johannine Comma" (1 John v, 7), a verse which Bentley authoritatively rejected, asserting that the doctrine of the Trinity did not need such textually corrupt support.[22]

Many believed that such variants in the New Testament were so numerous as to leave its true text beyond recovery; others believed, as did Swift and Evelyn, that it was long past time to end critical tampering. Both positions were rejected by Bentley, who believed that the Scriptures, like the buildings of Trinity, could be "restor'd to [their] Original Beauty." In a letter (15 April 1716) to William Wake, archbishop of Canterbury, Bentley detailed the manuscript evidence, and concluded:

I find I am able (what some thought impossible) to give an edition of the Gr. Test. exactly as it was in the best examples at the time of the Council of Nice. . . . So that that book, which, by the present management, is thought the most uncertain, shall have a testimony of certainty above all other books whatever; and an end be put at once to all var. lectt. now or hereafter. (W III, p. 477)

Four years later in the *Proposals,* sensitive to his controversial reputation as a conjectural critic, Bentley assured his potential subscribers that:

The Author is very sensible, that in the Sacred Writings there's no place for Conjecture or Emendations. . . . He declares, therefore, that he does not alter one

Letter in the Text without the Authorities subjoin'd in the Notes. And to leave the free Choice to every Reader, he places under each Column the smallest Variations of this Edition. . . . So that this Edition exhibits both it Self, and the Common ones.[23]

Though the *Proposals* were enthusiastically received — £2000 came in from subscribers — they were also viciously attacked. Conyers Middleton, Bentley's fell and mighty opposite at Cambridge, charged that Bentley had "*neither* TALENTS *nor* MATERIALS *proper for the work he has undertaken*" and that "*so much* VANITY, PEDANTRY, BLUNDER, *and* SELF-CONTRADICTION, *were hardly ever found together before in the compass of one single sheet.*" Worse, Middleton claimed, the *Proposals* destroyed "*at once the authority of all our published Scriptures; cries down by a sort of papal edict all our current editions . . . [and] raises an universal resentment and indignation.*"[24] Bentley's language in the *Proposals* and that of Middleton were to be reiterated when Bentley turned to *Paradise Lost,* and the poem was not absent from the uproar over the *Proposals.* In the *Full Answer* (mistakenly assuming that his attacker was John Colbatch), Bentley described his opponent as one who found "some squabble in the college to keep up his spirits" and on such occasions would "look something gay among us, [and] *smile horrible,* like Satan in Milton" (*W* III, p. 534).[25] Such satanic attacks apparently did not discourage Bentley, for as late as 1732, the year of the *Paradise Lost,* Bentley's colleague John Walker was still collating manuscripts for the edition; however, for a multitude of reasons, the project slowly faded.[26] Our inevitably increased knowledge of the textual evidence and of the monumental problems involved, E. J. Kenney points out, makes "the splendid assurance and the self evident simplicity of Bentley's plan appear chimerical; but the fundamental insight which underlies it [that the "establishment of a text according to its tradition is a strictly historical undertaking"] is right."[27]

Bentley's labors on the New Testament overlapped with his work on *Paradise Lost;* as the one prodigious project faded, its place was taken by the study of that other sacred text. The encounter between this critic and that poem was, no doubt, inevitable. That Bentley would be drawn to the text of the poem asserting "eternal Providence" is anticipated as early as the final sermons of the Boyle Lectures in which he had argued, as he wrote to Isaac Newton, "a divine Goodness from ye Meliority in our system."[28] In the printed version of the final sermon (5 December 1692), *Paradise Lost* is quoted to gloss Bentley's argument concerning the providential function of mountains, a passage to which I shall return below. This same sermon closes:

We have formerly demonstrated [in Sermon 5], that the body of a man, which consists of an incomprehensible variety of parts, all admirably fitted to their peculiar functions and the conservation of the whole, could no more be formed fortuitously that the *AEneis* of Virgil, or any other long poem with good sense and just measures, could be composed by the casual combination of letters. Now, to pursue this comparison; as it is utterly impossible to be believed, that such a poem may have been eternal, transcribed from copy to copy without any first author and original; so it is equally incredible and impossible, that the fabric of human bodies, which hath such excellent and divine artifice, and, if I may so say, such good sense, and true syntax, and harmonious measures in its constitution, should be propagated and transcribed from father to son without a first parent and creator of it. An eternal usefulness of things, an eternal good sense, cannot possibly be conceived without an eternal wisdom and understanding. (*W* III, p. 200)

This remarkable peroration, with its implicit rejection of Hobbes, its confident celebration of the Newtonian order, and its image pairing poem and the human body and both to their divine source, is worthy of its own commentary. And it is with this passage that Rudolf Pfeiffer has illustrated the unity of Bentley's scholarship, proving his belief in the original harmony of classical poetry "which — if corrupted by transmission from copy to copy — must be restored by reasonable criticism. So these Boyle Lectures reveal a characteristic blend of Christian theology with his humanistic scholarship and his firm grasp of principles."[29] Emphasizing as he does Bentley's work in "classical" poetry and embarrassed by Bentley's incredible critical lapse, Pfeiffer banishes mention of that "regrettable and much criticized edition" of *Paradise Lost* to the small print of a footnote (155 n. 5). Another classical scholar, however, has caught the discrepancy: E. Christian Kopff has said that Pfeiffer's chapter on Bentley "develops his insight [in an earlier essay] that Bentley's criticism was intimately related to his aesthetic and religious ideas of symmetry and order," an insight contradicted by Pfeiffer's exclusion of *Paradise Lost*.[30]

In bringing these principles to Milton's sacred poem, Bentley encountered a particularly responsive text, and the text one of its most intrepid readers. *Paradise Lost* called forth from Bentley not only a "rage for conjecture" but (in part its source) his views on the nature of Providence that he had expounded in the Boyle Lectures on behalf of Newton, the *Principia*, and latitudinarian Christianity.[31] Milton's poem, in its ambivalent position as a classical yet modern, secular yet sacred text, posed linguistic and interpretive issues that renewed the debate between the ancients and the moderns in which Bentley had played so influential a role and, more crucially, focused issues about language by which sacred truths might be either distorted or clarified. For Bentley, Milton's language demanded to be read with the purpose of preserving the truths that it embodied from those who would appropriate it for "atheistical" purposes, and from those Hobbesians who might claim that the so-called truths of the poem were "entangled in words, as a bird in lime-twiggs."[32] But the application of Bentley's theological and aesthetic principles in reading *Paradise Lost* had, if such were needed, even more specific promptings. If for Addison it was of no great importance whether Milton's poem was a "Heroick Poem" or a "Divine Poem,"[33] it was of no little significance to Bentley. The larger context has been summarized by Mark Pattison: the attacks on orthodox Christianity by the deists and others energized the defenders, including Bentley; as a consequence, the "whole of religious literature was drawn into the endeavor to 'prove the truth' of Christianity."[34] For Bentley, this literature included *Paradise Lost*, a point ignored by many of his critics, and one that helps us better understand why, to the uncomprehending irritation of his nephew, Bentley could not "forbear talking of Milton."[35]

The specific arguments concerning the Scriptures and *Paradise Lost* advanced by the deist John Toland and then by Collins provide a very specific context for Bentley's readings of Milton's text. In "The Life of Milton" (1698), Toland had co-opted Milton for the freethinking cause, arguing—for instance—that:

Milton shews the Insufficiency, Inconveniency, and Impiety of this method [using apostolic times to deduce diocesan Episcopacy] to establish any part of Christianity; and blames those Persons who cannot think any Doubt resolv'd or any Doctrin confirm'd unless they run to that indigested heap and fry of Authors they call Antiquity.[36]

Collins, who in the *Discourse* (1713) had also listed Milton as one of his band of freethinkers, returned in 1724 to an attack on the Scriptures. In *A Discourse of the Grounds and Reasons for the Christian Religion*, he argued against typology, insisting that using it to demonstrate the truths of the New Testament involved laughable interpretive procedures; since the "truths" of the New Testament were dependent upon the use of type and allegory, the Scriptures were thus "in an irreconcilable state and the difficulties against Christianity will be incapable of being solved."[37] In 1729, Collins took direct revenge for being bested by Bentley's 1713 *Remarks*, directing, in the same essay, shots across the bows of the Scriptures and *Paradise Lost*. He praises the satire against Bentley during the Phalaris controversy, noting that "Dr. *Bentley* is represented as *wrote out of Reputation into Preferment;* which, whether it be a more severe

Sarcasm on the Doctor, than on the Government, is hard to determine."[38] Collins had already ridiculed Providence as presented in the two sacred texts:

Moses introduces God speaking thus after the Fall, *Behold the Man is become like one of us, to know Good and Evil !* And I think this Passage shews, that the whole Affair of the *Fall*, of which we have so very brief an Account, was a very entertaining Scene; and would have appear'd so, if set forth at large; as indeed it does under the Hands of our Divines, who have supplied that short Narration by various Additions, founded on Conjectures. . . . To say nothing of *Milton's* famous *Paradise Lost.*[39]

It was, then, in these contexts that Bentley turned to *Paradise Lost*, a poem of good sense and just measures that required only reasonable criticism to reveal that its incomprehensible variety of parts formed a providential unity. Such criticism had, for Bentley, the meritorious purpose of answering the critics of sacred texts and of advancing "the conservation of the whole" of Milton's "Divine Narrative" (p. 157).

2. "THE CONSERVATION OF THE WHOLE": *PARADISE LOST* AS "DIVINE NARRATIVE"

If Bentley were unwilling to provide a new edition of the Scriptures, as Francis Hare had implored, he might gratify the community of the learned with a *"Critice Sacra"* — "an interpretation (and in its most specialized sense) the textual study of Scripture."[40] I have gone some way in implying that this request was fulfilled in the *Paradise Lost* in which Bentley — as Hare had requested — settled, mended, explained, and traced the literal sense of a sacred text, and in assuming that many of his contemporary critics and Bentley himself recognized this convergence. In a letter to *The Grub-street Journal*, "A. Z." recalls the "Paper-war" over Bentley's *Proposals* and breathes a sigh of relief that Bentley "could keep his hands off from the Holy Scriptures, and content himself to spend his rage upon MILTON."[41]

Suggestive as this is as an instance of his contemporaries' views, it is Bentley's own language that indicates his awareness of the connection between his sacred and Miltonic criticism. Bentley conceives of Milton as a sacred poet with God-like attributes; indeed, Bentley's "was perhaps the first evaluation of Milton . . . to see him as a universal personality . . . awesome in his isolation, greatness of mind, and integrity."[42] In his preface, Bentley describes this "first parent and creator":

But I wonder not so much at the Poem it self, though worthy of all Wonder; as that the Author could so abstract his Thoughts from his own Troubles, as to be able to make it; that confin'd to a narrow and to Him a dark Chamber, surrounded with Cares and Fears, he could spatiate at large through the Compass of the whole Universe, and through all Heaven beyond it; could survey all Periods of Time from before the Creation to the Consummation of all Things. (P. a3v; emphasis added by deletion of italics).

This apotheosis of the poet is matched by according the text, one *"worthy of all Wonder,"* scriptural status. In the *Remarks,* Bentley had answered the charge of textual corruption in the Scriptures: "If a corrupt line or dubious reading chances to intervene, it does not darken the whole context, nor make the author's opinion or his purpose *precarious"* (*W* III, pp. 359–60). Using Terence as an example, Bentley argues that for all the variations in that poet's received texts, their sense is "visible and plain thorow all the mist of *various lections"* (p. 360). He then turns from this secular illustration to the sacred:

And so it is with the sacred text; make your 30,000 [textual variants] as many more . . . all the better to a knowing and serious reader, who is thereby more richly furnished to select what he sees genuine. But even put them into the hands of a knave or a fool, and yet, with the most sinistrous and absurd choice, he shall not extinguish the light of any one chapter, nor so disguise Christianity but that every feature of it will still be the same. (P. 360)

This choice offered the "knowing and serious reader" anticipates his language in the 1720 *Proposals* and in the preface to the *Paradise Lost.* In his *Proposals,* Bentley had written that he "leaves the free Choice to every Reader." In his edition of the secular Horace, Bentley had substituted his conjectures for the received text; for *Paradise Lost,* however (as in the *Proposals*), he returned to a strategy appropriate for sacred text: *"all the Conjectures . . . cast into the Margin, and explain'd in the Notes. So that every Reader has his free Choice, whether he will accept or reject what is here offer'd him"* (a1v). The language of the preface contains other echoes of his language concerning the Scriptures. Corruptions and variants cannot "extinguish the light of any one chapter, nor so disguise Christianity but that every feature will be the same." Of *Paradise Lost,* with Terence again providing a link to the sacred, Bentley writes:

What native, unextinguishable Beauty must be impress'd and instincted through the Whole, which the Defoedation of so many Parts by a bad Printer and a worse Editor could not hinder from shining forth? It seems to have been in the Condition of Terence's beautiful Virgin, who in spite of Neglect, Sorrow, and beggarly Habit, did yet appear so very Amiable: [Phormio, lines 104–108]. (P. a3r–v)

And there is one final bit of prefatory evidence. Describing the dangers risked by a textual critic of the Scriptures, Francis Hare had said that if Bentley had essayed such a task "he would have been treated as a rash Man, and of no Judgment, of little Learning, and less Religion." In his preface, Bentley echoes Hare's description of the risks of tampering with sacred text. Having first queried how it was possible for the poem to have passed for sixty years as a *"perfect, absolute, faultless Composition: The best Pens in the Kingdom contending in its Praises, as eclipsing all modern Essays whatever"* (p. a3v), Bentley answers his own rhetorical question:

it's likely, he'll resolve it into This Cause; That its Readers first accede to it, possess'd with Awe and Veneration from its universal Esteem; and have been deterr'd by That from trusting to their Judgments; and even in Places displeasing rather suspecting their own Capacity, than that any thing in the Book could possibly be amiss. Who durst oppose the universal Vogue? and risque his own Character, while he labour'd to exalt Milton's? *I wonder rather, that it's done even now.* (P. a3v)

While recognizing the dangers, Bentley trusts his own "Judgments" and "Capacity," and engages the text in true Miltonic spirit: not reposing, as Milton puts it in *Christian Doctrine,* "on the faith and judgment of others in matters relating to God," but scrutinizing and ascertaining for himself "through a most careful perusal and meditation" on the text (Hughes, p. 900).

The poem's artifice is read to reveal its inherent "good sense," emending — if necessary — so that its verbal and theological unity is manifest. His approach to Milton's text was already inherent, as we have seen, in the final sermon of the Boyle Lectures, and it was focused by the specific attacks on sacred narrative and language. Collins had charged, for instance, that *"The* BIBLE . . . *is the most miscellaneous book in the world"* and that to master such a text required the ability *"to think justly in every science and art"* (W III, pp. 304, 305). Bentley retorted that to the extent such a charge was valid, Collins was a hopeless blunderer in such mastery (p. 305). While it had to be admitted that the Scriptures were diverse in content, *Paradise Lost* might be conserved from a like charge of the miscellaneous. In Bentley's reading, the "pragmatical Editor" (p. 132) who had corrupted Milton's text becomes a Collinsesque figure who cannot comprehend the poem's unity, but must insist on inserting "miscellaneous" content. Bentley, for example, deletes "[*And hence the Morning Planet gilds his horns*]" (VII, 366), initiating a long list of grammatical, scientific, and logical objections with the statement that "This

Line must needs be spurious: it betrays our Editor's Handy-work; who, by all his Insertions compar'd together, appears an injudicious Smatterer in Astronomy, Geography, Poetical Story, and old Romances" (p. 230). This sensitivity to the charge of hodgepodge in the Scriptures and Bentley's effort to remove similar "evidence" of it from *Paradise Lost* are anticipated in the Boyle Lectures: the deists/atheists, Bentley argues, see the universe (as Collins would later characterize the Bible) as "mere bungling and blundering; no art or contrivance to be seen in't; nothing effected for any purpose and design; but all ill-favouredly cobbled and jumbled together by the unguided agitation and rude shuffles of matter" (*W* III, p. 18). Since Bentley assumes that *Paradise Lost*, like the miracles of Christ to which he refers in the same sermon, was "not made out of vain ostentation of power, and to raise unprofitable amazement, but for the real benefit and advantage of man" (p. 19), the "miscellaneous" Renaissance learning of the poem is ruthlessly rooted out.

This demand for a verbal and theological unity is revealed in one of Bentley's more remarkable revisions:

> For still they knew, and ought to have still remember'd
> The high Injunction, not to tast that Fruit,
> *Whoever* tempted : which they not obeying
> Incurr'd, what could they less, the Penalty,
> *And manifold in sin, deserv'd to fall.* (X, 12–16).

"This," Bentley annotates, "is a sorry Line," defective both in diction and theology: "What's *Manifold in Sin?* Who would speak so for *Guilty of Manifold Sins?* And yet Sin was but one, the tasting the Forbidden Fruit: Unless you will by Aggravation split one into many; Pride, Unbelief, Uxuriousness, &c." (308–09). Discarding exactly the interpretation of the original lines confirmed by Milton (see *YP* VI, pp. 383–84; Hughes, p. 406), Bentley assigns the line to the editor and replaces it with one of his own, " a Verse, not worse at least than the Editor's: . . . DENOUNC'D ON DISOBEDIENCE, DEATH AND WOE" (p. 309). Without Milton's gloss but with his own stress on textual and providential unity, Bentley gives us an insight into how he was reading the "sense" of the poem. Sin speaks of being "join'd in connection sweet" with Satan (X, 359). Bentley does not annotate this line, but it is just this corrupting unity that he takes to be the right reading at Book X, line 16. Such a unity must be offset in the poem by a superior Providential unity, "*Sacred*, in opposition to *Evil thing*," as he glosses Book IV, line 562 (p. 127). Bentley had earlier stated this principle in his "Sermon Preached before King George I" (3 February 1717): "the all-wise Author of the universe . . . so contrived every part of his work, that they are all coherent and contributive to each other, and, by their mutual operations, conduce every one its share to the economy and beauty of the whole" (*W* III, p. 266). How this emphasis so profoundly affects his reading of the poem may be illustrated in brief by a set of emendations he makes on the lines, "And Earth be *chang'd* to Heav'n, and Heav'n to Earth, / One Kingdom, *Joy and* Union without end" (VII, 160–61). Bentley writes:

> I scarce know two viler Misprints in the whole Poem; because they lurk undiscover'd under the Similitude of Sense. But surely it's little Advantage for *Heaven*, *to be chang'd to Earth:* and *Joy and Union* come both odly together, and have no Cement with the preceding Words. The Author gave it;
>
> And Earth be CHAIN'D to Heav'n and Heav'n to Earth,
> One Kingdom JOIN'D IN Union without end. (P. 222)

As for the universe, so for Milton's poem. Bentley argues the unity of the poem, the "economy and beauty of the whole," in three fundamental ways: by equating Milton's text with Scripture; by comparing Miltonic and scriptural language, emending accordingly; and, most revealingly, by emending vexing places by readings in the poem that speak more clearly. Throughout, Bentley associates the narrative "truths" of *Paradise Lost* with those of the Scriptures. Bentley, for instance, rejects the comparison of Paradise to the gardens of Adonis and Alcinous (IX, 439–43) — the intruding editor again, and even "he confesses, those were but *feign'd*" (p. 282). "[W]hat Proportion," Bentley asks, "what Compare between Truth and Fiction?" (p. 283). Milton's inventions from the brief account in Genesis are accepted as a true history that must not be mixed with fictitious fables; thus, Bentley rejects the "pat Comparison" in Book XI, lines 8–11," of *Deucalion and Pyrrha* to our *Adam* and *Eve*" (p. 248). "Is *Adam* and *Eve's* History an *old Fable* too, by this Editor's own Insinuations?" (349). He supports an emendation I have already discussed — "*And Earth be* CHAIN'D *to Heav'n* . . . / . . . JOIN'D IN *Union*" — by again granting scriptural authority to Milton's narrative: "This Promise was at the Creation perform'd; for II, 1051, *Satan*, when he first got out of *Chaos, Beheld far off th' Empyreal Heaven,*[/] *And fast by hanging in a golden* Chain [/] *This pendant World*" (p. 222).

In one notable instance, Bentley goes so far as to elevate the poem to an authority *superior* to Genesis. Detailing the fifth day of creation, the poem reads:

> [And God created the great Whales; and each
> Soul living, each that crept, which plenteously
> The waters generated by their kinds;

And every Bird of wing after his kind:
And saw that it was good, and bless'd them, saying,
Be fruitful, multiply, and in the Seas
And Lakes and running Streams the waters fill;
And let the Fowl be multiply'd on th' Earth.]   (VII, 391–98)

Bentley deletes the entire passage, noting the problem of repetition here and in Genesis i, 20–21: "'Tis true, they are in *Genesis;* but they should not be in this Poem. Could *Milton* say, *God created great Whales, &c.* and himself afterwards create them again? Poetical Necessity forc'd him to omit that Verse in *Genesis;* which the busy Editor perceiving, was resolv'd to have it in" (p. 231). He ends here with an astounding question, demonstrating his objectivity in analyzing the textual defects in the Scriptures — as illustrated by his rejection of the "Johannine Comma" — and his willingness in granting authority to Milton's text, reasonably emended: "And why," he asks, "should *Raphael* be so tied up to the Letter in *Genesis,* who makes this Narrative thousands of Years before *Genesis* was writ?" (p. 231).

Boldly emending toward a unity, Bentley is also attentive to the demands of narrative consistency. Satan describes the moments just before his fall: "But see the angry Victor hath *recall'd* / His *Ministers* of Vengeance" (I, 169–70). Pointing out that Milton had apparently changed his mind during composition, Bentley alters the lines to read "hath *repress'd* / His *Instruments,*" arguing that in the first three books, the good angels pursue "the vanquish'd Rout"; in Book VI, line 801, however, "the Author chang'd this Idea for another, yet better; making the *Messiah* alone perform all himself. . . . These few Passages [II, 78, 996–97; III, 397] therefore must be alter'd, to make this noble Poem consistent" (p. 9). Verbal consistency based on the Scriptures is no less important than narrative unity. Bentley takes it as a given that Milton, "as he constantly does" adheres to biblical text, keeping close to the "Scripture Stile" (p. 189). In any number of places, Bentley simply points out the scriptural source of that style. He annotates the lines "as in the door he [Adam] sat / Of his cool Bowr" (V, 299–300), with the observation that "So *Abraham, Genesis* xviii. I. *Sat in the Tent-door in the heat of the Day*" (p. 158). More often, Bentley adjusts Milton's text to match that style. Struck by the unusual diction and what he takes to be a breach of decorum in the lines, "He [Raphael] arose; whom *Adam* thus / Follow'd with *benediction: Since* to part" (VIII, 644–45), he emends to "with *Valediction: loath* to part." "What's here?" Bentley asks, "*Adam* give Benediction, his Blessing, to an Arch-angel? No doubt *Milton,* so well vers'd in all the Scripture, could not forget that of *Hebrews* viii. 7. *And without*

all contradiction, the Less is blessed of the Better" (p. 264). In at least
one such emendation that has received recognition by modern editors,
Bentley suggests the substitution of *"Vessals"* for *"Vessels"* in the line in
which Moloch laments that the fallen angels must be "The *Vassals* of
[God's] anger" (II, 90; see Hughes, p. 234). Bentley confirms the original reading by quoting *"Our State of splendid* Vassalage" (II, 252) and
by Spenser's line, *"The* Vassals *of God's* Wrath" (*Tears of the Muses*, 126).
"But yet," Bentley suggests, "when I remember St. *Paul's* Words, *Rom.* ix.
22, *The Vessels of wrath fitted to destruction,* Σκεύη ὀργῆς, I suspect
that *Milton* here, as perpetually, kept close to the Scripture Stile; and
leave it to the Reader's choice, *Vassals* or VESSELS" (p. 40).

The "Reader's choice" of possible readings, with its echo of his words
in the *Proposals,* bring us to the most emphatic indication that Bentley
was treating *Paradise Lost* as if it were Scripture. He not only adjusts
the text to accord with its scriptural sources, but justifies emendation
by the "Scripture Stile" of *Paradise Lost* itself. Such procedure has the
sanction of both ecclesiastical and Miltonic authority. The "Confession
of Faith" established by the Assembly of Divines (1647) states that: "The
infallible Rule of Interpretation of Scripture is the Scripture it selfe: and
therefore, when there is a Question about the true and full sense of any
Scripture (which is not manifold, but one) it must be searched and known
by other places that speak more clearly."[43] It is this principle (with its
anticipation of Bentley's gloss on *"manifold in sin"*) that he applies to
the poem, a principle also sanctioned by Milton: "all places of Scripture
wherein just reason of doubt arises from the letter, are to be expounded
by considering upon what occasion every thing is set down: and by comparing other Texts" (*YP* II, p. 282).

In the passage in which Satan taunts Gabriel, "Thou and thy gay
Legions" in heaven *"practis'd distances* to cringe, not fight" (IV, 942,
945), Bentley objects to the odd phrase, "practis'd distances": "surely
Satan has not the privilege, as *Caliban* in *Shakespear,* to use new Phrase
and Diction unknown to all others. . . . 'Tis a rule indeed in Ceremony,
To know ones Distance, But *to practise Distances* is still a *Caliban* Stile"
(p. 142). He revises the offending phrase to *"practise Discipline,"* arguing from a place that speaks more clearly that "This biting Word of *Satan's* is thus retaliated by *Gabriel,* v. 954. . . . *Was this your* DISCIPLINE?
Which alone establishes the Emendation" (p. 142). Bentley uses this principle to undergird many of his emendations. "Love," Raphael instructs
Adam, "hath his seat / In Reason: *and is judicious, is* the scale / By which
to heav'nly Love thou may'st ascend" (VIII, 589–92). Bentley objects to
the measure, lack of elegance, and sense of the italicized words. He suggests in their place, *"Reason:* UNLIBIDINOUS": "No Man of Judgment and

Taste can doubt of this Restitution; and to convince the others I'll produce *Milton* himself, V. 448. *But in those Hearts* Love *unlibidinous reign'd*" (p. 263). Of Adam's lament, "That were to extend / His sentence beyond *Dust;* and Nature's Law" (X, 804–05), Bentley argues that "beyond *Dust*" is too obvious a point to need assertion. Bringing the phrase into accord with the Scriptures, Milton's clearer words elsewhere, and his own arguments in the Boyle Lectures, Bentley emends it to "*Just*": "God," he annotates, "cannot do unjustly. *Shall not the Judge of all the Earth do right?* [Genesis xviii, 25] That was *Abraham's* settled Notion. And *Milton* makes it *Satan's*, IX. 700, *God, therefore cannot hurt you, and be Just:* [/] *Not Just, not God*" (337).[44]

Bentley's emendations toward the clarity and simplicity of the "Scripture Stile" is a reflection both of the well-known prescription of the Royal Society — "positive expressions; clear senses . . . bringing all things as near the Mathematical plainness, as they can"[45] — and his own strong poetics set out in the edition: "The simplest and nearest Word is the best" (p. 174); "High Language [must be reconciled] with Philosophy and true Sense" (p. 190); "Simplicity and Grandeur" (p. 347). But such a poetics imposed upon Milton's poem also sought to resolve a debate about language, both scriptural and Miltonic. That debate derived in part from the discussion of Longinus's praise of the sublime fiat in Genesis, "Let there be Light, and there was Light." From that example of the sublime, two arguments emerged: one, that the sublime was achieved by elevated, even obscure language; the other, following Boileau, that "the greatest thought in simple language was the highest form of the Sublime."[46] Murray Roston has written that "scarcely a comment was made on the literary merit of the Bible at the turn of the [seventeenth to eighteenth] century which did not contain some reference to its noble *simplicity*."[47] Roston's generalization finds specific confirmation in Bentley's own views: "we have sure ground to believe that [the Bible] is the revelation of God; and we find in it propositions expressed *in plain words, of a determinate sense, without ambiguity*" ("Of Revelation and the Messias," 5 July 1696, W III, p. 225; italics added).

The argument concerning the scriptural sublime — obscurity versus simplicity — is mirrored in the equally contentious debate over Milton's language. Milton's subject, so Charles Gildon (1694) argued, required necessary obscurity: "Those *Antient*, and consequently *less Intelligible* Words, Phrases, Similes . . . do well suit with the *Venerable Antiquity* and *Sublime Grandeur* of his Subject."[48] If, however, *Paradise Lost* challenged the ancients by its sublime language and sacred subject, it did so — at least for some readers — *despite* its use of "*less Intelligible* Words." Praising Dryden's *The State of Innocence and Fall of Man* (ca. 1674–75),

Nathaniel Lee emphasized Dryden's refinement of Milton's rough chaos of language,[49] and Addison expressed a similar attitude: Milton's language was "sometimes obscured by old Words, Transpositions, and Foreign Idioms."[50] And John Hughes, in his preface to A *Complete History of England* observed that:

Mr. *Milton's* History, as well as his Poetical Works, proves this; where, in his Thoughts and Language, he appears with the Majestick Air of old *Greece* or *Rome*. This makes him indeed look particular, and perhaps to some uncouth, like the *Roman* Architecture heretofore, when the *Gothick* was in Fashion. But whether his or the more Modern Diction be the best, let the Controverters of old and new Books decide as they please.[51]

Bentley, the most renowned of "Controverters of old and new Books," addresses this issue of Milton's diction in emending "unless *an age too late*" (IX, 44): "What's the Meaning of an *Age too late*? If his *Own Age*, it's the same as what comes afterwards *Years* [line 45]: If *Saeculum*, an *Age* or *Century* too late; surely he could not think the World is super-annuated, and Mens natural Powers diminish'd. I should choose to lay the Blame on an impolite *Gothic* Tongue, inferior to *Greek* or *Latin*." (p. 268). Bentley emends to "unless A LANGUAGE RUDE."

Bentley's revisions emerge, as this passage demonstrates, from an aesthetic and historical understanding very different from Milton's, but they also reflect a solid foundation of opinion about the value of "noble *simplicity*" in both biblical and Miltonic language, a simplicity Bentley commends when it appears in *Paradise Lost*. At the moment of repentence, Adam says:

> What better can we do, than to the place
> Repairing, where he judg'd us, prostrate fall
> Before him reverent? And there confess
> Humbly our faults, and pardon beg, with tears
> Wat'ring the ground; and with our sighs the air
> Frequenting, sent from hearts contrite, in sign
> Of sorrow' unfeign'd, and humiliation *meek*.   (X, 1086–92)

This passage is repeated with only the slightest variation in lines 1098–1104, a transition from dialogue to narrative that in its plainness prepares for the austere diction of Books XI to XII. Bentley emends "meek" to "meet" in both lines (1092, 1104) — perhaps recalling the "fit and meet" at Book VIII, line 448, although Bentley, in any case, would hardly admire meekness! It is in the unadorned language and Milton's assurance "that what was once well said will bear repeating" that Bentley identifies the poem's "true Air both of Simplicity and Grandeur" (pp. 346–47).

For Bentley, this "Simplicity and Grandeur" necessitated a rejection of the fabulous, a resistance to the figurative, and a decided wariness about the allegorical. Anticipating Samuel Johnson's condemnation of "Lycidas," Bentley is unsparing in his ejection of the fables out of *Paradise Lost*. In this, he speaks the views both of the philosophes (who sought to unmask the lies of the learned myth merchants, including Milton)[52] and the Royal Society (who argued that the "*Wit* of the *Fables* and the *Religions* of the *Ancient World* . . . were only *Fictions*" that must give way to what is "*Tru* and *Real*").[53] Marvell's fear that *Paradise Lost* might ruin "The sacred truths to Fable and old Song" was, in Bentley's reading, a fear too nearly fulfilled. In excising these fictions, Bentley was continuing his defense of Christian truths against the deists whose "gospel" was, as he summarized it in the *Remarks*, that "Christianity [is] an imposture, the Scriptures a forgery, the worship of God superstition, hell a fable" (*W* III, p. 300). Collins had attempted to compromise Christian revelation by noting the infinite number of such revelations. In the *Remarks*, Bentley sought to turn the argument against Collins: "Think *freely* on all the various pretences to revelation; compare the counterfeit *scriptures* with the true, and see the divine lustre of the one, to which all the others serve as a foil" (*W* III, p. 331). In *Paradise Lost*, however, these fabulous foils seem too much like asserted truths that might compromise the text. Bentley's deletions of "counterfeit *scriptures*" are made throughout, but perhaps most bluntly in his partial rejection of the *locus amoenis*:

> Thus was the place,
> A happy rural seat of various view;
> Groves, **whose rich* Trees wept odorous Gums and Balm;
> Others, whose fruit burnish'd with Golden Rind
> Hung amiable', [Hesperian *Fables true*,
> *If true, here only'*,] and of delicious taste.   (IV, 246–51)

Bentley adjusts "**whose rich*" to "*some whose*" and then turns to the fabulous content, assigning it to the Editor: "Fables, says he, if true, here only true. Very quaint: but pray you, Sir, how can *Fables* be true *any where?*"[54] A passage that Bentley had cited in his preparatory notes as support for the initial "sacred" is, in its printed form, rejected for its fabulous content:

> [*In shady Bowr*
> *More sacred and sequester'd, though but feign'd*
> *Pan or* Sylvanus *never slept, nor Nymph,*
> *Nor* Faunus *Haunted*].   (IV, 705–708)

"Again," Bentley complains, "we have to do with this pragmatical Editor. What wrong would our Author have suffer'd by him, if he had not betray'd himself? *Pan, Sylvanus,* and *Faunus,* salvage and beastly Deities, and acknowledg'd *feign'd,* are brought here in Comparison; and their wild Grottos forsooth are *Sacred*" (p. 132).

The Collinsesque "Editor" is discovered in most of the intrusions of the fabulous. Bentley hooks the comparison of the "imbodied forces" of the fallen angels to "*what resounds / In Fable or Romance of* Uther's Son" (I, 579–87), thus freeing the poem from inappropriate fable and the burden of "Romantic Trash": "*Milton* indeed in his Prose works tells us, That in his Youth he was a great Lover and Reader of Romances: but surely he had more Judgment in his old Age, than to clog and sully his Poem with such Romantic Trash, as even then when he wrote was obsolete and forgot" (p. 26). For Bentley, such deletion is essential, since such "miscellaneous" fables and romances, which Collins had used to discredit Scripture, compromise the truths of the poem. "To stuff in here," Bentley continues, "a heap of barbarous Words . . . serving only to make his own Argument, which he takes from the Scripture, to be suppos'd equally Fabulous, would be such Pedantry . . . as I will not charge Him with: let his Acquaintance and Editor take it" (p. 26). He rejects, as a consequence of this view, the evocative comparison of Raphael to Mercury, "**Like* Maia's *Son* he stood, / And shook his Plumes" (V, 285–86). Bentley replaces the figurative and pagan with a choice of more literal descriptions: "*With gracefull meen,*" or "*Majestic there he stood,*" condemning a fabulous theology that would compare an archangel to a thievish god: "And why," Bentley asks his insistent question, "a Divine Narrative polluted thus with Fable and Lye?" (p. 157).

Collins's argument that the Gospels were precariously founded on type and allegory focused the issue of figurative and allegorical scriptural language. Bentley had addressed those issues in "Of Revelation and the Messias": the deists claim that "it is evident from the prophets, that the Messias is to be a temporal prince. . . . But the character of Jesus is as different from this description as a stable from a palace" (W III, p. 234). "'Tis true," Bentley continues, "we Christians endeavour to shew a similitude between them by figurative interpretations of Scriptures . . . [that] they [deists] call arbitrary and precarious" (p. 234). Bentley admits that the discourse of the prophets is indeed "thick set with metaphor and allegory" (p. 235), but he also points out the theological confusion caused by the mixture of the literal and figurative. He argues that the accurate interpretation of such bold comparisons is dependent on an essential literalness: "But then, in other passages of the same prophets, as it were on purpose to hint to us the true meaning of the former, the Messias is described plainly, without poetical colours, *to be a person of low condition . . .* and by other characters so clear and express" (p. 235). Bentley uses this view of the essential literalness in the Scriptures as a guide in emending Milton. Of Adam's lament, "Did I request Thee, Maker, from my Clay / To Mold me Man? did I sollicit Thee, / *From darkness* to promote me *or* here place / In this delicious Garden?" (X, 743–46), Bentley is impatient. He had already deleted the eleven preceding lines (731–41) because, among other reasons, Adam "was more concern'd for his *Reputation* with Posterity, than for all the Real Evils" (p. 335). Of the immediate line, Bentley argues, "*Darkness* is but metaphorical here; and can signify nothing but *Inexistence;* and so makes this Second Expostulation the very same with the First [lines 743–44]." Bentley emends the metaphorical to a clear and express "*When molded*" (p. 335).

As Bentley's citation of Spenser's allegorical lines in support of the "sacred" may suggest, he is not unalterably opposed to allegory; rather, he applies Isaac Newton's principle: "[Choose] those interpretations which are most according to the literall meaning of the scriptures unles where the tenour and circumstances of the place plainly require an Allegory."[55] In his *Remarks,* Bentley had berated Collins for the attempt to undercut Scriptures by literalizing allegory:

Repentence and anger attributed to the gods [Bentley quotes Collins]: this glances aside at those frequent expressions of our Bible, *the wrath of the Lord,* and *the Lord repented.* As if the whole herd of Christians did not know that these are not to be taken literally, but are spoken ἀνθρωποπαθῶς, *in a human manner,* accommodated to our capacities and affections; the nature of God being infinitely above all ruffles of passion. (*W* III, p. 403)

Bentley here has a controversialist's confidence that his fellow Christians can recognize allegory; however, in annotating *Paradise Lost,* he is attentive to its misleading potential. We miss in Bentley a detailed discussion of the allegory of Sin and Death that engaged so many of his contemporaries, but he rejects several of the comparisons leading up to it (for example, II, 635–43, 659–66): "Let the Editor here too take back his intended Comparisons. . . . and not contaminate this most majestic Poem with trash" (p. 61). He does point out that the allegory is just that: "the *pretended* Daughter and Son" (p. 65; italics added). Of the War in Heaven, Bentley is equally cautious. Although he had castigated Collins for literalizing "*the wrath of the Lord,*" Bentley carefully removes a comparable phrase in *Paradise Lost:* "So spake the Son: and into terror chang'd / His count'nance too severe to be beheld; / *And full of wrath bent on his Enemies.*" (VI, 824–26): "This Verse, in the midst of the elevated Stile, is so mean and flat, so superfluous too or rather cumbersome, that I need not say, it was the Editor's Handiwork" (p. 211). If he is here uncomfortable with allegory, though uncharacteristically awkward in its dismissal — he had, after all, allowed "God's anger" (II, 90) — he does recognize and impose the demands of the "tenour and circumstances" of biblical allegory. In the episode in which the fallen angels are driven out of heaven, the received text reads: "[They] as a Herd / Of Goats *or* timorous flock, together throng'd" (VI, 856–57). "If *or* is a admitted," Bentley argues, "then the other Flock must be Sheep; contrary to the Scripture Allegory, which places Sheep for Happiness, and Goats for Damnation (p. 212; see Matt. xxv, 32–33, 41). To avoid a misapplication of scriptural allegory, Bentley states that Milton "gave it therefore, *Of Goats, A timorous flock*" (p. 212).

Bentley's deletion of the allegorical "*full of wrath*" also reveals an even more fundamental reading: his insistence that Milton's poem must unambiguously portray God and the Son in their providential roles, a Providence Bentley had argued so emphatically in the Boyle Lectures. He does this in many more instances than can be considered here, but three examples may illustrate this emphasis. Milton's God describes the Son's role in the Redemption: "So Heav'nly love shall outdo Hellish hate, / *Giving to death*, and dying to redeem" (III, 298–99). In his preparatory notes, Bentley had experimented with "Yielding" for "Giving," noting the precedent of "now to Death I yield" (245); he finally decides that it should read "*Living to Teach*," commenting on the unusual grammatical usage of "Giving" and arguing the theological rightness of the emendation: "*Living to Teach*; Living to teach Mankind the Gospel, Dying to redeem them. Methinks, the Living Instruction should not be quite omitted, and all laid upon the Dying Satisfaction" (pp. 88–89).[56] In Book V, Bentley again emends toward clarification of the Son's providential function. The Son speaks of his understanding of his task in subduing the forces of the reprobate angels: "and in event / Know, whether I *be dextrous* to subdue / Thy Rebels, or be found the *Worst* in Heaven" (740–42). Missing Milton's pun, Bentley objects to "dextrous": "I wonder by what trick *Dextrous* crept in here; insinuating, as if he would *subdue* them by Slight and Strategem, and not by open and native Power. The simplest and nearest Word is the best; *Know whether I* PROVE ABLE *to subdue*" (p. 174). He then turns to the theological implications of "Worst":

If *Worst* relates to Moral Excellence, the Notion is absurd; if it mean (as it needs must) the *worst* or lowest in Power, then there's a properer Word, which I doubt not the Author gave;

Thy Rebels, or be found LEAST in Heaven.

Least in Heaven, an Expression warranted by both *Matthew* [v, 19] and *Luke* [vii, 28], Ἐλάχιϛος—μιχρωτερως ἦν τῇ βασιλεία τ̄ ὀνρωνῶν. (P. 174)

In the morning hymn (V, 144–208), Bentley emends to stress God's wisdom. Adam and Eve praise God's *"goodness beyond thought, and Power Divine"* (V, 159). "In this Verse," Bentley comments, "here's only God's *Goodness* and *Power* mention'd; his chief Attribute in the Creation quite drop'd. Would it not have been better thus? *Thy Goodness,* WISDOM, *Power,* ALIKE *Divine"* (p. 151). This alteration may be glossed by the opening paragraph of his eighth Boyle Lecture:

Having abundantly proved, in our last exercise [Sermon 7], that the frame of the present world could neither be made nor preserved without the *power* of God, we shall now consider the structure and motions of our own system, if any characters of divine *wisdom* and *goodness* may be discoverable by us. . . . the order and beauty of the systematical parts of the world, the discernible ends and final causes of them, the τὸ βελτίον, or meliority above what was necessary to be, do evince, by a reflex argument, that it could not be produced by mechanism or chance, but by an intelligent and benign Agent, *that by his excellent wisdom made the heavens.* (W III, p. 173)

3. "THE *SACRED* TOP": BENTLEY'S GOD'S PROVIDENTIAL EMBLEM

I have argued in the preceding pages that Bentley's "sacred" provides a thesis for many of his subsequent emendations, alerting us as it does to the sense of the sacred that Bentley brings to *Paradise Lost*. This, together with his emphasis on the wisdom and goodness discoverable in the "systematical parts of the world" that underpins his addition of "WISDOM" at Book V, line 159, enables us to return to the first emendation with some comprehension of why, for Bentley, the "top of *Horeb* or of *Sinai*" must be not "secret" but "sacred." But there was also another specific contemporary debate that Bentley sought to conclude with his authoritative emendation. In questioning Bentley's wisdom in replacing "secret," W. B. Stanford observed, in the passage quoted above, that Bentley knew better than most—or ought to have—that the word meant "'lonely, solitary, set apart'"; that he ought to have known that a mountain top was the ideal place for imparting esoteric illumination; that his revision reduced the phrase to a platitude. It is exactly because Bentley *did know* these implications and associations that he was compelled to emend. For Bentley, no less than for his contemporaries, mountains and their relation to Providence were of abiding concern — and debate;[57] and, for Bentley, "the *sacred* top" was not a platitude but the visible emblem of God's providential dealings with his creation.

One of Thomas Burnet's most influential arguments in *Telluris theoria sacra* was that before the deluge the earth was perfectly smooth; as the postdiluvian landscape emerged, the mountains thus created by the upheaval were revealed, in Burnet's poetic phrase, as "the ruins of a broken world."[58] In Bentley's first Boyle Lecture, he directly confronts Burnet's theory: "But some men are out of love with the features and mien of our earth; they do not like this rugged and irregular surface. . . . This with them is deformity, and rather carries the face of a ruin, or a rude and indigested lump of atoms that casually convened so, than a work of divine artifice" (*W* III, p. 193). Providing several arguments for an opposite view, Bentley concludes:

let them lastly consider, that to those hills and mountains we are obliged for our metals, and with them for all the conveniences and comforts of life. To deprive us of metals . . . [is] to bereave us of all arts and sciences, of history and letters; nay, of revealed religion too, that inestimable favour of heaven: for, without the benefit of letters, the whole Gospel would be a mere tradition and old cabbala, without certainty, without authority. (*W* III, p. 197)

In the *Paradise Lost,* beginning at Book I, line 6, Bentley applies the substance of these arguments to the poem's images of mountains. The rebel angels "pluck'd *the seated* Hills with all their load, / . . . and by the shaggy tops / Up-lifting bore them in their hands" (VI, 644–46). Bentley emends to "*th' high-seated* Hills," arguing for both particularity and holiness: "As VII. 585. *The holy Mount of Heav'ns* high-seated *top*" (p. 205). He revises the line in which the fallen angels find "all their Confidence / *Under the weight of Mountains bury'd deep*" (VI, 651–52). Avoiding the destructive actions of mountains and the Burnetian implication that the mountains themselves are fragmented into ruins, Bentley revises: "their Confidence / *Dash'd; all their Labours vain to fragments broke*" (p. 206). Of the lines,

> They view'd the vast unmeasurable Abyss
> Outrageous as a Sea, dark, wastful, wild,
> Up from the bottom turn'd by furious winds
> And surging waves, as *mountains* to assault
> *Heav'ns highth,* (VII, 211–15)

Bentley argues that:

> *Mountains,* an Idea from our Earth form'd by Providence, is too little to express
> the immense Billows of this infinite *Chaos;* and Mountains are quiet and peace-
> able, do not make *Assaults,* unless thrown by *Homer's* Giants, or *Milton's* An-
> gels. Perhaps [Milton] gave it, as MOUNTING *to assault;* though I should prefer
> THREATNING. (P. 224)

We hear in these revisions Bentley's forceful arguments in the Boyle Lectures on behalf of the sacredness of mountains, arguments for which
Paradise Lost is quoted in support:

> Who would part with these solid and substantial blessings for the little fantasti-
> cal pleasantness of a smooth uniform convexity and rotundity of a globe? . . . Are
> there then such ravishing charms in a dull, unvaried flat, to make a sufficient
> compensation *for the chief things of the ancient mountains, and for the precious
> things of the lasting hills* [Deut. xxxiii, 15]. . . . Are not all the descriptions of poets
> embellished with such ideas, when they would represent any places of superla-
> tive delight, any blissful seats of the Muses or the Nymphs, any sacred habitations
> of gods or goddesses? . . . They [poets] cannot imagine even Paradise to be a place
> of pleasure, nor heaven itself to be heaven without them. Let this, therefore, be
> another argument of the divine wisdom and goodness, that the surface of the earth
> is not uniformly convex. (W III, pp. 197–99)

The reference to the "sacred habitation of gods and goddesses," anticipating as it does his initial emendation in *Paradise Lost,* reminds us that
Bentley was not averse to a little myth merchanting of his own when
it served his argument. In the printed text of this sermon the penultimate sentence quoted here is glossed with two passages from *Paradise
Lost:* "Flowers worthy of paradise, which not nice art / In beds and
curious knots, but nature boon / Pour'd forth profuse on hill, and dale,
and plain" (IV, 241–43), and "For earth hath this variety from heaven /
Of pleasure situate in hill and dale" (VI, 640–41; W, 199).

4. *JACTA EST ALEA:* A CONCLUSION AND A BEGINNING

When in the 1720s Bentley turned from his work on the Scriptures
to Milton's poem, his first emendation summed up several contemporary
controversies and epitomized that "divine goodness and wisdom" that
he had argued in his sacred criticism from the Boyle Lectures to the *Paradise Lost* itself. But the bold emendation did something equally significant. In his design to reveal through reasonable emendation the "Original Beauty" of *Paradise Lost,* Bentley fulfilled in that vernacular but
sacred text the worst fears of the opponents of textual criticism of the

Scriptures and helped lay the groundwork for the postmodern formulations of the relations between text and critic. Sacred textual criticism's
attempt to "restore the fair proportions of the sacred edifice," Leslie Stephen noted, "was perilously close to destruction"[59] Because such criticism erased the bounds assigned to critical enquiry, it profoundly changed
the relation between text and critic. Rather than the text imposing its
reason upon the reader, the text submitted to the reason of the critic.
In their vituperative responses to Bentley's Milton, his opponents recognized, however imperfectly, that a dramatic shift had occurred; in his
final annotation, Bentley confirms it. With now no pretense of blame
for amanuensis, "pragmatical Editor," or printers, Bentley — quoting
Caesar's words on crossing the Rubicon, *jacta est alea* — "the die is cast" —
boldly rewrites the final lines of the poem "as close as may be to the
Author's Words, and entirely agreeable to his Scheme": "THEN *hand in
hand with* SOCIAL *steps their way* / *Through* Eden *took*, WITH HEAV'NLY
COMFORT CHEER'D" (pp. 397–98). This final revision reflects, as does the
initial "sacred," the "divine goodness from ye meliority in our system"
that Bentley had advanced in his apologetics; his annotation hints that
Bentley recognized that in bringing sacred criticism to the task of interpreting *Paradise Lost*, he had crossed the Rubicon of criticism.

University of New Orleans

NOTES

This essay is to the memory of F. Wylie Sypher (1904–1987), finest of teachers. I am
deeply grateful to him and to E. Christian Kopff who, long ago, first introduced me to
Bentley's Milton; to O. B. Hardison, Jr., who encouraged me to undertake a full-scale
study of the "base Baconian's" edition of *Paradise Lost;* to Jay A. Levine, whose essay
first suggested to me that the implications of *Critica Sacra* might be extended to Bentley's
reading of Milton; to Michael Cohen, who gave this essay the benefits of his astute criticism; to George Reinecke and Raeburn Miller, who aided me in reading Bentley's Greek;
and to Robert L. Fleury and Juanita R. Boudreaux, Office of Research, University of
New Orleans.

1. All quotations from *Paradise Lost* are from Bentley's edition (London, 1732),
including his original bracketing and italics; I have retained the italicization of his preface.
The lineation varies slightly from modern editions. Milton's other works are quoted from
John Milton, *Complete Poetry and Major Prose*, ed. Merritt Y. Hughes (New York, 1957),
and *Complete Prose Works by John Milton*, 8 vols., ed. Don M. Wolfe et al. (New Haven,
1953–82). Hughes is cited in my text by line number or page; Wolfe, by YP.

2. Robert Willis and J. W. Clark, *The Architectural History of the University of*

Cambridge (Cambridge, 1886), vol. II, p. 616; qtd. in G. M. Trevelyan, *Trinity College: An Historical Sketch* (Cambridge, 1972), pp. 59–60.

3. John Byrom, *Selections from the Journals and Papers of John Byrum, Poet-Diarist-Shorthand Writer*, ed. Henri Talon (London, 1950), p. 79.

4. William Empson, "Milton and Bentley," in *Some Versions of Pastoral* (London, 1935; rpt. New York, n.d.), pp. 149–91.

5. James Duff Duff, "Scholars and Antiquaries: I. Bentley and Classical Scholarship," in *The Cambridge History of English Literature*, eds. A. W. Waller and A. R. Ward (Cambridge, 1952), vol. IX, p. 338; Peter M. Briggs, "The Jonathan Richardsons as Milton Critics," *Studies in Eighteenth-Century Culture* IX (1979), 116.

6. Thomas Newton, ed., *Paradise Lost . . . Volume the First* (London, 1749), p. 7; T[homas?] T[yrwhitt], "The Life of Richard Bentley, D. D.", *The London Magazine*, January 1784, p. 42.

7. "Zoilus," *The Grub-street Journal*, 5 March 1730, p. 1; "Semicolon," *A Friendly Letter to Dr. Bentley. Occasion'd by his New Edition of* Paradise Lost (London, 1732), pp. 18–21; Zachary Pearce, *A Review of the Text of Milton's* Paradise Lost (London, 1732), pp. 1–3.

8. Jacob Tonson, Letter [to Jacob Tonson, II (?)], printed in *The Manuscript of* Paradise Lost: *Book I*, ed. Helen Darbishire (Oxford, 1931), p. xii. The "Specimen" is not listed in A. T. Bartholomew's *Richard Bentley, D. D.: A Bibliography* (Cambridge, 1908), and I have been unable to trace it. The reference to "Addisons notes page 285" is to *The Spectator*, no. 285 (26 January 1712): "If Clearness and Perspicuity . . . debased with common use." Joseph Addison, *The Spectator*, ed. Donald F. Bond (Oxford, 1965), vol. III, pp. 10–11; hereinafter cited by volume and page.

9. W. B. Stanford, *The Enemies of Poetry* (London, 1980), p. 44.

10. Bentley's maxim is quoted in James Henry Monk, *The Life of Richard Bentley, D. D.* (London, 1833), vol. I, p. 116.

11. E. J. Kenney, *The Classical Text: Aspects of Editing in the Age of the Printed Book* (Berkeley, 1974), pp. 100–01.

12. Norman Rabkin, *Shakespeare and the Problem of Meaning* (Chicago, 1981), pp. 63–64; Paul Maas, *Textual Criticism*, trans. Barbara Flowers (Oxford, 1958), p. 12.

13. A. E. Housman, ed. *M. Manilii Astronomicon*, recensvit et enarravit [examined and explained] A. E. Hovsman, Editio Altera [2nd ed. with addendum prepared by A.S.F. Gow], 5 vols. (Cambridge, 1937), vol. I, p. xvi.

14. Empson, "Milton and Bentley," p. 155.

15. Richard Bentley, *The Works of Richard Bentley, D. D.*, 3 vols., ed. Alexander Dyce (London, 1836; rpt. New York, 1966), vol. III, p. 248; hereinafter cited as *W*).

16. Bentley made his preparatory notes in *The Poetical Works of Mr. John Milton: Volume the First [Paradise Lost]* (London, 1720). This copy is in the Cambridge University Library, and the illustration of Bentley's notes from page 1 is made possible by permission of the Syndics of Cambridge University Library. I am grateful to them and to David McKitterick, now Librarian of Trinity College Library, for their assistance and consideration.

17. In the printed edition, Bentley deletes this first Miltonic parallel (IV, 706) as unacceptable; the reference to "Sinai's gray top," with its implicit argument *against* deletion of "secret," is considered in the edition (p. 1).

18. Francis Hare, *The Clergyman's Thanks to Phileleutherus forr his Remarks on a late Discourse of Free-Thinking. In a Letter to Dr. Bentley* (London, 1713), pp. 38–39.

19. Richard Simon, *Critical History of the Old Testament* (Eng. trans., 1682), pp.

8–10; see Jay A. Levine, "The Design of *A Tale of a Tub* (With a Digression of a Mad Modern Critic)," *ELH* XXXIII (1966), 201.

20. Jonathan Swift, *Irish Tracts and Sermons*, in *Prose Works*, ed. H. Davis (Oxford, 1939–68), vol. IX, p. 78; John Evelyn, *Diary and Correspondence*, ed. William Bray (London, n.d.), pp. 663–64.

21. Francis Hare, *The Difficulties and Discouragements, which attend the study of Scriptures* (London, 1714), p. 21; see Levine, "The Design of *A Tale of a Tub*," p. 203.

22. For Milton's views on the "Johannine Comma," see Hughes, pp. 938–39; for Newton's, *The Correspondence of Isaac Newton*, ed. H. W. Turnbull et al. (Cambridge, 1959–77), vol. III, pp. 83–122; Bentley, W III, pp. 484–85.

23. Richard Bentley, *H KAINH ΔΙΑΘHKH. Graece. Novum Testamentum Versionis Vulgate. . . . Proposals for Printing* (Cambridge, 1720), p. 2; rpt. in W III, pp. 497–98.

24. Conyers Middleton, *Remarks . . . upon the Proposals lately published by Richard Bentley. . . .* (London, 1721), pp. 3, 24, 5; in W III, pp. 497–98, 500.

25. Bentley is again quoting from memory; the passage to which he refers is "and Death / Grin'd horrible a ghastly smile, to hear / His famin should be fill'd" (II, 845–47).

26. For a fuller discussion of Bentley's work on the New Testament, see Adam Fox, *John Mill and Richard Bentley: A Study of Textual Criticism of the New Testament, 1675–1729* (Oxford, 1954).

27. Kenney, *The Classical Text*, pp. 100–01.

28. Newton, *Correspondence*, vol. III, p. 251.

29. Rudolf Pfeiffer, *History of Classical Scholarship from 1300 to 1850* (Oxford, 1976), p. 147.

30. E. Christian Kopff, review of *History of Classical Scholarship from 1300 to 1850*, *Classical Philology* LXXVI (1981), 314–18; see Pfeiffer, *Ausgenwählte Schriften*, ed. Winifred Buhler (Munich, 1960), p. 168, for Pfeiffer's earlier discussion of Bentley.

31. See Margaret C. Jacobs, *Newtonianism and the English Revolution* (Ithaca, 1976).

32. Thomas Hobbes, *Leviathan*, ed. A. W. Waller (Cambridge, 1935), p. 17.

33. Addison, *Spectator*, vol. II, no. 267, p. 538.

34. Mark Pattison, "Tendencies of Religious Thought in England, 1688–1750" in *Essays by the Late Mark Pattison*, 2 vols., ed. H. Nettleship (Oxford, 1889), vol. II, p. 47.

35. Thomas Bentley, letter to Zachary Pearce, 20 April 1731, in possession of the Alexander Turnbull Library, Wellington, New Zealand. I am grateful to them for a xerox of this letter. See below, note 54.

36. John Toland, "The Life of Milton," in *A Complete Collection of the Historical, Political, and Miscellaneous Works of John Milton . . . In Three Volumes, to which is Prefix'd the Life of the Author. . . .* (Amsterdam, 1698), vol. I, p. 12. Toland's "Life" contains two passages that reflect details of Bentley's involvement in the Phalaris controversy, then at its height. Toland quotes and praises Sir William Temple, Bentley's victim, "as the noblest Ornament of Politeness and Literature," (p. 43); more pointedly, I think, Toland describes Milton's continental travels where "he became acquainted with the celbrated *Lucus Holstentius* the *Vatican* Librarian, who us'd him with great Humanity" (p. 9). In the Phalaris controversy, Charles Boyle had insulted Bentley: "pro singulari sua humanitate" ("for his singular humanity") (Preface to *Phalaridis agrigentinorum tyranni epsitola*, [1695]), and the phrase "his singular humanity" was used repeatedly throughout the succeeding years to attack Bentley.

37. Anthony Collins, *A Discourse of the Grounds and Reasons for the Christian Religion* (London, 1724), p. 270. See Leslie Stephen, *History of English Thought in the Eighteenth Century*, 2 vols. (London, 1876); rpt. New York, 1962, vol. I, pp. 179–84.

38. Collins, A Discourse concerning Ridicule and Irony in Writing, in a Letter to the Reverend Dr. Nathanael Marshall (London, 1729), p. 62.

39. Collins, A Discourse concerning Ridicule, p. 23.

40. See Levine, "The Design of A Tale of a Tub," p. 200.

41. The Grub-street Journal, 25 May 1732, no. 125, p. 1.

42. Briggs, "The Jonathan Richardsons as Milton Critics," p. 126.

43. Assembly of Divines, The humble Advice of the Assembly of Divines . . . concerning a Confession of Faith (London, 1647), ch. I, pt. 9, p. 6.

44. Bentley's emendation reflects a passage in Sermon 6 of the Boyle Lectures: "freedom and necessity, that are opposites here below, do in heaven above most amicably agree and join hands together. . . . God cannot do what is unjust, nor say what is untrue, nor promise with a mind to deceive" (W III, pp. 125–26).

45. Thomas Sprat, History of the Royal Society, ed. with critical apparatus by Jackson I. Cope and Harold Whitmore Jones (St. Louis, 1950), p. 113.

46. Samuel Holt Monk, The Sublime: A Study of Critical Theories in Eighteenth-Century England (New York, 1935; rpt. Ann Arbor, 1960), p. 31.

47. Murray Roston, Prophet and Poet: The Bible and the Growth of Romanticism (Evanston, 1965), p. 51.

48. Charles Gildon, "Vindication of Paradise Lost" (1694), in Milton: The Critical Heritage (1628–1731), ed. John T. Shawcross (New York, 1970), p. 107.

49. Nathaniel Lee, "To Mr. John Dryden on his Poem of Paradise," in Shawcross, Milton, p. 83.

50. Addison, Spectator, vol. III, no. 297, p. 62.

51. John Hughes, ed. A Complete History of England. . . . , 3 vols., 2nd ed. (London, 1719), vol. I, p. a1r.

52. See Peter Gay, The Enlightenment: The Science of Freedom (New York, 1977), p. 215.

53. Sprat, History of the Royal Society, p. 414.

54. It is because of the family squabble over this emendation that Thomas Bentley wrote to Zachary Pearce (see above, note 34). R. Bentley had first proposed "Apples" to replace "Fables";

> Upon thinking of it in my way to Ashburnham House, when I left you [T. Bentley writes], I was convinced that Apples made the passage nonsense. I told my Uncle so, & satisfied him so far, that he said he would throw out the whole, & have it thus
>
> Hung amiable & of delicious tast.
>
> I will tell you as a friend, that I disputed with him that night about this place & some others, & indeed his whole design, till I put him quite out of humour, & till he called me Ignoramus & several other hard words. I told him I would never object again, since I saw he could not bear it, & hoped he wld take the ill language to himself, If I proved in the right. So we parted & I have never been with him since, for I know he can't forbear talking of Milton, & I can't bear the nonsense & absurdities he puts upon him. . . .

55. Isaac Newton, Yahuda MS I, qtd. in Frank E. Manuel, The Religion of Isaac Newton: The Fremantle Lectures 1973 (Oxford, 1974), p. 118.

56. Bentley's emendation may be related to the earlier gibe of Collins in the Discourse of Free-Thinking, that "We learn in the Old Testament, that Adam by eating the forbidden Fruit subjected himself and all his Posterity to Death. But the New Testament teaches us to understand by Death, eternal life in Misery" (p. 153).

57. See Francis Edward Litz, "Richard Bentley on Beauty, Irregularity, and Mountains," *ELH* XII (1945), 327–32; Marjorie Hope Nicolson, *Mountain Gloom and Mountain Glory: The Development of the Aesthetics of the Infinite* (Ithaca, 1959); Stephen Jay Gould, *Time's Arrow, Time's Cycle: Myth and Metaphor in the Discovery of Geologic Time* (Cambridge, Mass., 1987), pp. 21–59.

58. Thomas Burnet, *The Sacred Theory of the Earth. . . . The Two First Books Containing the Deluge and Concerning Paradise* (1681; English trans. London, 1684), p. 148.

59. Stephen, *History of English Thought in the Eighteenth Century*, vol. I, p. 170.

THE ICONOGRAPHY OF EDEN

Diane K. McColley

M AN IS a lumpe," John Donne wrote to Edward Herbert, "where all beasts kneaded bee; / Wisdome makes him an Arke where all agree . . . our business is, to rectifie / Nature to what she was."[1] It was a fundamental premise of seventeenth-century Christendom that our business in the world, and God's business in us, is to rectify nature — both the little arks we are and the larger ark of earth — to what she was "till disproportion'd sin," Milton has it, "broke the fair musick that all creatures made."[2] Milton stands alone as provider of a full, delicious, and dramatic rendering of "what she was" on which to model the work of rectification, along with a deeply considered account of the first shattering of Eden's lively peace. But visual artists also furnished diverse images of the first Creation and its ruin pertinent to its repair, and they too imbued this Edenic iconography with choices and implications that exercise those faculties of the beholder needed for the work of moral, familial, and what we would now call ecological rehabilitation.

The way a culture imagines its origins affects the ways its members identify themselves and their purposes. Our own time's images of cosmic and human origins tell of huge explosions, biological determinism, competition among species, and our likeness to other primates, over whom we have achieved some problematic technical superiority.[3] Milton's time, we know, spoke of a benevolent Maker, a purposeful and harmonious design, and human likeness to both the Maker and his making: hence our responsibility for the rest of nature and our capacity for arts and moral choices with cosmic reverberations. Owing to present preoccupations, the "Wisdome" contained in Edenic art is an endangered species. Twentieth-century humans reminded of the Genesis story are more likely to concoct and reject an image of the Fall of Man and the Fault of Woman composed of a few harsh strands than to hear "fair musick" worth rejoining. Even when we do regard seventeenth-century artists' responses to Genesis sympathetically, we are apt to miss what they freshly expanded: the details of an exuberant creation, blighted but mendable; the mutuality of male and female humankind in blessedness, betrayal, and recovery; the original delightfulness of man, woman, marriage, fecundity, and all the beasts; the grotesque apostasy into violence and greed and the

107

mutual sorrow and labor of the parents of the nations; the energetic arti-
faction of the Shaper and Saver of this diverse creation and humankind's
part in the Edenic arts of shaping and saving.

The topic of Adam and Eve in the Garden was prolifically depicted
and widely circulated by means of engravings during the sixteenth and
seventeenth centuries. It was an inviting one for Renaissance artists in
love with beauty and educated in anatomy, allowing them to celebrate
the human body unconfined to pagan story, revel in drawing animals
including the exotic ones discovered by explorers, paint lush landscapes,
and represent an important religious subject without offending the icono-
clasts. Moreover, in an age of violent controversy, the original goodness
of creation was a topic on which Catholics and Protestants could sometimes agree.

An artist setting about to draw Adam and Eve had many choices
to make. Which event in their lives should he select or make central?
Should the principal subject be their creation, their lives in innocence,
their fall, or its effects? If the Creation, which part, by what kind of
Creator, with what implications about the Book of Creatures and about
Edenic marriage? If the Fall, as Milton asks, what cause? Should their
bodies and the emblematic animals with them suggest pride, weakness,
vainglory, recklessness, stupidity, lust, understandable hubris, irresistibly
distracting erotic beauty? Should their stance and gestures imply complacency, collusion, dispute, a fearsome risk, a frivolous frolic, a de-
fection by savages, a mistake by essentially good and happy beings, a
fated compliance, a free choice? What kind of Serpent, if any, tempts:
a mere snake (the northern preference), a human-headed one, perhaps
resembling Eve (the southern tradition), a male, a demon, a charming
putto, a bristling monster (all occasionally used)? What should Eve's
part be: rational persuasion, sexual enticement, emotional blackmail,
overwhelming glamor, overweening ambition, childish sensuality? Which
of the two humans was more to blame, or was the act entirely mutual?
What effects should be suggested: a *felix culpa*, a poisoning of the whole
creation, a trivialization of life, a merely "human" or even "humaniz-
ing" frailty, a costly but correctable wrong? What symbols — every shape,
gesture, plant, animal, star, and stone having multiple emblematic
meanings — should be selected and given prominence? What commentaries, iconologies, iconographic traditions, and indeed iconoclasms should
the artist heed? All of these choices bore upon each image of the primal
choice; and often the artist embedded emblems of choice itself, bringing
home to viewers the pertinence of that image to all choice and exercising
their powers of vital and fine distinction.

The most frequently circulated images of Eden were, of course, Bible illustrations, which abounded in this period both as intrinsic parts of printed Bibles and as separate publications to be inserted by the binder. Since, in the former case especially, these illustrations had to be theologically acceptable, every implication is significant, and many are not what we may expect. A widely used modern dictionary of symbolism describes the Temptation, for example, as "Eve holding the fruit or in the act of plucking it, or, having taken a bite, offering it to Adam."[4] In the vernacular Bibles of the Reformation, this High Renaissance version of the Fall rarely appears. Usually, either Adam holds the fruit, or Adam and Eve fall simultaneously. If Eve holds the fruit, she has not taken a bite, and her gesture often implies rational persuasion: not a solely feminine attribute. During the first century of English Bibles, illustrations specifically and progressively combat all inclination to blame Eve more than Adam for the Fall; and this reform is part of a grander iconographic program that, refusing the notion that God made anything defective, proclaims original blessedness, woe for its loss and the ensuing murders and tyrannies, and hope of its regaining by the recovery of what Milton called "our beginning, regeneration, and happiest end, likeness to God."[5]

Creation images depict God in three principal ways. Two use human form, as benevolent Father or as Christ-Logos, energetically engaged in his work and often tenderly so, especially in the creation of Eve. The third depicts an invisible God by means of a "glory" or radiance, sometimes in triple or triangular form, usually around a Tetragrammaton, the four-letter Hebrew name of God vocalized as "Yaweh" or "Jehovah," and translated in English Bibles as "the Lord God." Only the earliest English Bibles contain the first two; authorized Bibles use the third.

The first Bible printed in English (Miles Coverdale's translation, 1535)[6] has four images of Adam and Eve. The title page (Thompson, fig. 3)[7] includes the Fall with Adam, not Eve, holding the fruit. At the beginning of Genesis, six images show Christ as Creator performing the six days' work, on the sixth stooping to raise Eve by the hand from Adam's side. The inset illustration to Genesis, chapter ii, is also a Creation of Eve, the Christ-Logos blessing her as she rises from Adam's side with joined hands. At the beginning of Genesis, chapter iii, comes another Fall: here Eve does hold the fruit toward which Adam reaches, distressed though open-palmed, but both are seated (unlike uxorious versions where Eve dominates a collapsing Adam), and Eve's gesture is one of persuasion, not seduction.

The Matthew Bible of 1537 has three pictures of Adam and Eve.

On the title page (Thompson, fig. 4), both grasp one fruit, Adam's hand on top. The inset Fall is the same as in the 1535 Bible. The large frontispiece to Genesis (Frye, fig. 212) does not depict the Fall itself, but what we might call a Moment of Choice for the viewer as well as the protagonists. Again, Eve's persuasive words are the subject. Her gesture, the goat behind it, and the monkeys above may prefigure the Fall, but nothing makes it certain to occur. There is no Serpent visible and no fruit in Eve's hand. She is not very beautiful; erotic passion is not what is happening. They are not upright, and Adam may be too comfortably seated for our comfort, but Eve does not dominate him as she does in the renditions of Raphael and Titian, more familiar to us now, and his choice is still open. The animals, conspicuous among them the hart of Psalm xlii, are abundant and benign, and on high God holds up two fingers — not the one finger of the Admonition — in blessing.

The "Great Bible" of 1539 is especially important because it went rapidly through six editions and was, as successive title pages state, first "apoynted to the vse of churches" (1540) and then "to be frequented and vsed in euery churche w'in this . . . realme" (1541). All six have the same illustration to Genesis, chapter iii: Adam holds one fruit while the Serpent (with human head) offers him another. Eve, *pudica*, holds no fruit, but faces us and points (accusingly?) toward Adam.

These illustrations concur with John Calvin's and St. Paul's doctrine that sin came "not by the woman, but by Adam him selfe." Calvin refutes the "common opinion" that Adam "was deceiued by her alluring entisements" rather than the deceptions of Satan, and holds that "before such time as the woman had tasted of the fruite of the tree, she told the communication which she had with the serpent, and insnared her husband with the same baites wherewith she herself was deceiued. . . . he did not transgresse the lawe which was giuen vnto him onely to obey his wife: but also being drawne by her into pestilent ambition . . . he did giue more credit to the flattering speaches of the deuell, then to the holy word of God."[8] Many artists, even before Calvin, indicated that Eve had not yet eaten by showing her with two fruits, or Adam and the Serpent with one each. English Bible illustrations either place blame squarely on Adam — still androcentric, perhaps, but not antifeminine — or else on the mutuality of the Fall, and on persuasion leading to free choice of deceptive ambition, not on passion or any weakness intrinsically linked with the feminine. They do not usually connect the Fall with sexual pleasure or imply that it was fortunate in any other way.

The sixteenth century produced two other important English Bibles: the Geneva Bible, translated by Marian exiles, and the Bishop's Bible, the official Bible of Elizabeth I.[9] Both sometimes had genealogies bound in, headed by a medallion of Adam and Eve engaged in a mutual Fall, and those printed by Christopher Barker, the queen's printer, as well as some Authorized Versions printed by Robert Barker, sometimes contain a frontispiece with Adam and Eve each holding a fruit and each holding banners proclaiming their equal participation in both sin and regeneration (Frye, fig. 109). The Forbidden Tree itself is labeled "Created good and faire, by breach of lawe a snare," and so becomes an emblem of the whole creation. Scrolls from the two fruits explain that "Desire to knowe hath wrought ovr woe. By tasting this th'exile of blisse," while the scrolls from their two free hands declare "By promise made restord we be to pleasures of eternitye." Although "desire to knowe" needs a careful gloss, and pun hunters will give it a scurrilous one, the main impression is of a regenerative typology. Around Adam and Eve diverse pleasant beasts in pairs roam the well-watered Garden. The snake who is disturbing this peace bears his comeuppance: "Dvste for to eate mvst be my meate." This image of a good Creation, an unfortunate Fall, and a gracious promise of restoration is the main theme of Reformation iconography of Eden.

Probably the most familiar image of Adam and Eve in the early seventeenth century was that in the Speed genealogies regularly bound into Authorized Bibles (and some Geneva Bibles as well) from 1611 to 1640,[10] including the 1612 quarto Milton owned. Apart from the 1611 folio, which reverts to an image of Eve taking the fruit from the Serpent's mouth while Adam reaches out his hand, much like Dürer's 1504 engraving (Frye, p. 164), the inset picture perpetuates the theme of a mutual and unfortunate Fall, though its inscription attributes the disobedience, in the redemptive Pauline text (Rom. v, 19, 21), to "one man." In another image of the Fall which Milton may have been acquainted with, the frontispiece to the Edinburgh Bibles printed by Robert Young in the 1630s,[11] both Adam and Eve grasp one fruit while Eve takes another, implying that they will eat the mortal feast together: a point Milton discards to avoid impugning Adam's intelligence, perhaps, though he preserves the emphasis on joint culpability in other ways. At their feet, a pair of turtledoves symbolizes the wedded love that is the "happier *Eden*" (*PL* IV, 507) of the Paradise being lost.

Title page design for the first century of English Bibles also moves toward a typology of regeneration. In early Bibles the left side depicts the Old Testament and the right side the New, often connected at the top by the Tetragrammaton. The 1535 title page (Thompson, fig. 3) has, on the left, Adam and Eve (with Adam holding the fruit), Moses

receiving the Law, and the reading of the Law. Opposite and antitypi-
cal to these are the resurrected Christ trampling serpent, demon, and
skull; his last charge to his apostles; and St. Peter preaching the gospel.
From the Name of God, Adam and Eve are addressed by a scroll (up-
side down to the reader): "In whate daye so ever thou eatest thereof,
thou shalt die," while Christ is acknowledged, in Latin, "This is my beloved Son, in whom I am well pleased." At the bottom Henry VIII gives
a Bible to his bishops, flanked by David and St. Paul. But the title page
to the Matthew Bible of 1537 (Thompson, fig. 4), taken from the Van
Liesvelt Dutch Bible (Antwerp, 1526), parallels the Giving of the Law
with the Annunciation, the mutual Fall with the Crucifixion, and Death
with the Resurrection. This program preserves a theme of salvation by
grace without suggesting a kind of *felix culpa* that would make grace
dependent on sin or allow too cheerful an attitude toward sin itself. Instead of presenting a Fall-and-Resurrection typology, it aligns Adam and
Eve with Death and makes the Fall a type of the Crucifixion: both Trees
are instruments of pain, though one brings death and the other redemption. This distinction between a fortunate Fall and salvation wrought
by great pain, but ultimately joyous, is confirmed in the verbal front
matter and annotations of English Bibles,[12] and the typology of a good
creation ill lost but well regained increases in the seventeenth century.

Title pages to the Authorized Version usually integrate Old and New
Testament figures to suggest that the Law and the gospel form a coherent regenerative process. The title page to the Bible issued by the university printer at Cambridge in 1630, while Milton was at Christ's, shows
a very small Fall overpowered by imagery of the good Creation and its
repair in the present world. Other small medallions show the Sacrifice
of Isaac halted by an angel; the Incarnation; and the Resurrection. At
the top, the Tetragrammaton sheds light on a shining world of the present, complete with sailboat, flanked by sun, moon, and stars as they typically appear in creation imagery. On either side, cherubs proclaim "God
saw everything that was made, and behold it was very good." Beneath
the globe, Justice and Peace embrace each other. Beside the title, Moses
with his rod that struck water out of desert rock faces David (where Aaron
stood in the 1611 titles) playing his harp, recalling the great psalm-singing
movement that united all classes in this period, and perhaps more pleasing to Milton than the figure of ecclesiastical authority it replaced. Below
the title Christ feeds his disciples, the symbolic sacrificial lamb before
him, flanked by the Evangelists, and at the bottom the hart of Psalm
xlii, a major figure in Edenic imagery, completes the hopeful program:
"Like as the hart desireth the waterbrooks, so longeth my soul after thee,
O God."[13]

Although Bible illustrations were not encouraged by the Parliamentarians of the 1640s and 1650s, some Authorized Versions printed by or for the Company of Stationers headed Genesis with a mutual Fall surrounded by happy animals in pairs. Also, lavish sets of engravings made their way into private copies, including a Genesis series of forty plates by the Dutch engraver Jacob Floris van Langeren (fl. Amsterdam, 1580–97?), published with four-language inscriptions by William Slatyer.[14] These are not the "Popish pictures" published by Robert Peake,[15] and nothing in their iconography would be likely to offend the most ardent Protestant who tolerates visual images of scriptural subjects at all. On the other hand, they do have two unusual features that come close to the spirit of *Paradise Lost*. In the background of the creation of Eve in which Eve, rising from Adam's side, is graphically "flesh of [his] flesh," Adam and Eve step together with open arms, while the voice of God says "It is not good for man to be alone," a point reconfirmed by the four-language commendation of woman as meet help. This rare motif is repeated on the set's title page, which includes the Fall and the expulsion but makes central the creation of Adam and another version of the joyous greeting. And between the creation of Eve and the Fall comes an exceedingly rare image: Adam and Eve praying on the Sabbath.[16] In other such series, the only event to come between the presentation of Eve to Adam and the Fall was the Admonition: a series of events that does not speak well for the virtue of "our first parents" or for God's gift of woman. The image Slatyer interprets as the Institution of the Sabbath does apparently derive from a drawing by Maerten de Vos of the Admonition, a popular subject of Dutch and Flemish art. Nicolaes de Brüyn's creation series uses it in that way. But another artist working after de Vos, Jan Theodore de Bry, produced an engraving (fig. 1) similar to de Brüyn's whose inscription (in French, here in counterproof) is the first verse of Psalm cxvii, "Praise the Lord all ye people": all people being incipient in Adam and Eve. The animals in de Bry's version mingle those often associated with the Fall (monkey, goat, and fox, grouped on the left) with more benign or ambiguous ones, associating the drinking hart with the kneeling pair. In the images of the Fall by both de Brüyn and van Langeren (and so presumably by de Vos, who was a wellspring of biblical imagery), Adam holds the fruit in such a way that one could not tell from the visual image alone who is tempting whom, an ambiguity also used by Rubens and traceable to Raphael.[17]

The publication in England of an engraving of Adam and Eve at prayer before the Fall is a significant event, because it gives sure evidence of a movement indicated as well by the joyous greetings of Adam and Eve and by the title page of the Cambridge Bible, affirming the

Figure 1. Jan Theodore de Bry, *God Speaking to Adam and Eve*. © Museum Plantin-Moretus en Prentenkabinet, Antwerp.

goodness of creation and the original blessedness of Adam and Eve, and so of the happy possibility of restoring nature to "what she was."

Depictions of Adam and Eve actually enjoying their lives in Eden are rare, but less rare than has been supposed, and once one is aware of the *topos* one sees even in the paradisal imagery of the standard Creation scenes a wave of gratitude, in the late sixteenth and early seventeenth centuries, for the beauty of creation and the delight of innocent love. But the *topos* of Original Blessedness has been overlooked not only because it is unusual but also because of our habit of pointing out the sinister side of ambiguities and forgetting their possibilities for rectitude.

Since all things are "created good and fair" but made snares by "dispro-portioned sin," all created things can be emblems of both good and evil and so engage the viewer in interpretive choices reenacting the primal choice of Adam and Eve. But it is easy, if we oversimplify their iconog-raphy, to suppose that the plants and animals of Eden are intended to represent either lost good (the hart) or evil (the goat), and to see in Adam and Eve and the beast imagery around them prefigurations of the Fall rather than configurations of delight. Another difficulty is that, in seventeenth-century versions especially, the Earthly Paradise teems with snakes, snails, toads, frogs, beetles, vultures, crocodiles, and other beasts not usually thought presentable. Since man as microcosm was thought to contain the natures of all created things, we need to interpret these hieroglyphs with care, lest we assume that the artists mean to tell us that God embedded repellent characteristics in humankind.

For the seventeenth-century iconologist, as well as the twentieth-century ecologist — to pick up the pun in Donne's doughy metaphor — all beasts needed be. Since, according to Genesis, God made all creatures and blessed them and pronounced them good, all may be considered originally innocent, including those that grew noxious when humans lost control of themselves and their charges. Those that have been allegor-ized as fallen passions, though they may be interpreted as prolepses of the Fall, may also represent the virtues, passions, and pleasures that are the stuff of regeneration. "Happy is hee," as Donne continues, who "can use his horse, goate, wolfe, and every beast / And is not Asse himselfe to all the rest."

It will enrich our understanding of paradisal imagery if we ask how one can use the goat, wolf, vulture, snake, and crocodile within. As Donne's poem implies, each human contains protoplastically all the ca-pacities the various animals display severally: skills, virtues, passions, and evil inclinations all have their traditional animal analogues. In the Gar-den of Eden, according to this view, all creatures near and (now) far lived together in harmony just as all affections were "rightly tempered" in the human soul. When "disproportion'd sin" broke their harmony, the affections went to war with each other, as the animals themselves did; in Milton's lines, "Discord first / Daughter of Sin . . . Death introduc'd through fierce antipathie." Where once "frisking playd / All beasts of th'Earth, since wilde" (IV, 340–41), "Beast now with Beast gan war, & Fowle with Fowle, / And Fish with Fish; to graze the Herb all leav-ing, / Devourd each other; nor stood much in awe / Of Man, but fled him, or with count'nance grim / Glar'd on him passing," while the Para-dise within undergoes like change, and Adam is in a "Sea of passion tost"

(X, 707–18). But "Wisdome," as Donne's poem says, can sort out these warring beasts, making a person not a chaotic lump or a storm-tossed sea, but an ark, a regenerate peaceable kingdom.

The tradition that associates the beasts with harmful passions derives more from the moralization of pagan myth than from Scripture. In the Psalms and the Book of Job the wildest animals demonstrate the awesome inventiveness and unlimited providence of their Creator, and analogies to the recalcitrance of goats or the uncleanness of swine come from the practical experience of a pastoral people rather than a systematic sense that animals resemble degraded humans. But the association of the beasts with sinful passions has deep classical roots. Circe, or sensuality, turns men into animals who represent the seven deadly sins: to use Spenser's identifications, the peacock is an emblem of pride, the lion of wrath, the wolf of envy, the camel of avarice, the goat of lechery, the swine of drunkenness and gluttony, and the ass of sloth.[18] Depictions of the Fall often give prominence to the animal that iconologists associate with the sin the artist thinks predominant. Goltzius puts a large goat in front of a voluptuous Adam and Eve; Burgkmair (Frye, fig. 216) blames the Fall on concupiscence (the monkey) and fraud (the fox); Dürer gives us liberty in the shape of a cat watching a mouse (Frye, fig. 164), or a phlegmatic temperament in the shape of a badger (Frye, fig. 218): a notion agreeable to Milton's sense that sin is "not properly an action, for in reality it implies defect;"[19] Jan Breughel, collaborating with Rubens, gives the peacock pride of place (Frye, p. vii).

But these emblems do not apply to the animal kingdom before the Fall set it in disarray. Sometimes they are proleptic of the Fall; in many a creation of Eve the cat scrutinizes the mouse with an unsettling intensity. But even then they participate in a long tradition of multiple significance. Warning against inflexible interpretation of scriptural signs, St. Augustine points out that the same similitude may be used "in a good sense" in one place and "in an evil sense" in another: "This is the situation where the lion is used to signify Christ, when it is said 'The lion of the tribe of Judah . . . has prevailed,' but also signifies the Devil, when it is written, 'Your adversary the devil, as a roaring lion, goeth about seeking whom he may devour.' Thus the serpent appears in a good sense in 'wise as serpents,' but in a bad sense in 'the serpent seduced Eve by his subtility.'"[20] According to Renaissance iconologists, the dog represents both envy and domestic fidelity; the monkey impudence, but also the cure of pride, perhaps by aping our affectations. The horse embodies both war and constancy, the lion courage and magnanimity as well as wrath. The goat is sometimes lust, but the mountain goat poised on a cliff in Dürer's engraving represents Christ, who, according to Physiologus, sees all things as from the mountain peaks.[21] The ostrich, curiously prominent in many versions, is in Physiologus a symbol of forgetfulness, surely an attribute of man's lapse, but also of those who forget "those things which are behind" in order to strive "for the prize of a heavenly vocation,"[22] and so prefigures regeneration. All beasts that are not purely good (as a few are seen to be even in the fallen world) have such multiple connotations, and which comes first to mind tells us something about ourselves.

Johannes Saenredam's engraving after Abraham Bloemart (fig. 2) presents a moment of choice for Adam and Eve and for the viewer. It is not a Fall; that comes next in Saenredam's series, and this has no Serpent and a different kind of tree. Gestures and attributes are ominous; yet each contains as much possibility for good as for evil, unless we have a predilection for evil. The beautiful bodies and clasped hands signify perfect health and marital consent, as well as warning of the beckonings of amorous excess. Eve's gesture is ominously reminiscent of the "persuasion" theme, Adam carries a broken branch, and their posture and exchange of glances suggests erotic absorption and ingratiation. Yet neither discussions of trees nor erotic attentiveness necessitate a Fall. The gourd is ambiguous, too. In Whitney's emblem[23] it signifies worldly pride or transitory happiness, but Whitney's has aspired to climb a tree, and Saenredam's lies meekly (if umbilically) on the ground. The gourd is an attribute of pilgrims, who use it as a water jar, including the Archangel Raphael (who, according to legend, planted the melon family in the Garden of Eden)[24] and Christ at Emmaus. God caused one to grow and shade the dejected Jonah, which gladdened him, and then smote it, to teach Jonah the value of life, and although Jonah's gourd withered, his prophecy was heeded and, therefore, abrogated, and Nineveh and all her cattle were spared. Here, too, the gourd may be seen as warning, not prediction, or as prefiguration of regeneration as well as fall.

The dominant beast, of course, is the vulture, or possibly eagle; its identity as vulture is strongly suggested by the turn of its head, the standard stance in iconologies. At first glance, a vulture portends death. It gnaws the vital organs of those who (like Prometheus) steal forbidden knowledge, and since it lives on carrion one supposes that it is waiting for Eve to persuade Adam to eat forbidden fruit so that death will enter the Garden and it can eat, too. But, of course, before the Fall all animals were vegetarians (PL X, 710–12); the lion ate straw, like the ox (Isa. xi, 11). In the *Hieroglyphica* of Valerian (1556), which was disseminated during the sixteenth and seventeenth centuries in several editions,

Figure 2. Jan Saenredam after Abraham Bloemaert, *Adam and Eve in Paradise*, 1604. © Centraal Museum, Utrecht.

and in the many versions of *Horus Apollo*, which summed up iconological lore in handy pocket books for painters, the vulture, the sacred bird of Egypt, is a symbol of mercy because it does not kill. It also signifies maternity, prescience, clarity of vision, and Urania, the Celestial Muse. It is a symbol of the Genius of Nature, as in Ripa's *Iconologia*, and of providence.[25] Simultaneously sinister and sacred, it is a perfect hieroglyph of the crucial choice still open to Adam and Eve in this engraving and open again to those who would rectify nature to what she was.

"The heart of man," Donne's poem says, "Is an epitome of God's great book / Of creatures"; and everything he made is, depending on how one uses it, "poysonous, or purgative, or cordiall." What is true of nature is also true of art that goes hand in hand with nature. Seeing nature and human nature as successively innocent, cursed, and blessed again, seventeenth-century literary and visual arts lead us literally and mimetically through these three stages. Their images are complex hieroglyphics of real and daily choices by which we preserve or spoil or renew the world. We can look at Saenredam's vulture and even Milton's lavish garden and see defect and disintegration; or we can go on to use these glyphic tests as purgatives and cordials by which to "rectifie / Nature" and those epitomes of nature we thereby learn we are.

Rutgers University

NOTES

Research support for this essay was provided by the Research Council of Rutgers, the State University of New Jersey.

1. John Donne, "To Sr. Edward Herbert. At Julyers," in *The Complete Poetry of John Donne*, ed. John T. Shawcross (New York, 1967).

2. John Milton, "At a Solemn Musick," in *The Student's Milton*, ed. Frank Allen Patterson (New York, 1930). All quotations from Milton are from this edition (*SM*).

3. Compare, for example, Michelangelo's *Creation of Adam* with Jay H. Matternes's careful reconstruction with details selected to suggest modern man's resemblence to Australopithecus afarensis in "4,000,000 Years of Bipedalism," *National Geographic* (November 1985), pp. 574-77.

4. James Hall, *Dictionary of Subjects and Symbols in Art* (New York, 1974), p. 5.

5. Milton, *Of Reformation*, in *SM*, p. 454.

6. Brief histories of early English Bibles include Craig R. Thompson, *The Bible in English, 1525-1611* (Charlottesville, 1958), and S. L. Greenslade, "English Versions of the Bible, A. D. 1524-1611," in *The Cambridge History of the Bible: The West from*

the Reformation to the Present Day, ed. S. L. Greenslade (Cambridge, England, 1963), chapter 4.

7. Parenthetical references are to Thompson, *The Bible in English*, and Roland Mushat Frye, *Milton's Imagery and the Visual Arts: Iconographic Tradition in the Epic Poems* (Princeton, 1978).

8. John Calvin, *A Commentarie vpon Genesis by John Calvin Englished by Thomas Thymme* (London, 1578), p. 92; first published in Latin (Geneva, 1554). The marginal gloss in this edition miscites the reference as Romans xv, 12. In the same paragraph, Calvin explains 2 Timothy ii, 14, "Adam was not deceiued, but the woman" as comparative, to show that Adam was not merely uxorious but consciously chose "pestilent ambition."

9. The first large Bishops' Bible (1568) has an illustration of the Fall in which Adam reaches for fruit Eve holds, as does the first large 1611 Authorized Version, but both of these were removed from subsequent editions. The first Bishops' Bible also has illustrations of the Creation of the World and the Creation of Eve from Virgil Solis's *Biblische Figuren* (Frankfurt-am-Main, 1562), but with the fatherly Creator replaced by the Tetragrammaton; in the case of the Creation of Eve new arms have been awkwardly attached to Eve to fill the gap. In subsequent editions, the Creation series (including Cain and Abel) was removed and a headpiece to Genesis substituted with Adam seated under a tree naming or exhorting the animals.

10. In 1610 John Speed obtained the right for ten years to insert his genealogies into every edition of the Authorized Version, a practice which continued until at least 1640: note to A. W. Pollard and G. R. Redgrave, *A Short-Title Catalogue of Books Printed in England, Scotland, & Ireland and of English Books Printed Abroad, 1475–1640* (London, 1926; second edition, revised and enlarged, begun by W. A. Jackson and F. S. Ferguson, completed by Katharine F. Pantzer, London, 1986), no. 23039.

11. See "Notes on Milton's Bibles," in *The Works of John Milton*, 18 vols., ed. Frank Allen Patterson et al. (New York, 1931–38), vol. XVIII, eds. Thomas Ollive Mabbott and J. Milton French, pp. 559–61. Some of the preliminary pages of Milton's copy of the 1612 Authorized Version in the British Library are now missing, including the Adam and Eve page of the Speed genealogies, but the subsequent pages are there in the standard format. A copy of the Robert Young edition is thought to have belonged to Mary Powell Milton.

12. See for example "The Summe of the whole Scripture," the prayer following the preface, and the note to the map showing "the situation of Gods garden" in Bishops' Bibles, and the "Argument" and annotations to Genesis in the Geneva version.

13. Coverdale's translation (spelling modernized); his much-loved rendering of the Psalter was frequently bound into later Bibles and was used in the Book of Common Prayer.

14. Pollard and Redgrave, *STC*, no. 226345. The British Library owns two copies of this set, bound into Bibles published in 1649 and 1663. I am grateful to Mervyn Jannetta of the British Library for help in tracing the source of these copies, which were not hitherto recorded in either the *Short-Title Catalogue* or the British Library catalogue. The Genesis series, along with other illustrations cited in this article, will be reproduced in my book-in-progress, "A Gust for Paradise in the Arts of the Age of Milton."

15. See A. S. Herbert, *Historical Catalogue of Printed Editions of the English Bible, 1525–1961*, revised from Darlow and Moule, 1903 (London, 1968), no. 476. Peake's New Testament series, also bound into the 1663 Bible in the British Library, has an iconic quality absent from the van Langeren set.

16. Reproduced in Diane K. McColley, "Eve and the Arts of Eden," in Julia M. Walker, ed., *Milton and the Idea of Woman* (Urbana, 1988), pp. 100–19.

17. Marcantonio Raimondi's engraving after Raphael shows Adam probably just hav-

ing received fruit from Eve but appearing to hold it out to her; reproduced in Bartsch, Adam von, *The Illustrated Bartsch*, gen. ed. Walter L. Strauss (New York, 1978), vol. XXVI, *The Works of Marcantonio Raimondi and of His School*, ed. Konrad Oberhuber (New York, 1978), no. 1. In Rubens's similar painting at his house in Antwerp, Eve holds the fruit (which is almost impossible to see) in such a way that Adam seems to be coaxing her to give it to him.

18. Edmund Spenser, *The Faerie Queene*, I, iv, 17–36, *The Works of Edmund Spenser: A Variorum Edition*, ed. Edwin Greenlaw, Charles Grosvenor Osgood, and Frederick Morgan Padelford, vol. 1 (Baltimore, 1932), pp. 47–52.

19. John Milton, *De doctrina Christiana*, in *SM*, p. 999.

20. Augustine, *On Christian Doctrine*, trans. D. W. Robertson, Jr. (Indianapolis, 1958), p. 100.

21. *Physiologus*, trans. Francis J. Carmody (San Francisco, 1953), no. XLIII.

22. *Physiologus*, no. XXXI.

23. Geffrey Whitney, *A Choice of Emblemes* (1586; rpt. New York, 1967), emblem 24.

24. 3 Baruch (Slavonic) iv, 7, in *The Old Testament Pseudepigrapha*, ed. James H. Charlesworth (New York, 1985), vol. II, p. 666. Paintings and engravings of Tobias and Raphael, often with a gourd flask, were very popular in this period.

25. *Orus Apollo de Ægypte* (?Paris, 1543); *Hori Apollonis: Selecta hieroglyphica* (Rome, 1606); Ioannis Pieri Valeriani Bellvensis, *Hieroglyphica, seu de sacris Aegyptiorvm aliarvmque gentium literis commentarii* (Lyon, 1610); *Les hieroglyphiques de Ian-Pierre Valerian*, trans. I. de Montlyart (1615; rpt. New York, 1976); Cesare Ripa, *Iconologia o vero descrittione dell' imagini vniversali* (Rome, 1593); *Nova iconologia di Cesare Ripa Pervgino* (Padua, 1618); *Iconologie . . . grauées . . . par Iacques de Bie [sic], et moralement expliquées par I. Bavdoin . . . de Cesar Ripa* (Paris, 1636).

FROM SHADOWY TYPES TO SHADOWY TYPES: THE UNENDINGS OF *PARADISE LOST*

Regina Schwartz

> So Law appears imperfet, and but giv'n
> With purpose to resign them in full time
> Up to a better Cov'nant, disciplin'd
> From shadowy Types to Truth, from Flesh to Spirit,
> From imposition of strict Laws, to free
> Acceptance of large Grace, from servile fear
> To filial, works of Law to works of Faith.[1]

I N T H E final education in *Paradise Lost*, Michael teaches Adam that his progeny are to be progressively enlightened, for the advent of Christ will bring them from a world of shadowy types to the revelation of truth, from the Old Testament realm of mere flesh to the life of the Spirit, and from the dispensation of law to the far more superior one of grace. The authoritative ring of these phrases—types to truth, flesh to spirit, law to grace—stems from their distinguished past at the center of theological speculation from Paul through Milton's own era. The doctrines they embody are the most fundamental and unassailable Milton could invoke: whatever complex controversies continue to rage between various sects, this much—the basic relation between the dispensations of the Old and New Testaments—is sure. And yet, for all of their definitive ring, these phrases are poorly suited to Milton's work. Replacing the carnal by the spiritual does not fit very well in a poem where angels eat with "keen dispatch of real hunger," and if Truth is imaged as Spirit here, elsewhere its haunting metaphor is as flesh: Truth comes into the world in *Areopagitica* as a *body*, and the second coming is not marked by the disappearance of that body or its replacement with Spirit, but by the recovery of its dismembered pieces, piece by fleshly piece. "From strict law to large grace": even the hierarchical distinction between law and grace is something Milton would qualify, for his effort is less to rank

123

them than to intermix the two, to make mercy colleague with justice, and to make justice executed with love (X, 59).[2] But the key phrase, "from shadowy types to truth" is my focus, for it implies arriving at a definitive understanding, a complete vision instead of a partial one, an authoritative answer instead of a hazy intimation, and yet it appears within a discourse — Michael's final narration to Adam in the last books of *Paradise Lost* — that is replete with conclusions that will not finish, moments of revelation that are incomplete, and flashes of insight that turn out to be dim apprehensions.[3]

Nonetheless, shadows that issue in truth became virtually a motto for typological thinking.[4] The Old Testament dispensation could offer only intimations of the genuine article. Melito of Sardis likened Old Testament types to small models the sculptor could use as a pattern while he works on the full-scale statue. Chrysostom spoke of types as the outline for a painting which is later filled in with color. These spatial metaphors blurred into temporal ones, for types are "filled in" in the "fulness" of time. Irenaeus isolated what he called the "consummative" nature of typology. Writing that "the Son of God became the son of David and the son of Abraham, perfecting and summing up this in himself that he might enable us to possess life," he asserted that God's plan for the Hebrew nation is consummated; that is, it is perfected and concluded by Christ.[5] Lancelot Andrewes's Christmas sermon of 1620 demonstrates the logic: "That which was thus promised to, and by the patriarchs, shadowed forth in the figures of the Law, the Temple and the Tabernacle; that which was foresaid by the Prophets, and foresung of in the Psalms, that was this day fulfilled."[6] "Fulfillment" makes a predictable appearance in typological readings. Andrewes's Christmas sermon of 1609:

And well also might it be called the fulness of time in another regard. For till then all was but in promise, in shadows and figures and prophecies only, which fill not, God knows. But when the performance of these promises, the body of these shadows, the substance of those figures, the fulfilling or filling full of all those prophecies came, then came the fulness of time: truly so called. Till then it came not; then it came.[7]

I

In the final books of *Paradise Lost*, Adam also uses the term *fulfilled*, and in the Irenaean sense of a culminating conclusion. He couples it with the frequently attendant metaphor of sight and blindness; having seen through a glass darkly, Adam now sees fulfillment face to face:

True opener of mine eyes, prime Angel blest,
Much better seems this vision, and more hope
Of peaceful days portends
        .   .   .   .
Here Nature seems fulfill'd in all her ends.   (XI, 598–602)

Adam certainly sounds like he is talking about Christ, but instead he is witnessing one of the most troubling—and carnal—scenes of the Old Testament: Genesis, chapter vi, where the sons of God cavort with the daughters of men. The scene does not portend peace, but complete moral chaos, for this is the terrible "wickedness" that provokes the Flood, the wickedness "for which / The world erelong a world of tears must weep" (XI, 627). Nature is not fulfilled, but corrupted, in all her ends, and Michael appears to be not the true, but the false opener of Adam's eyes. This is not an isolated instance of premature enlightenment. Adam soon becomes enthusiastic again, even alluding to his earlier error with the deep confidence that he is now correcting it. "Erewhile perplexed," he now sees clearly:

                    O sent from Heav'n,
    Enlight'ner of my darkness, gracious things
    Thou hast reveal'd, those chiefly which concern
    Just Abraham and his Seed: *now* first I find
    Mine eyes true op'ning, and my heart much eas'd,
    Erewhile perplexed.   (XII, 270–75; my emphasis)

But he still sees through a glass darkly, for here he is hastily mistaking Abraham and the Israelite nation to be born of him for Christ and the Heavenly Kingdom, mistaking, that is, the shadow for the truth: "but now I see / His day, in whom all Nations shall be blest." He responds to the narration of the birth of Christ with no less excitement, and little more insight. The true opener of his eyes (who showed him the sons of God with the daughters of men), the enlightener of his darkness (who enabled him to confuse Abraham for Christ), is now addressed, not only as the prophet of glad tidings (for Michael tells the nativity story), but also as the *finisher* of utmost hope. And what follows is Adam's third reference to his own clear-sightedness: "*Now* clear I understand" (XII, 376; my emphasis). But he is once again overconfident, for his next question—where and when the combat between Christ and Satan will take place—only reveals how clouded his vision still is (XII, 375–85). There will be no single duel; the battle for obedience must be fought perpetually in the hearts of Adam's progeny.[8] Even with the advent, his hopes are not utterly fulfilled, and the story is not finished.

If Adam's veil never fully lifts, it is not entirely his fault. Michael induces these moments of premature concluding by offering premature conclusions through his manipulation of typology, and Michael is a consummate typologist. He seizes upon each biblical event and personage as a type, and hence as an occasion to run ahead to its fulfillment. Abraham ("him God the most High voutsafes / To call by vision from his Father's house,"120–21) provides an opportunity for Michael to push his narrative forward from the patriarchal promise to the final promise ("in his Seed / All Nations shall be blest," 125–26), and from the earthly land promised to Abraham's descendants to the eternal paradise of the Promised Land: "This ponder, that all Nations of the Earth / Shall in his Seed be blessed; by that Seed / Is meant thy great deliverer (XII, 146–47). How could Adam avoid mistaking the shadow for the truth? This certainly sounds like an adequate explanation of the glorious mystery of ultimate deliverance. Then too, David, the seed of Abraham, offers a type of "the Woman's Seed to thee foretold / Foretold to Abraham" (XII, 327–28).

Michael's use of typology is perhaps most explicit when he turns to Mosaic law and finds an occasion to talk instead of grace, swiftly collapsing that enormous distance Adam's progeny must traverse between "strict laws and large grace." His narrative pace runs fast forward: in only *eight* lines, works of Mosaic law give way to faith, Joshua to Jesus, and the wide wilderness to the promised land.

> And therefore shall not Moses, though of God
> Highly belov'd, being but the Minister
> Of Law, his people into Canaan lead;
> But Joshua whom the Gentiles Jesus call
> His Name and Office bearing, who shall quell
> The adversary Serpent, and bring back
> Through the world's wilderness long wander'd man
> Safe to eternal Paradise of rest.   (XII, 307–14)

Surely now that he has depicted man's arrival, safe at last, at the eternal rest, there can be no more story. *Rest*—the term reverberates with the sabbath rest, the conclusion of the creation in Genesis, and the final rest of the heavenly creation in Revelation; all of the linear logic tied to a sacred history spanning alpha to omega is contained in *rest* and its allusions. But once again, Michael has used typology to frustrate, rather than fulfill, our expectation of an end. For Michael has not reached a place of rest in his narrative, any more than Adam and Eve do in theirs; he is only as far as Joshua (not even a third of the way through biblical history) and so he must backtrack to resume where he had left off, re-opening with a word that, having said it all, makes more saying possible: *meanwhile*. That *meanwhile* has the effect of canceling instantly the vision of rest, replacing the heavenly Paradise with an earthly Canaan much troubled by unrest:

> Safe to eternal Paradise of rest.
> Meanwhile they in thir earthly Canaan plac't
> Long time shall dwell and prosper, but when sins
> National interrupt thir public peace,
> Provoking God to raise them enemies   (XII, 314–18)

"Meanwhile," "but first," "but now"—all of these adverbial retreats from the envisioned future signal "not yet," and it soon becomes apparent that Michael's use of typology is controlled, not so much by the expected vocabulary of finality as by such key adverbs of deferral. When he waxes most typological—the Seed of Abraham foretells the Woman's Seed, the old law hints of the new grace, Joshua of Jesus, King David of the final King—we would most expect to hear of completion. Instead, Milton uses typology in the last two books of his epic to frustrate, rather than fulfill (or fill full) our expectation of an end. The technique is not restricted to those final visions and auditions to Adam: Milton's most classic use of the Adam/Christ typology in *Paradise Lost* are the very first lines of the epic.

> Of Man's First Disobedience, and the Fruit
> Of that Forbidden Tree, whose mortal taste
> Brought Death into the World, and all our woe,
> With loss of Eden, *till* one greater Man
> Restore us, and regain the blissful Seat   (I, 1–5; my emphasis)

Till dictates the temporal zone of this whole poem; the ensuing narrative will be located in that *till* between type and antitype, a *till* that forever defers fulfillment and conclusion. Strikingly akin to another of Milton's favorite adverbial phrases, *till* suggests the repeating, hence deferring, *yet once more*.

In Michael's clever narration of biblical history, little more has happened than the repeated inversion of fulfillment and prefiguration—tantalizing his hearers with an ending before he has offered the middle of his story—but then to invert the positions of fulfillment and anticipation is to undo the conclusion: *something comes next*, so the vision of Paradise is withdrawn as soon as it is offered. To put an end in the middle is not to end. All of this is consonant with *Areopagitica* where truth is not a place where we can arrive, having traveled from shadowy types to truth, but a "streaming fountain" whose waters must flow in a "perpetuall progression" (YP II, p. 543), and where the dismembered pieces of the body of truth have not all been recovered nor ever shall, until her master's second coming, and where Milton tells the Lords and Commons that we must not pitch our tents here (YP II, p. 549) for the promised land is still ahead. But I do not think that the effect is only to locate us in the midst, between alpha and omega, Egypt and Canaan, bondage and freedom; rather, Milton's "wide wilderness" swallows up the end and the beginning.

Michael does not only flip back and forth between type and antitype; meanwhile, his narrative is moving through the linear biblical plot. He does at last finish his lengthy summary of the Bible; and when he has narrated the key events of both testaments—not only through foreshadowing—when he has recounted the nativity through the resurrection when the Son shall "resume / His Seat at God's right hand" and described the conclusion of the world and the final judgment, he now seems qualified to genuinely conclude. This time when he explains that on that last eternal day "the Earth / Shall all be Paradise, far happier place / Than this of Eden, and far happier days" (XII, 463–65), he is narrating the world's great conclusion, rather than the typological fulfillment of an earlier event. Then, he pauses "As at the World's great period." Why is he *pausing* at the great period, instead of concluding? And why *as* at the world's great period, when Michael is indeed narrating the world's great period? With that *as*, Milton draws sudden attention to the fiction within his fiction: Michael has reached the end of the world only in *his* story. But Milton will not let that end conclude, and so he rather brutally recalls us to *his* story, and, leaving that satisfying vision of the final day of judgment when the righteous will be redeemed, he brings us back from the end of biblical time to its beginning, from Christ to Adam, who still has the world—and all its woes—before him. Milton thereby turns even the final eternal rest into only a pause. Milton the narrator is copying Michael's narrative technique, but doing it better (since he invented Michael's method to begin with); for Milton has framed the entire biblical typological narrative offered by Michael with his *own* typology, wherein the hearer prefigures, but is not identical to, the subject he learns about. The listening Adam is not (yet) Christ.

Michael's pause is easily mistaken for a period.[9] And if that pause at the world's conclusion is meant to be misread as grand finale, if it is designed—as I believe it is—to incite Adam's sense of an ultimate triumph, it certainly works:

So spake th'Arch-Angel Michael, then paus'd,
As at the World's great period; and our Sire
Replete with joy and wonder thus repli'd.
O goodness infinite, goodness immense!
That all this good of evil shall produce,
And evil turn to good.   (XII, 466–71)

Much that is not good is yet to come; the pause between Adam's fall and Christ's redemption will be a lengthy one.

II

Like Michael, then, the epic narrator holds out conclusions tantalizingly only to revoke them, and like Michael's, they are endings that allude to the apocalyptic end. Others have observed that the dramatic irony collapses in these last two books, that by the end Adam knows what we know. We also do *not* know what Adam does not know, sharing his propensity to reach conclusions prematurely. Soon after Adam and Eve repent, the Son mediates to secure man's future, rehearsing to the Father the remainder of sacred history to the end of time. His summary concludes:

let him live
Before thee reconcil'd, at least his days
Number'd, though sad, till Death, his doom (which I
To mitigate thus plead, not to reverse)
To better life shall yield him, where with mee
All my redeem'd may dwell in joy and bliss,
Made one with me as I with thee am one.   (XI, 38–44)

That last line is marked by one of the more emphatic devices of poetic closure, syntactic parallelism joined to antithesis[10] (made one with thee as I with thee am one), and with its vision of all separations reconciled— all in all—nothing prevents this summary conclusion from being just that: the summary. Nothing except that the Father has more to say on the subject, "But longer in this Paradise to dwell" is forbidden (XI, 48, 49). That "but now" has the effect of making the Son's apocalyptic vision disappear as abruptly as it was conjured—only to reappear again. For, having retreated from the Son's conclusion, the Father now proceeds to rush forward to precisely the same end the Son has just described. Death will become man's final remedy; after a life of "sharp tribulation," man will be resigned up to a second life "Wak't in the renovation of the just, / . . . with Heav'n and Earth renew'd." (XI, 65–66). This is not the last competition for the last word on last things. Now the Father's narrative has reached the world's "great period" — only to continue with an account of his present plan: "But let us" convene a synod. Next:

> He ended, and the Son gave signal high
> To the bright Minister that watch'd: hee blew
> His Trumpet, heard in Oreb since perhaps
> When God descended, and perhaps once more
> To sound at general Doom. (XI, 72–76)

There is much finality here. After "he ended," a trumpet is sounded — one, we are told, that was sounded only at the revelation to Moses and at the final judgment — and that sounds now in anticipation of that finality. And yet what ensues is not the final, but the *first* judgment, the decree to expel Adam and Eve from their garden; and the confidence in foretelling, "yet once more," has given way to doubt, "perhaps once more."

When the scene shifts to the garden, Adam speaks, we learn not a little ironically, "with welcome words renewed" (XI, 140); but he does not speak with the strains of iteration, but rather with that familiar tone of summary — a summary that concludes with the last words of the biblical account of the garden narrative, the renaming of Eve as the Mother of Life: "Whence hail to thee, / Eve rightly called, Mother of all Mankind, / Mother of all things living, since by thee / Man is to live, and all things live for man" (XI, 158–61). In that summary, Adam's echo of Ave Maria alludes to Eve's typological fulfillment (and I use that word advisedly). But the fulfillment is premature; Eve demurs from this title, content, like Blake's Thel, to stay in Paradise forever. "Ill worthy I such title should belong to me. . . . Here, let us live, though in fallen state, content" (XI, 163–80). Early in Book XI, by line 161 to be precise, the Son, the Father, and Adam have all reached the same apocalyptic conclusion — when all shall be all in all — but that conclusion has not been reached. And it will not be, not here, and not anywhere in *Paradise Lost*.

The narrative in the last two books is continually punctuated by concluding markers: "the angel ceased," "he ended," "he paused as at the world's great period," "Adam last replied," "the angel last replied." Each signals a plausible ending, alluding, as it does, to the final bliss at the end of time, and each sounds conclusive enough, but there are too many signals; the poem ends too many times and it describes the end too many times, so that finally — and that is precisely the wrong word here — these repetitions of an ending obtrude the very end they invoke. Our impatience for the narrative to get to the inevitable, when "one greater man restores us," becomes not unlike Adam's eagerness for death:

"why delays / His hand to execute what his Decree / Fix'd on this day?" (X, 771–73). And no wonder, since fictions of closure are linked to the death drive.

In Book XII, at least three appropriate endings are offered to us. All are visions of the end, of the apocalpytic conclusion, of the final peace, and all exact from us a premature sense of resolution. The first appears at Book XII, line 551, where Michael concludes his recitation of biblical history. This is not another instance of turning a foreshadowing event into a foretelling of the conclusion; this *is* the conclusion of Michael's precis of the entire New Testament. That breathless summary constitutes sixty-five lines; in it, Michael alludes to gospel accounts of the nativity, ministry, and passion of Christ, the development of the apostolic church, and with "their doctrine and their story written left," the corruption of the church that ensues in a world that goes on "under her own weight groaning" until the return of Christ:

> Last in the Clouds from Heav'n to be reveal'd
> In glory of the Father, to dissolve
> Satan and his perverted World, then raise
> From the conflagrant mass, purg'd and refin'd,
> New Heav'ns, new Earth, Ages of endless date
> Founded in righteousness and peace and love,
> To bring forth fruits Joy and eternal Bliss.   (XII, 545–51)

This is a perfect ending for *Paradise Lost*. It simultaneously alludes to the apocalyptic end of the world and to the end of the Bible. The fruit of "mortal taste" at the beginning of the poem gives way, at this end, to "fruits of joy and bliss." And how can anything possibly *follow* "eternal bliss"? Something does. The editorial frame, "He ended," becomes the ironic continuation: "He ended; and thus Adam last repli'd" (552). Then the angel "last replied" (574). Still, these are not the last words. Like all of those foreshadowings of the apocalypse that Adam mistook for the end of the story itself, once it is reached, that end of the story— the rehearsal of the apocalypse—is designed to lure us into a sense of premature closure for another story, *Paradise Lost*.

However, Adam's last words in *Paradise Lost* do seem to be "correct" last words; they do reflect definitive understanding, at least they are so validated by his instructor. For when he summarizes his lesson— and there are so many summaries in the final books of *Paradise Lost*— the angel congratulates him, "This having learnt, thou hast attain'd the sum / Of wisdom; hope no higher, though all the Stars / Thou knew'st by name" (575–77). But even then the angel *adds:* he adds the suggestion

that Adam "only add" something. Add to the sum of wisdom? What could
be such an addition?

> only add
> Deeds to thy knowledge answerable, add Faith,
> Add Virtue, Patience, Temperance, add Love,
> By name to come call'd Charity, the soul
> Of all the rest.   (XII, 581–85)

It turns out that Michael proposes no minor addition, not just "deeds
to thy knowledge answerable," not, that is, the enactment of the totality
of wisdom. Rather, the angel adds faith, virtue, patience, temperance,
and love; and this whole catalogue of virtues is offered as an *addition*,
a supplement, to Adam's so-called "sum of wisdom."[11] Just as the ends
refuse to end, so the summaries fail to summarize.

After Michael offers his additions to the sum of wisdom, he rehearses
the end again in a summary conclusion, and in doing so, offers another
perfectly appropriate ending for *Paradise Lost*. This one fulfills the expectation of mixing good with bad, achieves the delicate emotional poise
between regret and hope that we find in the final lines of the poem, and
even ends with the word *end:*

> Let her with thee partake what thou had heard,
> Chiefly what may concern her Faith to know,
> The great deliverance by her Seed to come
> (For by the Woman's Seed) on all Mankind,
> That ye may live, which will be many days,
> Both in one Faith unanimous though sad,
> With cause for evils past, yet much more cheer'd
> With meditation on the happy end.   (XII, 598–605)

The poem cannot end here, at the meditation on the happy end, and
it has not ended at equally plausible conclusions because Adam and Eve
have not yet been expelled. Milton torturously draws out our anticipation of that inevitable event, a delay mirrored by our lingering parents
who look back and move forward only with "wand'ring steps and slow."
This happy meditation of the happy future is broken by the expulsion
in the narrative present: "With meditation on the happy *end*. / He *ended*,
and they both *descend* the Hill; / *Descended*" (XII, 605–07; my emphasis). This is the most jolting retreat from the apocalyptic vision in the
final books: to move, in only one line, from imaginatively inhabiting that
paradisal end to the very expulsion from Paradise. The jolt is reenforced
by the incongruity of that easy rhyme, "the happy end" / "they both descend," one that is repeated in the past tense (ended, descended) just in

case we missed it the first time. Michael's biblical narrative technique —
the inversion of fulfillment (redemption) and figuration (expulsion) — is
here given its most deft use by another storyteller: the epic narrator.
Now the apocalpytic conclusion is held out to us only to be dramatically
revoked by the final action in *Paradise Lost*, rather than by a twice-
removed narration (the epic-narrator's account of Michael's narrative)
of another event recounted in another text, the Bible.

III

  Summary conclusions that continue, and so do not summarize or
conclude; moments of enlightenment that turn out to be veiled after all:
Milton has foiled all of the classic features of typology, and he has used
typology to do it.[12] The shadowy types allude to a truth he withdraws,
and the prefigurations to a fulfillment he obviates. But Milton not only
exploits the logic of provisionality characteristic of typology, he also manipulates its characteristic reference to another authority. To speak of
types at all is to encode particulars with the blueprint of another master-
narrative: the Bible. Milton embeds that master-narrative, first, within
Michael's version of the biblical story wherein paradise is lost and found
and lost and found, and then he embeds both within the epic-narrator's
story, *Paradise Lost*. The effect of his moving at will among the three
narratives is to subvert the plot of the master-narrative. In other words,
despite our efforts to drive *Paradise Lost* and the Bible together — an effort Milton himself invites — Milton has effected an immense structural
change in the biblical plot: he concludes, not with Revelation, but with
Genesis, with the expulsion. *Milton's poem ends where the Bible begins.*
That simple fact means that the function of those insistent allusions to
Revelation in the last books is to underscore that the apocalyptic paradise of bliss is denied rather than granted. Then again, Milton does not
quite conclude his narrative with the expulsion; more accurately, he
breaks off there, leaving that oft-invoked remainder of the biblical plot
hovering and thereby preventing even *his* conclusion from allowing *Paradise Lost* to conclude.

  The type for the hill of prospect where Adam surveys human history is not Sinai, despite the revelations there; nor is it the hill of the
Sermon on the Mount, even with all of the instruction; despite the extensive use of typology and allusions to redemption, it is not the Mount of
the Transfiguration where Jesus stood conversing with Moses and Elijah
and was then assumed. Milton tells us that this highest hill of paradise
was "Not higher that Hill nor wider looking round / Whereon for different cause the Tempter set / Our second Adam in the Wilderness, /

To show him all Earth's Kingdoms and thir Glory" (XI, 381–84). The
analogy is not to a place of definitive revelation, but to a place of temptation, and the temptation that Adam faces in the final books is to view
the prospect of what lay before him and want to possess it, as the Second
Adam is offered the kingdoms of the world. But Adam's tempter, Michael, does not offer him all the kingdoms; what he offers is all of biblical history. The temptation is for Adam to *possess* that entire story, to
"know" his future, rather than to determine it; it is in this sense that
despairing over the errors of his progeny and rejoicing over the righteous
remnant are equally misguided. The temptation is to believe that the
sum of wisdom can be gained from reading — or seeing and hearing —
the story Michael unfolds, and that wisdom can be thus summarized.
It is, in Stanley Fish's phrase, the "temptation of plot." The biblical plot,
with its exile from Paradise, the miseries of history punctuated by the
just men, and the return to paradise, does not tell the whole story because the moral life is internal:

> add Faith,
> Add Virtue, Patience, Temperance, add Love,
> By name to come call'd Charity, the soul
> Of all the rest: then wilt thou not be loath
> To leave this Paradise, but shalt possess
> A paradise within thee, happier far.   (XII, 581–87)

After Milton has written a story about the exile from Paradise — rather
even as he writes that narrative — he tells us that paradise need never
be left after all.

Jason Rosenblatt has shown that this "Hill of Speculation" also alludes to Pisgah, the hill where Moses stood looking into the Promised
Land before his death, and where he was told he could see that land
from his prospect, but could not enter into it.[13] The allusion is structurally important. Milton begins *Paradise Lost* by invoking the Muse who
inspired Moses to write the Bible; and he concludes his own bible with
the conclusion of the Pentateuch in mind, for the vision on Pisgah is in
the last chapter of the last book of the five books of Moses. That is, Milton alludes, in his ending, to the end of a work that does not end — the
last chapter of the Pentateuch is not the end of the Bible; rather, it goes
on to the Writings, the Prophets, and the New Testament.

The Pisgah scene also tells us something about the inaccessibility of
that other end, the promised redemption. And God said to Moses, "I have
let you see it with your own eyes but you shall not cross into it" (Deut.
xxxiv, 4). "Each place behold in prospect," Michael says to Adam, "as
I point them":

there by promise he receives
Gift to his Progeny of all that Land;
From Hamath Northward to the Desert South
(Things by thir names I call, though yet unnam'd)
From Hermon East to the great Western Sea,
Mount Hermon, yonder Sea, each place behold
In prospect, as I point them; on the shore
Mount Carmel; here the double-founted stream
Jordan, true limit Eastward.   (XII, 137–45)

The map is painstakingly drawn; the vision of the promised land could not be clearer. Adam looks, as Moses does from Pisgah, but unlike Moses, Adam does not see: ten lines earlier, Michael mentioned to Adam that while his instructor can see this vision of the promised land, the student cannot. Adam is asked not only to view a promised land he is denied access to, but to view one he cannot see; and he may even be asked to view one that is not there, for the dominant symbol of that land is the Jordan, a two-founted river in Milton's version; that is, one fed by two mythological, nonexistent streams: the Jor and the Dan.[14] If the Jordan has no tributaries, the Promised Land may not exist at its very source. Adam cannot get there, Adam cannot see there, because there is no "there" there. The disappearing act of conclusions is like this vision of the land of promise, of the promised end: like Adam, now we see it, now we don't. All of this brings me directly to a question that lurks behind this entire discussion: whether Milton imagines an end that is not accessible and cannot be articulated, or whether he refuses to imagine such an end. There is a wide gap in the history of philosophy and religion between an unattainable ideal and the absence of one at all. Representatives of these two poles are as far apart as Heidegger, for whom the ideal cannot be articulated, and Derrida, for whom the only ideal is within articulation; hence, there is no ideal per se.[15] But they may not be so very far apart; the difference between not seeing something and nothing being there to see may not be so great — especially to a blind man who depicts endless endings.

Milton could find ample precedent in the New Testament, not only for a totalizing typology — "Do not imagine that I have come to abolish the law and the prophets, I have come not to abolish but to complete them" (Matt. v, 17) — but also for deferral: "Now faith is the substance of things hoped for, the evidence of things not seen" (Heb. xi, 1). Here, belief becomes a testimony to absence. And Milton would go further, avoiding even the definition suggested by "substance." In *On Christian Doctrine*, he glosses this verse with "persuasion": "Faith is the [persuasion] of things hoped for, the demonstration of things that are not seen."[16]

In another formulation, in which even typology is expanded to include—
rather than preclude—this sense of deferral, Rudolf Bultmann writes that
"Faith is possible only by overcoming the old existence under the law"
(from shadowy types to truth, from strict laws to large grace), but he
goes on to say: "this existence under grace is never arrived at once and
for all, but is valid only as it is ever grasped anew."[17] Unlike so many
critics of the last two books of *Paradise Lost*, he does not deem it necessary to choose between linear and cyclical models of history.[18]

The book of Romans offers one of the texts most explicitly concerned
with conclusion—rather, with *the* conclusion. It depicts all of creation
groaning in labor, filled with the expectation of a delivery; but even in
this most eschatological of texts, amid the very anticipation of delivery,
the text becomes reflective about anticipation itself:

From the beginning till now the entire creation, as we know, has been groaning
in one great act of giving birth; and not only creation but all of us who possess the
first-fruits of the Spirit, we too groan inwardly as we wait for our bodies to be set
free. For we must be content to hope that we shall be saved—our salvation is not
in sight, we should not have to be hoping for it if it were—but, as I say, we must
hope to be saved since we are not saved yet—it is something we must wait for with
patience. (Rom. viii, 22–25)

Again, the ground of hope is that we are *not* saved (Rom. viii, 20–21);
faith is inspired by our not being delivered. But how does an eternal ges-
tation, a perpetual deferral of deliverance, differ from a miscarriage
where deliverance is also deferred, forever. Donne equates them. "Our
entrance into this life, from the womb, is an entrance from death," he
asserts in "Death's Duel":

neither is there any grave so close, or so putrid a prison, as the wombe would be
unto us, if we stayed in it beyond our time, or dyed there before our time. . . . The
wombe which should be the house of life, becomes death itselfe, if God leave us
there. In the wombe the dead child kills the mother that conceived it, and is a mur-
therer, nay a parricide, even after it is dead.[19]

Death in childbirth, the displacing of the Old Law, the expectation
of deliverance, and blindness and celestial sight come together in another
of Milton's works, the sonnet on his "late espoused saint." Again, the
apocalyptic conclusion is envisioned: the figure returns from the grave,
veiled, not only like Alcestis, but like the Old Testament when the Jews
read it, and she is purified only in the Old Law, awaiting the final puri-
fication of redemption. The speaker imagines the further and final pu-
rification of the new order of grace, imagines the figure unveiled, and
implicitly imagines the figures of the Old Law unveiled. But the figure

recedes: "I waked, she fled, and day brought back my night." Like the apocalyptic visions in the last books of *Paradise Lost*, now he sees it, and now he does not. Here, at the very center of a sonnet that dramatizes "not yet," is the familiar phrase, "yet once more" (7), suggesting the iterative nature of deferred endings. If the veiled figure appears and disappears to the mind's eye, the unveiled one never even assumes shape, like the mythically founted Jordan: "I trust to have / Full sight of her in Heaven without restraint." Sonnet XXIII depicts shadowy types to shadowy types, yet once more.

In all of these texts — Paul's letter to the Romans, Donne's final sermon, and Milton's sonnet — a perpetually postponed delivery signals death. One obvious inference we can draw from this deferral of delivery to the New Jerusalem is that it is symptomatic of Milton's disappointment that England had not ushered in the millennium. Yes, of course. Still, these visions are not offered *to* Milton and then taken away, they are offered *by* him. Hence, losing and finding and losing these visions again does not mean only that they are inaccessible. In Freud's *fort-da* game, the object hidden and retrieved is at hand. If Milton's Paradise is only "fix't as firm as Delos floating once" — hence, not so very fixed at all — it is *Milton* who fixes and unfixes his floating paradise at will. Milton effects a fundamental change in his Pisgah type-scene: Moses is *told* that he cannot enter paradise, but Milton *tells* — yet once more — that the earth will be all Paradise, "but longer in this paradise to dwell / Permits not."

Duke University

NOTES

A version of this paper was read at the 1986 MLA meeting in New York, "Milton, a General Session," chaired by William Kerrigan.

1. *John Milton: Complete Poems and Major Prose*, ed. Merritt Y. Hughes (New York, 1957). All references to Milton's poetry will be to this edition.

2. Milton's understanding and use of typology is, of course, neither uniform nor rigid; rather, it bends to suit his creative purposes. Even in his orthodox sounding statement in *The Reason of Church Government*, where the "hearts of the Jews are weaned from the old law," Milton would not have the shadow, here, the Temple of Ezekiel, be "fulfilled" in the church "unless we mean to annihilate the gospel." *Complete Prose Works of John Milton*, 8 vols., ed. Don M. Wolfe et al. (New Haven, 1953–82), vol. I, p. 757. (All references to Milton's prose will be to this edition, hereafter cited as YP in the text.)

Milton was not isolated in his uneasiness with the notion that the New Testament alone is *veritas* and *lux* and the Old Testament a mere *umbra* that has passed away: much of reformation theology depends upon the reappropriation, rather than discarding, of the Old Testament. See James S. Preus, *From Shadow to Promise: Old Testament Interpretation from Augustine to the Young Luther* (Cambridge, 1969).

3. On the subject of unending endings, I am generally indebted to Stephen Booth, *King Lear, MacBeth, Indefinition, and Tragedy* (New Haven, 1983), part I; Jonathan Goldberg, *Endlesse Worke: Spenser and the Structures of Discourse* (Baltimore, 1981); and D. A. Miller, *Narrative and its Discontents: Problems of Closure in the Traditional Novel* (Princeton, 1981).

4. On the theoretical implications of this phrase, see Schwartz, "Joseph's Bones and the Resurrection of the Text," *PMLA* CIII, 2 (March 1988), 114–24. Patristic variations on shadows and truth, figure and fulfillment are discussed in Erich Auerbach's classic essay, "Figura," in *Scenes from the Drama of European Literature* (New York, 1959), pp. 11–76, and in A. C. Charity, *Events and Their Afterlife: The Dialectics of Christian Typology in the Bible and Dante* (Cambridge, 1966). See also Barbara K. Lewalski, *Protestant Poetics and the Seventeenth-Century Religious Lyric* (Princeton, 1979), pp. 111–44; and William Madsen, *From Shadowy Types to Truth: Studies in Milton's Symbolism* (New Haven, 1968).

5. Melito of Sardis, "Homily on the Passion," ed. Campbell Bonner in *Studies and Documents*, ed. Kirsopp Lake and Silva Lake) London, 1940), vol. XII, p. 107. Chrysostom, Hom. 10:2 in Phil. Irenaeus, *Demonstration of the Apostolic Preaching* (London, 1920).

6. Lancelot Andrewes, *Sermons on the Nativity* (Grand Rapids, Mich., 1955), p. 237.

7. Andrewes, *Sermons on the Nativity*, p. 48.

8. Stanley Fish, "Things and Actions Indifferent: The Temptation of Plot in *Paradise Regained*," in *Milton Studies*, vol. XVII, ed. Albert C. Labriola and Michael Lieb (Pittsburgh, 1983), p. 163.

9. To speak of mistaken readings is to be indebted to Stanley Fish's *Surprised by Sin* (New York, 1967), but he depicts a reader progressively enlightened (his reader is superior to Adam in the final books) and even Adam's "O goodness infinite, goodness immense" expresses, for Fish, that Truth can be glimpsed: "The moment of supreme recognition, available to every Christian who ascends through meditation to a glimpse of the Truth, occurs for Adam when the full meaning of the prophecy of the seed is revealed to him in the image of the incarnation and the crucifixion." (p. 324). While Fish describes an education from error toward truth, I am arguing that the only error is to grasp any truth.

10. Barbara Herrnstein Smith, *Poetic Closure* (Chicago, 1968), pp. 166–71. His more recent work on *Areopagitica*, which unfortunately was not available until after I had written this essay, is more Derridean.

11. My reading here differs from many critics who see these premature resolutions and partial enlightenments in the last two books as stages in a steady progress of Adam's successful education. Georgia Christopher, *Milton and the Science of the Saints* (Princeton, 1982) p. 180, writes that "The poet's task in these last books is to demonstrate that real learning has taken place." Barbara K. Lewalski, "Structure and the Symbolism of Vision in Michael's Prophecy, *Paradise Lost*, Books XI–XII," *PQ* XLII, (1963), 25–35, writes that the prophecy at the end is designed to promote Adam's development; through it, "Adam is led to understand his sins and grow in virtue," until Adam does attain the sum of wisdom.

12. Joseph A. Wittreich, *Interpreting Samson Agonistes* (Princeton, 1986), pp. 174–238, makes precisely this point about Milton's use of typology in *Samson Agonistes*. "Typology could be used to expose typologies, enabling us to see through them; it could be

made to reveal what earlier it had concealed—the ambiguity and complexity of the Samson narrative in the Book of Judges" (p. 178).

13. Jason P. Rosenblatt, in "Adam's Pisgah Vision," *ELH* XXXIX (1972), 66–86, has traced the source for Milton's last two books to Mt. Pisgah through Pope's *Dunciad*. The "Argument" to the third book describes Settle taking Theobald "to a *Mount of Vision*, from whence he shews him the past triumphs of the empire of Dulness, then the present, and lastly the future . . . 'the present Action of the Dunciad is but a Type or Foretaste, giving a Glimpse or *Pisgah-sight* of the promis'd Fulness of her Glory.'" He has also helpfully documented the seventeenth-century commentary on the Pisgah episode, much of which equates the hill itself with the old law, which offers only a glimpse of the gospel; while Moses' limitation demonstrates that the Mosaic law cannot grant access to the gospel. Rosenblatt's remarks on closure are opposite my own.

14. Hughes notes that "the notion that the Jordan was formed by the confluence of two non-existent streams, the Jor and the Dan, seems ultimately to have stemmed from St. Jerome's commentary on Genesis xiv, 14." *John Milton, Complete Poems and Major Prose*, p. 457 n. 144–45. Carey and Fowler, *The Complete Poems of John Milton*, ed. John Carey and Alastair Fowler (London, 1968), p. 1034 n. 121–34, also trace the belief to George Sandys's *Relation* (1615), probably Milton's source. Allen Gilbert's entry in the *Geographical Dictionary*, p. 163, demonstrates that Milton would know that these were nonexistent, mythological source streams.

15. I am aware that this is only a hint, but a detailed excursus on the relation between Derrida and Heidegger is beyond the scope of this essay; my primary effort here is to situate Milton's sense of conclusion in the context of the Bible, Milton's own debt.

16. YP VI, p. 472. See Georgia Christopher, *Milton and the Science of the Saints* (Princeton, 1982), pp. 15, 16.

17. Rudolf Bultmann, "The Significance of the Old Testament for the Christian Faith," in *The Old Testament and Christian Faith*, ed. Bernhard W. Anderson (New York, 1963), pp. 15, 22.

18. Thomas Amorose, "Milton the Apocalyptic Historian: Competing Genres in *Paradise Lost*, Books XI–XII," in *Milton Studies*, vol. XVII, ed. Richard S. Ide and Joseph Wittreich (Pittsburgh, 1983), pp. 141–62. Amorose begins his own argument by contrasting the Greco-Roman conception of history as cyclical with the Judeo-Christian "linear model." These models tend to be emotionally charged in Milton criticism: Milton is either very disillusioned, having abandoned his earlier millenarian hopes to opt for a sense of history marked by the "endless recurrence of moral judgment," or he is most hopeful, with the final books showing a steady (linear) "annihilation of patterns of behavior that obstruct his freeing mankind from fallen history." Various combinations of linear and cyclic visions govern the majority of criticism of the final books of *Paradise Lost*.

19. John Donne, *Sermons*, 10 vols., ed G. F. Potter and Evelyn Simpson (Berkeley and Los Angeles, 1953–62), vol. X, "Sermon No. 11," pp. 231–32.

MILTON'S USE OF SONNET FORM
IN *PARADISE LOST*

Peggy Samuels

T HE SONNET tradition has had a complex relation to public, or
political, life. Donne's desire to "build in sonnets pretty rooms" is,
by self-admission, an alternative to taking his place in "chronicle," in
history. Sidney writes his sonnets when he is rusticated, and thematizes
the court in those sonnets only to reject it. Forcefully, perhaps with too
much force to convince, he replaces ambition for worldly gain with an
ambition to win Stella. Thus, one could see the sonnet in an antagonistic
relation to the political realm, as an attempt to escape, to counter, to
trivialize, to contain the political. On the other hand, sonnet composition also had its own political role. Renaissance sonnets were public and
pragmatic: they were spoken in order to gain for the author a reputation
as a wit or to gain favor from patrons or love from a lady.[1] Milton's sonnets foreground this political aspect of the sonnet tradition not only because their content was often political, but also because he wrote at least
some of them with a serious pragmatic purpose—to influence Fairfax,
Cromwell, Vane, the unidentified lady of *Sonnet IX*, and Cyriak. One
could see Milton, as Stuart Curran does, as the progenitor of the explicitly political sonnet in English, the vanguard of a tradition which, after
a long hiatus, continues with Coleridge's *Sonnets on Eminent Characters* and Wordsworth's *Sonnets Dedicated to Liberty.*[2] Anna K. Nardo
argues that Milton's sonnets are unified by their concern for the public
realm, praising, desiring, defining an ideal community, and Mary Ann
Radzinowicz calls the sonnets an illustration of "the stages of enlightenment through which individuals or societies must pass on their way
toward the achievement of political maturity."[3] But what about the embedded sonnets in *Paradise Lost?* These sonnets seem to echo the old
themes of the sonnet tradition—themes of love, subjectivity, subjection,
sacrifice, injustice, obedience, joy, the struggle between sweetness and
discipline. What function do these embedded sonnets have in *Paradise
Lost*, and how do they locate themselves in this question of the sonnet's
relation to the political realm?

The simplest way of looking at the function of the embedded sonnet is as a variation of the verse paragraph. While Milton's immediate precursor, Spenser, used stanzas to build his epic poem, Milton uses the verse paragraph, and the most intensified, controlled verse paragraph that he uses is the sonnet. Both Spenser and Milton needed some means of controlling a form that, even with the help of epic conventions, could be potentially disorganized, especially at the level of the individual line. In drama Shakespeare and other Renaissance writers had already used the sonnet to control prolixity of discourse. Milton, working with a long poem, especially one in which many of the lines are direct speech, was able to use the same means of control. Yet Milton deviated significantly from Spenser's practice. Spenser's stanzas, demarcated rather than embedded, compel the reader to take a look backward over the ground that has been covered in the stanza. One must treat the Spenserian stanza in accord with its etymology, as a standing place, a place where one can rest. Even more than the stanza, sonnets contain a generic expectation to fix and frame and thus to rest, but Milton disturbs this generic expectation. In his freestanding sonnets he makes stylistic innovations that break up the form. As has long been recognized, by F. T. Prince and William Stull for example, Milton, building on the Italian heroic sonnet tradition, roughens the form: he enjambs lines, overshoots the volta, frees the caesura, overturns normal syntax, and plays off syntax against rhyme.[4] More recently, James Mengert has described the "resistant" final lines of Milton's sonnets, which tend to qualify or disturb the sonnet's "finish," to unsettle its closure and its definitiveness of statement.[5] To these techniques, Milton adds a new strategy in *Paradise Lost*. He disturbs the sonnets' closure even more radically — after the close of an embedded sonnet, the poem continues: each stopping place proves to be only a false pause which must be fit into a larger perspective. Thus, in whatever ways Milton transgresses or corrects sonnet form in *Paradise Lost* (ways I will be discussing shortly), his major alteration of the form is not accomplished *within* the embedded form but *by embedding it*.

The theoretical consequences of embedding a short form are crucial here. Any short lyric, by the nature of its limited scope, increases the semantic pressure on the limited words available. That is, the short lyric moves more quickly to moments of totalization. (Again, one can think of Donne's attempt to pronounce love, or the sonnet, the totality.) Or, looked at another way, the sonnet has a tendency to make a definitive statement; it leans toward or ingests the epigram.[6] However, if the sonnet is set within a sequence, the attempt at totalization or definitive statement and the closure of the individual sonnet are immediately placed in question. One need only think of Shakespeare's sonnet sequence to feel how the mere act of beginning another sonnet retrospectively pronounces the previous sonnets on the same subject incomplete. Thus, whether one thinks of the sonnets in *Paradise Lost* as a sequence or merely as individual embedded sonnets, Milton has put in question the closure of any one of these sonnets by embedding it in another form.

To consider the political implications of embedding the sonnet, one must recall, for a moment, that political problems are, in some sense, problems of form. Milton, and many of his contemporaries, placed politics within a religious frame (social relations had to be interrogated within a religious context); thus social and political criticism was accomplished by means of formal innovation, reframing. Milton draws on the power of the sonnet, that discourse of subjectivity, but by embedding it he politicizes the personal; he places it in a larger perspective and thus renders it incompletely understood when taken solely on its own terms. The sonnet which comprises the final lines of *Samson Agonistes* presents a paradigmatic case here: what will be this sonnet's frame? We must interpret the chorus' closing statement, the chorus' private resolution, by taking note of the larger structure in which it is embedded.[7]

To begin to see this process in action, I will look at Eve's first sonnet, which, more than any of the other embedded sonnets, calls attention to its own form, taking its own form — to a greater degree than most sonnets do — as its subject.[8]

> Sweet is the breath of morn, her rising sweet,
> With charm of earliest Birds; pleasant the Sun
> When first on this delightful Land he spreads
> His orient Beams, on herb, tree, fruit, and flowr,
> Glistring with dew; fragrant the fertil earth
> After soft showers; and sweet the coming on
> Of grateful Eevning mild, then silent Night
> With this her solemn Bird and this fair Moon,
> And these the Gemms of Heav'n, her starrie train:
> But neither breath of Morn when she ascends
> With charm of earliest Birds, nor rising Sun
> On this delightful land, nor herb, fruit, flowr,
> Glistring with dew, nor fragrance after showers,
> Nor grateful Eevning mild, nor silent Night
> With this her solemn Bird, nor walk by Moon,
> Or glittering Starr-light without thee is sweet.   (IV, 641–56)[9]

Clearly, this sonnet takes to an extreme the stylistic marks of sonneteering: balance, parallel phrasing, repetition, the "turn" of thought, and compression. (The repetition and compression are intensified by the sonnet picking up many of its images from the five previous embedded sonnets: sweetness, morning, birds, sun, moon, stars all appear in those other sonnets.) The closure of the sonnet, its sense of self-containment, derives from the first word and the last coinciding, as the whole has been contained within an immense epanalepsis. Eve's feat in compressing all of Eden into a mere sixteen lines is only surpassed by her ability to describe Eden twice in those sixteen lines. The exact repetition of every item from octave to sestet (here nine and seven lines rather than eight and six) performs what one might call "compression squared." Not only has Milton accomplished the usual sleight-of-hand by creating a compressed sonnet, but he has performed the feat again in front of our eyes by compressing what took place on top into the smaller space of the bottom.[10] Yet, in performing this extreme compression, Milton suggests a morality of compression when he has Eve leave out of the repetition the tree, the only item that Eve will consider sweet without Adam ("herb, tree, fruit, flowr" becomes "nor herb, fruit, flowr"). My sense that Milton is making some kind of moral distinction here is supported in the two lines that follow Eve's sonnet. She asks: "But wherfore all night long shine these [the stars], for whom / This glorious sight, when sleep hath shut all eyes?" Eve's question is an objection to wasted motion. Her sense of perfection will not allow this waste. Yet, as Adam makes clear in his response when he tells Eve the use of these lights, Eve's sense of perfect compression is essentially an attitude of selfishness. It does not consider what is outside of herself, and, I believe, it passes judgment on the preceding sonnet, pronouncing it too self-contained, too exclusionary, as sonnets traditionally had been.

Perhaps the stakes in this debate are greater than they at first appear. As Sir Thomas Browne writes in *Religio Medici:*"God is like a skilfull Geometrician, who when more easily and with one stroake of his Compasse, he might describe, or divide a right line, had yet rather doe this, though in a circle or longer way, according to the constituted and forelaid principles of his art."[11] Compression is an integral element in design, and when we encounter Eve's questioning of God's design, a question which impugns his knowledge of compression, which sees his acts as too diffuse, as not going immediately enough to the goal, we find ourselves back inside the problem of evil. In any case, Eve's error in believing that the lights are meant for her proves again to be her error in Book IX when she is confronted by the serpent.

As it was Eve's exclusion of an item in the compressed form which seemed prophetic of her sin, it makes sense to compare another speech of Eve's on the same subject, to determine what else was left out of the compressed form.

Forsake me not thus, Adam, witness Heav'n
What love sincere, and reverence in my heart
I bear thee, and unweeting have offended,
Unhappilie deceav'd; thy suppliant
I beg, and clasp thy knees; bereave me not,
Whereon I live, thy gentle looks, thy aid,
Thy counsel in this uttermost distress,
My onely strength and stay: forlorn of thee,
Whither shall I betake me, where subsist?
While yet we live, scarse one short hour perhaps,
Between us two let there be peace, both joyning,
As joyn'd in injuries, one enmitie
Against a Foe by doom express assign'd us,
That cruel Serpent: On me exercise not
Thy hatred for this miserie befall'n,
On me already lost, mee then thy self
More miserable; both have sin'd, but thou
Against God onely, I against God and thee,
And to the place of judgment will return,
There with my cries importune Heav'n, that all
The sentence from thy head remov'd may light
On me, sole cause to thee of all this woe,
Mee mee onely just object of his ire.

    (X, 914–36)

Aside from demonstrating the many sorrowful complexities that have entered into Eve's consciousness since the Fall, the passage (particularly the lines which claim all things distressful without Adam's presence) demonstrates what Eve had excluded from the parallel moment in her previous sonnet: God, desire for Adam's counsel, and concern for Adam's welfare.

All of this is not to say that Milton was somehow *against* sonnets, or against compression, but it is to say that Milton problematizes, takes as his subject, what is implied in the sonnet form and in its thematic tradition. It is standard practice to see that in the course of its history the sonnet has borne along with it a dialectic between restraint and liberty — a crucial subject for Milton. In *Eikonoklastes* he writes: "the People, exorbitant and excessive in all thir motions, are prone ofttimes not to a religious onely, but to a civil kinde of Idolatry in idolizing thir Kings."[12] For Milton, excess enthralls not only in *Eikonoklastes* where he was attempting to make "judgment uninthrall'd," but, as Christopher Hill has documented, increasingly throughout his career Milton blamed the revolutionaries' lack of self-restraint for the failure of the revolution.[13] However, as the divorce tracts and *The Tenure of Kings and Magistrates* reveal, a blind adherence to a falsely conceived restraint errs equally with license. Perhaps Milton suggests through Eve's rigorously "ruled" sonnet that restraint itself can be too sweet. Some of the ways in which Milton attacks the false restraint of the sonnet form have been well discussed: his playing off syntax against rhyme, his enjambment of lines, his flexible use of the volta, his use of both the Italian and English forms. In the embedded sonnets, however, Milton invents new methods of breaking sonnet form. These new methods use the technique described above; that is, they interrogate the closure or perfection of the sonnet by drawing attention to what it excludes.

Satan's first sonnet is interrogated or implicitly criticized both by the surrounding verse and by the two other sonnets which are parallel to it in subject.

> Is this the Region, this the Soil, the Clime,
> Said then the lost Arch-Angel, this the seat
> That we must change for Heav'n, this mournful gloom
> For that celestial light? Be it so, since he
> Who now is Sovran can dispose and bid
> What shall be right: fardest from him is best
> Whom reason hath equald, force hath made supream
> Above his equals. Farewel happy Fields
> Where Joy for ever dwells: Hail horrours, hail
> Infernal world, and thou profoundest Hell
> Receive thy new Possessor: One who brings
> A mind not to be chang'd by Place or Time.
> The mind is its own place, and in it self
> Can make a Heav'n of Hell, a Hell of Heav'n.   (I, 242–55)

The closure of this sonnet is attacked eight lines later when Satan claims: "Better to reign in Hell, then serve in Heav'n." Any reader can see that Satan contradicts himself, or at least finds his own reasoning insufficiently compelling, by pronouncing hell a heaven and then claiming it is better to reign in hell, but only a reader who pays attention to genre can feel the full force of a conclusion not sufficiently concluded. Only by noticing that Satan has spoken a sonnet can one notice that the pleasing, pseudoconvincing form of the sonnet is false and thus gain an added perspective on Satan's false logic.

As we have seen, the blank verse which surrounds the sonnet comments on and undermines that sonnet. Milton also uses another strategy to transform the traditional sonnet, a strategy which intensifies his often-remarked methods of creating parallels, mirrorings, and inversions. The satanic sonnet, Satan's response to being vanquished by God, is mirrored in the Son's sonnet, *his* response to being vanquished. The inversion is accomplished elegantly by means of the volta: "on me let Death wreck all his rage; / Under his gloomie power I shall not long / Lie vanquisht; *thou* hast givn me to possess / Life in my self for ever, by thee I live" (III, 241–44; italics mine). The descent into death, the self vanquished, is only relieved by a volta, a turn, to God, to "thou." In contrast, Satan's volta simply remarks a willed rupture: "Farewel happy Fields / Where Joy for ever dwells: Hail horrours, hail / Infernal world, and thou profoundest Hell / Receive thy new Possessor" (I, 249–52). The rhythm, of course, exaggerates this self-willed quality, this fiat, of Satan's speech. Again, one can remark the parallels without noticing the sonnet, but the sonnet form is a precise and elegant intensification of Milton's strategy.

The sonnet traditionally imitated the process of the mind moving through an argument with itself. The sonnet is therefore the perfect tool for that Milton of whom Radzinowicz writes: "The physician-artist with the palpable design to change the reader's mind must discover a form that imitates and encourages thinking itself, its processes and its progression."[14] The sonnet can reveal the mind arguing with itself and the path of logic in the sonnet can reveal where the speaker's mind goes awry, takes a wrong turn, makes the wrong choice. I use the word "turn" deliberately, for as we have just seen the volta can represent a wrong turn or wrong choice. The sonnet's form mimics or formalizes the mind's process. To the extent that politics for Milton means individuals making choices, the sonnet becomes one of his tools for dramatizing those choices.

In a gesture similar to what occurs at the volta, the Son's sonnet breaches its own closure to assert that Christ will rise from the grave. The last lines of the sonnet speak of being death's due, of lying in the loathsome grave, of dwelling with corruption, but the lines immediately following the sonnet proclaim: "But I shall rise Victorious, and subdue / My Vanquisher" (III, 250–51). (One could see the fourteen lines following the sonnet as a second sonnet with its volta (III, 260) marking the rise of the redeemed, the end of history, the ultimate consequence of Christ's own rising.) This movement-beyond-bounds of the Son's sonnet is paralleled in the narrator's only sonnet, in the proem to Book III. Milton ends his sonnet by completing the description of his own blindness, "And wisdom at one entrance quite shut out" (III, 50). The lines that follow Milton's sonnet, like the lines which follow the Son's, breach the closure of the sonnet, as Milton prays for the defeat to transform itself into triumph, for physical blindness to be transfigured into an inner, less earthly, sight.

Milton's linking the Son to his own triumph is revealed not simply by his praying for a kind of grace, and not only by the formal parallel between the two sonnets just mentioned, but also by another formal parallel between the proem and a later sonnet. Donald Davie has written most perceptively about the tension and surprise in Milton's line breaks and diction in this proem.[15] Davie particularly remarked on: "Thus with the Year / Seasons return, but not to me returns / Day (III, 40–42), where one expects spring and receives instead, after the delay of the line break, "day." The parallel moment comes in Adam's last sonnet, spoken to the Archangel Michael:

> O sent from Heav'n,
> Enlightner of my darkness, gracious things
> Thou hast reveald, those chiefly which concern
> Just *Abraham* and his Seed: now first I find
> Mine eyes true op'ning, and my heart much eas'd,
> Erwhile perplext with thoughts what would becom
> Of mee and all Mankind; but now I see
> His day, in whom all Nations shall be blest.   (XII, 270–77)

The terms which Adam uses, "Enlightener of my darkness," "Mine eyes true op'ning," "my heart much eas'd," wondering "what would becom of mee," all seem poignantly recalled from Milton's proem. The same surprising tension is built into the line break placed at "but now I see" with the same word coming unexpectedly, "His *day*." There can be little doubt that Milton used this symmetry to suggest a rich parallel between his day and His day.

As these parallels confirm, Milton creates, as Lee Johnson has pointed out, an extensive system of parallels among the sonnets in *Paradise Lost*.[16] Johnson mentions as one example the trilogy of Christ's offer of sacrifice (III, 236–37), Eve's apology to Adam in which she also offers to sacrifice herself (X, 914–36), and Satan's failure to do so in his sonnet rejecting repentance (IV, 78–92). The use of the parallel sonnets is not, as Johnson claims, primarily to Christianize the epic by using a nonclassical form at key moments. The series of sonnets comes much closer to Radzinowicz's description of the sequence of freestanding sonnets: "Milton's political meaning appears in the sonnets as a representation of a sequential or historical process; the sequence illustrates the stages of enlightenment through which individuals or societies must pass on their way toward the achievement of political maturity."[17] By "political" Radzinowicz means, of course, political in the wide sense in which Milton viewed the public realm — as intimately connected to the state of the individual soul. In examining the thematic motifs that link the sonnets, one can observe the kind of sequence of alternatives Radzinowicz mentions. Space does not permit me to explore these fully, but let me demonstrate with one example.

The series of sonnets reveals a consistent thread exploring various conceptions of "place." In the first sonnet, Satan attempts to define his new place—both in the sense of viewing his new physical location and in the sense of revising his understanding of his own position vis-à-vis God (I, 242–55). Increasingly through the sonnets' reference to "place," one comes to understand that "place" will depend on relation to God. In the following sonnets "place" is a predominant theme: Uriel ends his triple sonnet—a long description of place—with a reference to Adam's abode, his place, and to Satan's and his own (Uriel's) way (III, 694–735); Satan asks "is there no place / Left for Repentance" (IV, 79); Raphael elliptically describes Adam's place in the great chain of being (V, 491–505); God, speaking to his Son, ends his sonnet saying, "lest unawares we lose / This our high place, our Sanctuarie, our Hill" (V, 731–32); the rebellious angels lose their place in Raphael's sonnet narrating the Son's moment of triumph (VI, 859–66); Raphael tells Adam "thine and of all thy Sons / The weal or woe in thee is plac't" (VIII, 637–38); Sin leaves her place in hell (X, 365); Eve offers to return to the "place of judgment" (X, 932); Michael tells Adam to leave his place in Paradise (XI, 259–62); Adam fears that the men of Babel have overreached their proper place (XII, 64–77); Adam asks why God deigns "to dwell on Earth" with sinners (XII, 280–84); Michael tells Adam he shall "possess / A Paradise within thee, happier farr" (XII, 586–87); and finally Eve tells Adam "thou to mee / Art all things under Heav'n, all places thou" (XII, 618). This insistence on "place" is Milton's revision of the Renaissance sense of the term "place" as position in a social hierarchy. Anna K. Nardo has written about Milton's attempt to replace wordly hierarchy with a more ideal, godly community. As Nardo says, the process is an intensely personal one; in order to establish his own sense of place, Milton, "to convey the meaning of his blindness . . . had to dramatize a progress from egocentricity to dependence on God."[18] Perhaps Milton's insistence that place be defined more carefully—as dependent on virtue, on love of God and man, on obedience—is a reworking of the strain of ambition running through the Elizabethan sonnet. Arthur F. Marotti has made much of the homologic relation between ambition and love in the sonnet. He tends to read this confluence as a sign that talk of love should be translated as really talk of ambition.[19] Milton picks up both of these threads—ambition and love—in one hand and twists them together. The proper ambition is the ambition to love God and to deserve God's love.

The parallels, mirrorings, inversions of theme and form in these sonnets provide enough support, I believe, to make a case for the sonnets comprising a sequence. The problem in making the case is the proverbial one in any attempt to define genre or sequence: one creates a definition of the sequence by looking at the members in it, but in order to do so one must already have some idea of which sonnets, or verse paragraphs, belong in the sequence, and which must be excluded — choices which seem to imply an already existent definition of the sequence. It is not my purpose in this paper to make a case for the sonnets comprising a sequence, but I would like to suggest the effect on interpretation that the existence of such a sequence might have.

If the sonnets are, as I have said, an intensification of the Miltonic strategies of mirroring and inverting, then one could see the sequence as constituting a smaller system of mirrors, a kind of miniature of the epic *Paradise Lost*. The miniature would comprise an internal skeleton of key moments in Milton's poem. The consequence of the existence of a sonnet sequence embedded in *Paradise Lost* would be to raise the status of passages we might not have taken with equal weight before we noticed a sequence. I am thinking specifically of the first sonnet Adam speaks to Michael:

> O execrable Son so to aspire
> Above his Brethren, to himself assuming
> Authoritie usurpt, from God not giv'n:
> He gave us onely over Beast, Fish, Fowl
> Dominion absolute; that right we hold
> By his donation; but Man over men
> He made not Lord; such title to himself
> Reserving, human left from human free.
> But this Usurper his encroachment proud
> Stayes not on Man; to God his Tower intends
> Siege and defiance: Wretched man! what food
> Will he convey up thither to sustain
> Himself and his rash Armie, where thin Air
> Above the Clouds will pine his entrails gross,
> And famish him of Breath, if not of Bread?   (XII, 64–78)

The passage demands to be included in the sequence because of its parallels to the other embedded sonnets. Most intensely, it recalls Raphael's sonnet about the "light Fare" of angels and of men; and it continues thematic motifs to be seen in other sonnets, such as questions of authority, obedience, rebellion, dominion, place, hope, despair, the question of proper limits and crossing boundaries, and relation to God. By seeing this sonnet as a member of the sonnet sequence, one is pressed to give its subject—a political subject, a statement about the proper relation between man and man in the state—equal emphasis with the issues addressed in other sonnets. Could this be a reference not only to kingship, but to the lack of popular support for the rash New Model Army which could not survive without bread given to it by the people? In any case, the political note here is sounded with much force, and using the sequence as a tool of emphasis, Milton seems to be increasing that forcefulness.

Another speech which gains in status from its inclusion in the sequence is God's sonnet to Abdiel in Book VI, lines 29–43. The sonnet to Abdiel, with its bipartite structure of what has been accomplished and what remains to be accomplished, recalls Milton's sonnets to Fairfax and Cromwell with their "O yet a nobler task awaits thy hand," and "Yet much remains to conquer still," and the less explicit demand in the sonnet to Vane, "on thy firm hand religion leans in peace." These resonances with the other freestanding sonnets, and the autobiographical note one cannot help but hear in the speech, lend extra weight to God's speech to Abdiel, but it is by the speech's inclusion within the embedded sonnet sequence that one senses an emphasis internal to the poem being placed on this passage. Likewise, the inclusion of a section of Milton's proem to Book III in the sequence confirms one's impression of the weight to be given to Milton's own role in the poem, his insistence that the unfolding of a story bears an intimate relation to some work of unfouling the subject which it treats. In other words, this emphasis, created by using the sonnet form, picks up on that pragmatic, political strain in the sonnet tradition; it makes the very serious claim (similar to *Sonnet* VIII) that poetry is a kind of action of equal stature to other crucial moments in the poem.

Paying attention to what Jauss calls "the horizon of expectations" of the sonnet inflects the embedded sonnets in directions that would, without that attention, be much less visible.[20] One could, for example, see the entire sequence of embedded sonnets as a sequence of love lyrics, an attempt to catch by a series of variations the definition of love (a complex rendition of Herbert's "Prayer" on a grand scale). This method tells us not only that, as Johnson pointed out, Satan's sonnet to the sun is a lyric of hate, a demonic parody of the love lyric, but also that Satan's other sonnets betray a bleak absence of love. To attend to Satan's sonnets as sonnets is to raise one's expectations to find love and therefore to increase one's sense of love's absence. Conversely, expecting to find love treated in Adam's sonnet to Michael (quoted above) presses the reader to widen his definition of love to encompass man's relation to man and to God.

Milton draws on many of the generic conventions subtler than the sonnet's alliance with love. The frequent idolization of the loved one in the sonnet tradition allows one to read Satan's third sonnet ("O then at last relent: is there no place / Left for Repentance") as a reversal of sonnet idolatry in which Milton gives us a startling view of the subjectivity of the one idolized: "Ay me, they little know / How dearly I abide that boast so vain, / Under what torments inwardly I groan: / While they adore me on the Throne of Hell" (IV, 86–89). Perhaps most startling is that part of the sonnet tradition Milton chooses to eliminate from his embedded sonnets. The convention of adoring the inaccessible speaks volumes in its absence, for Milton seems to be saying that in these embedded sonnets which explore the relation of God to his creation inaccessibility is not a major concern. The theme occurs only once, in Raphaels' sonnet to Adam: "what surmounts the reach / Of human sense, I shall delineate so, / By lik'ning spiritual to corporal forms, / As may express them best" (V, 571–54). The intimation of insurmountable distances is softened somewhat by the succeeding lines: "though what if Earth / Be but the shaddow of Heav'n, and things therein / Each t' other like, more then on earth is thought?" The sonnets which treat distance belong to Satan, and in them distance is examined and found to be self-willed.

So, what is the function of the sonnets and what relation do they have to the political? The sonnets, on the simplest level of poetic construction, help Milton to control prolixity of discourse. But further, by embedding the sonnets, Milton increases the sense in his poem that there can be no resting at false solutions. By embedding these sonnets, Milton creates a form to express the human situation: subjectivity embedded in a larger structure. The embedded sonnet sequence drives the reader to compare, evaluate, and reframe — political moves in that self-containment, compression, and closure become questionable, leading the reader to incorporate private moments in a larger perspective. Milton breaks the traditional form of the sonnet in order to attack false restraint and false solutions. The formal constraints of the sonnet form — the volta, quatrains, closure — give another dimension to those speeches (and another perspective on the characters of those speeches) which Milton writes in sonnet form. The argumentative structure of the sonnet is a perfect tool for Milton's project to show judgment enthralled, or, better, judgment in the process of enthralling itself. The sonnet tradition gives Milton a form which already has inscribed within it many of the crucial themes of *Paradise Lost*. Attention to those generic conventions and their absence inflects many of the speeches in otherwise barely perceptible directions. The sonnet sequence intensifies the use of comparisons, reveals false positions, and makes parallels that might otherwise go unnoticed. Finally, the presence of a series of sonnets in *Paradise Lost* raises the status of some passages (some political ones especially), giving them more weight than one might ordinarily attach to them.

Thus, the use of the sonnet in *Paradise Lost* is significantly more various than Barbara Lewalski or Rosalie Colie have seen it to be in their nevertheless enlightening comments on Milton's use of genre. Colie remarks that "[Milton's] way was generic . . . so that this first struggle of the first human beings with their moral temptations — with themselves — could be seen against the range of human possibilities, represented in the poem as the kinds."[21] It is quite true, and important, that Milton uses what Colie calls "the *social* force and function of the kinds, as abbreviations for a 'set' on the world, as definitions of manageable boundaries, some large, some small, in which material can be treated and considered."[22] However, Milton does not simply critique the sonnet, or its "set" on the world, by juxtaposing it to different forms; he has available to him another means of critique: he varies and transforms the kind and breaks the form. Perhaps other genres Milton confines to certain sections of his epic, but the sonnet seems to be a more versatile tool in his hands. He does not use the embedded sonnet, as both Nardo and Lewalski suggest, to show that there is room for pure forms, and therefore for redemption, even in a fallen world.[23] Milton's idea of the sonnet was too complex for him to use it to represent redemption. To ignore the variety of embedded sonnets in *Paradise Lost* and Milton's resistance to the form is to bar oneself from an entire range of meanings; it is to exile oneself from sweetness by an unnecessary restraint.

City University of New York Graduate Center

NOTES

1. See Daniel Javitch, "The Impure Motives of Elizabethan Poetry," *Genre* XV (1982), 225–38, and Arthur F. Marotti, "'Love is not Love': Elizabethan Sonnet Sequences and the Social Order," *ELH* XLIX (1982), 396–428.

2. See Stuart Curran, *Poetic Form and British Romanticism* (New York, 1986), chapter 3.

3. Anna K. Nardo, *Milton's Sonnets and the Ideal Community* (Lincoln, Neb.: 1979), and Mary Ann Radzinowicz, *Toward "Samson Agonistes": The Growth of Milton's Mind* (Princeton, 1978), p. 143.

4. F. T. Prince, *The Italian Element in Milton's Verse.* 2nd ed. (New York, 1962), and William Stull, "Sacred Sonnets in Three Styles," *SP* LXXIX (1982), 78–99.

5. James G. Mengert, "The Resistance of Milton's Sonnets," *ELR* XI (1981), 81–95.

6. See Rosalie Colie, *The Resources of Kind: Genre Theory in the Renaissance,* ed. Barbara K. Lewalski (Berkeley and Los Angeles: University of California Press, 1973).

7. See John T. Shawcross, "Irony as Tragic Effect: 'Samson Agonistes' and the Tragedy of Hope," in *Calm of Mind: Tercentenary Essays on "Paradise Regained" and "Samson Agonistes" in Honor of John S. Diekhoff,* ed. Joseph A. Wittreich, Jr. (Cleveland, 1971).

8. Perhaps the generic self-reference of this sonnet can also be seen in its theme of sweetness. Colie, in her chapter entitled "Small Forms: Multo in Parvo" has suggested that "sweetness" is a generic signal for "sonnet." This is certainly true for Shakespeare, and it seems possible that it might be true for Milton as well.

9. *The Complete Poetry of John Milton,* ed. John Shawcross; rev. ed. (Garden City, N.Y., 1971), p. 333. I have used this edition for the quotations from Milton's poetry.

10. John Fuller's description of the Italian sonnet, *The Sonnet* (London, 1972), p. 3, reveals the extent to which Milton may be creating a kind of meta-sonnet in Eve's lyric: "The eight lines of closed rhyme produce a certain kind of musical pace which demands repetition. Any expectation of stanzaic continuation is, however, violated by the six lines of interlaced rhyme which follow: the sestet is more tightly organized, and briefer, than the octave and so urges the sonnet to a decisive conclusion."

11. Sir Thomas Browne, *Religio Medici,* ed. Jean-Jacques Denonain (Cambridge, 1955), p. 22.

12. *Complete Prose Works of John Milton,* 8 vols., ed. Don M. Wolfe et al. (New Haven, 1953–82), vol. III, p. 343.

13. Christopher Hill, *Milton and the English Revolution* (London, 1977), 16off. and parts III and IV.

14. Radzinowicz, *Toward "Samson Agonistes,"* p. 5.

15. Donald Davie, "Syntax and Music in *Paradise Lost,*" in *The Living Milton,* 2nd ed., ed. Frank Kermode (New York, 1968), p. 73.

16. Lee Johnson, "Milton's Blank Verse Sonnets," in *Milton Studies,* vol. V, ed. James D. Simmonds (Pittsburgh, 1973), pp. 129–53.

17. Radzinowicz, *Toward "Samson Agonistes,"* p. 143.

18. Nardo, *Milton's Sonnets and the Ideal Community,* p. 157.

19. See Arthur Marotti, "Love Is Not Love," *ELH* XLIX (1982). This is, I believe, unnecessarily reductive for the Elizabethan sonnets; it is to collapse one side of the homology into the terms of the other. Milton, of course, is writing long after the specific historical conditions that Marotti sees as determining this strain of the sonnet, the strain that uses the language of love to speak of ambition.

20. In spite of Milton's transformation or adaptation of the sonnet, appropriating it for political purposes, and in spite of the Renaissance public use of the sonnet, one would have to say that generic expectation in the late seventeenth century still placed the sonnet as a love lyric, as an expression of subjectivity, as a private not a public discourse. Even if the history of the form included DuBellay's *Regrets,* Tasso's *Heroical Sonnets,* Donne's *Religious Sonnets* and Drayton's metaphysical sonnets, the perceived history of the form was influenced more actively by an outdated sense of the genre, one considerably less flexible. That is, writers still wrote "against" a simpler paradigm than actually existed.

21. Colie, *The Resources of Kind,* p. 120.

22. Ibid., p. 115.

23. Anna K. Nardo, *Milton's Sonnets and the Ideal Community,* p. 163; Barbara K. Lewalski, *"Paradise Lost" and the Rhetoric of Literary Forms* (Princeton, 1985), p. 254.

"HAIL WEDDED LOVE": MILTON'S LYRIC EPITHALAMIUM

Sara Thorne-Thomsen

I**N BOOK** IV of *Paradise Lost*, the narrator's greeting, "Hail wedded Love,"[1] signals the beginning of a lyric epithalamium inspired by the example of perfect conjugal love just witnessed by the narrator in his and our first view of Adam and Eve in the Garden. This epithalamium is Milton's only contribution to a tradition which traces its literary roots back to the lyrics of the biblical poet David and the Greek poet Sappho. Originally used to identify a song of praise sung at the door of the bridal chamber of a newly married couple, the term *epithalamium* came to be applied to any poem celebrating marriage. In general, the lyric epithalamium describes the wedding day of a particular couple and focuses on the attributes of the bride and bridegroom as well as on the personal and public aspects of the marriage. The symbolic potential of this popular, if limited, genre, was recognized early by poets. The epithalamium, therefore, flourished not ony as a lyric compliment to a particular bridal pair, but was also used by many poets before Milton as an integral part of a larger work, in which it retains its original function as a poem of praise and assumes a symbolic function as well. Like the epithalamiums of many of his predecessors, Milton's "Hail wedded Love" operates on several levels. It keeps its original role as a poem of praise and, at the same time, defines the essential nature of married love crucial to our understanding of the importance of marriage to man, to God, and to the cosmic order. It also epitomizes what Milton is doing with the epic genre as he fuses classical and Christian elements into a cohesive whole in *Paradise Lost*.

How an epithalamium functions depends on how the poet exploits the traditional background, which consists of the conventional formulae and topoi associated with this genre as well as the marriage songs of his predecessors. Gary M. McCown has located Milton's epithalamium in the epithalamic tradition of Catullus and the hexameral poets, whose epic epithalamiums never achieved the same popularity in England that they had on the Continent, and John G. Demaray has located it in the tradition of the epithalamic masque.[2] Milton, however, evokes and ex-

ploits the larger tradition which includes a more extensive lyric background than that afforded by Catullus's poems alone, important though
these are to it. Theocritus's Idyll xviii, David's Psalm xlv, Solomon's Song
of Songs, and Edmund Spenser's often imitated "Epithalamion" also gave
impetus to the genre in England. By including an epithalamium in Book
IV of *Paradise Lost* Milton is continuing in an epic tradition which embraces *The Aeneid* and *The Faerie Queene*, both of which have epithalamiums in their fourth books.[3] The commentaries of Julius Caesar Scaliger, George Puttenham, and several biblical exegetes, which set forth
generic conventions as well as moral attitudes and theological teachings
concerning love and marriage, provide insight into Milton's epithalamium
as well as into those of his predecessors and the ways he draws on them
to inform his own celebration of marriage. Drawing upon the entire
epithalamic tradition in complex and interesting ways, Milton makes a
unique contribution to the genre as he revalues it in order to highlight
the special role that the narrator's song, beginning "Hail wedded Love,"
plays in his epic.

I. THE CLASSICAL LYRIC EPITHALAMIUMS

The classical epithalamium had its beginnings as a literary genre
in the lyrics of Sappho and appears to have been a popular form of poetry among the ancient Greeks.[4] Theocritus's Idyll xviii, celebrating the
marriage of the mythological figures Helen and Menelaus, is the only
pre-Roman lyric to survive intact.[5] Located in the pastoral world not
so much by virtue of setting and structure but by virtue of its place in
a collection consisting primarily of pastoral poems, Idyll xviii depicts
twelve maidens at the door of the bridal chamber of Helen and Menelaus, who dance and sing of the bride, the bridegroom, and the marriage to the couple within. It is the earliest example of an epithalamium
in the strict sense of the word—a song sung at the chamber door. In *Paradise Lost* we will see that "Hail wedded Love" is also an epithalamium
in the strict sense. Since it is the only English epithalamium in which
the narrator clearly locates himself at the door of the bridal couple's
chamber, it is evident that Milton is placing his nuptial song in a direct
line with the earliest classical example of this lyric kind and, thus, restoring the genre to its original state. This restoration emphasizes the
original state of the married love that we have just witnessed in our first
view of Adam and Eve in the Garden, as well as the ideal conception
of marriage that the epithalamium itself sets forth.

The three epithalamiums of the Roman poet Catullus are the only
other lyric marriage songs from the classical period to survive largely in-

tact. Two of these poems, Carmina lxi and lxii, are more important to the development of the epithalamic genre in Renaissance England than Theocritus's Idyll xviii, because they give the genre its conventional form and images. The third poem, Carmen lxiv, offers an example of how an epithalamium can be used within a larger poem.

Of the three, Carmen lxi influenced more subsequent nuptial poems and did more to provide the genre with its conventions than any other surviving epithalamium. It develops as a dramatic monologue in which the poet-speaker acts as a master of ceremonies who invokes the marriage god Hymen, exhorts the reluctant bride, praises both the bride and the bridegroom, predicts a good marriage, offers some wanton jests — the so-called *fescennina iocatio* (carm. lxi, 123), — promises offspring, and bids the couple a good night and all others good night. This bare outline, which points out the aspects of the poem that become conventions of the genre, gives an inadequate picture of the richness and brilliance of the poem.[6] As is characteristic of the dramatic monologue, we see not only the bridal couple and the other participants in the festivities, but also the speaker himself, who appears as a kind of jolly and benevolent human substitute for Hymen as he choreographs the marriage dance and orchestrates the most important event, the consummation of the marriage. The poem emphasizes the significance of marriage as both a private and public occasion. Marriage is an event which must be celebrated as one of the most important in the life of a man and woman, because from it are born children who provide solace to their parents, who are a tribute to their mother's chastity, and who carry on the family name. Through children a Roman gains immortality and Roman society is maintained. As Shakespeare says many centuries later in *As You Like It*, "Tis Hymen peoples every town."

With Carmen lxii, which differs from Carmen lxi in form and approach, Catullus expands the potential of the genre. Instead of focusing on the marriage of a particular couple, it focuses on marriage as an institution worthy of praise. It assumes the amoebean form as a group of young men and a group of virgins join to contest the virtues of marriage. Hesperus, the evening star, whose appearance signals the beginning of the nuptial ceremonies in this poem, becomes a conventional image in later epithalamiums. The debate between the young women, who argue against marriage, and the young men, who support the idea of marriage, ends with two striking similes, both often imitated in the Renaissance. The unwed girl is first compared to an unplucked flower and then to an unsupported vine. This second simile, with which the young men win the debate, extols marriage as the only means by which a chaste maiden achieves perfection. With this lyric, Catullus opens the genre to the possibility of writing an epithalamium that focuses more on the idea of marriage than on the bridal couple, as well as the possibility of using a double perspective to make a point about the idea of marriage. Milton utilizes both these possibilities in Book IV of *Paradise Lost:* "Hail wedded Love" does focus more on the idea of marriage than on the bridal couple, and the poet and Satan act as a kind of double chorus.

With the lyric epithalamium in Carmen lxiv, Catullus further develops the potential of this occasional genre to include cosmic implications. Carmen lxiv, technically an epyllion, or little epic, depicts the wedding day of the mythological figures Peleus and Thetis, whose union was later allegorized as the marriage of earth and water.[7] Within the framework of the wedding festivities are embedded an aside on Theseus's desertion of Ariadne and a proper epithalamium sung by the Parcae. This wedding song predicts happiness for the bridal couple, but unhappiness for the rest of the world; the bloody havoc wreaked at Troy by their mighty son, Achilles, will mark the beginning of the perversion of human and social values. It serves as a projection of the cosmic discord that is to follow in later ages because of the madness of Achilles's acts, which confound right and wrong and cause the goodwill of the gods to be turned from mankind. The song of the Parcae provides an example (for Virgil, Spenser, and Milton) of how an epithalamium may be used in an epic to comment on an issue of greater importance than the marriage with which it is immediately concerned.

II. A Renaissance Theory of the Classical Epithalamium

Citing the wedding poems of Catullus as excellent examples of the epithalamic genre, Julius Caesar Scaliger devotes a lengthy chapter in his influential treatise, *Poetices libri septem,* to a definition and description of the epithalamium, which he classifies as poetry of praise.[8] His discussion provides the generic formulae and yields a wealth of material about marriage customs in general. Drawing from the principles of Greek and Roman rhetoricians like Menander and Himerius, who had contrived the rules for writing poems and orations from the lyrics of Sappho and Catullus in particular,[9] Scaliger divides the epithalamium into six parts: an explanation of the desires of the bridegroom and the bride for each other; a description of the appearance of the bridal couple as well as their parents; good predictions for the marriage; jokes and wanton jests gently aimed at the pair; promises of children; and an exhortation to sleep —sleep to the guests but wakefulness to the newly married couple.[10] Recognizing the limitations of a genre used for such a specific occasion as marriage, Scaliger advises the poet to choose his material imaginatively from literary tradition and popular custom so that all epithalamiums will not sound alike. He singles out particular images and aspects of the literary tradition as well as of ancient custom that he thinks can be used imaginatively in a nuptial song. After describing how the ancients used the crow and the turtledove to predict an auspicious wedding, Scaliger adds, "non parum gratiae ex hisce avibus Poemati adiungetur" ("from these small birds no small amount of pleasing material will be added to the poem") (p. 151). The bridal attendants also can provide something "ad quos etiam carmen divertere tuum poterit" ("to which your song will be able to turn aside") (p. 152). The poet can also talk about the beauty of the nuptial torches, and about how one was allowed to burn all night in the bridal chamber, but the rest were extinguished lest the bedding ceremony resemble a funeral. Scaliger also offers advice about the use of *Fescennina licentia*, because how the poet uses the *Fescennina iocatio* serves to indicate the quality of his mind. Here he bids the epithalamist not to imitate Catullus but to preserve proper decorum. He explains numerous and varied marriage customs "ut multis e locis argumenti varietas excipi queat ("so that variety of argument can be taken from many places"), and to show the would-be epithalamist that by culling matter not only from Scaliger, but also "ex aliis antiquorum ritibus qui apud diversas nationes observarentur" (from other rites of the ancients that used to be observed from diverse nations"), he can bring "multum luminis poemati" ("much light to his poem") (pp. 151, 153). Scaliger urges the poet not only to choose his material imaginatively but also to apply the formal outline in such a way that he emphasizes one particular aspect of the marriage over all the others, as the song of the Parcae does when it dwells on Achilles, son of Peleus.

III. Biblical Models of the Epithalamium

The biblical epithalamic tradition is as important to the development of the lyric epithalamium in the English Renaissance and to the understanding of Milton's lyric in *Paradise Lost* as the classical epithalamiums and Scaliger's discussion of the characteristics of the genre. The biblical epithalamiums, Psalm xlv and the Canticles, introduce further images to the genre and expand its significance. The commentaries on them tend to place more emphasis on the emotional aspects of marriage and its cosmic significance than do the classical epithalamiums and Scaliger's discussion of the genre.

Both Psalm xlv and the Song of Songs were treated as epithalamiums by Christian exegetes. As E. Faye Wilson points out,

Beginning at least as early as Origen the *Canticle* was considered to be an epithalamium in the form of a drama celebrating the Incarnation: the wedding of Christ, the bridegroom, to the flesh, the bride, in the marriage chamber of the Virgin Mary. Or to put it in other ways, the marriage of Christ and the Church, of the human soul and the *Logos*, of Christ and the human soul, or later of Christ and the Virgin Mary, the mystical type of both. Origen thought of the dialogue as between four participants: the bride and the bridegroom; and two choruses, one composed of companions of the bridegroom, angels and saints, and the other of companions of the bride, the faithful of the church on earth. The 44th *Psalm* [Psalm xlv], beginning at least with St. Augustine, was subjected to the same sort of interpretation. He clearly identifies it with the sort of epithalamia being composed and recited at weddings by the rhetoricians of his day.[11]

This tendency to allegorize both the Song of Songs and Psalm xlv persisted in the Renaissance. Maintaining the traditional belief that Psalm xlv ought to be read as an allegory, Victorius Strigelius in 1562 writes:

And the kind of song *is* κωμάσικον, a song of mirth, iolity & love, or *it is* ἐπιθαλάμιον *a marriage song wherein the holy ghost is a maker up of the marriage betweene* Christ *and his* Church. . . . Now then this ground of purpose in the *Psalme* being thus confirmed (that it speaketh expresly of the *Messiah* and of the *true Church*) let us compare, if it please you, the *Mariage* together with the league that is between *Christ* and his *Church:* for there are five speciall properties or tokens of sincere *Matrimony:* namely the first *mutuall love:* the second *faith:* the third *society or partaking in weale and in woe:* the fourth *procreation of issue:* and the fift *defence from the husband to the wife.* And first of all indeede, the loue of *man* and *wife* ought to be feruent without dissimulation and compulsion, sincere without suspitions and finally, sweetly delightfull without bitternes and disdaine. That such kind of loue was in the sonne of God towards his *spouses* the Church, his taking of humane nature vpon him doth well witnes.[12]

Thus, human marriage takes on a special significance in the ordering of the cosmos, since it becomes a reflection of a mystical union. Strigelius's explication of Psalm xlv typifies the approach of the exegete who is more interested in interpreting the mystical significance of the biblical epithalamiums than in discussing them as poetry.

The exegetes found it necessary to explain away the sexual subject matter of the Song of Songs by describing this collection of erotic verses in terms of a marriage between Christ and the church or the individual soul. Richard Sibbes describes the relationship of Christ and the church in terms of vacillation and recovery on the part of the church, while Christ remains constant. The steps he enumerates are the following: the church's strong desire for a communion with Christ; some declining in her affection; her recovery and regaining of love; another declining of affection and alienation from Christ; and finally a recovery of affection on the church's part because Christ has remained constant.[13] This description, which recalls the reluctance of the bride in Catullus's Carmen lxi and Carmen lxii, confirms that the dramatic element of the Song of Songs, first noted by Origen, has not been lost. Origen himself acknowledges the similarities between the Song of Songs and pagan epithalamiums like those of Catullus, but accounts for them by assuming pagans imitated the Bible, not vice versa: "In this book . . . is at once a drama and a marriage song. And it is from this book that the heathens appropriated the epithalamium, and here is the source of the type of poem; for it is obviously a marriage-song that we have in the Song of Songs."[14]

Although Origen's remarks draw attention to the fact that there are grounds for comparison between classical and biblical sources for the epithalamium, the biblical commentators and English translators of the Song of Songs tend to avoid direct comparisons. However, they are willing to call attention in other ways to various generic qualities which link the Song of Songs to the classical tradition. Joseph Hall calls the Canticles a "Pastoral-marriage-song (for such it is)." Samuel Slater entitles his translation *Epithalamium or Solomon's Song* and in the dedicatory epistle refers to Solomon's Song as "that mysterious Marriage Song." Nathanael Homes calls the Canticles "divine *Bucholicks* or *Pastorals*" and explains that "Speeches and Elogies after the nature of *Epithalamia*, marriage songs, are used to express the *union* between Christ and his Church."[15]

Poets were more willing to make direct comparisons between the Psalms and the Song of Songs and classical works. Both Sir Philip Sidney and Milton compare classical and biblical poetry and remark on the poetic excellence of the Psalms and the Song of Songs.[16] Numerous translators attempt to show this excellence. Of the many sixteenth- and seventeenth-century translations of Psalm xlv, the most interesting is that of Sidney's sister, the countess of Pembroke, who, with her brother, thought of the Psalms as a collection of lyric kinds and therefore experimented in her translations with different forms and meters. Rendering Psalm xlv into eight stanzas, she uses an elaborate rhyme scheme that emphasizes both the elegance and the importance of the occasion, as well as the importance of the inner nature of both the bridegroom and the bride:

> The queene that can a king her father call,
> Doth only she in upper germents shine?
> Nay, under clothes, and what she weareth all,
> Golde is the stuffe, the fashion art divine,

> Brought to the king in robe imbroidred fine,
> Her maides of honor shall on her attend
> With such, to whom more favoure shall assigne
> In nearer place their happie daies to spend.[17]

Other features of this epithalamium that the countess's translation underscores are the marriage procession and the role of the speaker, who not only sings "The praise of him that doth the scepter swaye" (2), but also sings the name of the bride "in lasting verse" (63). These are features of the psalm adopted by English epithalamists. The narrator of Spenser's "Epithalamion" shows a similar awareness of his role and the role of the poem. As an epithalamium, Psalm xlv is more solemn and stately than either Carmen lxi or Carmen lxii of Catullus. There is no playfulness or mirth in the tone as it is rendered into English in its several versions. While the poet is aware of his role as one who praises and immortalizes the participants, there is no suggestion that he is orchestrating the consummation of the marriage. This psalm offers an example of a more serious kind of lyric epithalamium in which the poet is an admiring onlooker, rather than a participant in the events of the day. The narrator in Book IV of *Paradise Lost* adopts a similar attitude for his epithalamium.

The Song of Songs inspired a variety of translations intended, as William Baldwin notes, as an indictment of "the baudy balades of lecherous love that commonly are indited and songs of idle courtiers in princes and noblemens houses."[18] John Wharton continues the explicit indictment of the courtly versifiers (and the implicit indictment of courtly love) in his introduction to Jud Smith's rendering of the Canticles into English:

For surely (gentle Reader) if thou couit to heare anye olde bables, as I may terme them, or stale tales of Chauser, or to learne howe Acteon came by his horned head? If thy mynde be fired to any such metaphoricall t[r]opes, this book is not apt nor fit for thy purpose. But if thou are contrary wise bent, to heare, or to reade holsome documents, as it becometh all Christians, then take this same. . . .

Would to God that all our rebald songs were abrogated and cast quit away, and that we would once call to mynde this sweete saying of our Lord God (O that my people would have harkened unto mee.) Therefore let us followe the good consail of the Apostle, that is: To cast awaye the workes of darknesse, and put on the Armour of lyght, which lyght is the true word of the most hiest.[19]

Such comments express a reaction against the courtiers' love songs and other unwholesome secular poetry that will be echoed by Milton in the epithalamium in *Paradise Lost*.

In the next century, Francis Quarles paraphrases the Canticles, treating it as a collection of songs inviting us "to the wedding." Quarles

claims that his lines are not "loose and lascivious," but his paraphrase
does acknowledge the eroticism of the Song of Songs in the exchanges
between the Bride and the Bridegroom. For example, praising the Bride,
the Bridegroom exclaims:

> The deare-bought fruit of that forbidden Tree,
> Was not so daintie, as thy Apples bee,
> These curious Apples of thy snowy brests,
> Wherein a paradise of pleasure rests;
> They breathe such life into the ravished Eye,
> That the inflam'd beholder, cannot die:
> How orient is thy beautie! How devine!
> How darke's the glorie of the earth, to Thine![20]

The marginal notes gloss the "snowy brests" as "the old and new Testaments," "the ravished Eye" as "the sanctified and zealous reader" and
"cannot die" as "the second death," and, thus, undercut the eroticism
of the lines. Quarles's paraphrase, undoubtedly influenced by Spenser's
"Epithalamion," suggests that it was now possible to take considerable
liberty with the Song of Songs. His free rendering of Canticles ii, 12 ("The
time of the singing of *birds* is come, and the voice of the turtle dove is
heard in our land")[21] into "The Birds (sweet Heralds of so sweet a Spring) /
Warble high notes and Hymenaeans sing," with "Birds" glossed as
"Angels," calls to mind the moment in *Paradise Lost* when the narrator
tells us that the angels were the first to sing the nuptial song for Adam
and Eve, as well as Adam's statement to Raphael that he first heard birds
sing his hymenal. Quarles shows that it is possible to introduce classical
elements into a biblical song just as Spenser has earlier shown that it was
possible to introduce biblical images into a classical form. Milton, as we
will see, also fuses classical and biblical elements in his epithalamiums
in *Paradise Lost*.

The biblical epithalamiums, however, are even more important for
Paradise Lost for the thoughts and comments they provoked from the
exegetes on the subject of marriage and the place of marriage in God's
greater scheme of things. The institution of marriage was held in high
regard in the Renaissance, where it was given a role different from that
held in classical times. Nathanael Homes explains:

And lastly it may be very requisite to open this Book, the rather, because of the
resemblances of *Marriage, Love, Husband, Wife*, etc. For that the most hearers
are, or may be, or have been married persons, and so are here taught by most ex-
perimental comparisons, 1. How to perceive Christs love to them that are spiritually married to him by faith. 2. How to love Christ, and be a kind Spouse to him.

3. How from this pattern, for Husbands and Wives reciprocally to love one another.[22]

An understanding of love and how to love is important to man, because, as James Durham says to his reader, "love alone fills Heaven unto all eternity so that it is certain that Love is the souls most adorning Ornament, it's [sic] most Heavenly frame."[23] Human marriage is a reflection of divine marriage and love. Psalm xlv, the Canticles, and the exegetical tradition supplied Milton with examples of divine epithalamiums presenting married love (not courtly love) as the means for reaching to a higher love.

IV. PUTTENHAM'S SYNTHESIS OF THE EPITHALAMIC TRADITIONS

The only critical work besides Scaliger's *Poetices libri septem* to consider the epithalamium at length as a distinct genre is *The Arte of English Poesie*, attributed to George Puttenham. Obviously influenced by Scaliger's work, Puttenham departs from Scaliger's treatment of the genre in what appears to be an attempt at synthesizing the classical and biblical traditions. He places more emphasis on the moral implications of love and marriage than on form and topoi and then cites an odd model for writers to imitate.

Puttenham begins with his theory governing the use of the genre:

As the consolation of children well begotten is great, no lesse but rather greater ought to be that which is occasion of children, that is honorable matrimonie, a loue by al lawes allowed, not mutable nor encombred with such vaine cares and passions, as that other loue, whereof there is no assurance, but loose and fickle affection occasioned for the most part by sodaine sights and acquaintance of no long triall or experience, nor vpon any other good ground wherein any suretie may be conceiued: whereof the Civill Poet could do no lesse in conscience and credit, then as he had before done to the ballade of birth: now with much better deuotion to celebrate by his poeme the chearefull day of mariages as well Princely as others, for that hath alwayes bene accompted with euery countrey and nation of neuer so barbarous people, the highest and holiest, of any ceremonie apperteining to man: a match forsooth made for euer and not for a day, a solace prouided by youth, a comfort for age, a knot of alliance and amitie indissoluble: a great reioysing was therefore due to such a matter and to so gladsome a time.[24]

Equating marriage with eternal peace and friendship, Puttenham distinguishes between married love and "that other love," which is fickle and causes "vaine cares and passions," and, echoing the biblical exegetes, he explains that marriage is "the highest and holiest, of any ceremonie apperteining to man."

Then, advocating a form consisting of three parts to be sung at different times during the wedding night, Puttenham draws on popular custom for the first part, which must be "loude and shrill" to cover the outcries of the ravished virgin, and on material found in Scaliger's outline of the classical genre for the second part. The third part, sung to the couple in the morning before the bride must "come forth *Sicut sponsa de thalamo,*" is "a Psalme of new applausions" (pp. 66–67). The description of the last part suggests that Puttenham is thinking of biblical models as well as classical epithalamiums. Not only does his use of the term *Psalme* here apparently mean praise and recall the psalmic epithalamium, but his sly reference to "*Sicut sponsa de thalamo*" from Psalm xix also evokes the Bible as a source of inspiration for the epithalamium.

In his choice of Johannes Secundus as the model for the writer of an epithalamium, Puttenham completes his attempt to conflate the classical and biblical traditions: "*Catullus* hath made of them [epithalamiums] one or two very artificiall and civill: but none more excellent then of late yeares a young noble man of Germanie as I take it, *Johannes Secundus* who in that [his epithalamium] and in his poem *De Basis* passeth any auncient or moderne Poetes in my iudgment" (p. 68). Johannes Secundus's epithalamium, a frankly erotic lyric which candidly depicts what goes on in the marriage bed on the wedding night, affords the bridegroom a charming lesson in lovemaking. His *De basis*, however, is not an epithalamium at all, but a series of erotic poems on the theme of the kiss, full of imagery from both the Song of Songs and classical love lyrics, particularly those written by Catullus to Lesbia. Like both the Song of Songs and the Lesbia poems, *De basis* is a loosely linked group of lyrics. Such praise of Secundus and Puttenham's surprising association of the epithalamium with a collection of erotic poems that are not epithalamiums at all can only be explained if the Canticles, as well as Catullus's poems, are his models; his not mentioning the biblical lyrics explicitly must be a deliberate omission, because it was stylish, especially among court poets, to look to the poetry of the Greeks and Romans for models.[25] The choice of *De basis*, in particular, suggests that Puttenham found no lyric epithalamium which fused the two traditions satisfactorily.

V. Spenser's "Epithalamion"

Edmund Spenser's "Epithalamion" represents the first satisfactory synthesis of classical and biblical traditions in this genre in England and fulfills his interest in making the inherited genres distinctively English. Spenser managed all this in his "Epithalamion" by combining native custom with both classical and biblical traditions to create a poem that is, as de Selincourt remarks, "Spenser's highest poetic achievement."[26] This poem, which was often imitated but never surpassed, set a precedent for the English epithalamist and provides an exemplary model against which we can test our expectations for Milton's epithalamium.

Like Catullus's Carmen lxi, which begins with an invocation to the god Hymen, Spenser's "Epithalamion" also begins with an invocation, but to the "learned sisters" (1) rather than to Hymen. Unlike Catullus's invocation, it does not tell us what kind of poem this is. Instead, the title names the genre and explicitly locates the poem in the classical epithalamic tradition. The poem's opening directions to the muses,

> And hauing all your heads with girland crownd,
> Helpe me mine owne loues prayses to resound,
> Ne let the same of any be enuide:
> So Orpheus did for his owne bride,
> So I vnto my selfe alone will sing,
> The woods shall to me answer and my Eccho ring,   (12–18)

affirm Spenser's debt to the classical tradition by locating himself and the poem in the lyric tradition of Orpheus and establishing it as a dramatic monologue in the tradition of Catullus's Carmen lxi. These lines also evoke the opening lines of Psalm xlv in the Countess of Pembroke's translation:

> My harte endites an argument of worth,
>   The praise of him that doth the Scepter swaye:
> My tongue the pen to paynt his praises forth,
>   Shall write as swift as swiftest writer may.

Like the Psalmist, Spenser is himself fully aware of his role as a singer and poet able to make the subject of his praises immortal with his epithalamium. But Spenser's poem differs from both Carmen lxi and Psalm xlv, because he conflates speaker with bridegroom, thereby making his "Epithalamion" both a public and a personal expression of joy. Thomas Greene, who assesses the place of Spenser's poem in the classical tradition, points out that this fusion of the poet-speaker with the bridegroom is Spenser's most "original stroke."[27] When Spenser's poem is looked at only as part of the classical tradition this is indeed his most original contribution to that tradition. However, when it is looked at in the tradition of the Song of Songs, which was interpreted as a series of utterances by several speakers, one of whom is the Bridegroom who, as we have seen, praises the Bride, this "original stroke" may be seen as an effort by Spenser to combine the public celebration of the classical tradition with the more personal joy of the biblical songs.

In structuring the "Epithalamion" Spenser basically follows an outline derived from Scaliger and Carmen lxi, reshaping it in places to suit
the needs of his poem. According to Scaliger's model the first part of the
poem should show the love and eagerness of the bridegroom and the reluctance of the bride. In Spenser's poem, the bride's slowness to awake
shows her reluctance, while the bridegroom's love and eagerness become
evident in his desire to have the muses and nymphs attend his bride and
in his desire to have a perfect day. The Bridegroom's cry, "Wake, now
my love, awake," (74), which echoes the Canticles' "My beloved spake,
and said unto me, Rise up, my love, my fair one, and come away" (ii,
10) is followed immediately by "for it is time, / The Rosy Morne long
since left Tithones bed, / All ready to her siluer coche to clyme, / And
Phoebus gins to shew his glorious hed" (74–77), an obvious classical bor-
rowing, which is, in turn, followed by further echoings of the Song of
Songs. Together they afford an example of Spenser's use of biblical and
classical material side by side in this poem, thereby creating a rich and
exquisite blending of two traditions.

For the next section of the epithalamium, Scaliger instructs the poet
to praise both the bride and the bridegroom for their "praestantia cor-
poris" ("physical appearance") and "animi studiis" ("zeal of mind"). In
stanzas 7–11, the bridegroom/speaker praises his bride for her physical
beauty with, as Baroway suggests (pp. 25–31), allusions drawn from the
Song of Songs. He next praises his bride for "The inward beauty of her
liuely spright" (186), an echo of Psalm xlv. As the speaker, the bridegroom cannot overtly praise himself, but he does so indirectly by stating
that such a beautiful, good, and modest lady could not love a man of
base affections and that contemplation of her beauty elevates his spirit.
Spenser transforms Scaliger's third part, in which the poet makes favorable predictions about the marriage, into a description of the church service (stanzas 12–13), which, beginning with "Open the temple gates unto
my love" (204), echoes the Song of Songs (v, 2). He then juxtaposes this
biblical echo with the pagan custom of decking the doorposts. Here the
auspicious birds of Scaliger's discussions become the "Angels" (231), who
"forget their service" (231) in their admiration of the bride's beauty, as
Quarles glossed the birds of Canticles as angels. By interpreting Scaliger's
vague "beneominabatur" as the church service, Spenser here is adapting
the lyric epithalamium to his own customs. In doing this, he is also following Scaliger's advice to look to native practices for original material,
even as Milton did later.

The fourth part of the epithalamium, according to Scaliger, consists of jollity and wantonness. This is the fescennine part of the poem,

and here the poet/bridegroom must be careful about what he says because his words are an indication of his character. Spenser's poem deals with this problem in two ways. Jollity is translated into the festivities after the ceremony (stanzas 14–15), and gentle wantonness is expressed in the speaker's own desire for day to end and night to come (stanza 16). As the poet decorously shows his desire to consummate the marriage, he retains the fescennine element without being crude. Actually, if the entire poem is considered, its sensuous language and rhythms, plus the poet's desire for sexual consummation, create not a *fescennina iocatio*, but a kind of fescennine atmosphere for the entire poem, so that while the poem is not ribald, it is, nevertheless, frankly sexual.

To complete the poem, Spenser adjusts the model again to suit the needs of the bridegroom. Instead of ending his epithalamium with promises of offspring and then with the bedding of the couple and the exhortation to the others to sleep, the poet dismisses the bridal attendants and then promises offspring when he and his bride are alone in bed. To continue the poem beyond the usual point becomes possible only because of Spenser's fusion of the bridegroom and the poet. This innovative ending (stanzas 18–23) is another of Spenser's original contributions to the epithalamic genre, and one which subsequent English epithalamists try to imitate in their poems.

Spenser's magnificent synthesis of lyric epithalamic traditions is based on a view of marriage like the one Puttenham assumes: marriage is "the highest and holiest, of any ceremonie apperteining to man: a match forsooth made for euer and not for a day, a solace prouided for youth, a comfort for age, a knot of alliance and amitie indissoluble." Marriage is then that human institution which not only, to use Shakespeare's classical terms, "Peoples every town," but also, as Spenser indicates, peoples heaven and reflects the cosmic order:

> And ye high heauens, the temple of the gods,
> In which a thousand torches flaming bright
> Doe burne, that to vs wretched earthly clods,
> In dreadful darknesse lend desired light;
> And all ye powers which in the same remayne,
> More then we men can fayne,
> Poure out your blessing on vs plentiously,
> And happy influence vpon vs raine,
> That we may raise a large posterity,
> Which from the earth, which they may long possesse,
> With lasting happinesse,
> Vp to your haughty pallaces may mount,

And for the guerdon of theyr glorious merit,
May heauenly tabernacles there inherit,
Of blessed Saints for to increase the count.
So let vs rest, sweet loue, in hope of this,
And cease till then our tymely ioyes to sing,
The woods no more vs answer, nor our eccho ring.   (409–26)

Spenser's "Epithalamion" reconciles classical and biblical traditions of the wedding song in a statement about marriage, which stresses its importance as a social, religious, personal, and sexual event closely tied to nature and the ordering of the cosmos. It is a dramatic statement of the speaker's own emotional involvement and commitment to marriage, which, above and beyond being an occasion for public rejoicing, becomes, as Greene notes, "above all a private emotional event" for the speaker (p. 228).

Instead of exhausting the epithalamic genre in England, as it might well have, Spenser's "Epithalamion" apparently sparked an interest in the occasional genre, introducing a flurry of activity as the epithalamium was tried by poets great and not so great. Not only did it continue to be popular as a lyric compliment to a particular couple; it also became part of masques celebrating royal marriages, plays, and even epic poems. The list of those who attempted one or more includes Donne, Jonson, Herrick, and Marvell, as well as numerous less well-known poets.

VI. MILTON'S "HAIL WEDDED LOVE"

Milton's epithalamium in Book IV of *Paradise Lost* draws upon the entire lyric tradition of the epithalamium, classical and biblical, Elizabethan and Jacobean, as well as criticism and commentary that had grown up around that tradition over several centuries. Milton uses and adapts the epithalamic genre to a celebration of the marriage state itself, rather than specifically of the wedding night — for, of course, Adam and Eve are assumed to have consummated their marriage at some earlier time before the narrator presents them to us.

In comparison to the classical and biblical epithalamiums and to Spenser's "Epithalamion," Milton's "Hail wedded Love" seems both brief in length and stark in its use of epithalamic imagery. Like Catullus's Carmen 61 and Spenser's "Epithalamion," Milton's nuptial song begins with an invocation, but neither to the classical god of marriage, Hymen, whose presence was necessary for the proper sanctioning of a marriage, nor to the muses, who aid the poet in his composition. However, instead of rejecting this classical god, as Spenser does when he calls upon the muses in his "Epithalamion," Milton transforms Hymen into "wedded Love," thus identifying the genre of this lyric by recalling Catullus's "o Hymen, Hymenaee." This modification of Hymen to "wedded Love," which is then identified as "mysterious Law," confirms that this epithalamium belongs to a Christian rather than a pagan world, and, at the same time, stresses the importance of the concept of married love, which the narrator, like Catullus in Carmen lxii, is now going to praise as an ideal that reaches beyond the immediate human marriage that we have just had depicted for us in the lines preceding this epithalamium. In this way, the poet recalls the exegetical tradition associated with Psalm xlv and the Song of Songs, in which human marriage becomes a reflection of a mystical union and of divine love, as well as a means for understanding and reaching a higher love. By using features from two of Catullus's nuptial songs in such a way as to recall exegetical comments on Psalm xlv and the Canticles, Milton fuses the classical poems which gave the genre its conventions with biblical exegesis, thus resolving a tension that existed between classical modes of expression and Christian thought.

This fusion continues as the poet continues his definition of "wedded Love" as:

>   true source
> Of human offspring, sole propriety
> In Paradise of all things common else.
> By thee adulterous lust was driv'n from men
> Among the bestial herds to range, by thee
> Founded in Reason, Loyal, Just, and Pure,
> Relations dear, and all the Charities
> Of Father, Son, and Brother first were known.
> Far be it, that I should write thee sin or blame,
> Or think thee unbefitting holiest place,
> Perpetual Fountain of Domestic sweets,
> Whose bed is undefil'd and chaste pronounc't,
> Present, or past, as Saints and Patriarchs us'd.   (IV, 750–62)

In a tone which echoes the solemn and nostalgic tone of the epithalamium in Catullus's Carmen lxiv, the narrator describes what married love is—that love that distinguishes man from beast and affords an example from which other kinds of love are learned. By alluding to "Saints and Patriarchs," the poet suggests that married love nowadays is not all that it once was and that Christian tradition rather than classical tradition provides more reliable examples of chaste marriage. (A classical figure like Penelope might epitomize chastity in marriage, but Odysseus was not a model husband.)

Although pagan poets produced marriage poems worthy of imitation, the concept of marriage in the pagan world was a limited one, a fact emphasized by the Odysseus-Penelope marriage and by the nuptial poetry itself. In Book XI Milton underscores the limited pagan concept of marriage when Michael shows Adam the future and Adam beholds

> A Bevy of fair Women, richly gay
> In Gems and wanton dress; to the Harp they sung
> Soft amorous Ditties, and in dance came on:
> The Men though grave, ey'd them, and let thir eyes
> Rove without rein, till in the amorous Net
> Fast caught, they lik'd, and each his liking chose;
> And now of love they treat till th'Ev'ning Star
> Love's Harbinger appeared; then all in heat
> They light the Nuptial Torch, and bid invoke
> *Hymen*, then first to marriage Rites invok't;
> With Feast and Musick all the Tents resound.   (XI, 582–92)

Charmed by what he sees, Adam is rebuked by Michael, for these women, though beautiful, are "empty of all good wherein consists / Woman's domestic honor and chief praise" (XI, 616–17) and are bred for lust. Here the love seems to be no more than Puttenham's "other loue, whereof there is no assurance, but loose and fickle affection occasioned for the most part by sodaine sights and acquaintance of no trial or experience," and which should never be celebrated with a marriage song since it represents a union based on passion and lust. And it is here, where the union of man and woman is based on passion and lust, that we find unmodified features of the classical epithalamium: the evening star, the nuptial torch, and the invocation to Hymen. When these classical topoi finally appear as part of a world of limited values and ideals, we understand why Milton rejects them for use in an epithalamium in the pure and as yet uncontaminated world of the Garden. When we return to "Hail wedded Love" and find the narrator declaring that Love "here [in Eden] lights / His constant Lamp" (IV, 763–64), we see that he uses but modifies the standard epithalamic image of the nuptial torch to emphasize the importance of the marriage commitment in the life of man, as well as in the scheme of the universe.

For Milton, Love "Reigns . . . and revels" in the Garden and in the chaste marriage bed, and

> not in the bought smile
> Of Harlots, loveless, joyless, unindear'd,
> Casual fruition, nor in Court Amours,
> Mixt Dance, or wanton Mask, or Midnight Ball,
> Or Serenate, which the starv'd Lover sings
> To his proud fair, best quitted with disdain.   (IV, 765–70)

Love and even marriage as practiced in the royal courts and among the nobility is no longer, as it was in Psalm xlv, a true example of love, and is therefore not to be imitated or praised. Milton implies a criticism of the epithalamic genre in the court masque, which so often celebrated an empty or tawdry version of married love, glittering in the glow of artificial light. He also implicitly criticizes other genres associated with the world of the court and used to proclaim and celebrate illicit love.

In the final lines of "Hail wedded Love," the narrator turns to Adam and Eve, who have not, so far, been the center of attention, as would be usual in the conventional epithalamium. Since this is not the wedding night of Adam and Eve, Milton does not image forth the consummation of the marriage, a frequent practice of epithalamists, nor does he urge the couple to vigorous sexual activity on their wedding night. Instead he imagines them asleep in their bower and urges them to "Sleep on" (IV, 773). This exhortation inverts the ending that Scaliger recommends for the epithalamium, as he instructs the poet to urge sleep for the guests, but wakefulness for the bridal couple. Finally, with words that evoke "at, boni / coniuges, bene vivite et / munere assiduo valentem / exercete iuventam" ("but, good pair, live well / and in constant duty exercise / your vigorous youth"), the happy ending of Catullus's Carmen lxi, the narrator closes on a sad and forboding note as he continues to address the couple, who will be "yet happiest if ye seek / No happier state, and know to know no more" (IV, 774–75). In this he recalls the speaker in Catullus's Carmen lxiv, who implies that the actions of Achilles, the offspring of Peleus and Thetis whose marriage the poem celebrates, affect subsequent generations in their relationship not only with the gods, but also with other individuals. The omniscient narrator of *Paradise Lost* knows what lies ahead not only for this happily married couple whose actions affect the subsequent generations of mankind, but also for their descendants, who suffer many of the same afflictions described in Carmen lxiv.

Although Milton's epithalamium, like Theocritus's Idyll xviii, is sung, as Puttenham says, "at the chamber dore of the Bridegroome and Bride" (p. 65), and although it does begin with an invocation, nevertheless it is not conventional when placed in the lyric tradition. It does not describe the events of the wedding day; it does not base its argument on the desires of the bridal couple, as Scaliger says all nuptial songs should; and the poet does not orchestrate the most important event, the consummation of the marriage. Instead of a lush poetic endeavor similar to the lyrics written by earlier epithalamists, this sober, plain, and nostalgic lyric reads more like a commentary on Psalm xlv or the Song of Songs, as it defines not only married love but also the place of love and marriage in Milton's poetic universe, much as biblical commentators define the place of love and marriage in God's schematic ordering of the cosmos.

But though Milton has largely eschewed classical epithalamic topoi for "Hail wedded Love," such classical influences are evident elsewhere in Book IV. As McCown points out, in the article cited above (note 2), classical topoi from Catullus's Carmen lxi and lxii are transferred from the epithalamium proper into the scenes leading up to "Hail wedded Love." The evening setting (540–43, 555–57, 598–606), the praises of the bridal pair (289–318), the wedding feast (325–55), and the entertainment provided by the animals, who replace the human well-wishers and whose humorous antics replace the ribald fescennine joking (340–52), are all derived from Catullus's poems. The vine, pliant in Carmen lxi and in need of support in Carmen lxii, is used to describe Eve's "golden tresses," which curl "As the Vine curls her tendrils, which impli'd / Subjection" (304–11). These Catullan elements are a part of the perspective that the narrator shares with Satan. Along with the narrator, we delight in all that we see, until Satan begins to lament his situation:

> Sight hateful, sight tormenting! thus these two
> Imparadis't in one another's arms
> The happier *Eden*, shall enjoy thir fill
> Of bliss on bliss, while I to Hell am thrust,
> Where neither joy nor love, but fierce desire,
> Among our other torments not the least,
> Still unfulfill'd with pain of longing pines.   (IV, 505–11)

These lines remind us that this shared perspective is a limited one, as they focus on the idea of desire which Scaliger says should be the subject of an epithalamium. Satan, however, turns Scaliger's discreet expression of modest and lawful desire into a burning, tormenting passion, similar to that expressed by the sonnet lover and to that which Puttenham excludes from a marriage song, as being an unsound basis for marriage. With his closing words, "Live while ye may, / Yet happy pair; enjoy, till I return, / Short pleasures, for long woes are to succeed" (IV, 533–35), Satan parodies the usual epithalamium ending.

By placing features of the classical epithalamium in a perspective shared with Satan, Milton again suggests that the view of marriage presented in the classical epithalamium is indeed limited. In this way, Milton prepares us for the revalued and expanded view of marriage presented in "Hail wedded Love." He also prepares us, by the departure of Satan, to see Adam and Eve from the perspective of a chastened narrator. The focus shifts from the physical perfections of Adam and Eve to their conversation and evening prayer. Eve's love lyric to Adam (635–58) recalls the praises sung by the bride to the bridegroom in the Song of Songs with its richness of imagery and its sensuous tone. Her phrase, "Sweet is the breath of morn, her rising sweet" (641), echoes the Canticles (ii, 17). Indeed Milton seems to be guided by his statement that the Song of Songs is "a divine pastoral drama . . . consisting of two persons and a double chorus" (*YP* I, 815), for Adam and Eve are the two persons and Satan and the narrator (who, like the youths and maidens in the marriage debate in Catullus's Carmen lvii, provide a double perspective on marriage) make up the double chorus. The choric function of Satan becomes particularly evident in the closing lines of "Hail wedded Love," for the narrator's exhortation to Adam and Eve, "Sleep on, / Blest pair; and O yet happiest if ye seek / No happier state, and know to know no more" (IV, 773–75) sadly echoes Satan's bitter closing parody (quoted above) directed at Adam and Eve.

In spite of the faint classical echoes at the beginning and ending, "Hail wedded Love" is a celebration written in a different and more lofty key, emphasizing the importance of marriage to the world of the Garden, to the universe, and to the poem itself. This epithalamium, which sounds like one of the biblical commentaries on Psalm xlv or the Song of Songs, explains the difference between chaste marriage and short-lived amours in terms of biblical patriarchs and court figures. The implied criticism of literary genres which were popular at court for expressing illicit love suggests that the Bible, not the court, is the place to look for examples of true love and marriage. Indeed, as Halkett points out, "true marriage . . . is an emblem of natural order, just as, to the divines, it was an emblem of the authority of Christ over the Church" (p. 57). Wedded love sums up and reflects the true nature not only of human order but also of cosmic order. For, as we see in *Paradise Lost*, love binds people to people, individual to individual, angel to angel, Father to Son, and Son to mankind. The true marriage that the narrator sees imaged forth here in Adam and Eve's marriage expresses for us in terms that we can understand what Halkett calls "the divine harmony inherent in the composition of things, the capstone of the universal order" (p. 53). Consequently, when anything happens to disrupt this harmony, the natural order, be it human or cosmic, is disrupted with disastrous consequences.

VII. MILTON'S EPITHALAMIUM AND THE EPIC TRADITION

Milton further emphasizes the importance of conjugal love, and hence the importance of the lyric "Hail wedded Love" to *Paradise Lost* as a whole, by locating his epithalamium in Book IV. In so doing he is continuing in an epic tradition which embraces *The Aeneid* and *The Faerie Queene.* Each of these epics contains an epithalamium which comments on the larger implications of marriage in these poems. If we look at Milton's epithalamium as the culmination of an epic tradition that begins with Virgil's celebration of the "marriage" of Dido and Aeneas in Book IV of *The Aeneid* and continues with Spenser's celebration of the marriage of the Thames and Medway Rivers in Book IV of *The Faerie Queene,* we can see how Milton has adapted these epic precedents for using an epithalamium to underscore central themes of the epic to his own poetic purposes.

Virgil—who, like the poets of the Renaissance, had Catullus's epithalamiums as his models—announces the consummation of Dido's love for Aeneas in Book IV of *The Aeneid* with rain, hail, and thunder. Juno identifies this storm as an epithalamium as she and Venus plot together in feigned friendship to unite Dido and Aeneas:

> His ego nigrantem commixta grandine nimbum,
> . . . .
> Desuper infundam, et tonitru caelum omne ciebo.
> . . . .
> Hic Hymenaeus erit.

[On them will I pour down from above black rain mixed together with hail, and I will wake all the heaven with thunder. . . . This will be their nuptial song.][28]

And indeed, when a storm brings Dido and Aeneas together in a cave, we find an epithalamium, or rather a parody of an epithalamium:

> Interea magno misceri murmure caelum
> Incipit; insequitur commixta grandine nimbus;
> Et Tyrii comites passim et Troiana iuventus
> Dardaniusque nepos Veneris diversa per agros
> Tecta metu petiere; ruunt de montibus amnes.
> Speluncam Dido dux et Troianus eandem
> Deveniunt. Prima et Tellus et pronuba Iuno
> Dant signum; fulsere ignes et conscius Aether
> Conubiis, summoque ululerunt vertice Nymphae.   (IV, 160–68)

[Meanwhile the sky begins to be disturbed with a great rumbling; violent rain mixed with hail follows. The Tyrian company, the Trojan youth, and the Dardanian grandson of Venus in their fear sought shelters scattered through the fields; streams rush down the mountains. The leader Dido and the Trojan come to the same cave. Primal Earth and the bridesmaid Juno give the signal; fires flashed and the air was witness to their marriage, and on the highest peak, the Nymphs shrieked.]

Like the conventional epithalamium, this one does describe the events of the day. Yet unlike Catullus's epithalamiums, it has no joyful human or divine attendants. Instead, the youths (who make up the choruses in Catullus's Carmina lxi and lxii) have fled in fear of the storm, which reflects the nature of this union, both on the human and cosmic scale. A violent rainstorm replaces the cheerful human festivities; thunder substitutes for the chorus of young people; the empty air, not Hymen, presides over the wedding ceremony; the Primal Earth and Juno, instead of Hymen or the evening star, give the signal for the "festivities" to begin. A cave and lightning replace the nuptial couch and the nuptial torch. The consummation of the marriage is celebrated not by maidens who sing the epithalamium proper at the door of the bridal chamber, as they do in Theocritus's Idyll xviii, but by the owl-like shrieks of the nymphs. C. M. Bowra argues that the "powers of earth and sky carry out in their own way the ceremony of an ancient marriage" and that Dido consequently "believes that the marriage is real," even though she "does not wed Aeneas as a Roman woman weds a Roman man, . . . she weds him with the approval of nature."[29] But only Dido, blinded by what Virgil calls "furor" (Puttenham's "other love"), believes that hers is a legitimate marriage, for Virgil embeds usual epithalamic topoi into other parts of Book IV to comment on this so-called marriage. An early remark made by Dido, "si non pertaesum thalami taedaeque fuisset" ("if I were not weary of the bridal bed and torch," IV, 18), indicates that she knows quite well what the elements of a proper marriage ceremony, Roman or otherwise, ought to be. And Aeneas himself will later point to the absence of the traditional nuptial torch when he tells Dido that they were never married: "nec coniugis unquam / Praetendi taedas aut haec in foedera veni" ("I never held out the bridegroom's torch nor entered in this pact," IV, 338–39). Just as the normal epithalamic motifs have been parodied or set aside in this hymeneal, so also have the conventional values of marriage been set aside by Dido and Aeneas in their parody of a marriage. Their union cannot be permanent; nor does it provide any of the solaces that Catullus's Carmina lxi and lxii suggest are a part of marriage. Instead it brings about personal discord, disgrace, and destruction, as well as world discord, since the enmity between Rome and Carthage is linked to it. Eventually, in Book VIII, Virgil reminds us with the depiction of the battle of Actium on Aeneas's shield that a union based on lust causes personal disgrace and creates national, international, and even cosmic discord.

Virgil's epithalamium, therefore, serves to condemn the actions of Dido and Aeneas, who, "turpique cupidine captos" ("caught in base desire," IV, 194), neglect their responsibilities to their people. It also condemns the kind of "marriage" their union represents, especially as it was lived out for Virgil and his contemporaries in the union of Antony and Cleopatra. But it also serves by implication as a positive comment on marriage of the kind depicted by Catullus in Carmen lxi—a marriage in which physical attraction is important, and which, when properly sanctioned, forms the foundation of a stable society and state. Book IV of *The Aeneid* provides the Renaissance poets with an example of an epithalamium that vividly reflects the nature of the Dido-Aeneas union, and also plays an integral role in the epic, implicitly introducing the ideal of the true and valid marriage into a poetic universe which focuses largely on the actions of warriors responsible for the founding of the Roman nation.

In *Paradise Lost* Milton echoes Virgil's epithalamium for Dido and Aeneas in two places. The first use adapts the Virgilian imagery to a positive statement about marriage sanctioned by God and nature. In Book VIII of *Paradise Lost* we find the first use as Adam describes his wedding day and night to Raphael in epithalamic terms which owe much to Virgil:

> To the Nuptial Bow'r
> I led her blushing like the Morn: all Heav'n,
> And happy Constellations on that hour
> Shed thir selectest influence; the Earth
> Gave sign of gratulation, and each Hill;
> Joyous the Birds; fresh Gales and gentle Airs
> Whisper'd it to the Woods, and from their wings
> Flung Rose, flung Odors from the spicy Shrub,
> Disporting, till the amorous Bird of Night
> Sung Spousal, and bid haste the Ev'ning Star
> On his Hill top, to light the bridal Lamp.   (VIII, 509–19)

Epithalamic elements here include a description of the physical appearance of the bride, which comments on her character, the good omens given by nature, the leading of the bride to the nuptial chamber, and the desire for the evening star to appear. The argument, however, is based not on the desires of the bridal couple, but on the desire of nature and the creatures of nature, who orchestrate the event, to have the union consummated. These verses, which recall with positive imagery the epithalamium in *The Aeneid* and the Song of Songs, place Adam and Eve's union into harmony with nature and the cosmos.

In Book IX, after the Fall Milton emphasizes the significance of marriage when he borrows negative images from Virgil's parody to describe

the perversion of Adam and Eve's marital love. Here the poet describes
their desire for each other, which, according to Scaliger, forms the argument of the epithalamium, but he stresses the lustful nature of their desire as emphasis is placed on their sexual encounter:

> Earth trembl'd from her entrails, as again
> In pangs, and Nature gave a second groan,
> Sky low'r'd, and muttering Thunder, some sad drops
> Wept at completing of the mortal Sin
> Original;
>   . . . .
>   but that false Fruit
> Far other operation first display'd,
> Carnal desire inflaming, hee on *Eve*
> Began to cast lascivious Eyes, she him
> As wantonly repaid; in Lust they burn:
> Till *Adam* thus 'gan *Eve* to dalliance move.
> Eve, now I see thou are exact of taste,
> And elegant, of Sapience no small part,
>   . . . .
>
> So said he, and forbore not glance or toy
> Of amorous intent, well understood
> Of *Eve*, whose Eye darted contagious Fire,
> Her hand he seiz'd, and to a shady bank,
> Thick overhead with verdant roof imbowr'd
> He led her nothing loath; Flow'rs were the Couch,
> Pansies, and Violets, and Asphodel,
> And Hyacinth, Earth's freshest softest lap.   (IX, 1000–41)

Milton's critique of Adam and Eve's actions is carried forward as earth-
quake, thunder, and rain (like that which marked Dido and Aeneas's
perversion of married love) accompany their action, and we are reminded
that love based on lust brings discord to the universe as well as to the
couple. After this, we are not surprised to find Adam and Eve quickly
at odds with each other and out of harmony with the atmosphere of the
Garden. Thus the genre, as used by Virgil and defined by Scaliger, offers Milton a vehicle for criticizing a lustful union.

Like Book IV of *The Aeneid*, Book IV of *The Faerie Queene* contains an epithalamium, a fact which invites us to consider the Thames-
Medway epithalamium (XI, 8–35) as part of an epic continuum. Like
the epithalamium in *The Aeneid*, this one too is unusual: it does not portray a human marriage nor recount all the events of the wedding day,
but instead depicts the marriage of the Thames and Medway rivers, focusing on the guests as they arrive and on the bridal couple with their

numerous attendants, much in the manner of Psalm xlv. Spenser (like Virgil) announces that these stanzas constitute an epithalamium by beginning, as Scaliger advises, with an explanation of the desires of the bridal couple and the bride's initial reluctance:

> Long had the *Thames* (as we in records reed)
> Before that day her wooed to his bed;
> But the proud Nymph [Medway] would for no worldly meed,
> Nor no entreatie to his loue be led;
> Till now at last relenting, she to him was wed.   (IV, xi, 8)

Then the poet digresses to a catalogue of the wedding guests, a device borrowed from Catullus's Carmen lxiv, but much enlarged upon here, before he introduces the bridal couple. Instead of continuing on to the usual culmination, the bedding of the bridal couple, the nuptial poem ends with the second part of Scaliger's outline, praises of the bridal couple's appearance, because it is designed to summarize and epitomize on a mythological and cosmic level the marriages that occur in this book, or that will occur at some future time. The narrative of *The Faerie Queene* moves from the concept of love in the individual, where it involves personal harmony, to love as a social phenomenon, where it involves harmonious relationships with others; the Cupid of Scudamour's shield, who "with his killing bow / And cruell shafts" (IV, x, 55) kindles "lustfull fires" (III, i, 39), is conspicuously absent. Instead of love founded in lust, which creates both internal and external discord as we have seen in *The Aeneid*, love among the nobler men and women of *The Faerie Queene* is spiritually based, as is also love among friends. Spenser uses an epithalamium because his larger subject in the third, fourth and fifth books is marriage and social unity.

Just as Virgil layers into *The Aeneid* the unions of Dido and Aeneas and of Antony and Cleopatra, so too has Spenser layered numerous unions into Book IV of *The Faerie Queene*. But because Spenser can people his fairyland with as many characters as he needs, he can work by both positive and negative example. In contrast to the spiritual bondings of Canacee and Triamond, Cambina and Cambell, Poeana and Placidas, Florimell and Marinell, and Britomart and Artegall, we see the lustful longings of the baser characters like Braggadochio and the False Florimell, whose pairing ends in nothing, and the marriage of Amoret and Scudamour, which is described in Book IV though it actually took place earlier.

In Book IV, marriage which brings man and woman together as one becomes a symbol for this larger network of familial bonds and bonds

between friends. We see the brothers Priamond, Diamond, and Triamond become one in the body of Triamond for a short time. We also
see the friends Cambell and Triamond become one as Cambell dons the
wounded Triamond's armor to "purchase honour in his friends behalve"
(IV, iiii, 27). The lookalike friends Amyas and Placidas become one as
Placidas pretends to be Amyas for his "friends good" (IV, viii, 60). Ultimately, then, the Thames-Medway epithalamium summarizes and epitomizes the concept of friendship in Book IV. We can see, therefore, why
Spenser transmutes the traditional epithalamium by focusing, not on the
personal pleasure of the bridal couple anticipated in the consummation
of the marriage, but on the guests: for him, marriage is primarily a social concept. Through it the world is filled with individuals who come
together in inviolable bonds of friendship. In the epithalamium, the reunion of the three rivers, who spring from the same source into harmonious accord, symbolizes all the reconciliations in Book IV:

> The first, the gentle Shure that making way
> By sweet Clonmell, adornes rich Waterford;
> The next, the stubborne Newre, whose waters gray
> By faire Kilkenny and Rosseponte boord,
> The third, the goodly Barow, which doth hoord
> Great heapes of Salmons in his deepe bosome:
> All which long sundred, doe at last accord
> To ioyne in one, ere to the sea they come,
> So flowing all from one, all one at last become.   (IV, xii, 43)

With this epithalamium, unique within the generic tradition and
yet part of that tradition, Spenser moves marriage beyond the limited
human realm, where it may not always be as exemplary as the noble
unions in Faeryland, and makes it the symbol for cosmic harmony. This
mythological version of an epithalamium, which celebrates marriage as
Puttenham's "highest and holiest, of ceremonies apperteining to man,"
becomes the generic means of expressing cosmic harmony, as the ocean
gods, the rivers of the world, the rivers of Ireland, and the rivers of
England converge in Proteus's hall to rejoice in the convergence of the
Thames and the Medway.

In his epithalamium in Book IV of *Paradise Lost*, Milton derives
from Spenser's epithalamium the use of an epithalamic form in an epic
as a means of symbolizing cosmic harmony and rendering this harmony
accessible to his audience. Even before the epithalamium proper, the narrator sounds the note of cosmic harmony in the larger structure of Book
IV as he describes Adam and Eve's wedding night:

Here in close recess
With Flowers, Garlands, and sweet-smelling Herbs
Espoused *Eve* deckt first her Nuptial Bed,
And heav'nly Choirs the Hymenaean sung,
What day the genial Angel to our Sire
Brought her in naked beauty.   (IV, 708-13)

Like the epithalamium in *The Faerie Queene*, Milton's contribution transmutes the generic tradition. Like Spenser, Milton works through positive and negative example, but unlike Spenser, he does it in his epithalamium by distinguishing between married love and what Puttenham calls "that other love." Milton depicts married love, the only proper state of love in Paradise, as the "true source of human offspring" (751) as well as the source of "Relations dear" (756) — marital, familial, and congenial, which are "Founded in Reason, Loyal, Just, and Pure" (755). Married love is the paradigm of divine love in human society. As the source of brotherly love and perpetual domestic bliss, married love reflects the heavenly love portrayed in Book III. Marriage places man in harmony with the cosmos and, as William Haller points out, becomes "the projection of the divine order, of the order of nature and of the soul, into human society."[30]

In contrast to this chaste and ennobling love is "adulterous lust," which is found "Among the bestial herds" (754) or "in the bought smile / Of Harlots, loveless, joyless" (765-66) or "in Court Amours, / Mixt Dance, or wanton Mask, or midnight Ball, / Or Serenate, which the starv'd Lover sings / To his proud fair, best quitted with disdain" (767-70). Milton's epithalamium asserts that through wedded love fallen man has the opportunity to recreate Paradise: "Here Love his golden shafts imploys, here lights / His constant Lamp, and waves his purple wings, / Reigns here and revels" (763-65). This emblem of a Love who uses only his golden shafts suggests Cupid, but not the cruel Cupid of Scudamour's shield, who causes the adulterous lust or sterile loves of the courtly lover. This love, whose golden shafts suggest instead Golden Age bliss, and whose lamp suggests constancy, is found only in marriage.

After defining "wedded love" and its beneficent powers, an effort which turns both the speaker and the reader away from Adam and Eve to comprehend a general lesson, the speaker returns to them as he ends his epithalamium with the customary exhortation to the couple: "Sleep on, / Blest pair; and O yet happiest if ye seeke / No happier state, and know to know no more" (773-75). Since Adam and Eve have, of course, consummated their marriage before the poet enters the Garden, Milton

turns the traditional ending, in which the speaker looks forward cheer-
fully and even exuberantly to the consummation of the marriage, into
a sobering moment to remind us of what is to come.

As Milton uses the generic elements of the nuptial song in *Paradise
Lost*, he redefines the appropriate argument for an epithalamium and
thereby turns marriage into a symbol for cosmic harmony, as Spenser
did before him. Like Virgil and Spenser, he uses the genre in Book IV
of his epic to introduce the ideal of true marriage into his poetic universe
and, by purifying it, to show that "wedded Love" is a paradigm for divine love. Unlike Spenser, Milton does not remove his epithalamium to
the realm of mythology, and, therefore, he holds out the possibility that,
even amid the realities of a fallen world, one can live in harmony with
oneself, one's spouse, one's children, and one's friends, as well as with
God and the universe.

As we have seen, Milton's epithalamium draws upon the entire generic tradition of the epithalamium, lyric and epic, classical and Christian. Moreover, Milton uses his epithalamium to set up and then to resolve a tension between pagan and Christian values, as well as between
pagan and Christian approaches to the genre. In his epithalamium he
does not entirely reject classical elements, but he does translate them
into acceptable Christian terms. This fusion of classical and Christian
elements in the epithalamium epitomizes the ways in which Milton combines his sources throughout *Paradise Lost*.

Virginia Polytechnic Institute and State University

NOTES

1. John Milton, *Paradise Lost*, in *Complete Poems and Major Prose*, ed. Merritt
Y. Hughes (Indianapolis, 1957), IV, 750. Subsequent citations of *Paradise Lost* are from
this edition and are cited by book and line numbers in the text.

2. Gary M. McCown, "Milton and the Epic Epithalamium," in *Milton Studies*,
vol. V, ed. James D. Simmonds (Pittsburgh, 1973), pp. 39–66. John G. Demaray, "Love's
Epic Revel in *Paradise Lost*: A Theatrical Vision of Marriage," *MLQ* XXXVIII (1977),
3–20. In *Milton and the Idea of Matrimony: A Study of the Divorce Tracts and "Paradise
Lost"* (New Haven, 1970), John Halkett, using a nongeneric approach, draws from the
divorce tracts to discuss Milton's conception of the ideal mate and marriage and how it
is finally expressed in *Paradise Lost*.

3. The epithalamium in Book IV of *The Aeneid* is, of course, a parody. How it
functions in the epic will be discussed in a later section of this chapter.

4. In *Sappho and Alcaeus: An Introduction to the Study of Ancient Lesbian Po-*

etry (Oxford, 1955), pp. 119–26, Dennys Page discusses Sappho's epithalamiums. Sappho apparently composed a collection of wedding songs, but only fragments of these epithalamiums have survived. Page notes about these fragments: "the nature of the wedding ceremonies was such that songs of different types were sung at different stages of the proceedings; it is not surprising to find that Sappho's book of Epithalamians was miscellaneous in style and especially in meter" (p. 123). Numerous fragments from other Greek lyricists also have survived, mainly in treatises of the Greek rhetoricians.

5. Two more epithalamia have survived complete in *The Peace* and *The Birds*, comedies by Aristophanes. They serve as examples of this lyric kind used within a larger work, but are not important to the use of the genre in *Paradise Lost*. In *The Poetry of Marriage: The Epithalamium in Europe and Its Development in England* (Los Angeles, 1970), Virginia Tufte notes that the first English translation of Idyll xviii was published at Oxford in 1588 (p. 16).

6. Arthur Leslie Wheeler, in *Catullus and the Traditions of Ancient Poetry* (Berkeley, 1934), chapter 7, discusses the elements from Greek literary tradition and from actual Roman ritual used by Catullus. Among these is the traditional fescennine ribaldry in a refined form.

7. Although it is not technically an epithalamium, the whole of Carmen lxiv was treated as a narrative or epic epithalamium by the subsequent Latin epithalamists, Statius and Claudian, who used it as a model for their epic epithalamiums, and by Julius Caesar Scaliger in his encyclopedic work on poetic theory, *Poetices libri septem*, facsimile, 1561 (Stuttgart, 1964). The epic epithalamium differs from a true epic (*The Aeneid* or *Paradise Lost*) in that it focuses only on the marriage celebrations of a particular couple.

8. The very length of Scaliger's chapter on the epithalamium undoubtedly revived interest in the possibilities of this occasional genre. Scaliger's own preference for the epithalamiums of Catullus, especially Carmen lxi, may explain why this genre developed along lyric lines in England rather than along epic lines as it did on the Continent, where poets imitated the epic epithalamiums of Statius and Claudian. For a complete survey of the development of the epithalamium between Catullus and Sir Philip Sidney, the first English Renaissance poet to write an epithalamium, see Tufte, *The Poetry of Marriage*, and McCown's unpublished dissertation, "The Epithalamium in the English Renaissance" (Chapel Hill, N.C., 1968).

9. A. L. Wheeler, in "Tradition in the Epithalamium," *AJP* LI (1930), 205–23, discusses the rhetorical tradition.

10. Scaliger, *Poetices libri septem*, p. 150. All translations from the text are my own, and spelling has been modernized.

11. E. Faye Wilson, "Pastoral and Epithalamium in Latin Literature," *Speculum* XXIII (1948), 40–41.

12. Victorius Strigelius, *A Third Proceeding in the Harmonie of King Davids Harp*, trans. Richard Robinson (London, 1595), pp. 1–5. In *A Brief Explication of the First Fifty Psalms* (London, 1655), David Dickson explains that Psalm xlv is " a song, describing the mystical marriage of the *Messiah Christ Jesus* our Lord, and his Church, . . . and . . . is set down not in a typical manner, but in a simple similitude of the marriage of a King & Queen indefinitely, whose marriage useth to be the most glorious of all earthly marriages, and fittest to lead us up to that incomparably glorious spiritual marriage of Christ & his Church" (pp. 283, 293).

13. Richard Sibbes, *Bowels Opened or, A Discovery of the neere and deere Love, Union and Communion betwixt Christ and the Church, and consequently betwixt Him and every beleeving Sovle* (London, 1639), pp. 4–5.

14. Origen, *The Song of Songs. Commentary and Homilies*, trans. R. P. Lawson (London, 1957), p. 268.

15. Joseph Hall, *An Open and Plain Paraphrase, vpon the Song of Songs* (London, 1609); Samuel Slater, *Epithalamium or Solomon's Song* (London, 1653); Nathanael Homes, *A Commentary Literal or Historical, and Mystical or Spiritual on the Whole Book of Canticles* (London, 1652), p. 463.

16. Sir Philip Sidney, *The Defense of Poesy*, in *Selected Prose and Poetry*, ed. Robert Kimbrough (New York, 1969), pp. 110–11; Milton, *The Reason of Church Government*, in *Complete Prose Works of John Milton*, 8 vols., vol. 1, ed. Don M. Wolfe et al. (New Haven, 1953), pp. 812–16, hereafter cited as *YP*.

17. Sir Philip Sidney and the Countess of Pembroke, *The Psalmes of David Translated into Divers and Sundry Kindes of Verse* (London, 1823), printed from a copy of the original manuscript transcribed by John Davies of Hereford in the reign of James 1. Most translators of the Psalms rendered them into ballad stanzas because they expected them to be sung during church services. Both John Hopkins in Thomas Sternhold and John Hopkins, *The Whole Book of Psalmes: Collected into English Metre* (London, 1603) and George Wither, *The Psalmes of David Translated into Lyrick Verse* (The Netherlands, 1632), render Psalm xlv into ballad stanzas.

18. William Baldwin, *The Canticles or Balades of Solomon, phraselyke declared in English metres* ([London], 1549), Dedication to Edward VI.

19. Jud Smith, *A Misticall Devise of the spirituall and godly love betwene Christ the Spouse and the Church or Congregation* (London, 1575), To the Christian Reader.

20. Francis Quarles, *Sions Sonets* (London, 1625), Sonet XII, stanza 5. Quarles's paraphrase indicates that by 'sonet' he means 'little song.' He prefixes an epithalamium of his own composition to this paraphrase. The sonets vary in length and preserve the dramatic, pastoral, and lyric associations.

21. All references to the Bible (except where otherwise noted) are to the Authorized Version (King James) and will be noted in the text hereafter by book, chapter, and verse numbers.

22. Homes, *Commentary . . . on the Whole Book of Canticles*, p. 470.

23. James Durham, *Clavis Canticii: or, an Exposition of the Song of Solomon* (London, 1669).

24. George Puttenham, *The Arte of English Poesie*, facsimile, 1589 (Kent, Ohio, 1970), pp. 64–65.

25. Puttenham dedicates his treatise to Queen Elizabeth and appears to be directing it to the would-be court poet.

26. Edmund Spenser, *Poetical Works*, ed. J. C. Smith and E. de Selincourt (Oxford, 1970), p. xxvi. This edition is used throughout, with citations in the text. In his letter to Ralegh on *The Faerie Queene*, Spenser explains that he has "followed all the antique Poets historicall" (p. 407). Although this statement is usually interpreted as meaning that Spenser was imitating classical poets, his poetry clearly shows that he also had the Christian tradition in mind. On Spenser's interest in "Englishing" the inherited genres, see E. K.'s prefatory remarks on *The Shepheardes Calendar* (pp. 416–18). On his use of Catullus's Carmen lxi, see the introduction in Edmund Spenser, *Epithalamion*, ed. Cortland van Winkle (New York, 1926). His use of imagery from the Song of Songs is discussed in Israel Baroway, "The Imagery of Spenser and the Song of Songs" *JEGP* XXXIII (1934), 23–45.

27. Thomas M. Greene, "Spenser and the Epithalamic Tradition" *CL* IX (1957), 222.

28. George Long, ed., *P. Vergili Maronis Opera* (London, 1872), IV, 120, 122, 127. All subsequent quotations from *The Aeneid* will be noted by book and line number in the text. The translations are my own.

29. C. M. Bowra, *From Virgil to Milton* (London, 1954), p. 54.

30. William Haller, "Hail wedded Love," *ELH* XIII (1946), 97.

OPPOSITES OF WIFEHOOD:
EVE AND DALILA

Ricki Heller

T HROUGHOUT HIS life, Milton's fierce desire for knowledge directed his studies to classical sources that had been forgotten or disregarded by many of his contemporaries. As a consequence of his foraging in ancient history, Milton's own theories often seemed avant-garde; such is the case with his argument for divorce, in many ways perfectly compatible with twentieth-century attitudes toward the subject. His theories of marriage and divorce are also reflected in Milton's other writing, and most clearly illustrated in the two poems that present accounts of married life—namely, *Paradise Lost* and *Samson Agonistes*. As if to include the entire gamut of possibilities in wedlock, Milton chooses to depict marriage from opposite ends of the spectrum: Adam and Eve fulfill the requirements for an ideal union as set out in the divorce tracts, while Samson and Dalila represent the classic paradigm for divorce. In the poetry, in fact, it is the marriage relationship that informs the action. The fall in each case is precipitated by a breach in the proper conjugal harmony, and it is the wife in each instance who attempts to restore the balance by reconciling with her husband and resuming marital relations. Eve, because she is the ideal wife for Adam, succeeds in regaining her position as Adam's wife. Contrarily, Dalila, by claiming the same wifely motivation, exposes her essential unfitness as Samson's mate, and negates each of the characteristics of a true wife. Paradoxically, each woman achieves the same end, acting as a catalyst to her husband's eventual recovery and spiritual regeneration.

To remain steadfast in his beliefs, even in the absence of positive or intelligent response to his work, Milton did require, as William Parker suggests, "almost fanatical courage."[1] Even more than courage, Milton was supported by his firm belief that what he advocated was the veritable wish of God, as he recognized this in his heart and the written law (even when he had to contort Scripture to suit his purpose). Insisting that God's law could work only toward the good of man, Milton was unable to accept the existing divorce laws that could enforce marriage between essentially incompatible individuals. Without compatibility, marriage was impossible; and "God commands not impossibilities."[2]

A good marriage should, in accordance with God's law, bring its members closer to him. While Milton perceives the functions of marriage as manifold, he enumerates these in order of importance: "first a mutuall help to piety, next to civill fellowship of love and amity, then to generation, so to household affairs, lastly the remedy of incontinence" (Tetr., p. 599). In a good marriage, the partners will naturally work toward love and worship of God. Conversely, an improper union not only induces personal acrimony, but it is offensive to God, and may initiate a loss of religious faith. Even a pious man may be tempted to "mutin against divine providence"[3] when yoked to an unfit wife. In such a case, Milton contends, proper devotion to God may be restored through divorce. He writes:

Him I hold more in the way to perfection who forgoes an unfit ungodly & discordant wedloc, to live according to peace & love, & Gods institution in a fitter chois, then he who debarrs himself the happy experience of all godly, which is peaceful conversation in his family, to live a contentious, and unchristian life not to be avoided, in temptations not to be liv'd in, only for the fals keeping of a most unreal nullity, a mariage that hath no affinity with Gods intention, a daring phantasm, a meer toy of terror awing weak senses, to the lamentable superstition of ruining themselves; the remedy whereof God in his law voutsafes us. (Tetr., pp. 666–67)

As a consequence of their basis in spiritual concordance and individual temperament, Milton's views were considered libertine, even heretical. His disgusted opponents accused him of condoning, even advocating, "divorce at pleasure."[4] To interpret Milton's attitude this way, however, is to overlook his genuine belief that God preferred divorce to an unhappy marriage, and his sincerity when he sanctions divorce for "whatever [is] unalterably distastful, whether in body or mind" (Tetr., p. 620). We must focus on the word "unalterably" here, for Milton states unequivocally that divorce should be effected only as a final solution to the problem, when every other alternative has already been attempted and there remains no hope for reconciliation. He insists that "divorce is not rashly to be made" (Tetr., p. 680), and would rebuke those who seek divorce without valid reason and deliberation (Tetr., p. 669). What Milton claims in his prose tracts is borne out in his poetry, where he illustrates the permanence and restitution of true marriage, as well as the dissolution of faulty wedlock.

John Halkett attempts to adumbrate "the extent to which the ideal of matrimony in Milton's divorce tracts is embodied in Paradise Lost."[5]

Halkett compares Milton's own conception of marital perfection to that of contemporaneous marriage handbooks, and concludes that Adam and Eve fulfill the major criteria of "Fitness" (individual suitability to one another) and "Conversation" (proper performance as man and wife within the marital unit). The permanence of their union is established by their ideal enactment of Milton's paradigm defining marriage as a "divine institution joyning man and woman in a love fitly dispos'd to the helps and comforts of domestic life" (Tetr., p. 612).

Because they are the only couple whose marriage is ordained by God, their fitness is natural and inevitable. In the divorce tracts, Milton writes, "That there was a neerer alliance between *Adam* and *Eve*, then could be ever after between a man and wife, is visible to any" (Tetr., p. 601). God's promise to Adam that "What next I bring shall please thee, be assur'd, / Thy likeness, thy fit help, thy other self, / Thy wish, exactly to thy heart's desire"[6] is realized the instant Adam sights Eve and recognizes the perfect spiritual harmony between them. He is irresistibly attracted to her, exclaiming:

> I now see
> Bone of my Bone, Flesh of my Flesh, my Self
> Before me; Woman is her Name, of Man
> Extracted; for this cause he shall forgo
> Father and Mother, and to his Wife adhere;
> And they shall be one Flesh, one Heart, one Soul.
>
> (*PL* VIII, 494–99)

Milton's interpolation of the key words "heart" and "soul," not included in the analogous biblical passage (Gen. ii, 23), redefines the bond of marriage to conform with his own spiritual focus and his belief that love, the "soul of wedloc," most unites the partners. More than their physical connection, it is the immediate love they feel for each other that renders them fit mates who wish to join in matrimony.

Eve's own inescapable attraction to Adam is clear in her account of their initial meeting. For Milton, the mutual attraction of both parties, naturally leading to consent in marriage, is more important to its "fruitfulnes and prosperity" than even God's providence.[7] Consent is a necessary condition for true love, for "there can be no love or good will, and therefore no marriage, between those whom mutual consent has not united" (*CD*, p. 368). As Dennis Burden suggests, Eve does, indeed, consent to follow Adam when she yields to his touch and concludes that "beauty is excell'd by manly grace / And wisdom, which alone is truly fair" (*PL* IV, 491–92).[8] From this point onward, Eve's existence as Adam's wife determines her behavior, and her happiness is contingent upon her execution of this role.

Milton's emphasis on a spiritually based love relegates the physical function of marriage to a status below that prescribed by contemporaneous marital commentators. In the divorce tracts, he asserts that "to consent lawfully into one flesh, is not the formal cause of Matrimony, but only one of the effects" (Tetr., p. 611). Concerning the physical expression of love, it is imperative that "this union of the flesh proceed from the union of a fit help and solace" (Tetr., p. 606); a sexual relationship without spiritual alliance is empty and ungratifying. The perfect love of Adam and Eve expresses the union of two bodies and its concomitant converging of souls. Milton displays the nature of true married love that is "unlibidinous" (PL IV, 449), pure, and innocent. In the epithalamion beginning "Hail wedded Love," he emphasizes that in the marriage of Adam and Eve "adulterous lust was driv'n from men" (PL IV, 753). As an outgrowth of their spiritual compatibility, the physical union is expressed and enjoyed mutually.

The result of their perfect fitness for each other is the "mutuall solace and help" (Tetr., p. 601) that Adam and Eve furnish for each other. While Milton's views on marriage were, in many respects, extremely innovative, he was, nevertheless, influenced by his ideological context and the prevalent belief in woman's subordination to man, created below him in the hierarchy of nature. He clarifies this distinction between the two in his first description of the couple:

> Not equal, as thir sex not equal seem'd;
> For contemplation hee and valor form'd,
> For softness shee and sweet attractive Grace,
> Hee for God only, shee for God in him.   (PL IV, 296–99)

Together they fulfill what Milton terms the "golden dependance of headship and subjection" (Tetr., p. 591).[9] Eve's awareness of her status as Adam's subordinate is reflected in her willing submission to his unquestioned authority. She calls him "my Guide and Head" (PL IV, 442) and "Author and Disposer," continuing,

> what thou bidd'st
> Unargu'd I obey; so God ordains,
> God is thy Law, thou mine: to know no more
> Is woman's happiest knowledge and her praise.
>   (PL IV, 635–38)

While Eve is necessarily Adam's subordinate, Milton endows her with a function equal to Adam's in Paradise. She attends to the domestic duties as wife, preparing meals and even exhibiting superior knowledge in such matters.[10] While her faculty of reason is less developed than her husband's, she nevertheless experiences intellectual advancement and growth toward wisdom, prompted by her husband's instruction and guidance. Her intellectual competence is essential if she is to supply the proper "conversation" for a satisfying marriage. Adam, in pleading his case to God, expresses the need for a partner of equal mental faculties to his own, since "Among unequals what society / Can sort, what harmony or true delight?" (*PL* VIII, 383–84). Eve's intellectual parity with her husband is confirmed when the couple is visited by Raphael. Both Adam and Eve attend to the angel's discourse with equal interest and comprehension, until Eve departs of her own accord. Here, Milton insists:

> Yet went she not, as not with such discourse
> Delighted, or not capable her ear
> Of what was high: such pleasure she reserv'd,
> *Adam* relating, she sole Auditress;
> Her Husband the Relater she preferr'd
> Before the Angel, and of him to ask
> Chose rather: hee, she knew, would intermix
> Grateful digressions, and solve high dispute
> With conjugal Caresses, from his Lip
> Not words alone pleas'd her.   (*PL* VIII, 48–57)

Halkett (p. 112) suggests that this episode also underscores Eve's inherent fitness as Adam's spouse, because she prefers the more "amiable and attractive" conversation befitting husband and wife to the "grave" discussion of Adam and Raphael. In other words, she is instinctively prompted to behavior that enhances her role as Adam's wife.

Perfectly compatible in every way, then, Adam and Eve cannot help but fulfill Milton's primary edict in marriage — namely, a "mutuall help to piety" (Tetr., p. 599). The "meet and happy conversation" (DDD, p. 246) of their quotidian existence is everywhere characterized by their intimate love and knowledge of God, and this permeates everything they do. From the hymn of appreciation that precedes their act of physical love, to the restorative prayer following Eve's dream, to their sundry other extemporaneous expressions of piety and devotion, their entire prelapsarian existence is replete with "adoration pure / Which God likes best" (*PL* IV, 736–37).

If Milton was to render convincing on a human level the severing and reuniting of the first marriage, he had to ensure that, in every way, Adam and Eve's initial fitness was not undermined before the fall. For this reason, their love for each other is unwavering, and even directs them toward a temporary lapse in their devotion to God. It is only when they once more recognize and reclaim this steadfast nucleus of conjugal love that they are able to return to the proper worship of God.

In the crucial precursor to her fall, the parting scene in Book IX, Eve acts in accordance with Milton's marital ideal and upholds the wifely prototype. Even though she suggests that the couple divide their work, Eve is not here attempting to usurp her husband's natural authority. She honestly believes that the separation will attain a praiseworthy end—dinner rightfully merited through honest labor. Furthermore, her request supplies Adam with the option to either "advise / Or hear what to my mind first thoughts present" (PL IX, 211–12). Eve innocently assumes that her husband will correct her, as he has in the past, if her assumption is illogical or impractical. Adam errs when he lauds her suggestion in terms of her role as wife (PL IX, 232–35), and she misinterprets his subsequent hesitation as an expression of his own doubt in her conjugal faith and love. When Adam concludes, "Go; for thy stay, not free, absents thee more" (PL IX, 372), it is his own love for her that refuses to detain her against her will. Halkett (p. 124) believes that Adam here is "rightly showing his love for her in not forcing her to remain; he is exercising his authority with love and gentleness." But Adam has abrogated his husbandly authority by refusing to act as Eve's "Guide and Head" (PL IV, 442); even if her faith and love are constant, they cannot supply her with the necessary reasoning to counter Satan's sophistry. Even at her parting, Eve is properly deferential to her husband, "yet submiss" (PL IX, 377); she leaves only because she interprets Adam's speech as conferring permission to go.

In depicting Eve's fall per se, Milton is careful to stress that her error is caused by faulty reason, and not by any diminished love for her husband; she believes, before she eats, that the knowledge she acquires will benefit them both. In Eve's pathetic attempt to parry Satan's specious reasoning, she continues to identify herself in terms of her marriage, with reference to "us" and "we" throughout her speech. She feels that both she and Adam have been slighted by being deprived of the fruit; her intentions toward her husband remain pure. It is only after she has ingested the apple, immediately exhibiting the depravity of the deed, that Eve considers withholding the knowledge from Adam. Her decision to share the fruit, too, she believes is prompted by love; but her fall has turned the emotion inward, and she no longer considers the ramifications of her actions as these would affect her husband. Immediately, her own knowledge of a wife's status in wedlock is also affected. When she approaches Adam, proffering the forbidden fruit, she argues to reestablish their erstwhile conjugal balance:

> Thou therefore also taste, that equal Lot
> May join us, equal Joy, as equal Love;
> Lest thou not tasting, different degree
> Disjoin us, and I then too late renounce
> Deity for thee, when Fate will not permit.   (*PL* IX, 881–85)

But part of the very harmony of the marriage was Eve's own "different degree" that placed her as her husband's subordinate. Here she not only oversteps her authority as Adam's wife, but asks him to accept her command over God's.

Adam's impetus to join his wife in iniquity is his own reaffirmation of his love's spiritual bond. Because his own soul is ideally attracted to hers, Adam is unable to imagine existence bereft of her perfect companionship. His immediate reaction to her speech implies his own dependence on the marriage relationship (*PL* IX, 896–916). His decisive thought, "no, no, I feel / The Link of Nature draw me: Flesh of Flesh / Bone of my Bone thou art, and from thy State / Mine never shall be parted, bliss or woe" (*PL* IX, 913–16), eliminates the crucial third element, the "soul," from the connecting triad. For the first time, Adam feels that their spiritual natures do not coincide, since Eve has already eaten while he remains at this point "yet sinless" (*PL* IX, 559).

In *The Logical Epic*, Burden suggests that Adam's action here is prompted by his feeling constricted in the bond of indissoluble wedlock. Had Adam consciously deliberated about his plight, Burden argues, he would have reached the conclusion offered in Milton's divorce tracts: "God had previously shown by creating Eve in the first place that the loneliness which Adam dreaded was something for which he would provide. But the important thing is that Adam has a remedy and Milton of all people must know it. The remedy is divorce" (p. 169). However, by offering such a solution in this case, Milton would have aligned himself with those who condemned him for advocating divorce at whim.

Milton insists in the divorce tracts that nullification of marriage should be effected as a final recourse only. Where natural fitness exists to unite a couple in true wedlock, this same fitness may later be the salve to heal a marital wound. Contrary to the extant divorce laws of his day, Milton is even willing to forgive adultery where fitness prevails, and urges reconciliation in such circumstances, forgiving the sin so that it "may soon be repented, soon amended, soon, if it can be pardon'd, may be redeem'd wth the more ardent love and duty in her who hath the pardon" (Tetr., p. 674).[11] While Eve's transgression is, indisputably, the greatest possible sin she could commit, to Milton's mind hers is the only marriage for which divorce does *not* present a viable solution to the predicament. The natural conjugal love born of fitness has been established by God himself. In marriage after Adam and Eve's, this bond need not necessarily be perceived as a permanent alliance in nature, since "if it were in nature, no law or crime could disanull it" (Tetr., p. 601). Since their marriage *was* formed in harmony with the law of nature and God's law, it must survive even this crime.

The immediate effect of the fall is reflected in the temporary disruption of the couple's pristine happiness. Their ideal love, transmogrified through sin, emerges as lust without the spiritual harmony to lend it meaning. We witness "Carnal desire inflaming" (PL IX, 1013) as "in Lust they burn" (PL IX, 1015). Without the proper expression of love, they cannot fulfill their offices of marriage; rather than act as a mutual comfort and help, they attempt to incriminate each other as responsible for their sin. Adam feels "estrang'd" (PL IX, 132) from his wife without the conjugal link of love to join them. Without Eve's reparative expression of affection and her attempt, in her repentance, to resume her role as Adam's wife, there would indeed be "no end" to the couple's "vain contest" (PL IX, 1189).

Eve's simple and open admission of guilt when the Son descends to judge the pair (PL X, 162) is the first step toward regeneration.[12] As the couple renew their love for each other and regain their proper offices as husband and wife, they are able to move toward acceptance of God's will and recognition of his love.

Though Adam repels her initial advance, Eve's heartfelt sorrow and repentance impel her to persist in her pleas for reconciliation. In her selfless acceptance of responsibility and commensurate punishment for sin, Eve also reasserts her desire to be accepted once more as Adam's wife. Her own love for him is evidenced in her complete faith and submission to Adam, as she pleads:

> Forsake me not thus, *Adam*, witness Heav'n
> What love sincere, and reverence in my heart
> I bear thee, and unweeting have offended,
> Unhappily deceiv'd; thy suppliant
> I beg, and clasp thy knees; bereave me not,
> Whereon I live, thy gentle looks, thy aid,
> Thy counsel in this uttermost distress,
> My only strength and stay: forlorn of thee,
> Whither shall I betake me, where subsist?
> Yet while we live, scarce one short hour perhaps,
> Between us two let there be peace, both joining,
> As join'd in injuries, one enmity
> Against a Foe by doom express assign'd us,
> That cruel Serpent: On me exercise not

Thy hatred for this misery befall'n,
On me already lost, mee than thyself
More miserable; both have sinn'd, but thou
Against God only, I against God and thee,
And to the place of judgment will return,
There with my cries importune Heaven, that all
The sentence from thy head remov'd may light
On me, sole cause to thee of all this woe,
Mee mee only just object of his ire.   (*PL* X, 914–36)

By recognizing the ineradicable bond of love that motivates her, as well as her need of Adam's superior knowledge and counsel, she reaffirms her willingness to resume her wifely position. It is in Eve's nature to act as Adam's wife; she cannot exist without him. A restitution of their marriage, Eve recognizes, would restore the spiritual harmony they lacked since their fall and allow them to work once more toward marital felicity and "peace."

Eve's insistent appeals to Adam, because he perceives her love, serve to soften his heart and elicit his forgiveness. Himself repentant, he agrees to "strive / In offices of Love" (*PL* X, 959–60), once more acting as husband and wife. Following this scene of mutual contrition and love, Adam and Eve once more perform their proper functions within marriage. Adam protects and comforts Eve, denying her propositions that they attempt "to abstain / From Love's due Rites" (*PL* X, 993–94) or to commit suicide, while Eve exhibits her former "humility, submission, and desire to aid" (Halkett, p. 134). Their conjugal harmony restored, they begin the slow process of regeneration and conformity with God's will.

By the time they accept their expulsion from Eden, Eve has completely recovered her status as an ideal wife, willing to follow her husband with complete trust in his direction. Because of her identity as Adam's fit mate, Eve is able to effect this recovery, leading to both her own and Adam's salvation. In Milton's version of the biblical story, it is the inexorable core of fitness and marital love that allows the couple to overcome their despair and proceed in their journey toward God (Halkett, p. 137). Consonant with Milton's own conception of ideal marriage, the temporary schism between Adam and Eve is completely repaired, and their marriage is no less perfect even in their fallen state.

Beginning *in medias res, Samson Agonistes*, which contains Milton's second poetical account of marriage, presents us with a union that has already been fractured before the poem opens. Like Eve, Dalila returns to her husband intending to reinstate the conjugal relationship and gain her husband's renewed love and forgiveness. What Dalila proposes, however, is not a return to true marriage but a travesty of its real form, "the empty husk of an outside matrimony" (DDD, p. 256). For, without the most important criterion for a happy marriage in Milton's scheme— true and mutual love born of fitness—the dissolution of the conjugal bond is not only desirable, but mandatory.

In contrast to those critics, such as William Empson,[13] who would interpret Dalila's motives as laudable, we must consider that Milton altered the biblical account, making Dalila Samson's wife rather than concubine, for a specific purpose. Milton is impelling us to evaluate Dalila in terms of her capacity as Samson's spouse.[14] When assessed in comparison with Eve's perfect fulfillment of Milton's criteria for a genuine "help meet," Dalila is clearly, and in every way, the antithesis of a fit mate.

Even before her entrance, Dalila's fitness as Samson's wife is made questionable, since he expresses his own despair at having married her. While his first marriage, he believed, he elected through "intimate impulse" (SA 557), he perceives marriage to Dalila as a mistake:

> the next I took to Wife
> (O that I never had! fond wish too late)
> Was in the Vale of *Sorec*, *Dalila*,
> That specious Monster, my accomplisht snare.   (SA 227–30)

Stanley Fish also suggests that the ambiguity of the situation is increased by Manoa's implication that neither marriage was "of God" (SA 420).[15] Yet it is Dalila herself who confirms Samson's estimation once she appears to request his pardon.

The first description of Dalila, uttered by the awestruck chorus, contains none of the elements we would expect to be associated with a repentant wife. Mary S. Weinkauf has pointed out that the comparison to a ship and Dalila's ornate appearance were both associated with immodesty by Milton's audience.[16] Furthermore, despite her tears, Dalila is perceived as "gay" (SA 712) and "stately" (SA 714); nor is her measured speech and equanimity consonant with the genuine sorrow and humility of true repentance.

Dalila's opening speech, like Eve's, claims contrition and "conjugal affection" (SA 739). She requests her husband's forgiveness, offering "recompense" (SA 746) for her sin. Mary Ann Radzinowicz, in the article cited above (note 12), comments that Eve's regeneration is contingent upon her submission to her husband and her complete admission of guilt. Since Eve was "made for God in Adam, her renovation cannot proceed without reconciliation to him" (p. 171). In order to restore her own spiritual equilibrium, Eve must reaffirm her role as Adam's wife. But Dalila's persistent pleas for forgiveness reveal that she has no conception of her function as wife; rather than truly repent and regain Samson's love, Dalila requests his pardon in order to avoid future obloquy.

We are she truly repentant, Dalila would, like Eve, be willing to accept the responsibility for her sin and the consequent punishment for it. Instead, despite her assurance, "not that I endeavor / To lessen or extenuate my offense" (*SA* 766–67), she repeatedly deflects the blame for her actions, first to the female sex in general, then to Samson himself, and finally to the "Magistrates / And Princes" (*SA* 850–51) of her country. We are reminded of Eve's previous desire that "all / The sentence from thy [Adam's] head remov'd may light / On me, sole cause to thee of all this woe" (*PL* X, 933–35). Without a confession of guilt leading to repentance, Dalila is unable to elicit Samson's love.[17]

Despite his vehement rejection of her, Dalila persists in her professions of her own love. In his treatment of her character, Anthony Low asserts that Dalila "thinks she has acted, and is acting, out of love."[18] However, her impression of love includes none of the spiritual unity and restorative functions of true love. While Samson acknowledges that he had previously loved his wife (*SA* 878), his recognition of her perfidy in wittingly betraying him has negated his love. As he tells her later, "thou and I long since are twain" (*SA* 929). Dalila, nonetheless, is willing to pursue the outward pretense of marriage. However, Milton explains in the divorce tracts that without love "the true bond of marriage, if ther were ever any there, is already burst like a rott'n thred" (Tetr., p. 631). Furthermore, "not to be belov'd and yet retain'd, is the greatest injury to a gentle spirit" (DDD, p. 253). If Dalila is willing to continue cohabiting with Samson although she knows he is no longer attracted to her, her own profession of love becomes suspect.

That Dalila cannot comprehend love's most important dimension, spiritual affinity to another, is made clear by her emphasis on love's physical expression. Without the spiritual component, physical union is meaningless. What she excuses as "jealousy of Love" (*SA* 791) was prompted by fear of Samson's "absence in my widow'd bed" (*SA* 806). Her final plea that "Life yet hath many solaces, enjoy'd / Where other senses want not their delights" (*SA* 915–16) does not consider the possibility of spiritual companionship as a true solace for his despondency. When all her other endeavors fail to regain Samson's love, Dalila resorts once more to an attempt at physical contact. As Mary Ann Radzinowicz observes, love for Dalila is merely "intercourse of the body," while Samson understands that it must include "companionship of mind."[19] His rejoinder, "But Love constrain'd thee; call it furious rage / To satisfy thy lust: Love seeks to have Love" (SA 836–37), demonstrates his own apprehension that love must be spiritual and reciprocal.

Because her love is not genuine, Dalila's attempts to resume her role as Samson's wife betray her inherent unfitness for the office and her inability to provide the conjugal help and solace he requires. The actions she interprets as proper wifely duties — namely, dispensing her "nursing diligence" (SA 924) to her husband — only serve to denigrate Samson's proper status as husband and place her in the unnatural position of marital authority. This, Halkett suggests (pp. 86–87), is the greatest offense that a wife can commit against her husband, and implies lack of love.

In each of her requests to care for Samson, Dalila discloses her own intention to be his protector and guide, rather than the reverse. Were her love sincere, she would strive to elevate his status, rather than perpetuate Samson's weakness and dependence upon her. Dalila's attempts at reconciliation focus on what she is able to supply in material terms; moreover, she recognizes no need of his participation in the marriage. She would mitigate his suffering through her own "ability" (SA 743) and "power" (SA 917). Again, the contrast to Eve's pleas for reconciliation exposes Dalila's inversion of the proper conjugal balance.

In order to renew her relationship with Adam, Eve reassumes her marital status and acknowledges the necessity for Adam's guidance, which provides her "strength and stay" (PL X, 921). Furthermore, she seeks reunion in order to conquer the sense of hopelessness she and Adam feel and to rise above despair. Dalila's vow to nurture Samson, however, would benefit her alone. In his bitter denunciation of her offer, Samson recognizes that Dalila's interpretation of marriage, lacking mutual love and respect, would only fulfill her desire to dominate him. In this regard, it is interesting that the only form of reciprocity Dalila suggests involves an admission of Samson's own guilt and infirmity. She proposes:

> Let weakness then with weakness come to parle
> So near related, or the same of kind,
> Thine forgive mine; that men may censure thine
> The gentler, if severely thou exact not
> More strength from me, than in thyself was found. (SA 785–89)

Without any redemptive spiritual bond, weakness is the greatest alliance that Dalila sees joining herself and her husband.

Since she is incapable of love for her husband and unwilling to accept her proper place as Samson's subordinate, Dalila violates the primary function of wife, and draws him away from his love of God. The fact that Dalila did not share Samson's religion would not, a priori, render her unfit as a wife if her love compelled her to follow her husband in his piety. According to Milton's divorce tracts, in a marriage between an infidel and a devout man, "where the religion is contrary without hope of conversion, there can be no love, no faith, no peacefull society . . . nay there ought not to be, furder then in expectation of gaining a soul; when that ceases, we know God hath put enmity between the seed of the woman, and the seed of the serpent" (Tetr. p. 682). Dalila's lack of repentance, in itself, emphasizes her disregard for God; moreover, she establishes her allegiance to the Philistine god in her attempt to divert blame for her deed, saying,

> the Priest
> Was not behind, but ever at my ear,
> Preaching how meritorious with the gods
> It would be to ensnare an irreligious
> Dishonorer of *Dagon:* what had I
> To oppose against such powerful arguments? (SA 857–62)

She would have Samson genuflect to Dagon by condoning her actions, thereby betraying his own true God.

Acknowledging her utter depravity in considering her husband an "enemy" (SA 882), Samson correctly charges Dalila with ignorance of a wife's proper role:

> Why then
> Didst thou at first receive me for thy husband
> Then, as since then, thy country's foe profest?
> Being once a wife, for me thou wast to leave
> Parents and country; nor was I their subject,
> Nor under their protection but my own,
> Thou mine, not theirs. (SA 885–88)

If she felt genuine conjugal attraction, Dalila's desire to fulfill her wifely function would preclude any previous attachments. He recognizes that to remain tied to her in matrimony would be tantamount to accepting "the lowest slavery that a human shape can bee put into" (Tetr. p. 626). When Samson states, "This Gaol I count the house of Liberty / To thine whose doors my feet shall never enter" (SA 949–50), he affirms the spiritual disjunction between himself and Dalila. He has, in effect, issued his own divorce decree.

Only once she realizes that Samson's condemnation of her is irrevocable does Dalila expose her true motives for seeking reunion. The facility with which she "chose / Above the faith of wedlock bands" (SA 985–86), in her first betraying Samson and finally parting from him, confirms her ineptitude as his wife. Lacking true repentance or love, Dalila's pleas to reinstate the marital relationship are her only means of justifying her heinous deed; when Samson will not validate her actions, she contents herself with the meaningless "double-mouth'd" fame of notoriety (SA 971).

Samson's final indictment of "Matrimonial treason" (SA 958) fittingly concludes his encounter with his wife. Throughout, Dalila's arguments have appealed to her resumption of her role as Samson's spouse, serving to evoke his own recognition of her complete unfitness as such. In response to his denunciation of Dalila, the chorus muses:

> Yet beauty, though injurious, hath strange power,
> After offense returning, to regain
> Love once possest, nor can be easily
> Repuls't, without much inward passion felt
> And secret sting of amorous remorse.   (SA 1003–07)

Samson's reply, "love-quarrels oft in pleasing concord end, / Not wedlock-treachery endangering life" (SA 1008–09), is proof that he understands the true nature of marriage; he has assessed Dalila's fitness as his wife and found her wanting. He might have forgiven Dalila had her contrition been sincere and her love genuine. By dissolving the "disastre of a no-marriage" (Tetr., p. 605), Samson renews his alliance with God's will. His divorce from an unfit wife is the pivotal act in Samson's regeneration. When he receives Harapha, Samson has already regained his "trust in the Living God" (SA 579) and his faith that he will experience God's mercy and "final pardon" (SA 1171–72).

In both poetical marriages, Milton provides the dramatic rendition of what he proposes in the divorce tracts. While he was an avid proponent of divorce, he reserved its execution to those situations in which it was truly necessary. Compelled by the biblical account to reunite Adam and Eve after their fall, Milton depicts the reconciliation as a reaffirmation of the marriage bond. Their initial fitness as mates remains unimpaired and serves to restore their love for each other and God. In Samson's case, Milton altered the biblical tale so that he could represent the circumstances for divorce. While the biblical story makes no mention of Dalila after Samson's fall, Milton specifies that Samson banishes her because she has not fulfilled her wifely duties. In his case, divorce is a necessary step toward religious faith and love. By depicting antithetical views of married life, Paradise Lost and Samson Agonistes serve to support Milton's conviction that marriage, if it is to benefit its partners, must create a spiritual unity that will naturally join them and urge them toward reconciliation even after a marital rupture.

University of Toronto

NOTES

1. William Riley Parker, *Milton: A Biography*, 2 vols. (Oxford, 1968), vol. I, p. 240. Further references to this work will appear in the text.

2. John Milton, "Tetrachordon," in *Complete Prose Works of John Milton*, 8 vols., ed. Don M. Wolfe et al. (New Haven, 1953–82), vol. II, p. 606. Hereafter referred to in the text as Tetr.

3. John Milton, "The Doctrine and Discipline of Divorce," in *Complete Prose Works*, vol. II, p. 254. Hereafter referred to in the text as DDD.

4. Ernest Sirluck, introduction to *Complete Prose Works*, vol. II, p. 142.

5. *Milton and the Idea of Matrimony: A Study of the Divorce Tracts and "Paradise Lost"*. (New Haven, 1970), p. vii. Further references to this work will appear in the text.

6. John Milton, *Paradise Lost*, in *John Milton: Complete Poems and Major Prose*, ed. Merritt Y. Hughes (Indianapolis, 1957; rpt. 1981), vol. VIII, pp. 449–51. Further references to this and other poetry will be from this edition and will appear in the text.

7. John Milton, *Christian Doctrine*, trans. John Carey, in *Complete Prose Works*, vol. VI, p. 368. Hereafter referred to in the text as CD.

8. *The Logical Epic* (London, 1967), p. 85. Further references to this work will appear in the text.

9. Yet Milton does account for exceptions to this rule, stating in "Tetrachordon" that "the wiser should govern the lesse wise, whether male or female" (589).

10. Halkett, p. 110, suggests that Eve's correcting her husband regarding the storage and preparation of food in Book V (321–30) represents Milton's desire to "show some natural superiority of Eve over Adam in the management and disposition of household goods."

11. It is interesting, in this regard, that Halkett observes, "Eve's submission to Satan might be considered a form of infidelity to Adam" (p. 125).

12. For a full account of Eve's process of repentance and renovation, see Mary Ann Radzinowicz, "Eve and Dalila: Renovation and the Hardening of the Heart," in *Reason and Imagination: Studies in the History of Ideas, 1600–1800*, ed. J. A. Mazzeo (New York, 1962), pp. 155–81.

13. "A Defense of Dalila," *Sewanee Review* LXVIII (1960), 240–55.

14. To suppose, as many critics do, that Milton portrayed Dalila as Samson's wife so that he could attack his own first wife is to attribute to Milton vengeful motives without warrant. As Parker, *Milton*, p. 317, points out, any parallels to be drawn between Milton's life and works would imply Eve as the embodiment of Mary Powell, since she was a first wife who strayed once and returned to win her husband's love and forgiveness.

15. "Question and Answer in *Samson Agonistes*," *Critical Quarterly* XI (1969), 243.

16. "Dalila: The Worst of All Possible Wives," *Studies in English Literature* XIII (1973), 142. Weinkauf focuses on the prevalent attitudes of the era, sometimes without accounting for Milton's own views in the divorce tracts.

17. Samuel Hornsby, "Penance of the Hyaena," *Philological Quarterly* LVII (1978), 353–58, also suggests that Dalila's insincerity is underscored by her choice of the word "penance" to describe her motivation. In *Christian Doctrine*, Milton differentiates between "penance" and "repentance." Only the latter includes sincere sorrow for sins committed and results in renovation (Hornsby, 355). Laurie P. Morrow, "The 'Meet and Happy Conversation': Dalila's Role in *Samson Agonistes*," *Milton Quarterly* XVII, no. 2, 38–42, also points to Dalila's refusal to acknowledge her sin as the contrast Samson needs to himself become fully repentant. Ironically, Morrow describes the couple's bitter invective as being just the "meet and happy conversation" which Milton argues "marriage ideally ought to be. The similarity between Samson's and Dalila's faults makes the 'meet' companions indeed, and their conversation is ironically a 'happy' one, for it results in Samson's recognition that he can receive God's forgiveness" (41). But this recognition results from Samson's understanding of the irreconcilable differences between them, not their similarities.

18. *The Blaze of Noon: A Reading of "Samson Agonistes"* (New York, 1974), p. 152.

19. *Toward "Samson Agonistes": The Growth of Milton's Mind* (Princeton, 1978), p. 37.

MAKE WAR NOT LOVE:
ON *SAMSON AGONISTES* AND
THE CAUCASIAN CHALK CIRCLE

Jacqueline DiSalvo

IN TYPICAL Miltonic fashion the hero of *Samson Agonistes* comes to understand the political and military failure of his mission of liberation as a moral failure of disciplined self-government. Thus, having resisted the indulgence of drink, but relinquished his military power in succumbing to other sensual temptations, he remorsefully asks: "What boots it at one gate to make defense, / And at another to let in the foe, / Effeminately vanquish't."[1] Milton's confusing imagery here fuses sexuality, gender, and war. Samson yields to an assault upon a sexual orifice femininely conceived as a "gate," failing "to make defense" against Dalila, a female ravisher. The irruption of Samson's defenses by the Philistines was made possible because he has forfeited his manhood, being first penetrated, not just by Dalila, but by his own desire, projected as a female aggressor. This perplexing account reverses inside and outside, male and female roles in sex, and such inversions only make sense because in Milton's discourse desire is feminine. So (although the image of an actual female assailant continues throughout the text), Samson is "effeminately vanquish't" not just by a woman, but as a woman. Since Milton's poem presents the feminine as subversive of military valor and such valor as masculinity writ large, an analysis of that text will allow us to question the relationship of gender and war.

Historical readings of *Samson Agonistes* have presented it as manifesting either the politics of the English revolution and its New Model Army or the politics of gender. Arguing the former, Christopher Hill has written that "Milton's additions to and deviations from the story in Judges are all most easily explained if we assume that he is thinking of Samson as in some sense a symbol of the Good Old Cause or its army."[2] Arguing the latter, John Guillory has said the work reflects the seventeenth-century transformation of the sexual division of labor and "sets the vocation of the husband against the demands of the housewife." In this structure, he contends, "it does not matter . . . that Samson's vocation . . . takes the form of violent struggle against the Philistines."[3] But Dalila's appeal to "make love not war" echoes a female role that goes back as far as *Lysistrata*. So, having analyzed *Samson* both as a drama of the English revolution and as a psychodrama of gender, rooted in the same split spheres of vocation and domesticity, I couldn't help thinking that this linkage between sexuality, gender and war mattered very much. This essay, therefore, will attempt to meld these two readings of Milton's work, as a drama of sexuality and gender and of revolution, into a single, composite interpretation.

In this context, I was struck by the extent to which the plays of Bertolt Brecht involve the same contraries of women and warriors. Nor is a comparison of these authors so peculiar as it might first seem: both were political polemicists whose writings were conceived as adjuncts to contemporary movements for revolutionary change, and both seemed to envision to that end a reconstructed drama. Among Puritans Milton is exceptional in imagining a reformed drama, having speculated, before Parliament closed the theaters, whether "Dramatic constitutions . . . shall be found more doctrinal and exemplary to a Nation" (YP I, 814–15). Renaissance and Jacobean drama had already been a vehicle of political criticism. After an era of innovative political practice, what is so new in *Samson*, as later in Brecht, is drama as a guide to radical political action, not merely as a critique of the established order.[4]

With Milton, Brecht shared a perspective in which gender is contextualized by political struggle; however, Brecht advocated a politics which was in many ways directed against the institutions and values originating in the seventeenth-century revolution which Milton celebrated. Thus, a comparison of these two revolutionary dramatists provides a lens through which one might see what is historically specific in Milton's representation. To reveal the issues involved in the construction of Milton's discourse, therefore, one might place it against the foil of a subsequent radical art which both adopts and reorganizes it.

In attempting to sever *Samson*'s legacy of militant resistance from the ideologies of gender and class in which it is entangled, I found that into my hand leaped the double-edged sword of the figure of the woman warrior, so often the protagonist of Brecht's plays. In such women, Brecht offered a contrasting approach to militancy which snythesized the values Milton so deliberately sets asunder. This study, therefore, by letting Brecht read Milton, proposes to decenter Milton's representation of gender and revolution in *Samson Agonistes* by relocating from its margins the image of the female militant which disrupts the text.

Samson's conflation of gender and war makes it susceptible in many respects to a critique by feminist pacifists. However, the comparison to

Brecht, who shares some feminist assumptions about woman and peace, introduces a more dialectical perspective, since Brecht also endorses a Miltonic view that distinguishes wars of conquest from wars of liberation. Consequently, Brecht also privileges militancy as a strategic necessity over the purely private, domestic values identified with women. Nevertheless, this association of women and peace leads to opposite strategies: Milton sets warriors against women while Brecht forces women to become warriors. The reason for this contrast, I will argue, is the following: Milton fuses masculinity and war so that "manhood," defined by the unconscious assumptions of a masculine psychology of separation, becomes a metaphor in which the exigencies of struggle are merged with and become a cover for a political ideology of individualism; Brecht uses the figure of the woman warrior to force a disjunction between militancy and masculinity in order to distinguish the means of struggle from its political ends, which he symbolizes as maternal.

I. Venus Against Mars

The motif of masculine war versus feminine love was a commonplace in the Renaissance, but its uses were ambiguous. In arguments for male supremacy, misogynists like Joseph Swetnam vaunted that "a man triumphes at warres, but a woman rejoyceth at peace." Feminists like Constantia Munda, in response, defended their sex for its more peaceable values.[5] The myth of Mars seduced by Venus was, Stevie Davies reminds us, "a favorite one in the period," often taken to signify "the triumph of the subtle and cosmic power of Love over the martial and aggressive power of the heroic tradition of arms."[6] But the opposite conclusion might easily be drawn, admonishing men to beware, lest they be seduced from the glorious arms of war to the emasculating arms of a woman. Shakespeare exploits these ambiguities in *Antony and Cleopatra,* and, as Guillory cogently demonstrates, Milton's allusions identify Dalila with Cleopatra and her opposition of the "venereal" to the martial.[7] Among these alternatives *Samson Agonistes* privileges war over love, criticizing Dalila's betrayal of Samson allegedly for love:

> I knew that liberty
> Would draw thee forth to perilous enterprises
> . . . .
> Here I should still enjoy thee day and night,
> Mine and Love's prisoner. (803–08)

Since Shakespeare's text weaves the mythic opposition of Mars and Venus into a whole web of Renaissance associations, the interpolation of *An-*

tony and Cleopatra into *Samson Agonistes* implicitly, and at times explicitly, invokes the entire complex. In this chain of intertextuality, we can begin to observe Milton's fusion of male gender and revolutionary war.

Antony is termed "this Herculean Roman" (*Ant.* I, iii, 83), but Shakespeare's portrayal of him draped in female garments recalls not the triumphant but the humiliated hero in the story where he is similarly garbed by Omphale and forced to slave at her loom. But Samson is also a Herculean strong man, emblematically associated with Hercules's pillars. The Omphale motif is imported via Shakespeare into the story of his effeminate submission to Dalila (with change of coif substituting for change of dress): as Antony loses himself in "dotage" (*Ant.* I, ii, 19), Samson is "enslav'd / With" it (*SA* 1041–42). Moreover, the myth is given an even more ominous cast by the Chorus, whose denunciation of Samson's traitorous wife for "cleaving mischief" (1039) alludes to Hercules's wife Deineira, who sent him an envenomed robe in her attempt to regain his love. Thus Milton's conflation of these mythic variants reconstructs a complex in which Antony, Hercules, and Samson are seduced by women to an effeminacy that both endangers their lives and undermines their heroism.

But Shakespeare also introduces another hero who anticipates Milton's emphasis on the national and political significance of such a threatened mission. The central parable for such temptation was, of course, the *Aeneid*, cited in Shakespeare's comparison of Antony and Cleopatra to Dido and Aeneas as the root myth for his Roman tragedy. In his celebration of the valiant institution of Roman civilization, birthplace of Christianity, Virgil provided both the foundation and model for Renaissance civic and national aspirations. Within that saga, Dido, queen of Carthage, had proposed to subvert the march of civilization and Providence itself by tempting Aeneas to abandon his martial mission for her love.

But Milton, who had Virgilian aspirations, intimates a link between Samson and Aeneas in his prose. He had claimed a Virgilian legacy for his *Defences* of the Civil War: "as the epic poet . . . undertakes to extol, not the whole life of the hero whom he proposes to celebrate . . . but usually one event of his life (. . . the arrival of Aeneas in Italy) . . . so let it suffice . . . to have celebrated at least one heroic achievement of my countrymen" (YP IV, i, p. 685). Milton clearly hoped the Puritan revolutionaries would, like Aeneas, initiate a new stage of civilization. Significantly, *Areopagitica* substitutes the biblical Samson for the classical Aeneas as the image of that renovation in a "noble and puissant Nation rousing herself like a strong man after sleep, and shaking her invincible locks" (YP II, p. 558). Joseph Wittreich has demonstrated the politically charged use of the Samson story in Milton's era when its iconography was batted back and forth between left and right.[8] In the 1640s radicals commonly identified themselves with Samson, as did John Lilburne, the Leveller, who threatened his persecutors that he would "by his death, so doe them (Sampson like) more mischiefe then he did them all his life."[9] Thus too Milton in the *First Defence* had defended Cromwell by comparison to "the heroic Samson" who, "though his countrymen reproached him . . . still made war single-handed on his masters, and, whether prompted by God or by his own valor, slew . . . not one but a host of his country's tyrants. . . . Samson therefore thought it not impious but pious to kill those masters who were tyrants over his country, even though most of her citizens did not balk at slavery" (YP IV, i, p. 402).

Several studies have argued a political significance for Milton's dramatization of the Judges story as well. Mary Ann Radzinowicz presented it as a moral analysis of political defeat, that "prophesied a potential political movement through the educative power of the tragedy itself," which debated "questions of religious, domestic and civil liberty." Christopher Hill has catalogued numerous references to the revolution and its army. I have elsewhere proposed that Milton's drama be seen as his poetic *Defence of the English People*, a call for fidelity to those values by which the "armed saints" of Cromwell's New Model Army had hoped to fulfill a providential mission to establish an English republic. By presenting Samson's battle as one against a decadent, luxurious, idolatrous, reveling Philistine aristocracy, I argued, Milton parallels it to that of Cromwell and the New Model Army and endows the Puritans' armed struggle against monarchy with biblical precedent, sanction, and moral principles.[10]

But, having suggested the contemporary significance of Milton's Mars, we must now return to Venus. If Samson represents not just a revolutionary warrior, but the revolution, then by rendering Dalila as a biblical equivalent of Dido, the enemy of the militant austerities of masculine heroic achievement, Milton seems to offer the startling judgment that the revolution itself was "effeminately vanquish't." However, before we can understand the significance of his opposition of revolutionary virtue to feminine domesticity and love, we must develop a theory of gender difference relevant to *Samson Agonistes*.

II. SAMSON AND THE SEXUAL DIVISION OF LABOR

As Guillory and I have both argued, the work's fundamental conflict involves the split spheres of Samson's masculine vocation and Dalila's feminine domesticity.[11] Samson insists he is "no private person but a person rais'd" for glorious public achievement while scorning Dalila's defense that for her also "to the public good / Private respects must yield" (868) with his contention that her role as wife should have precluded other duties. *Samson* revolves around these split spheres and the threat of seduction by Dalila to "effeminate" idleness at the "household hearth" (566). Underlying this discourse is what Roberta Hamilton has described as the contemporary "decline of the family as a unit of production" in which husband and wife labored together to produce a common income. A new sexual division of labor arose which was based upon "the separation of production from consumption, work from home, housework from work and public from private."[12]

This structural division, I have argued, is also the basis of the gender psychology of Milton's drama. Feminists once tended to minimize difference entirely as mere social convention aimed at female subjection. More recently many have come to accept a socially relative gender difference while still rejecting biologically fixed variations and inequality. Such distinctions have been traced to the sexual division of labor based upon the primary role of women in "mothering," not merely as child bearing, but as physical and emotional nurturance for the privatized family. Psychological theorists such as Nancy Chodorow have pointed to this differentiation of parental roles, and particularly to the different relations of boys and girls to a female mother, as the basis for different gender psychologies. Gender formation requires that boys go through an early crisis of "dis-identifying" with the mother. This process of excessive separation requires the repression of emotional and sensuous needs focused upon the mother in order to acquire a gender identity as "not-feminine." The oedipal crisis and later socialization to male vocational roles build upon this profound early differentiation. Contrarily, girls, by maintaining identification with the mother, already embody a relational orientation that prepares them for nurturance.[13]

In these terms I have read *Samson* as a psychodrama in which Samson must resolve an apparently aborted childhood masculine psychogenesis. Samson's fall through excessive dependency on Dalila repeats that earlier failure of separation. Milton's curious erasure of Samson's mother from the Judges story and the fact that Samson's attachment to Dalila has left him "helpless as a child" as the play opens are two of many indications that Milton invests the romantic bond with such an infantile component. Samson experiences what Chodorow calls a dissolution of gender, and Milton a fall into "foul effeminacy" (*SA* 410). Samson must then reverse this regression through the plot's psychoanalytic process.

Dalila invites him to return to a symbiotic state in which, as his mother-nurse-lover, she will merge nurturance and eroticism. By rejecting this offer he can "dis-identify" with Dalila, his mother, and the "effeminate" desires for the relationship and pleasure which he has focused on women. By separating a second time and thus reasserting his autonomy, Samson simultaneously recovers his manhood and his political mission. Given the overlapping associations Guillory and I have traced (with vocation a masculine prerogative defined in opposition to a maternal role and its correlate feminine psychology), what this convergence proves is that his vocation was always fundamentally one to masculinity anyway.

III. THE WAR AGAINST WOMAN

It is no indifferent matter, however, that this is a military vocation, for in Milton's drama of violent action and inner identity, the congruence between Samson's masculinity and his militarism is repeatedly underscored. He has a vocation to war before he is even born. "Himself an Army" (*SA* 346), he wages war single-handedly against the Philistines, despising his countrymen's attempts to curtail his belligerence and negotiate a contemptible peace. He describes his inner state as war with "Thoughts my Tormentors arm'd with deadly stings" (623) and as a "fort of silence" (236) under seige by women, for the language of Samson's psychological conflict is invariably military. Relations with women are viewed as a combat in which he is "overpowr'd" (880) by an enemy whose emotional initiatives are described in military terms as a match for his military prowess. The woman of Timna "wrested" his riddle; Dalila "assay'd with . . . amorous reproaches" "With blandish't parlays, feminine assaults / Tongue batteries . . . / To storm me overwatch'd" (403–05) to make him her and love's "Prisoner" (808).

Nor are these just metaphors, for at the center of Milton's plot is a conflation of gender and war in the representation of woman as the enemy equally of Samson's nation, vocation, and manhood. Samson's hair signifies on one level his martial strength, on another the fear of castration or feminization. His secret, thus, is at once a military secret, giving the Philistines power over him, and "secrets of men" (492) — that is, of manhood as harboring a feminine core of identity. Dalila is able to penetrate both aspects and undermine his prowess by discerning and manipulating the dependency and desire it subsumed. In her acknowledged design to sabotage his military vocation and bind him to her bed in possessive attachment, she makes domesticity an obstacle both to the liberty of masculine action and to the independence of the male ego itself. In becoming thus "enslav'd by dotage," Samson suffers what he perceives as an emasculation which threatens both his male autonomy and his military mission, and which does in fact result in physical as well as psychological slavery. With all the doubling going on here, all the wars become one: Samson has a war with women which is an interior war with his own "feminine" side, a self-division revealed by maternal allusions to be rooted in the boyhood battle to become "not mother," a conflict which has left him in an all too common male condition of being at war with the world, a psychic stance he acts out as warrior par excellence in a vocation whose primary enemy has become, even in strictly military terms, not opponents' armaments, but the traitorous arms of a woman.

Some feminists may imply an essentialist picture of men as biologically greedy and warlike and women as cooperative and peaceful, but others, by rooting gender difference in the "split spheres" of an ongoing sexual division of labor, have attempted to develop a more contingent relationship between gender and other social values. Thus, Nancy Chodorow presents the process of male individuation as having wider social consequences. Freud's picture of human nature becomes for her an account mainly of masculine nature, emerging from the frustrations of separation, frozen in the conflict of self and other, and hence determined aggressively to control objects in the world, asserting self against others in "primary mutual hostility."[14] Similarly, Carol Gilligan holds men's excessive separation responsible for their tendency to see human society in adversarial terms and to formulate an ethic of restraints necessary to defend clashing rights and interests. In contrast, she found women, operating on symbiotic expectations, as tending to emphasize an interdependency which requires that apparent discord be overcome through attempts to meet the needs of all involved.[15] Within this framework, the male perspective is better suited to the world of competition and contracts as well as that of conflict and war. Three characteristics — individualism, asceticism, and aggression — are pointed to by such commentators as linking a male realm of capitalist production, masculine psychology, and the role of warrior.

IV. SAMSON'S MANLY MILITARISM

Such parallels were common to Puritan discourse, where the image of the "warfaring Christian" frequently used military discipline as a prime example of the moral life. Samson was typically a symbol of a failure of discipline; thus had John Downame compared Christian souls to soldiers going forth to battle and warned them against listening to the siren music of the world, lest they awake strengthless from Dalila's lap to be defeated by Satan.[16] Similarly, Milton's dramatization of the conflict between "liberty" and "bondage" in the multiple layers of his text attributes Samson's military defeat to a failure of autonomy and asceticism. Hence, the strategic necessity for such virtues in the struggle for liberation provides a narrative cover for the representation of masculine psychology and an individualistic political ideology as mutually legitimating discourses.

The hardships of military life do provide a pragmatic rationale for stoicism and discipline; Samson's dereliction with Dalila violates his commitment as a liberator and is a form of sleeping on the watch that can't be indulged in battle. Milton always praised the moral advantages of the New Model Army and Cromwell, their commander, who, having first "acquired the government over himself" was thereby assured of victory over others. Samson partly exemplifies such austerity since "Desire of wine and all delicious drinks / Which many a famous Warrior overturns / Thou couldst repress" (*SA* 540–42). Yet his downfall, as we have already observed, was a failure of such discipline, for "what avail'd this temperance not complete"? (558).

There is, however, a gender aspect to such asceticism which has been traced to male psychogenesis and that repudiation of infant emotional sensuous pleasure in its mother which is intensified in boys by the requirements of gender and the oedipal crisis' repression of their childhood sexuality. For Samson both personal autonomy and military effectiveness are endangered by an "unmanly" desire. Thus, when he "fell / Of fair fallacious looks, venereal trains, / Soft'n'd with pleasure and voluptuous life" (534), it was because a woman had seduced him to the "foul effeminacy" which "held me yok't / Her Bondslave" (410–11).

Freud claimed that the weaker oedipal formation in girls (who retained their primal maternal love object) had rendered them less "moral." What is crucial here, however, as Gilligan argues, is the definition of morality. Such asceticism has not only been identified with masculinity but also with the disciplined work ethic of capitalism whose rise, according to Norbert Elias, required a massive relinquishing of sensuality. Thus, according to Chodorow, male psyches, created by alienation from the maternal sphere, are uniquely suited to "the alienated capitalist work world" because the same repressions, denial of feeling and of attachment, promote inner direction, rational planning, and a generalized achievement orientation.[17]

Feminists have seen the male ego ideal, with its emphasis on competitive success, violence, and domination of women, as a form of psychic compensation for such renunciation. Karen Horney found fierce aggression to be the consequence of infant separation and frustration.[18] But since greater aggression has been the most consistent characteristic differentiating males from females, feminists have related it to the exaggerated separation of male psychogenesis. Samson only repudiates his desire by transmuting it into aggression against its object, rejecting Dalila's touch with a "rage to tear thee joint from joint" (SA 953). Moreover, since primal separation from a woman has an oedipal component, the text implies a psychological level to Samson's bellicosity, its infantile component revealed in Milton's doubly phallic language when with "his sword of bone / A thousand foreskins fell" (143–44). His need for military invincibility seems a direct inversion of his being emotionally overwhelmed by women. Not only is his combative challenge to Harapha typical of masculine competition, but its immediate source is his antecedent fury at Dalila, whose murder among the Philistines is conveniently hidden in his political massacre. Since the virility he then acts out as violence has strong erotic overtones ("I feel some rousing motions in me," SA 1382), masculine violence appears as an eroticized aggression.

Our ideological suspicion is most aroused, however, by Milton's conflation of Samson's battle for national liberation with masculine self-sufficiency. Not only is slavery to sensuous and emotional desires seen as the root of all bondage, but their suppression also requires a wariness of all relations in which their fulfillment is sought. In the close intertwinement of his marital and political affairs, he is in a perpetual state of flight from women, his enemies, and even his own people, who "love Bondage more than Liberty" (270).

"Liberty" is, of course, the most privileged term in Miltonic discourse. Samson, "who stood aloof . . . insupportably" (135–36), is a literal embodiment of independence; as a "Nazarite" he is not only vowed to asceticism but is by definition "separate" "to God" from human relationships. As Milton's Defence stressed that Samson "made war singlehanded . . . though the greater part of his country refused not tyranny," his drama underscores his hero's "Single Rebellion" (1210), as a "single combatant" (344), emphasizing his alienation even from his own people. Among the judges, however, Samson was unique in being an individual champion rather than a military leader, for Israel's victories depended more on tribal solidarity than on stubborn individual integrity.

But isolation characterizes all dimensions of Samson's existence, separating him from the mother suppressed in Milton's text and the father who would compromise his integrity, from his alien wives, especially in his "divorce" of Dalila, as well as from a community which threatens to draw him into their "servitude" (SA 269), social cohesion in Milton invariably suggesting a passive conformity. Even Samson's revival fails to free him from the "Dungeon of [him]self" (156) as he departs, "cut off" (764, 1157) from all human contact to violently confront a world made up entirely of enemies.

But, as Gilligan suggests, the world men tend to see as a collection of individual atoms is also a world of collision and combat.[19] The anarchic Samson seems forced into a state of perpetual violence in defense of an autonomy so total that any human connections—to family, wife, nation—would circumscribe it. A circular narrative pattern of redundant escape and captivity, in which he must repeatedly break out of a confinement his violence itself had provoked, intimates a relationship between that violence and his autarchy. After he attacks the Philistines in vengeance over his first marriage, the Jews turn him over to them, but he escapes, killing a thousand enemies; he is then free until his liaison with Dalila allows the pattern of vengeance and escape to be recapitulated—the Philistines avenging his violence with captivity, Samson avenging his captivity to both Dalila and her nation with violence. Finally, the drama's paradoxical imagery of liberation and bondage, victory and defeat, culminates in his final act as, by thrusting asunder the pillars containing him in hope of breaking Israel's bonds, he achieves "death who sets all free" (1572). The necessary concomitant of his demand for a total asocial "liberty" is perpetual combat, and death is its only adequate fulfillment.

Thus, while Samson's discipline and aggression might be partly justified by his martial mission, his individualism seems more a cause than a requisite of such militancy. Ultimately in Milton's poem the significance of such independence is, as its overdetermination reveals, ideological. Politically Samson becomes a "league breaker" to accomplish "Israel's Deliverance" (*SA* 225) from its Philistine "yoke" to national self-determination, but independence also signifies manly autonomy, physical freedom from his captors, military assertiveness against his enemies, emotional detachment from Dalila, religious nonconformity toward idolatry, moral responsibility, spiritual election, political integrity against Hebrew collaboration, and civil resistance to tyranny. Although Milton poses Samson's resistance to Dalila, Manoa, and his people in terms of the virtues required of a liberator, such self-sufficiency seems to have more to do with the individualistic ideological premises of his revolution. Its economic foundation is suggested in Samson's preferring "to drudge and earn my bread" (573) to the "thraldom" of dependency on his father or wife. In contrast, as we shall see, to Brecht, Milton's and Samson's political goals involve neither the meeting of human needs nor the supplanting of domineering relationships by more cooperative or supportive ones. And that, finally, is why Milton represents revolutionary virtues as a hypermasculinity whose primary threat is the "feminine" and maternal vocation to nurturance and interdependence.

V. Feminism and Pacifism

Associations between masculine emotional paranoia, misogyny, and aggression have produced in feminists like Dorothy Dinnerstein the suspicion that this psychology has perverted the whole enterprise of a male-defined civilization and that misogynist rage at the mother has fostered a cultural predilection for war. Popular discourse has always linked masculinity with war: you send a boy to the army to "make a man out of him." Since Virginia Woolf's *Three Guineas* argued that women, in their alienation from male power, comprised a "Society of Outsiders" whose liberation was a prerequisite for peace, a growing feminist literature has linked women to peace movements and patriarchy to war.[20]

Again, feminists seeking a historical analysis that produces strategies for change root these associations in the sexual division of labor. In "Public Nurturance and the Man on Horseback," Elise Boulding traces the origins of patriarchy to a new relationship between militarism and domesticity emerging from an era whose beginnings, interestingly, can be found in Israel in the period of Judges. Boulding identifies the complex changes through which hunter-gatherer and horticultural communities evolved into complex stratified societies with a transformation of the division of labor, first to rank based on skill and then to class differences in access to resources. With population growth and heightened conflict between peoples, rewards were allocated particularly for military ability. A specialized warrior class emerged which doubled as administrators, and "eventually the elected battle leader became the military king." Boulding sees a concomitant change in the sexual division of labor, arguing that among nomads both sexes often received combat training since everyone rode horses, but among settled peoples training became limited to men. In these new forms of warfare and settled life, the maternal role and a new segregation of the domestic sphere excluded women, "Thus the role of the man on horseback was invented," and "the practice of settled life . . . life to another social invention . . . the specialized hearth-tending role for the female . . . a euphemism for assigning all personal care of children and adults to women."[21]

These and other assumptions of contemporary feminist treatments of war can be illustrated by Marge Piercy's poem, "The Emperor" with its condemnation of "Evil old men . . . / Who rule the world," through "the Male Principle of corner and kill": "You are the God of the Puritans / playing war games on computers: / you can give birth to nothing / except death."[22] Piercy draws her archetypes from a prevailing feminist myth of the overthrow of a mother/love Goddess by a father/ruler/warrior God (Jehovah-Zeus-Mars). While historical development is far more complex, feminist historians like Boulding allow the poet to assume some reality behind this myth of an ancient triumph of patriarchy over an earlier, presumably less sexist, more egalitarian and pacific realm.

Since the sexual division of labor is a legacy bequeathed to modern society, so is its mythical expression, and the ancient Royal Father God becomes "God of the Puritans." Piercy's archetypal patriarch symbolizes the superimposition on these archaic symbols of all the gender polarities which we have found in Milton: the split spheres of production and reproduction and of war and nurturance, the psychological differences of gender, and the conflicts within the male psyche. Thus, the triumphant "Male Principle" is identified with a cruel lust for power and empire, manifest as "the Father Who Eats His Young" in war (missiles, war games, bombs), and technological domination of nature, till "the wheel of all seasons is broken / and life spills out in an oil slick to rot the seas." All of which proceeds from an obsession with "profit":

> All roads lead to the top of the pyramid on the dollar bill
> where hearts are torn out and skulls split to feed
> the ultimate ejaculating machine,
> the ruling class climax by missile.
>
> . . . .
>
> It is reason enough to bomb a village if it cannot be bought.
>
> (8–11, 15)

As in Dinnerstein, Piercy's sexual imagery traces such social disaster to a perverted male psyche, paranoid about relationship:

> Heavy as dinosaurs, plated and armored,
>
> . . . .
>
> You exiled the female into blacks and women and colonies.
> You became the armed brain and the barbed penis and the club.
>
> . . . .
>
> withered your emotions to ulcers,
> strait-jacketed the mysteries
> and sent them into shock therapy.　　　(16, 19–20, 23–25)

Thus have these patriarchs created a world of total war, an ecological, political and emotional wasteland, by excluding the female principle of reproduction and nurturance, which is life-giving and interdependent, for

> There is in the dance of all things together no profit
> for each feeds the next and all pass through each other,
> the serpent whose tail is in her mouth,
> our mother earth turning.   (27–30)

Since the two most exclusive gender roles remain those of male soldier and female mother, feminist theorists argue that just as men are accommodated to war, psychological and vocational conditions orient women toward peace. Prolonged identification with the mother in girls allegedly lessens the frustration and the hostility that men project in violence. Moreover, Sara Ruddick finds the maternal role itself to predispose women against war. Women are socialized to a vocational role of "maternal practice" committed to preservation of vulnerable beings and their protection from harm through peaceful resolution of conflict. Carol Gilligan argues that the feminine "ethic of care rests on the premise of non-violence" and Ruddick that "maternal practice" produces "a distinctive kind of thinking . . . incompatible with military strategy but consonant with pacifist commitment to non-violence." Therefore, she anticipates "new possibilities for peace" when "transformation of gender and sexuality is joined with an ancient preservative love."[23]

VI. IDEOLOGY AND STRATEGY

Upon such feminist-pacifist assumptions it might seem possible to construct a consistent, if antithetical, reading of Milton's drama. However, what distinguishes the activist Milton from most other writers is a perspective simultaneously analytic and strategic which sustains a tension between commitment to ethical ideals and to a political praxis determined to advance them in concrete historical circumstances. Here comparison to the similarly activist Brecht provides a corrective against any overly idealist bias.

Thus, Brecht offers a dialectical critique of feminist pacifism which can put Samson's conflicts in perspective. For, while Brecht himself employs a kind of feminist mothering theory in his own materialist vision of history, he rejects any simple extrapolation from gender differences to political strategies for social change as hopelessly utopian. In foregrounding the relationship of gender structures to war, feminists sometimes imply that criticism of those structures aimed at changes in culture, life-style, and individual psychology will alter power relations such as militarism. Dinnerstein proposes a reversal of Miltonic discipline, a "mobilization of eros" in order to undo both psychic and political repression. Ruddick and others suggest that one can derive "non-patriarchal" strategies, such as pacifism, directly from "feminine" role and psychology.[24]

The fact that aggression pervades masculine psychology is not, how-ever, an automatically reversible proposition, for the reformation of that psychology will not necessarily eliminate all causes of war. What provoked this present study was the way such analyses, and purely ethi-cal or psychological readings of *Samson*, including my own, have often ignored the more direct strategic problems posed by power. But Sam-son, "in power of others, never in my own" (79), confined by physical as well as psychological "bonds," is above all about achieving power. Milton depicts a world of danger and domination and gives us the bleak-est image of history as tragedy: the Hebrew nation ruled by the Philis-tine whip, the bulk of it fearfully licking their masters' boots, while a resistor like Samson is displayed in torment as a threat to any followers. In the biblical picture of a surrounded and embattled Israel, forced to fight ceaselessly for living space and self-determination, Milton found a resonance with his own historical moment: his Good Old Cause aban-doned, and, as Mary Ann Radzinowicz sharply summarized it, "Crom-well torn from the desecrated grave, Milton driven into hiding, Vane delivered to the block."[25] In both worlds, signified by Samson, "Eyeless in Gaza at the Mill with slaves" (41), his people "debas't / Lower than bondslaves," torture is the fruit of conquest, and slavery, complete sub-mission to force, the only alternative to revolt. Increasingly, pacifist readings have found Samson a repudiated hero, symbolizing Milton's re-pudiation of a strategy of armed revolution.[26] Such readings generally ignore, however, how totally the Samson world is circumscribed by counterrevolutionary terror, the brute, coercive violence echoed in its language of constraint, with Samson "chain'd," "imprison'd," "ensnar'd," "entangl'd," bemoaning a tightening circle of hostile forces: "How many evils have enclos'd me round?" (194). Particularly, Samson's options for action are restricted as he is reminded when he tries refusing to perform at the Philistine feast:

> Art thou our Slave,
> Our Captive, at the public Mill, our drudge,
> And dars't thou at our sending and command
> Dispute thy coming, come without delay
> Or we shall find such Engines to assail
> And hamper thee, as thou shalt come of force. (1392–98)

Milton's treatment of Samson may express his revulsion at violence, and insist that revolution must be different than mere conquest, but this grim drama never offers pacifism as a possibility. The only challenge to the total idolatry of force, which Samson's submission to Dagon would rep-resent, is a courageous, disinterested, self-sacrificial and forceful resistance: "My Nation was subjected to your Lords, / It was the force of Conquest; force with force / Is well ejected when the Conquer'd can" (1205–07).

Like Milton, witnessing the triumph of a blood-thirsty counterrevolution over a people in 1660 unwilling to continue the fight, Brecht, a German refugee, watching democratic forces hesitate while the Nazis took over all Europe, wrote dramas of resistance from exile. The words of his dying *St. Joan of the Stockyards*, "Only force helps where force rules" (254), echo Samson's. Joan is typical of Brechtian woman warriors who give up saintly pacifism for a realistic militancy. Canonized during the depression for denouncing striking workers' militancy by the same bosses she has opposed, Joan dies recanting:

> Again the world runs
> Its ancient course unaltered
> When it was possible to change it
>
> . . . .
>
> I stayed on the sidelines.
>
> . . . .
>
> O goodness without consequences! Intentions in the dark!
> I have changed nothing.
>
> . . . .
>
> Take care when you leave this world
> You were not only good
> But are leaving a good world.[27]   (*St. Joan*, pp. 250–52)

Thus, Brecht's and Milton's plays seem to trace the same circumference of historical necessity but in opposite directions. Where Milton's male hero must repudiate his "impotence of mind" (*SA* 52) and bring his military prowess under the direction of virtue and faith, Brecht's female heroines must learn the powerlessness of a virtue and sanctity unwilling to utilize force.

VII. THE WOMAN WARRIOR IN BRECHT

This striking contrast can be instructive, for the figure of St. Joan (and Brecht wrote three St. Joan plays—see also *The Vision of Simone Machard*, his St. Joan of the French Resistance, and *St. Joan of Rouen*) provides a kind of inverted image of Samson, working the transformations of gender upon Milton's armed saint. Whereas Samson must set his masculine mission against an "effeminate" retreat, Brecht's heroines must reject, not their domestic realm, but its seclusion from the world of struggle, embracing "masculine" militancy as the indispensible means to their "feminine" ends. Within this dialectic, the values of individualism, asceticism, and aggression which characterized Samson's male militarism are completely reoriented.

While noting the presence of these motifs of woman and war, motherhood and militancy, throughout Brecht's plays, we can focus our analysis on their development in *The Caucasian Chalk Circle*. Here Milton's implicit superimposition of contemporary political reference on a historical biblical narrative is replicated in the explicit structure of Brecht's play within a play. In a prologue, two Russian communes are presented returning to a valley from which they have successfully routed Nazi troops and meeting to decide which group—the goat herders forced to retreat from their former habitat, or the fruit growers who entered to defend it—shall inhabit the liberated territory. Amid their deliberations, the tale of Grusha is performed as a kind of historical parable: an invasion has driven former rulers into exile, and in their haste they have abandoned an infant prince who falls by default into the care of this young servant girl.

Like *Samson*, both Brecht plots depict a history caught up in the tribulations of conquest and resistance. But Brecht typically reduces that nightmare to a wrenching confrontation between infant vulnerability, maternal protection, and military brutality. Thus, against a backdrop of general carnage, he foregrounds Grusha's pursuit, baby in arms, by military "Ironshirts" as she attempts to save the hunted child from marauders threatening to run a lance through it. Imaging the human condition as a conflict between nurturance and war, Brecht asks "How will this human child escape / The bloodhounds, the trap-setters" (*Circle*, p. 47)? So too from the Salvation Army soup kitchens in *Happy End* and *St. Joan of the Stockyards*, to *The Good Woman of Setzuan*, torn between feeding her own child and her poor neighbors, to the canteen wagons of Mother Courage and Widow Begbick, trailing after the armies, Simone Machard defying the Nazis and opening an innkeeper's storeroom to refugees, and the women making soup at the Paris commune barricades, maternal women are at the poetic center of Brecht's plays in narratives which unravel the problematics of nurturance. Compassion is his constant theme and nurturance the touchstone of a vision of life both grimly materialist in its insistence upon human vulnerability and optimistic about human cooperation. When he looks at human nature in its barest animal contingency, Brecht sees not just a world of predators but a mother feeding her brood. In the legendary context of the *Circle*, Grusha, the maid, comes to embody an archetypal maternity, an affirmation of the human interdependency incarnate in primal symbiosis, an ethos of "maternal care" required for the survival of needy and dependent human beings: "Help the helpless child, the helpless girl" (p. 54). Grusha hears the child calling "help me," and because "in the bloodiest times / There are kind people" and "he who hears not a cry for help . . . will never hear / The gentle call of a lover," she "bent down and sighing took the child": "Fearful is the seductive power of goodness" (pp. 45–46).

The language here is erotic, for "till night came, till dawn came" Grusha "sat with the child . . . too long she saw / The soft breathing, the small clenched fists / Till toward morning the seduction was complete" (p. 46). The implicit interconnections of symbiosis and sexuality, which in Milton's discourse represent a threat to autonomy and self-determination, become in Brecht an explicit affirmation of human interdependence and a solidarity rooted in the natural drives for survival and pleasure. Grusha faces practical choices between love and survival, lover and child; she must separate from her soldier fiance to flee the Ironshirts, marry a repulsive old peasant out of economic necessity, and risk losing her lover when he returns to find her married with a child. But Brecht's description of the lovers' engagement, after Grusha has been observed bathing half-naked in the river, indicates that his women make such sacrifices as admirably sensuous creatures. Sympathetic heroines like Shen Te, Widow Begbick, and Pirate Jenny are frequently prostitutes, and in contrast to the temperate Samson, Brecht's nurturers run saloons:

> In Widow Begbick's rolling bar
> Whatever you want's for sale
> All India has seen her car
> Before you gave up mother's milk for ale.
>
> (*A Man*, vol. 2, p. 12)

Suckling pleasures are linked here to adult ones, for Brecht's maternal ethos, with its sensitivity to human neediness, provides the basis for a humanistic hedonism. Thus, in contrast to Samson's denunciations of "lascivious lap[s]" and "venereal trains," Brecht rejects a moralism that divides women into saintly wives and whores.

Rather, he strategically mirrors but ideologically demystifies Milton's ethos of revolutionary self-denial. Several plays explicitly address this Samson theme. In the brutal parody of *A Man's a Man*, the ruthless sergeant, Bloody Five, echoes its castration symbolism when, humiliated by the erotic desires distracting him from combat, he proves his manhood by shooting it off. Brecht understands the *Samson* complex of militarism and manhood, ascetic repression and eroticized violence, and brutally satirizes it in the boast of Grusha's Ironshirt pursuer: "A good soldier has his heart in it. When he receives an order, he gets a hard on, and when he sends his lance into the enemy's guts, he comes" (p. 50). In *Drums in the Night*, Brecht's youthful distaste for asceticism is seen in his sympathetic portrayal of a returning veteran who abandons the Spartakus uprising to retreat with his fiancée to the "big wide bed," which symbolizes desire in the play. But in his last work, *Days of the Commune*, Samson's equivalent is a woman communard who refuses to be seduced from her cause, rejects a lover's temptations and even turns him over as a spy. Still, the sensuousness of these commune women alongside lovers on the barricades contrasts with Milton's moralism. Brecht adopts a pragmatic stance toward discipline summarized in *The Caucasian Chalk Circle* by the reminiscence that in fighting the fascists "All pleasures have to be rationed" (p. 20). Desires, seen not as excessive but simply as frustrated by social obstacles, need not be morally condemned, just practically adjusted. In contrast to Milton, he could find no better image for enlightened self-interest than a sensuous maternal love, the pleasure in her child which made even Grusha's sacrifices a pursuit of mutual satisfaction.

At the same time, though giving mothering qualities mostly to women risks sex-role stereotyping, Brecht is careful to deny biology as destiny.[28] Nurturers like Grusha often are not biological mothers. Rather her refusal in a Solomon-like test to tear the child from its blood mother (who seeks his inheritance) proves her the "true" mother. In replacing the physical bonds of birth and nursing, Brecht distinguishes his celebration of motherhood from patriarchy with its hereditary claims. When, in addition, Grusha is freed from a desperate marriage of convenience by an iconoclastic judge, the mystifications of monogamy and the "natural family" are negated as well. Brecht's families typically appear as matrilineal units of mothers and children, and his later plays emphasize the autonomy of the female character, ignoring her as wife or lover, defined in relation to a man, in favor of the single maid in his St. Joans or such widows as the Mother, Mother Courage, and Widow Begbick.

Consequently, Brecht's plays construct a social definition of maternity. His women nurture those ejected from the domestic sphere: orphans, fighters on the battlefield and the barricades, beggars outside the door and in bread lines. Works like *The Caucasian Chalk Circle* break down the boundary between public and private so central to Miltonic discourse. Thus, the destitution of Grusha, mothering a child outside the family, begging strangers for food and shelter, forced into a marriage of near prostitution for survival's sake, is contrasted to the new socialist conditions of the prologue. There the fruit growers have convinced the shepherds to give up their valley for an irrigation project whose increased abundance will feed them all, for where there is common nurturance, resources devolve to those who use them most maternally: "Thus what there is shall go to those who are good for it, / Thus, the children to the motherly, that they prosper, / Carts to good drivers, that they be driven well, / And the valley to the waterers, that it yield fruit" (p. 128).

Maternal bonding comes to symbolize an end to the split spheres in what might aptly be conceptualized by Boulding's "public nurturance."[29] However, whereas for her it only means the intervention of feminine values and leadership in a kind of welfare state, Brecht's vision proposes a total structural reorganization of the sexual division of labor. The maternal principle comes to define collective life in a new relationship of community and nature. Society becomes responsible for "mothering" its members and its resources, and production, reorganized for a shared abundance, is subordinated to reproduction, as the life-long rearing of human beings.

Such a goal also determines Brecht's relation to feminist-pacifist strategies. In such depictions of women, Brecht endorses much of Ruddick's and Gilligan's delineation of "maternal thinking" as well as the social significance of its ethic of preservative love and mutual gratification. Moreover, Brecht's maternal women often demonstrate precisely that affinity for reconciliation and repugnance toward violence advocated by such feminists. But Brecht presents the issue of force ultimately as one of means and ends and uses the distinction to restructure the Miltonic contraries of warriors and women, advocating "masculine" means to attain "maternal" ends. For, until the battle for a new society is won, Brecht considers it less likely that men will give up their hard-boiled military grit, than that women will have to take on "masculine" stoicism, independence, militancy, and toughness. His working-class women, women of the streets and camps, are pragmatic realists who have known few luxuries of a domestic haven and its private virtues anyway. Grusha foregoes her betrothed for a marriage of convenience; the charitable *Good Woman of Setzuan* must disguise herself for business as her hardheaded male cousin, and the Salvation Army's Hallelujah Lil must unite with the female gangster in *Happy End*, for, as its song goes, "Don't get soft, baby. For God's sake, never get soft, baby. If a small shot's noise should cause a bother, don't let it get you down; I mean you're not his father" (p. 40). Hence, it bodes a "happy end" when the charity of the Salvation Army acquires the forces of poor outlaws and "just to conquer one small bowl of soup for every poor man," forms "an army that is great and strong," "the army of the poor" (p. 70). So while Brecht shares many assumptions about the positive virtues of "maternal thinking" and derives from them his ultimate social goals, he would reject a feminist projection of them into a pacifist strategy. Like Milton in the face of reactionary terror, Brecht feared that pacifism might sometimes be, at its best, self-indulgent, at its worst a form of collaboration.

He shared, if not Milton's stereotypes, the fear underlying them — that women's powerlessness and isolation from political reality in the domestic sphere would make them oppose the "perilous enterprise" of revolution, as Dalila did. In their focus on the day-to-day survival of their families, historically women had often been very conservative, seeking a modus vivendi with the status quo. Thus, like Dalila in her submission to the Philistine rulers, Mother Courage and her canteen wagon have actually become an adjunct to the army. Political acquiescence is usually embodied by Brecht either in soldiers rendered automatons by the military or in the women who "travaillée pour l'armée," literally or metaphorically, by feeding or breeding such cannon fodder. In her opportunist attempt to preserve her own children by cooperating with military slaughter, Mother Courage brings about their deaths. Her ostensibly shrewd amoral willingness to sing her "Great Capitulation" and "march in lockstep with the rest" makes the shortsighted food provider a servant to the cannibalism that feeds on her young.

In the militant antiwar and antifascist movements of the two World Wars, Brecht's heroines combine the virtues of peacemaker and warrior. For, though Brecht's women modify Samson's ethos of autonomy and asceticism, they must finally learn his capacity for aggressive valor. In asking a peasant mother with a soldier son to hide the babe from Ironshirts, Grusha may appeal to maternity against force: "Do you want him to run children through with a lance? You'd bawl him out. No fooling with lances in my house . . . is that what I've reared you for"? (p. 55). But she also learns that, against force, maternity must be defended with force when a moment later, "looking around in despair she sees a log of wood, seizes it and hits the corporal over the head . . . quickly picks up the child and rushes off" (p. 56). In Brecht's dialectic, motherhood, the irreducible condition of an interdependent humanity, is rendered futile by the state of total war of unjust societies. Numerous plays evidence a pattern of nonviolent women forced into militant resistance. In *Señora Caraar's Rifles* a mother is determined to keep her sons out of the Spanish Civil War, but motherhood itself forces her into the fray. When her son is killed by the Fascists, she not only turns over rifles to the republicans but joins the battle. As Hitler's armies approach, Brecht's St. Joan of the Resistance, Simone Machard, feeds refugees and blows

up gasoline supplies. *The Mother* denounces Russian women for acquiescence to World War I ("There is no animal that would sacrifice its
young the way you do yours . . . for a rotten cause. You should have
the wombs torn out of you," [p. 128]), but has also had to overcome her
own hostility to her son's radical militancy and learn that real peace
has to be fought for. In the pursuit of "preservative love" and peace,
such women must become warriors, and the mothering of their own children must expand to include all who share their fate:

> Still Mother
> Even more Mother now, Mother of the many fallen,
> Mother of the struggling, Mother of the unborn, she now
> Cleans up the government. Puts stones into the rulers'
> Extorted meal. Cleans weapons. Teaches
> Her many sons and daughters the language of struggle
> Against war and exploitation.[30]

VIII. MILTON'S REJECTION OF WARRIOR WOMEN

As Simon Shepherd shows, the figure of the warrior woman had
previously enjoyed its greatest vogue in the period from Spenser's Britomart to the militant women Levellers.[31] Armed and fighting women filled
the literature of the Renaissance and early seventeenth century, from allusions to armed goddesses like Diana, to Ariosto's Bradamante and Mar-
fisa, the folk heroines Long Meg of Westminster and Moll Cutpurse, and
the stage women found in Middleton, Fletcher, Webster, and Heywood.

Thus Milton, who turned the entire cosmos into a battlefield, might
easily have portrayed a woman at arms, but one of the reasons his potentially male or female angels all seem "Masculine Spirits" is their soldierly
male mien. Eve is compared only to a Diana who has been thoroughly
disarmed. His reference to the woman warrior in *Comus* is only meta-
phoric, describing the chastity of the Lady: "She that has that is clad
in complete steel / And like a quivered nymph with arrows keen / May
trace huge forests" for none "Will dare to soil her virgin purity" (*Comus*
419–26). While such references intimate a political dimension for his
Puritan heroine, Milton explicitly restricts her to passive resistance; unable to liberate herself, her battle seems limited to defending matrimony
with the morality of self-control. Moreover, Milton attacks (as an anti-
British invention) the woman warrior Boadicea, the liberator of Britain
from the Romans, celebrated by Milton's contemporaries, excoriating "the
wild hurrey of a distracted Woeman, with as mad a Crew at her heeles,"
for representing "the rankest note of Barbarism, as if in Britain Woeman
were Men, and Men Woeman" (YP V, pp. 79–80).

It is significant, therefore, in a work structured around the feminine subversion of war, that Dalila offers an alternative reconstruction of the text, which rereads its condemnation of her emotional "assaults" as traces of her stature as a woman warrior.[32] For in war and politics, she reminds us, praise and blame are "double-mouth'd" and, however she "may stand defam'd" in Israel, in her own country,

> I shall be nam'd among the famousest
> Of Women, sung at solemn festivals,
> Living and dead recorded, who to save
> Her country from a fierce destroyer, chose
> Above the bands of wedlock
>
> . . . .
>
> Not less renown'd than in Mount Ephraim,
> Jael, who with inhospitable guile
> Smote Sisera sleeping through the Temples nail'd.   (SA 982–90)

Introducing multiple levels of cultural and historical relativity, Dalila destabilizes Milton's construction of his text around the split spheres of masculine war and feminine domesticity. For, unlike Samson and the Chorus who bemoan how among wives there is "One virtuous, rarely found / That in domestic good combines" (read "is submerged"), the Philistines apparently can appreciate a woman's public, militant achievement. Moreover, by comparing herself to Jael, Dalila insinuates such relativity into biblical history itself, opening up that great historical gulf before Samson in which (as in Boadicea's era) women not only defended but judged Israel. For the story of Jael's defeat of Sisera appears in the most ancient "Song of Deborah," prophet and judge, celebrated in Judges v as the "mother of Israel" who led Barak into battle. Milton's own songs contain no praise for such militant biblical heroines. Rather, in recounting the Judges xiii legend of a woman undermining Samson and the liberation of Israel, Milton celebrates a text whose effect was to rewrite and reverse the discourse of those "days of Jael" in which, Boulding suggests, greater tribal solidarity meant the lesser gender hierarchy evidenced in woman elders and warriors.[33]

What, then, is at stake in these representatives of woman in Milton, Brecht, and the Bible as alternatively a nemesis of militant liberators or liberator herself? The fact that Milton not only repudiates feminine "softness" in his warriors but also condemns militancy in his women reveals a fundamental overdetermination in his discourse. On one level, John Guillory (p. 111) is right in saying that a warrior Dalila threatens both gender hierarchy and the preservation of a separate and supportive domestic sphere. But this comparison to Brecht suggests other strategic and ideological concerns as well.

The fact that Milton presents an opposition to women and domesticity and Brecht locates the conflict within them is significant. Dalila's identification with Jael cannot redeem her; most likely it suggested to Milton the ominous militarism of royalist women. Yet, the civil war might just as easily have given Milton reasons to appropriate Jael, or to tell the story of Deborah and Barak, and present, as an alternative to woman as enemy, woman as comrade, not just domestic "helpmeet." Antonia Fraser notes that in that era "biblical women who had assumed some kind of active role, such as Esther, Deborah and Jael, became popular images of liberty." Elizabeth Lilburne and the Leveller women petitioners to Parliament were described as "gallant Lacedemonians or bold Amazons . . . marching with confidence to counter Tyrannie." The petitioners themselves justified their activism by citing militant women patriots such as Boadicea, for "by the British women this land was delivered from the tyranny of the Danes." In 1649, Parliament was admonished with biblical precedents that "God is pleased often times to raise up the weakest meanes to work the mightiest effects . . . we could not forebeare to make this our humblest application to you," for "God hath wrought many deliverances for severall Nations, from age to age by the weake hand of women. By the counsell and presence of Deborah, and the hand of Jael, Israel was delivered from the King of Canaan, Sisera and his mighty hosts." Thus, as John Lilburne had identified himself with Samson, his wife, Elizabeth, ever agitating for his freedom and his cause, becomes a Deborah or Jael. Lilburne said that Elizabeth, "though a Feminine," was "yet of a gallant true Masculine Spirit."[34] Although Milton named his daughter Deborah, it is hard to imagine him celebrating such militant female heroism. The Lilburnes exemplified a radical marital alternative. In treating Samson's politically disastrous choice of alien wives, Milton never even considers such a possibility — a political as well as personal marriage of fellow patriots.

More than just sexist prejudice lies behind Milton's aversion to the woman warrior. It seems to me that Brecht separates and Milton fuses issues of masculinity and militancy because Brecht separates, while Milton's individualism fuses means and ends. In Milton the strategic failure of "manhood" as commitment and discipline, with its resultant military and political catastrophe, covers a polemic for an ideology of "manhood" as a metaphor for a bourgeois revolution. In his conflation of masculinity and war a key factor is the merger of his politics of resistance in a "masculine" psychology of self-sufficiency threatened by "feminine" attachments. Now, in the context of post-Restoration isolation, fidelity to the cause did require great personal integrity, which Milton might well have experienced primarily as a matter of personal noncompliance with the new conformity. But such autonomy has as much to do with the individualistic ends of a revolution which for Milton, the Independent, primarily sought to liberate individual economic and intellectual self-activity from authoritarian constraints. Similarly, in his emphasis on individual morality, on "manly" discipline against "effeminate" voluptuousness, the strategic demands of revolutionary sacrifice serve as a cover for the ideology of accumulation we have come to know as "the Protestant ethic." Thus manhood signifies an individualism which fuses moral with military discipline, and these means of individual psychic freedom and resistance with the goal of political liberty.

In contrast, Brecht's mother-warriors are an attempt to use the conflict between women and revolution both to dramatize the tension between means and ends and to provide a metaphor which can dialectically undermine such Miltonic fusions by signifying different means and ends through which that conflict can be overcome. Thus Brecht uses maternity, with its ethos of interdependence and gratification, to represent his socialist ends, a society of mutual aid, whose communality, either in Brecht's version or in Deborah's tribes, would be as alien to Milton's perspective as Winstanley's Diggers were in his own time. Moreover, by making his revolutionaries women, Brecht replaces Milton's strategy of personal integrity with one of social solidarity and struggle that reconciles the tactical necessities of discipline with the ultimate goal of gratification.

But Milton and Brecht, as contemporary feminists, are responding to a real tension between the realms of nurturance and violence, a tension which problematizes the relationship of women both to war and revolution. Their contrary discourses—Samson must reject a domestic haven, and Brecht's women must leave it; Milton's heroes must eschew "effeminate" softness, and Brecht's heroines add toughness—both privilege valor in a public realm of struggle over private satisfaction. Both authors even see attempts by Manoa or Mother Courage to ensure their children's survival as reactionary and self-defeating. Feminists, therefore, should realize that Milton's subordination of the feminine, within acceptance of sexual division of labor, signifies not just male domination but a prioritizing of commitment to the more austere revolutionary virtues. Samson's masculinity, after all is not so much rewarded with authority and power as sacrificed for his people's liberation. Brecht asserts that in their struggle for power and liberation, women will have to take on, in addition to their other grave burdens, an equality of such sacrifice. As liberation fighters, they must accept the harsh realities of political combat, both as valor in the face of violence and a stoic postponement of gratification. Finally, like Milton's making a biblical saint his revolutionary hero, Brecht's foisting of such necessities on nonviolent, nurturant, and erotic women, offers an apologia for the disparity between means and ends in what is not the best of all possible worlds:

> Alas we
> Who wished to lay the foundations of kindness
> Could not ourselves be kind
> But you, when at last it comes to pass
> That man can help his fellow man,
> Do not judge us
> Too harshly.[35]

Milton and Samson might ask no less. Our ultimate assessments of this poet must do justice to the complexities he embodies. As he is, in many ways, a father of the institutions, psychologies, and ideologies of a culture whose limitations we must criticize and alter, our reading of him must be an agon in which we struggle to liberate our own consciousness. But he is also the original for such struggle. It is well that criticism has acquired enough detachment from Milton's values to begin to deconstruct them. A critique of Milton's ideology, however, must not ignore the praxis which was its context. We should never forget that, as his war with tyranny was never a mental war alone, but took place on a battlefield where everything was at stake, we can never underestimate the ways in which his words were governed by that practice. And the dangers of tyranny are not so remote that we have outlived our need for the militant resistance which may still remain the most uncomprehended dimension of his deeply coded polemical poems. Milton may be read differently in safety, where his assumptions can be dissected with detachment, than in struggle when he is read for inspiration and warning by that "fit audience though few," embattled and under attack as he was. As a feminist Miltonist, I may often criticize him, as here for the ways he exalts warriors to denigrate women, but I do so with some humility, realizing that the effort to resolve such contradictions will require his virtues of courage and fortitude, or what one might call a valiant Miltonic feminism.

Baruch College

NOTES

1. Quotations from *Samson Agonistes* are from John Milton, *Complete Poems and Major Prose*, ed. Merritt Y. Hughes (New York, 1957), pp. 589–60. The prose is quoted from *Complete Prose Works of John Milton*, 8 vols., ed. Don M. Wolfe et al. (New Haven, 1953–83), and subsequent references will appear in the text as YP, followed by volume and page number.

2. Christopher Hill, *Milton and the English Revolution* (New York, 1977), p. 437; see also Hill, *The Experience of Defeat* (New York, 1984).

3. John Guillory, "Dalila's House: *Samson Agonistes* and the Sexual Division of Labor," in *Re-Writing the Renaissance: The Discourses of Sexual Difference in Early Modern Europe*, ed. Margaret W. Ferguson, Maureen Quilligan, and Nancy J. Vickers (Chicago, 1986), p. 110.

4. A more conservative ideology is found, not only by traditional scholars but in recent new historicists, e.g., Jonathan Goldberg, *James I and the Politics of Literature: Jonson, Shakespeare, Donne and Their Contemporaries* (Baltimore, 1983); Stephen Greenblatt, *Renaissance Self-Fashioning: From More to Shakespeare* (Chicago, 1980). The argument for a radical tradition is found in Jonathan Dollimore, *Radical Tragedy: Religion, Ideology and Power in the Drama of Shakespeare* (Brighton, 1984); Margo Heinemann, *Puritanism and the Theatre: Thomas Middleton and Opposition Drama Under the Stuarts* (Cambridge, 1980); Christopher Hill, *The Collected Essays of Christopher Hill: Writing and Revolution in Seventeenth Century England* (Amherst, Mass., 1985); Leah Marcus analyzes the politics of "Milton's Anti-Laudian Masque" in *The Politics of Mirth* (Chicago, 1986).

5. Joseph Swetnam, *The Araignment of Lewde, idle, froward and unconstant women: Or the vanitie of them, choose you whether* (1615), p. 39; Constantia Munda, *The Worming of a mad Dogge; or A Soppe for Cerberus the Iaylor of Hell* (1617); see Linda Woodbridge, *Women and the English Renaissance: Literature and the Nature of Womankind, 1540–1620* (Urbana, Ill., 1984).

6. Stevie Davies, *The Feminine Reclaimed: The Idea of Woman in Spenser, Shakespeare and Milton* (Kentucky, 1986), p. 15.

7. Guillory, "Dalila's House," p. 112, compares Dalila's description as a ship (*SA* 710–24) to Cleopatra's barge: "Milton follows Shakespeare in most details – ship, sails, amorous winds, scent, train."

8. Joseph Wittreich, *Interpreting "Samson Agonistes,"* (Princeton, 1986), finds Samson also criticized by both Puritans and Royalists after the 1640s.

9. John Lilburne, *The Resolved Man's Resolution* (1647), p. 1.

10. Mary Ann Radzinowicz, *Toward "Samson Agonistes": The Growth of Milton's Mind* (Princeton, 1978), p. 102; Jackie DiSalvo, "'The Lord's Battells': *Samson Agonistes* and the Puritan Revolution," in *Milton Studies*, vol. IV, ed. James D. Simmonds (Pittsburgh, 1972), pp. 39–62.

11. For my full analysis of Samson's psychology, see "Intestine Thorn: Samson's Struggle with the Woman Within," in *Milton and the Idea of Woman*, ed. Julia Walker (Champaign, Ill., 1988).

12. Roberta Hamilton, *The Liberation of Women* (London, 1978), p. 24.

13. Nancy Chodorow, *The Reproduction of Mothering: Psychoanalysis and the Sociology of Gender* (Berkeley and Los Angeles, 1978).

14. Sigmund Freud, *Civilization and Its Discontents* (New York, 1961), p. 59.

15. Carol Gilligan, *In A Different Voice: Psychological Theory and Women's Development* (Cambridge, Mass., 1982). For male gender role, see also Clyde W. Franklin, *The Changing Definition of Masculinity* (New York, 1984); Jean Lipmen-Blumen, *Gender Roles and Power* (Englewood Cliffs, N.J., 1984); and Joseph Pleck, *The Myth of Masculinity* (Cambridge, Mass., 1982).

16. John Downame, *Christian Warfare* (London, 1609), p. 34.

17. Gilligan, *Different Voice*, pp. 19–23; Norbert Elias, *The Civilizing Process: The History of Manners* (1939; English trans. 1978); Chodorow, *Reproduction of Mothering*, p. 186.

18. Karen Horney, "The Dread of Women," *International Journal of Psychoanalysis* XIII (1932), 348–60. Freud alternately traced aggression to childhood repression and separation and postulated it as the projection of an essential instinct.

19. Gilligan, pp. 43–48.

20. Dorothy Dinnerstein, *The Mermaid and the Minotaur: Sexual Arrangements and the Human Malaise* (New York, 1976), and "Afterword: Towards the Mobilization of Eros," in *Face to Face: Fathers, Mothers, Masters, Monsters — Essays for a Non-Sexist Future*, ed. Meg McGavran Murray (Westport, Conn., 1983), pp. 293–309; Virginia Woolf, *Three Guineas* (New York, 1937), p. 172. Feminist antiwar writing appears in three anthologies: Wendy Chapkins, ed. *Loaded Questions* (Amsterdam, 1981); Pam McCallister, *Reweaving the Web of Life: Women and Non-Violence* (Philadelphia, 1982); Judith Steihm, *Women and Men's Wars* (Oxford, 1983), and *Women's Studies Quarterly* XII (1984), special issue on "Teaching Peace, War and Women in the Military."

21. Elise Boulding, "Public Nurturance and the Man on Horseback," in *Face to Face*, p. 275.

22. *To Be of Use* (Garden City, N.Y., 1969), pp. 99–101.

23. Gilligan, *Different Voice*, p. 174; Sara Ruddick, "Preservative Love and Military Destruction: Some Reflections on Mothering and Peace," in *Mothering*, ed. Joyce Trebilcot (Totowa, N.J., 1984), pp. 259, 233; see also "Maternal Thinking," in Trebilcot, p. 213 and "Pacifying the Forces: Women in the Interest of Peace," *Signs* VIII (1983), 471–89.

24. Dinnerstein, in *Face to Face*, pp. 293–309; Ruddick, "Preservative Love," pp. 231–262; in McCallister, *Reweaving the Web*.

25. Radzinowicz, *Toward "Samson Agonistes*," p. 96.

26. Criticism is divided about whether Samson is a hero and whether or not Milton approves of his use of force. The theme of a hero's regeneration was introduced by William R. Parker, in *Milton's Debt to Greek Tragedy in "Samson Agonistes"* (Baltimore, 1937), and came to dominate interpretation after discussion by A.S.P. Woodhouse, "Tragic Effect in *Samson Agonistes*," and John Steadman, "Faithful Champion: The Theological Basis of Milton's Hero of Faith," both in *Milton: Modern Essays in Criticism*, ed. Arthur Barker (New York, 1965), pp. 447–66, 467–83. John Carey, *Milton* (London, 1969), and Irene Samuel, "*Samson Agonistes* as Tragedy," in *Calm of Mind*, ed. Joseph Wittreich (Cleveland, 1971), pp. 235–57 first read Milton's drama as an ironic critique of its violent hero. For a pacifist reading, see Michael Wilding, "Regaining the Radical Milton" in *The Radical Reader*, ed. Wilding and Stephen Knight (Sydney, 1977), pp. 119–43; for Milton's antiwar stance, generally see Stella Purce Revard, *The War in Heaven* (Ithaca, 1980), and James Freeman, *Milton and the Martial Muse: "Paradise Lost" and European Traditions of War* (Princeton, 1980); for a rebuttal, see Robert Thomas Fallon, "*Captain or Colonel": The Soldier in Milton's Life and Art* (Columbia, Mo., 1984). Now Wittreich, *Interpreting "Samson Agonistes"* has presented impressive textual and contextual argu-

ments for a pacifist reading with an unregenerate Samson. Agreeing that *Samson* is radical drama, he disagrees with my sense of its meaning, but shows that the existence of alternative Samsons in the seventeenth century and in the ambiguities of Milton's text makes any reading a matter of interpretive choices.

27. Brecht's plays are cited in the text by volume and/or page numbers in the following editions: *Brecht: Collected Plays*, ed. Ralph Mannheim and John Willett (New York, 1972–77), vols. I–IX; *The Caucasian Chalk Circle*, trans. Eric Bentley (New York, 1947); *Days of the Commune*, trans. Clive Barker and Arno Reinfrank (London, 1982); *Guns of Carrar*, trans. George Tabori (New York, 1971); *Happy End*, trans. and adapted Michael Feingold (London, 1982); *The Mother*, trans. Lee Baxendall (New York, 1965); *Mother Courage* and *St. Joan of the Stockyards* in *Seven Plays*, trans. Eric Bentley (New York, 1961).

28. For criticism of Brecht's treatment of women see Sara Lennox, "Women in Brecht's Works," *New German Critique* XIX (1978), 83–96; see also Bernard Fenn, *Characterization of Women in the Plays of Bertolt Brecht* (Frankfort am Main, 1982). For Brecht's political vision, see Keith A. Dickson, *Towards Utopia: A Study of Brecht* (Oxford, 1978) and Claude Hill, *Bertolt Brecht* (Boston, 1975). I am indebted to Michael Strong for insights into Brecht's political aesthetic.

29. Boulding, "Public Nurturance," pp. 287–89.

30. *Gassammelte Werke*, vol. XVII, p. 1094, translated in Lennox, p. 86.

31. Simon Shepherd, *Amazons and Warrior Women: Varieties of Feminism in Seventeenth-Century Drama* (New York, 1981).

32. If my associations are valid a pacifist *Samson* would have to find a feminist subversion of sexual hierarchies as well; if Samson is a villain, Dalila, as William Empson argued in *Milton's God* (London, 1965), is a heroine and "effeminacy" is his salvation. Joseph Wittreich, *Feminist Milton* (Cornell, 1988) has now followed the logic of his pacifist reading to its feminist implications.

33. Among the Jews, settlement was only partial and gradual during the Judges period when they inhabited the hills outside not yet conquered Canaanite cities. Boulding's argument in "Public Nurturance," pp. 273–91, for military training of women in nomadic eras, therefore, supports those for greater gender equality in early Israel in David Bakan, *And They Took Themselves Wives: The Emergence of Patriarchy in Western Civilization* (New York, 1979) and Jo Ann Hackett, "In the Days of Jael: Reclaiming the History of Women in Ancient Israel," in *Immaculate and Powerful: The Female in Sacred Image and Social Reality*, ed. Clarissa W. Atkinson, Constance Buchanan, and Margaret R. Miles (Boston, 1985).

34. Antonia Fraser, *The Weaker Vessel* (New York, 1984), pp. 222, 239; Document in British Museum, E. 556(22); *The Humble Petition of divers well-affected Women inhabiting the City of London, Westminster, the Borough of Southwark, Hamblets and places adjacent* (London, 1649), pp. 4–5, B.M. E.551(14); John Lilburne, *Jonah's Cry Out of the Whale's Belly*, (London, 1647), p. 4; see also P. Higgins, "The Reactions of Women, with Special Reference to Women Petitioners" in *Politics, Religion and the English Civil War*, ed. Brian Manning (New York, 1974), pp. 178–222.

35. "To Posterity," in *Bertolt Brecht: Selected Poems*, trans. Hoffman Reynolds Hays (New York, 1959), p. 177.

MILTON'S *SAMSON* AND THE "NEW ACQUIST OF TRUE [POLITICAL] EXPERIENCE"

Barbara Kiefer Lewalski

WHATEVER CONSENSUS once obtained about *Samson Agonistes* no longer exists. For a time, Miltonists at least agreed to disagree with Dr. Johnson that the work lacks a middle — though in that middle they sometimes traced Samson's regeneration, and sometimes his tragic unregeneracy.[1] Now the middle bids fair to disappear again (at least in an Aristotelian sense) as many critics find in its place a radical disjunction between divine and human action.[2]

Moreover, all the old disputes about other aspects of Milton's dramatic poem are still with us. In terms of genre, most critics view the work as tragedy, but describe its "spirit" variously as classical, or Hebraic, or Christian; others see it as religious or liturgical drama or prophetic tragicomedy.[3] In terms of typology, some view Samson as a figure of Christ crucified; others as a Hebrew severely limited in his moral vision by the rigor and vengeance of the Old Law; and still others as a type of the embattled elect Christian throughout history and at the apocalypse.[4] In terms of date, the work has been assigned to the 1640s, to the months just following the Restoration in 1660, and also to the 1670s, as Milton's last poem.[5] Read as his last poem, it is seen as a fit conclusion to his lifelong development as a Christian humanist concerned with reasoned moral choices, and also as a radically prophetic, apocalyptic vision.[6] It is viewed as a near allegory of Milton's personal situation — Milton Agonistes — and as a treatment of the common human condition.[7] Some think the work profoundly political, others that it honors a withdrawal from the public sphere to utter inwardness.[8] When read in political terms, it is construed as a near allegory of the English Revolution and its aftermath; or as a covert call to the English Puritans to rise again; or as a repudiation of the English Revolution and of all military action.[9]

How should we try to come to terms with this cacophony of critical voices? The literary historians' usual recourse to contemporary contexts to help resolve interpretive issues has become highly problematic in

233

the wake of Joseph Wittreich's exhaustive account of the many conflicting seventeenth-century versions of Samson—elect and reprobate, suicide and Christic sacrificial type, God-appointed liberator and private
revenger or rebel.[10] *Samson* readily invites readings as a deconstructionist text, which proliferates alternative interpretations by using antitheses
and either/or constructions, and destabilizes meanings by eschewing any
authoritative vantage point. It also invites emphasis on the construction
of meaning by readers: on one view the poem's myriad unresolved questions baffle and frustrate reasoned analysis, forcing a leap of faith; on
another, the many interpretative possibilities make readers choose which
meanings they wish to give privilege to, in accordance with their own
needs and values, moral and literary.[11]

Anyone who would join—or rejoin—this critical debate at this juncture should declare his or her assumptions at the outset. The Milton I
read continually invites readers' choices, but does not mean those choices
to be undecidable, or purely arbitrary, or entirely dependent upon faith,
or wholly determined by readers' present state of moral knowledge. Milton seeks, I take it, to guide readers' choices by literary means which
encode his own choices among the multiple Samson traditions and among
the many generic and tonal possibilities. Yet our access to those Miltonic
choices is tortuously indirect, undermining supposedly authoritative or
comprehensive readings. That said, it remains important to weigh and
argue interpretative probabilities, using the best scholarly and critical
resources we can muster.

My purpose here is not to offer a new interpretative key, but rather
to follow some implications of a key word centrally important in this
text and indeed everywhere in Milton, the term *experience*. The Chorus's
final speech makes two claims: that they (and presumably we) have at-
tained tragic catharsis, "calm of mind, all passion spent;" and that they
(and presumably we) have gained a "new acquist / Of true experience."[12]
I began this essay by asking the question: What is this "true experience"
in regard to the public and political realm? That specification is warranted by the fact that Milton's hero insists so forcefully upon his role
as liberator: "I was no private but a person rais'd / With strength sufficient and command from Heav'n / To free my Country" (1211–13). *Experience* is hardly a new term in Milton criticism, but Miltonists have
chiefly focused on Milton's own life experience as reflected in his works,
or on the reader's experience in responding to Milton's texts, rather than
on Milton's concept of experience or the thematics of experience in his
poems.[13] Kathleen Swaim's suggestive analysis of a dichotomy between
experience and faith in *Samson* is a notable exception, though I mean

to argue here for a broader conception and a much more positive valuation of experience in that work.[14]

Milton's *Art of Logic* describes experience as one of the four "helpers" to reason: it judges the "common agreement" of particular instances and so provides "the principles" of any field of knowledge.[15] His tracts and poems appear to recognize four principal kinds of experience:

1. That afforded by history and cultural tradition: in *Of Education* he recommended language study because "every nation affords not experience and tradition anough for all kinde of learning" (YP II, p. 369).

2. The experience of others, made available through observation and testimony: in *Of Education* Milton proposed to augment his pupils' studies in various arts and sciences by the "helpfull experiences" of their practitioners — hunters, fowlers, fishermen, shepherds, gardeners, architects, engineers, mariners, anatomists — as well as by travel throughout England and abroad (YP II, pp. 393–94, 412–14).

3. Personal experience, what happens in one's own life: Milton's pupils were to gain personal experience in warfare, tactics, and various martial arts through war games and exercises (YP II, pp. 411–12); and Milton's divorce tracts appeal continually and poignantly to what "lamented experience daily teaches" about the desperate unhappiness of union with an intellectually unfit wife (YP II, p. 312; see also II, pp. 249–50, 742–43).

4. Interior psychological or spiritual experience — of two kinds: "the experience of a good conscience" defined in several tracts as the ground of the moral life (YP I, p. 935, II, pp. 224–25); and the illumination of the Spirit of God, such as Jesus responds to in *Paradise Regained*.[16] All of these kinds seem to be involved in Il Penseroso's final stage of life — "Till old experience do attain / To something like Prophetic strain." And also in Milton's proposed qualification for the epic poet, who cannot "sing high praises of heroick men, or famous Cities, unless he have in himselfe the experience and the practice of all that which is praise-worthy" (YP I, p. 890).

In the political sphere Milton continually invokes experience to help interpret signs and events. The *Areopagitica* calls upon England's historical experience of God's ways to gloss present political signs: "Now once again by all concurrence of signs . . . God is decreeing to begin some new and great period in his Church, ev'n to the reforming of Reformation it self: what does he then but reveal Himself to his servants, and *as his manner is*, first to his English-men" (YP II, p. 553; emphasis added). *The Ready and Easy Way* urges "seasonable use of gravest autorities, experiences, examples" (YP VII, p. 448) to stiffen resistance to the king's restoration, and marshals them from ancient and contemporary history. In *Paradise Lost* the angels appeal to their own past experience to evaluate a new political event: God's proclamation of his Son as their king. Satan reads that event as a sign of divine tyranny, since there is no basis in angelic experience for assertions of the Son's agency in their creation: "who saw / When this creation was? remember'st thou / Thy making?" (*PL* V, 856–58). Abdiel's very different interpretation is founded on the angels' direct and constant experience of divine providence: "Yet by experience taught we know how good, / And of our good, and of our dignity / How provident he is" (V, 826–28). For Milton, "true experience" is one guide to sound interpretation and right political action.

Samson Agonistes is filled with ambiguous signs and events requiring interpretation and political response from both the characters in, and the readers of, the dramatic poem. They include the wonders surrounding Samson's birth, his Nazarite breeding, the extraordinary strength that attaches to his unshorn hair, his awesome deeds, his catastrophic fall, his sense of being repudiated by God, his claims to "inner impulses" and "rousing motions," and his final destruction of the Philistines and himself. The poem achieves thereby a brilliant mimesis of the confusions attending moments of political crisis and choice. At issue are such questions as these: How is a nation to recognize a liberator raised up by God to promote change? What signs are reliable indexes of God's favor or God's rejection of leader or of nation? How can the would-be liberator know himself to be chosen (or repudiated)? What imperatives for political action follow from apparent signs of God's special interventions? How far can we generalize from particular cases to general principles, or see the past as guide to the present, or guard against deception or delusion? How does human political action relate to the course of providential history? In this work several characters weigh these issues in the light of various kinds of experience—past and present, societal and personal, secular and spiritual, objective and subjective—first in regard to Samson's catastrophic fall, and then his death.

At the outset the political question for both Samson and the Chorus is whether Samson ever had a divine mission to liberate his people. At issue is the right interpretation of past experience: how to validate and evaluate the external and internal signs that apparently testified to Samson's mission. Samson's long opening soliloquy shows him almost wholly engulfed by present pain and loss. We soon recognize his tendency to dwell upon immediate personal experience—external signs of God's favor or rejection, subjective emotional states, inner motions. Accordingly, his present anguish causes him to read the external signs that once seemed to be clear evidence of his vocation—his "birth from Heaven foretold /

Twice by an Angel" (23-24) and his "Heav'n-gifted strength" (36) — as an ironic or perverse mockery: "Ask for this great Deliverer now, and find him / Eyeless in *Gaza* at the Mill with slaves" (40-41); "God, when he gave me strength, to show withal / How slight the gift was, hung it in my Hair" (58-59).

The chorus of Danites, by contrast, tend to privilege the maxims, proverbs, and exemplary histories that codify the common cultural experience of the nation or of humankind, and to resist indications that something truly extraordinary is now happening to them. In their first ode, characteristically, they seek a formula for Samson's profound fall from glory to abject misery, and they find it in the tragic formula of the wheel of fortune:

> O mirror of our fickle state,
> Since man on earth unparallel'd!
> The rarer thy example stands,
> By how much from the top of wondrous glory,
> Strongest of mortal men,
> To lowest pitch of abject fortune thou art fall'n.   (164-69)

In their ode and agon with Samson the Danites dwell upon his wonderful past deeds but do not once refer to them as God-given signs of his political mission. They also resist his claim to an "intimate impulse" from God prompting his first marriage as an occasion to begin Israel's deliverance, and his later inference that his marriage to Dalila was sanctioned for the same political end. They imply rather that these claims are discredited by the sad result: "Yet *Israel* still serves with all his Sons" (240).

This challenge goads Samson to claim his past. He now insists that his deeds were an unmistakable sign of his special political vocation, and blames Israel's continued servitude on the blindness and political cowardice of her governors, "Who seeing those great acts which God had done / Singly by me against their Conquerors / Acknowledg'd not" (243-45), and failed to give support. Moreover, as he voices Milton's own characteristic principle that inner servitude gives rise to political bondage, Samson is able, as he was not before, to locate his personal experience within general human patterns:

> But what more oft in Nations grown corrupt,
> And by thir vices brought to servitude,
> Than to love Bondage more than Liberty,
> Bondage with ease than strenuous liberty;
> And to despise, or envy, or suspect
> Whom God hath of his special favor rais'd
> As thir Deliverer.   (268-74)

When the Chorus corroborates this generalization with the similar examples of Gideon and Jeptha, Samson pointedly insists on his place in
that historical pattern: "Of such examples add mee to the roll" (290).

For their part, the Danites' engagement with Samson during this
agon evidently leads them to come to some terms with the extraordinary. Their ode—"Just are the ways of God, / And justifiable to
Men"—acknowledges Samson's deeds and even his inner promptings as
divinely inspired, and explains the technical illegality of his marriages
to Gentile women on the principle that God is able to dispense with his
own laws.[17]

The political question in the agon between Samson and his father,
Manoa, focuses on what the divinely appointed liberator should do in
defeat. At issue now is the interpretation of present signs, the validity
of inward experience, and the relevance of past experience in new and
profoundly changed circumstances. While Manoa never doubts that Samson's former deeds of strength were signs of his God-given political mission, he does doubt Samson's divine promptings to marriage outside the
tribe. Like the Chorus, he judges by results:

> I cannot praise thy marriage choices, Son,
> Rather approv'd them not; but thou didst plead
> Divine impulsion prompting how thou might'st
> Find some occasion to infest our Foes.
> I state not that; this I am sure; our Foes
> Found soon occasion thereby to make thee
> Thir Captive and thir triumph.   (420–26)

Manoa's ransom plans are based on the commonsense view that the blind
Samson must perforce retreat to a private life, and he meets Samson's
anguished objections by reference to sinners' customary experience of
God's ways,

> Who evermore approves and more accepts
> (Best pleas'd with humble and filial submission)
> Him who imploring mercy sues for life,
> Than who self-rigorous chooses death as due.   (510–13)

But Samson's primary reference point is always his inward, subjective
experience. If his refusals sometimes sound "self-displeas'd / For self-
offence, more than for God offended" (514–15), as Manoa and Irene
Samuel claim,[18] the reason is that as yet he experiences no inward assurance of God's pardon and therefore finds no reason to try to prolong a
purposeless life. Manoa sees Samson's decision to remain at the mill as

suicidal, but Samson explains it as a legitimate and reasonable choice of work over idleness—to "drudge and earn my bread" (573).

Manoa and Samson now seek to interpret a new sign—Samson's restored hair as emblem of his restored strength. Samson can find no meaning in it, save as a public talisman of his uselessness and failure: "these redundant locks / Robustious to no purpose clust'ring down, / Vain monument of strength" (568–70). But Manoa, appealing to past experience, finds in this sign an augury of Samson's miraculous restoration to his former self and former role:

> But God who caus'd a fountain at thy prayer
> From the dry ground to spring, thy thirst to allay
> After the brunt of battle, can as easy
> Cause light again within thy eyes to spring,
> Wherewith to serve him better than thou hast;
> And I persuade me so; why else this strength
> Miraculous yet remaining in those locks? (581–87)

Reliance on past experience helps Manoa grasp the essential meaning of the sign—that God has some further use for Samson—but his failure to discriminate past from present circumstances leads him to expect a similar easy miracle now. By contrast, Samson's overwhelming present experience of sin's terrible effects—"faintings, swoonings of despair, / And sense of Heav'n's desertion" (631–32)—preserves him from Manoa's facile optimism, but leads him to find an absolute disjunction between past and present, election and reprobation: "I was his nursling once and choice delight, / His destin'd from the womb, . . . / But now [he] hath cast me off as never known, / . . . Nor am I in the list of them that hope" (633–47). Yet his strong instinct not to retreat into privateness and passivity leaves him poised to respond should that inner weather change.

Watching this encounter, and experiencing Samson's misery vicariously, the Chorus has now learned to value inward spiritual experience. Their ode—"Many are the sayings of the wise / . . . Extolling Patience as the truest fortitude"—moves quickly to admit that such proverbial wisdom offers little help to the afflicted, "Unless he feel within / Some source of consolation from above" (652–64). Echoing Job and the psalmist—"God of our Fathers, what is man"—they are led by Samson's situation to the distressing conclusion that an apparently arbitrary God often brings just and unjust alike to a miserable end.

The central political issues in Samson's agon with Dalila are the apparent cultural relativism underlying all justifications for political action, and the difficulty of assessing the truth of character beneath rhetorical claims and stereotypes. Here the interpretative focus shifts from the signs associated with Samson to the enigma of Dalila's self-presentation. The fact that Dalila is in many respects Samson's counterpart confronts Samson, the Chorus, and the reader with the difficulty of knowing inner states from external appearances. They must make what they can of Dalila's claims to repentance, her explanations based on common stereotypes, her justifications grounded upon obedience to civil and religious authority.

Dalila says nothing whatever about Samson's woeful change, or past glories, or pitiful condition; she never voices shock, she engages in no laments, she poses no metaphysical questions to the universe. Like Samson himself, Dalila speaks constantly of herself and her motives, but for all that she seems to have no interiority, no inner life. Instead she is like a figure in an emblematic pageant whose costume, words, and actions require interpretation. A feminist reading might identify Dalila as a site of all the stereotypes of the female in a patriarchal society, a woman who has so entirely internalized those cultural norms that she can only voice and enact them. I think Milton deliberately presents her in just such terms: she takes great care about her appearance, sailing in like a ship, "bedeckt, ornate, and gay," with perfume and damsel train (712–21); she weeps delicately, "like a fair flower surcharg'd with dew" (728). And she bases her excuses on feminine stereotypes: curiosity to know and tell secrets, woman's frailty, and domestic love which sought to keep her husband safe at home. But Milton does not excuse woman or man on grounds of cultural constraints from the responsibility of developing a personal conscience and an integrated self. We note that Samson continually holds Dalila and himself to the same harsh moral standard: "all wickedness is weakness" (834).

It seems clear that Samson is testing Dalila's claims against his own inward experience — the painfulness of his own struggles toward self-knowledge and true repentance — and that he finds that standard confirmed as it reveals her shallowness and deception. He also appeals to past experience, and finds it a true guide when circumstances are similar. From his past experience with Dalila and other such women, Samson promptly concludes that she is putting on a performance: "these are thy wonted arts, / And arts of every woman false like thee" (748–49). And he bitterly offers his own case to the human store of such experience, "to Ages an example." The Chorus and the reader must make their judgments wholly from this encounter, as they see how Dalila's claims of repentance, conjugal affection, and desire to make amends are gradually undermined by her constant rhetoric of self-exculpation and her myriad shifting excuses.

Dalila grounds her political arguments on the relativity of religious and national values. She also appeals to the authority of the state, claiming that the Philistine magistrates and priests urged her to betray her husband as a civic and religious duty. Finally, she appeals to authoritative maxims based on common experience:

> at length that grounded maxim
> So rife and celebrated in the mouths
> Of wisest men, that to the public good
> Private respects must yield, with grave authority
> Took full possession of me and prevail'd;
> Virtue, as I thought, truth, duty so enjoining. (865–70)

In some ways there seems little to choose between Dalila's proclaimed motives and Samson's own, since his marriage were intended to advance Israel's cause against the Philistines.[19] Samson, however, challenges Dalila's relativism by appealing to widely shared human values. With all the polemic of the English civil war echoing in the background, he flatly denies ultimate authority to civil and religious leaders, or to *raison d'etat*. He appeals first to the inward experience of love: had Dalila genuinely loved him as he did her she could not have betrayed him. He does not state but obviously means her to remember that he did not betray or harm her by his actions against Philistia. Next, he appeals to the law of nature and nations, which privileges the marital union and the loyalty of wife to husband above the claims of the magistrates or the state. The authority of Philistia's gods he refers to the judgment of reason: gods so powerless that they must resort to ungodly deeds contradict themselves, and so "Gods cannot be."[20]

Though Dalila begs forgiveness with what sounds like sincerity, and offers the recompense of loving care, Samson insists that their divorce is final—"Thou and I long since are twain" (929). His ground is again past experience: if Dalila could betray him "in my flower of youth and strength" she would certainly do worse now when he is blind and helpless. Forbidding her approach lest rage and passion overcome him, he grudgingly forgives her "at distance," and predicts that her story will become an exemplum of matrimonial treason. But her counterinterpretation of that exemplum from the Philistine perspective makes a powerful point about the relativity of fame and civic honor:

> I shall be nam'd among the famousest
> Of Women, sung at solemn festivals,
> Living and dead recorded, who to save
> Her country from a fierce destroyer, chose
> Above the faith of wedlock bands, my tomb

With odors visited and annual flowers.
Not less renown'd than in Mount *Ephraim*,
Jael, who with inhospitable guile
Smote *Sisera* sleeping through the Temples nail'd.   (981–90)

We are left to evaluate that comparison by supplying the appropriate distinctions. Jael violated, for religious and national purposes, the classical code of hospitality protecting a guest, while Dalila violated the intimate claims of love, and the high claims of marital fidelity assumed to be grounded in natural law.

The Chorus has learned something about illusion, deception, and hypocrisy from their experience with Dalila, but not much else. Not until the end do they recognize the "sting" of this "manifest Serpent" (997–98), and even then they are amazed by Samson's ability to resist her beauty and the power of former love. Their ode queries, with Freud-like bafflement, what do women want? And what is woman's nature? Taking Samson's matrimonial troubles as the norm, they offer their own masculine counterpoint to Dalila's feminine stereotypes, proclaiming man's "despotic power / Over his female" as God's universal law. The larger political questions and the subtlety of Samson's distinctions have largely escaped them; and they seek refuge from their confusion in a simplistic misogyny.

In the agon with Harapha Samson again takes up his calling as divinely appointed liberator, offering it to the trial of battle and defending it by reasoned political argument. The political issue here concerns the grounds for armed revolt and warfare against an enemy, which Samson locates both in inward experience and in recognized public sanctions.

The foundation of all is Samson's inward sense of restored vocation. When Harapha comes to "survey" him, Samson at once offers him single combat — "The way to know were not to see but taste" (1091). That challenge, in these unlikely circumstances, testifies to his renewed faith and hope, which now allow him to interpret his restored hair and strength as signs of God's renewed favor. He can now fuse his past with his present state as he proclaims the original and continuing source of his strength: "My trust is in the living God who gave me / At my Nativity this strength / . . . Which I to be the power of *Israel's* God / Avow" (1140–51). And he meets Harapha's taunts of God's repudiation with new confidence in God's pardon and his restored vocation:

> these evils I deserve and more,
> Acknowledge them from God inflicted on me
> Justly, yet despair not of his final pardon

> Whose ear is ever open; and his eye
> Gracious to re-admit the suppliant;
> In confidence whereof I once again
> Defy thee to the trial of mortal fight,
> By combat to decide whose god is God,
> Thine, or whom I with *Israel's* Sons adore. (1169–77)

The matter of public sanctions for armed revolt is raised when Harapha declares Samson a rebel, murderer, and covenant-breaker — echoing royalist denunciations of the Puritans, both during and after the Interregnum, for regicide and for breaking the Solemn League and Covenant. Samson's responses echo the basic radical Puritan (and Miltonic) justifications. First, appeals to the natural law which always allows rebellion against conquerors—"Force with force / Is well ejected when the Conquer'd can" (1206–07). And second, the liberator's public office, and the God-given strength which testifies to his divine mission:[21]

> I was no private but a person rais'd
> With strength sufficient and command from Heav'n
> To free my Country;
>
> . . . .
>
> I was to do my part from Heav'n assign'd,
> And had perform'd it if my known offense
> Had not disabl'd me, not all your force. (1211–19)

In pressing his challenges upon Harapha Samson evidently recognizes that if his arguments and his divine mandate are denied the would-be liberator can only appeal to the trial of battle. When Harapha's long series of excuses reveals him at last as a "baffl'd coward," the chorus shares so intimately in the experience of Samson's psychological recovery that—for the moment—they almost imagine him charging forth to liberate them:

> Oh how comely it is and how reviving
> To the Spirits of just men long opprest!
> When God into the hands of thir deliverer
> Puts invincible might
> To quell the mighty of the Earth, th'oppressor,
> The brute and boist'rous force of violent men
> Hardy and industrious to support
> Tyrannic power. (1268–75)

But then, recalling the harsh realities of Samson's blindness, they relegate him again to the common norm, the patient conquest over the self which is the usual exercise of saints.

The encounter between Samson, the Philistine officer, and the Chorus explores the claims and possible conflict of three kinds of authority — civil power, religious law, and the experience of inward illumination. The language and political issues recall the post-Restoration plight of the radical Puritans, faced with an idolatrous established church and Test Acts; as Mary Ann Radzinowicz argues, Samson provides an exemplary model for life and action in such situations.[22] Samson refuses the Philistine command to perform feats of strength at the Dagonalia on grounds of religious law — "Our Law forbids at thir Religious Rites / My presence" (1320–21) — and also inward sanctions — "my conscience and internal peace" (1334). While the fearful Chorus shows a disposition to yield to civil power in everything, like the ordinary, unheroic men they are, Samson holds fast by the higher authority of the religious law against prostituting holy things to idols — placing in that category his divinely restored strength. He distinguishes carefully between his refusal to submit in this religious matter and the performance of civil duty involved in his "honest and lawful" labor at the mill, "to deserve my food / Of those who have me in thir civil power" (1365–67). And he answers their case for outward conformity — "Where the heart joins not, outward acts defile not" (1368) — by differentiating actual overwhelming force from mere commands: "Commands are no constraints. If I obey them, / I do it freely; venturing to displease / God for the fear of Man" (1372–74).

Finally, he proposes divine illumination as the highest authority, affirming God's power to dispense "me or thee" from religious laws "for some important cause," and claiming an inward experience of "rousing motions" as a sign of such illumination, disposing "To something extraordinary my thoughts" (1377–83). These words indicate to the chorus the true ground of his decision to go to the temple, though he misleads the officer by ironically pretending to accept the prevailing ideology of civil absolutism: "Masters' commands come with a power resistless / To such as owe them absolute subjection; / And for a life who will not change his purpose?" (1404–06). Samson's posture as he leaves is one of openness to further illumination.

This scene has proved a major crux for critics, with its antinomian implication that all law is abrogated for the elect. But neither Milton nor Samson are radical antinomians. Samson insists three times over that the experience of inward illumination dispensing him from the letter of the law will meet the public test of fulfilling its spirit, its essential moral and religious content: "Nothing to do, be sure, that may dishonor / Our Law, or strain my vow of *Nazarite*" (1385–86); "in nothing to comply / Scandalous or forbidden in our Law" (1407–08); "of me expect to hear / Nothing dishonorable, impure, unworthy / Our God, our Law, my Nation, or myself" (1423–25). By analogy, in the *Christian Doctrine* Milton grounds his radical arguments for Christian liberty upon the entire abrogation of the Mosaic law as a law of works, yet insists that the "substance of the law, love of God and of our neighbor" is now inscribed "on believers' hearts," bringing forth good works by faith, and that it demands of Christians "a more perfect life than was required of those . . . under the law" (YP VI, pp. 530–36).[23]

The Chorus' prayer as Samson departs indicates that they now credit his inner illumination: they sense that the Spirit is leading him, and they expect that prophetic signs and wonders may again attend him. The poetic language of this prayer is a far cry from their earlier formulas and maxims, suggesting that their vicarious experience of Samson's struggle has worked some change in their consciousness:

> Go, and the Holy One
> Of *Israel* be thy guide
> To what may serve his glory best, and spread his name
> Great among the Heathen round:
> Send thee the Angel of thy Birth, to stand
> Fast by thy side, who from thy Father's field
> Rode up in flames after his message told
> Of thy conception, and be now a shield
> Of fire; that Spirit that first rusht on thee
> In the camp of *Dan*
> Be efficacious in thee now at need.   (1427–37)

At this juncture, the issue for interpretation shifts to Samson's death. Like the reader, Manoa and the Chorus have no direct access to this event: they experience it only at a distance, through several filters, and the resulting ambiguities elicit from them most of the interpretative possibilities offered by the exegetical tradition. When deafening shouts and screams of unknown cause interrupt Manoa's ironically hopeful plans to ransom Samson, he reads them as a sign that "they have slain my Son." For its part, the Chorus conjures up a Manoa-like scenario in which Samson has his eyesight miraculously restored and is "dealing dole among his foes." But Manoa now terms this idea presumptuous, probably because he cannot really believe in the present accomplishment of his nostalgic hopes.

Then Manoa and the Chorus have a text to interpret, the distraught messenger's report. Manoa's questions at first extract piecemeal answers, leading him to construe Samson's death as revenge and suicide—"O lastly over-strong against thyself! / A dreadful way thou took'st to thy revenge" (1590–91). At last the messenger provides a detailed account of what he saw and heard: Samson patiently performing feats of "incredible, stupendious force" (1627); Samson's request to rest between the pillars of the temple; his last ironic words to his captors; his destruction of the temple with all the Philistine nobility inside; the escape of the "vulgar" who stood outside. But the messenger cannot read Samson's spiritual state from the external signs: the head inclined and eyes fast fixed may equally suggest "one who pray'd, / Or some great matter in his mind revolv'd" (1636–38). Milton's much mediated presentation of this scene forces characters and readers alike to distinguish between what is necessarily hidden from them (Samson's spiritual condition, his regeneration) and what they can know clearly: that God has again enabled Samson to strike a blow for the liberation of Israel. That political insight is consonant with the qualifications Milton uses in his political tracts to judge leaders: not whether they are or seem to be regenerate, but whether they love liberty and advance its cause.[24]

What then do the Danites finally gain from their experience with Samson? For one thing, they seem now to recognize the complexity of human motives, as they offer multiple constructions of his last act: it was "dearly bought revenge, yet glorious"; it was the culmination of his divine mission; it was not suicide, since he was "self-kill'd / Not willingly, but tangl'd in the fold / Of dire necessity."[25] For another, they now display a new reach of spiritual imagination, evidenced, as Kathleen Swaim has shown, by the high poetry and richly evocative emblems and imagery in their final ode,[26] especially the striking paradox of Samson's restored vision in blindness:

> But he though blind of sight,
> Despis'd and thought extinguish't quite,
> With inward eyes illuminated
> His fiery virtue rous'd
> From under ashes into sudden flame.   (1687–92)

Manoa's "acquist" of true experience is more limited. As before when he expected Samson's blindness to be miraculously cured, so now he still remains a little too ready to discount the tragic — "Nothing is here for tears" (1721). As before when he thought to ensconce Samson as a kind of icon on the family hearth, so he now expatiates on the glorious monument he will build to Samson in his father's house. And as before he still blames Samson's troubles chiefly on "his lot unfortunate in nuptial choice, / From whence captivity and loss of eyes" (1743–44). But now he also construes Samson's death in complex rather than simple terms: it accomplished full revenge on his enemies; it was the fit end to a life heroic; and it demonstrated that God was "not parted from him, as was fear'd" (1719). Most important, Manoa can now imagine a new future, in which Samson's story might inspire other valiant youth to "matchless valor and adventures high," and his great deed might provide Israel with a new political opportunity: "To *Israel* / Honor hath left, and freedom, let but them / Find courage to lay hold on this occasion" (1715–16).

What "true political experience" does Milton's dramatic poem offer its readers—of the seventeenth or the twentieth century? I take it they are not led to repudiate political life—even revolution and battle when circumstances warrant—since the whole thrust of this work affirms Samson's divine calling to liberate his people. Joseph Wittreich's argument that such repudiation is implied by the contrast between Samson's tragic warfare and the spiritual victories of Christ in *Paradise Regained* I find unpersuasive.[27] In Milton's works, some heroes are called to do battle in God's cause. Christ on earth was not; he had another office. But in *Paradise Lost* the Son of God, the archangel Michael, and the angelic host were so called in the battle in heaven. So were Samson and the Old Testament judges. The English Puritans also were and might be again.

On the other hand, I do not think readers are invited to construe *Samson* in Christopher Hill's terms, as a covert political allegory whose polemical intent is to call the English people to arms or at least to prepare them for such a call, with hope of better success next time. For all the echoes of civil war polemic, and the many ways in which Samson's situation replicates that of Milton and the defeated Puritans, the thematics of experience we have been tracing tell against any direct equation of past and present history, inviting instead a complex and subtle assessment of the uses of the past. Milton presents the biblical story of Samson not as a political allegory but as a paradigm which can subsume later revolutions and struggles for liberty—including the Puritan revolution—into the flow of providential history, but which should also lead readers to make careful discriminations between one historical moment and another.

Readers will hardly derive from this work an optimistic assessment of the possibilities for political liberation. The Samson paradigm insists that all human heroes are flawed, that the signs of the times and the lessons of experience are inordinately hard to read, that political advances are all too likely to collapse under the weight of human sin and weakness. Milton's drama reprises the tragic historical vision of Books XI and

XII of *Paradise Lost:* "So shall the World go on, / To good malignant, to bad men benign" (*PL* XII, 537–38) until the apocalypse. The external paradise is forever lost, and neither Samson nor God's Englishmen will restore it. God is seen to raise up his champions—his Samsons, or Gideons, or Cromwells—and they achieve some temporary successes. But then the weight of sin in themselves and in the world overcomes them, as Samson so trenchantly observes:

> But what more oft in Nations grown corrupt,
> And by thir vices brought to servitude,
> Than to love Bondage more than Liberty,
> Bondage with ease than strenuous liberty.   (268–72)

Modern readers will hear prediction in these lines, and heavy irony in Manoa's belief that the Israelites will be encouraged to "lay hold" on the opportunity for freedom provided them by Samson's great act. We know from the biblical record that Israel continued in corruption and servitude and that the Danites were apparently reprobate—that they disappeared entirely from the biblical account and were omitted from the lists of the twelve tribes in the Book of Revelation.[28]

Yet the Samson paradigm allows no retreat from the political arena. In the play's historical moment that future is not yet fixed, and choices are still possible. If the Israelites (or the English) could truly value liberty, could reform themselves, could read the signs and events with penetration, could benefit from the "new acquist / Of true experience," liberation might be possible: the chance is always there. Accordingly, liberators must always respond to the call of God (or history) if it comes to them, must seek to educate and reform their societies, and may always (as Milton argued in *The Ready and Easy Way*) reclaim their freedom by armed struggle when they are in bondage, if they have power.[29]

The sententious maxims the Chorus pronounces at the end resonate against the entire drama. It is of course true—and obvious—that only "in the close" can we "best" know the champions to whom God—or history—bear witness. But the drama has demonstrated that political choices must be made and actions taken *in medias res*, in circumstances always characterized by imperfect knowledge and conflicting testimony. The thematics of true political experience in this work offer readers no definitive answers, but instead present a process for making such choices in such circumstances. That process displays the impossibility of judging leaders (or others) on grounds of regeneration or spiritual condition, directing attention instead to the uses of many kinds of experience in evaluating more accessible qualities: honesty, openness, evidence of repentance for wrongdoing, self-knowledge, personal integrity, moral values, service to the cause of liberty, God-given power. In the long interaction between leader and people Milton portrays the Danites learning by stages to open themselves up to the new: to inward experience, illumination, prophecy. And he portrays a prophet/liberator (Samson) learning to reclaim his inward experience and special mission, but offering them finally to be judged by others in accordance with recognized moral and cultural norms: "Our God, our Law, my Nation."

Milton surely expected his English contemporaries to find some "new acquist of true [political] experience" in the tragedy of Samson. He probably hoped that his later readers might do so too, in their own terms and times.

Harvard University

NOTES

1. Johnson, *The Rambler*, #139, 16 July, 1751. Essays tracing Samson's regeneration include Arthur Barker, "Structural and Doctrinal Pattern in Milton's Later Poems," in *Essays in English Literature from the Renaissance to the Victorian Age, Presented to A.S.P. Woodhouse*, ed. Millar MacLure and F. W. Watt (Toronto, 1964), pp. 169–94; and Arnold Stein, *Heroic Knowledge* (Minneapolis, 1957), pp. 137–202. For the unregenerate Samson, see Irene Samuel, "Samson Agonistes as Tragedy," in *Calm of Mind: Tercentenary Essays on "Paradise Regained" and "Samson Agonistes,"* ed. Joseph A. Wittreich (Cleveland, 1971), pp. 237–57.

2. Stanley Fish, "Question and Answer in *Samson Agonistes*," *Critical Quarterly* (Autumn 1969), 252, declares "this is a play without a middle, or at least without a middle one can point to and analyze." See also Boyd M. Berry, *Process of Speech: Puritan Religious Writing and "Paradise Lost"* (Baltimore, 1976), p. 9; and Edward W. Tayler, *Milton's Poetry: Its Development in Time* (Pittsburgh, 1979), pp. 106–09.

3. The case for tragedy is argued by, among many others, A.S.P. Woodhouse, "Tragic Effect in *Samson Agonistes,*" *UTQ* XXVIII (1959), 205–22; Raymond Waddington, "Melancholy Against Melancholy": *Samson Agonistes* as Renaissance Tragedy," in *Calm of Mind*, pp. 259–87; and Anthony Low, *The Blaze of Noon: A Reading of "Samson Agonistes"* (New York, 1974). The several subclassifications are suggested, respectively, in William Riley Parker, *Milton's Debt to Greek Tragedy in "Samson Agonistes"* (1937; rpt. Baltimore, 1970); Harold Fisch, *Jerusalem and Albion: The Hebraic Factor in Seventeenth-Century Literature* (London, 1964), pp. 140–47; and John M. Steadman, "Faithful Champion: The Theological Basis of Milton's Hero of Faith," *Anglia* LXXVII (1959), 12–28. Arguments for other genres include Una Ellis-Fermor, "*Samson Agonistes* and Religious Drama," in *The Frontiers of Drama* (London, 1945), 17–33; T.S.K. Scott-Craig, "Concerning Milton's *Samson*," *Renaissance News* V (1952), 45–53; John C. Ulreich, Jr., "'Beyond the Fifth Act': *Samson Agonistes* as Prophecy," in *Milton Studies*, vol. XVII, ed. Richard S. Ide and Joseph Wittreich (Pittsburgh, 1983), pp. 281–318.

4. For these respective positions see, e.g., F. Michael Krouse, *Milton's "Samson Agonistes" and the Christian Tradition* (Princeton, 1949); William G. Madsen, *From Shadowy Types to Truth* (New Haven, 1968), pp. 181–202; and Barbara K. Lewalski, "*Samson Agonistes* and the 'Tragedy' of the Apocalypse," *PMLA*, LXXXV (1970), 1050–62.

5. The positions, respectively, of W. R. Parker, "The Date of *Samson Agonistes*," *PQ* XXVIII (1949), 145–66, and *Milton: A Biography* (Oxford, 1968), vol. II, pp. 903–17; A.S.P. Woodhouse, "*Samson Agonistes* and Milton's Experience," *Transactions of the Royal Society of Canada*, (3rd ser.), XLIII (1949), 157–75; and (in a resounding reaffirmation of the old chronology) Mary Ann Radzinowicz, *Toward "Samson Agonistes"* (Princeton, 1978).

6. The positions, respectively, of Radzinowicz, *Toward "Samson Agonistes,"* and William Kerrigan, *The Prophetic Milton* (Charlottesville, 1974), pp. 188–258.

7. For these views see James Holly Hanford, *John Milton, Englishman* (London, 1950), pp. 233–63; and Balachandra Rajan, "To Which Is Added *Samson Agonistes*," in *The Prison and the Pinnacle*, ed. Rajan (Toronto, 1973), pp. 84–110.

8. See, e.g., Radzinowicz, *Toward "Samson Agonistes,"* pp. 167–79; Anne Davidson Ferry, "Samson's 'Fort of Silence,'" in *Milton and the Miltonic Dryden* (Cambridge, Mass., 1968), pp. 127–77.

9. For these positions, see Jackie DiSalvo, "'The Lords Battells': *Samson Agonistes* and the Puritan Revolution," in *Milton Studies*, vol. IV, ed. James D. Simmonds (Pittsburgh, 1971), pp. 39–52; Christopher Hill, *Milton and the English Revolution*, (London, 1977), pp. 428–48; Samuel, "*Samson Agonistes* as Tragedy."

10. Joseph A. Wittreich, *Interpreting "Samson Agonistes"* (Princeton, 1986).

11. Wittreich makes the case for a deconstructionist reading (but does not adopt it) in an unpublished monograph, "Deep in the Heart of *Samson Agonistes*: Method or Madness in Milton Criticism." For essays emphasizing ambiguities in the drama, see R. A. Shoaf, "Samson: Son of the Same, Victim of Confusion," in *Milton: Poet of Duality* (New Haven), pp. 169–89; and Virginia Mollenkott, "Relativism in *Samson Agonistes*, *SP* LXVII (1970). Fish, "Question and Answer in *Samson Agonistes*," argues the need for a leap of faith. For studies emphasizing readers' choices, see Wittreich, "Deep in the Heart of *Samson Agonistes*"; and Susanne Woods, "Elective Poetics in *Samson Agonistes*" (Paper presented at the annual meeting of the Modern Language Association, New York, 28 December 1986).

12. Milton's poems are cited from *John Milton: Complete Poems and Major Prose*, ed. Merritt Y. Hughes (Indianapolis, 1957), and identified by line number in text and notes.

13. E.g., Robert T. Fallon, "Milton's Epics and the Spanish War: Towards a Poetics of Experience," in *Milton Studies*, vol. XV, ed. James D. Simmonds (Pittsburgh, 1981), pp. 3–28; and Fish, "Question and Answer."

14. Kathleen Swaim, "The Doubling of the Chorus in *Samson Agonistes*," in *Milton Studies*, vol. XX, ed. James D. Simmonds (Pittsburgh, 1984), pp. 225–45.

15. *Complete Prose Works of John Milton*, 8 vols., ed. Don M. Wolfe et al. (New Haven, 1953–82), vol. VIII, pp. 213–14. Subsequent references to Milton's prose tracts in text and notes are to this edition, cited as YP followed by volume and page numbers.

16. *PR* 1.290–92: "And now by some strong motion I am led / Into this Wilderness, to what intent / I learn not yet."

17. For a suggestive contrast between the Chorus' pietistic faith in an arbitrary God and Samson's development of a rational faith in a rational God consonant with Milton's theology in *De doctrina Christiana*, see Joan S. Bennett, "Liberty Under the Law: The

Chorus and the Meaning of *Samson Agonistes*," in *Milton Studies*, vol. XII, ed. James D. Simmonds (Pittsburgh, 1978), pp. 141–63.

18. Samuel, "*Samson Agonistes* as Tragedy," p. 246.

19. See, e.g., Mollenkott, "Relativism in *Samson Agonistes*," pp. 98–100.

20. Some of these discriminations are noted by Bennett, "Liberty Under the Law," pp. 154–56.

21. Hill offers a suggestive discussion of such echoes in *Milton and the English Revolution*, pp. 434–38.

22. Radzinowicz, *Toward "Samson Agonistes*," pp. 174–79.

23. This analogy is also discussed in Bennett, "Liberty Under the Law," pp. 141–63.

24. I have discussed this issue in "Milton: Political Beliefs and Polemical Methods, 1659–1660," *PMLA* LXXIV (1959), 191–202.

25. Lines 1660–66. The last distinction alludes to the moral principle that an unintended evil which necessarily attends a good act is not sinful.

26. Swaim, "The Doubling of the Chorus," pp. 231–42.

27. Wittreich, *Interpreting "Samson Agonistes*," pp. 319–85.

28. Northrop Frye, *Spiritus Mundi: Essays on Literature, Myth, and Society* (1976; rpt. Bloomington, Ind., 1983), p. 222.

29. YP 7.455: "They who seek nothing but thir own just libertie, have alwaies right to winn it and to keep it, when ever they have power, be the voices never so numerous that oppose it."

OF *PARADISE REGAINED:*
THE INTERPRETATION OF CAREER

Ashraf H. A. Rushdy

THE FIELD that comprises what is now called hermeneutics, to be differentiated from the traditional science of sacred interpretation, has become so vast yet subtle that it is difficult to speak of interpretation without some frame of reference. To use such a word in one's title, then, is perhaps to invite expectations which the following study has neither the desire nor the capacity to fulfill. Rather, I concern myself with Milton's poem and, more specifically, his artistry in one aspect of that poem. And yet that aspect of the poem compels one toward consideration of the relationship between ontology and epistemology. Milton conceived somewhat the same problems that a Hirsch or a Derrida or a Gadamer encounters in his philosophy. The solution at which Milton arrives through the dialectic of the poem's characters, to compare small things with greatest, is closer to Hirsch's than Gadamer's and *positively* anathematizes the playful irresponsibility of Derrida. The temptation to theorize instead of to explicate is always great — Jonathan Culler even thinks it exemplary and worthy of submission — but this study is concerned more with Milton's *Paradise Regained* than any instituted mode of discourse which permits me the pretension of understanding that poem. Long before critics were conscious of *langue* they were able to *parole* nonetheless. While reference will be made to theorists of hermeneutics, it is the agency of interpretation as it is demonstrated in the poem itself that interests me. And so although many definitions of our epigonic age are available to me, I choose to implicate that of an earlier theorist, a lexicographer whose view of reality consisted of things, in his term, "extra-dictionary."[1]

To interpret, according to Samuel Johnson, is "to explain; to translate; to decipher; to give a solution; to clear by exposition; to expound." This, of course, implicates a "something" to be interpreted, and an entity which interprets. The interpreter must perforce bring with him certain mental baggage to bear upon the "something." And the something, once interpreted, takes its place, in its translated form, amidst this luggage. Thus, Dr. Johnson defines the "interpretative" as that "collected by interpretation."

Temptation, to adapt the terms to our immediate concern, is an offered information, a source of ends or means that must needs be assayed and acknowledged, then rejected or accepted. The act itself of tempting is to offer the information. The act of being tempted is that of interpreting the temptation, with its manifold aspects and accoutrements. In Book IX of *Paradise Lost*, Satan offers Eve some remarkable rhetoric, some information about the virtues of the interdicted tree in some well-wrought sophistry. Eve then reflects on these words — those that won too easy entrance into her heart — and, in the act of reflecting, she interprets them. Many of the machinations of her mind are directly affected by the words of Satan; it is no little part of the temptation for Eve to play with the linguistics Satan has offered. This is a neat trick of Satan's, this play on evil not known, not repulsed, we hear her thinking. As she revolves in her mind the offer to eat of the fruit of the tree, she interprets the possible outcome of the deed and the language in which the offer is couched. The act of interpretation cannot be divorced from the temptation. One must know before one rejects; it is otherwise nothing but a blank virtue acting in blind and meaningless abstinence. Nor is this the state only of postlapsarian man. Adam and Eve were expected to know the temptation and yet choose credulity in God over Satan. To recognize the temptation without succumbing to it would have constituted *knowing* good by itself; their fatal lapse caused knowledge of good *by* evil.

And so is it the case in *Paradise Regained*. The temptations are offered to the Son, and it is in his interpretation of them that the heart of the poem resides. This is why so much of the poem, and so much commentary on the poem, is interested in the long replies Jesus makes to each of the temptations of the kingdoms. He is offered Roman glory; he interprets the notion of glory and relates it to a proper immediate cause. Athenian learning is offered with resistless eloquence. But it is left to the Son to interpret the offer, both in terms of the stuff of the offer and the relation it holds to the ultimate cause, and then to resist it. Such eloquence as the Adversary employs is noxious because of its seeming clarity. It is an offer made in a text that surreptitiously ignores the context. The Son's temptation is one essentially requiring a divine skill in hermeneutics (in the original sense, of course).

The idea that Jesus rejects each temptation without considering it is based on a shallow reading of the poem; and it is one upon which is based the condemnation of the characterization of the hero of this poem.[2] The suggestion is that the temptations are paradigmatic, requiring established and ready answers. Take one temptation, take another, they are interchangeable, as any paradigm is. This is a view as damaging as it is false. Jesus does consider each various temptation. He examines and interprets the offer in relation to itself—the merits and failings involved in it as a separate entity—and in relation to the primal cause. More than a little the Son exercises his skill in etiology.

The idea of interpretation, though, plays an even more important role in the poetic than in the formal temptations. The concept of interpretation is, I suggest, radical to the poem. This study is especially concerned with one type—the interpretation of the biographical. It is sadly little considered how much of the poetry is devoted to biographical and autobiographical accounts. Each of the main characters delivers an autobiography and each offers a biography of his adversary. Indeed, considering the various schemes imposed on this poem, it is surprising that hardly anyone has suggested what seems to me to be manifestly the case: that the interpretation of one's career—in both the sense of "vocation" and "motion" toward or away from God—is the basic temptation in the poem, underlying all the offers of Satan, and finding local expression as well.[3] To cite but one example, which will receive more expansive treatment momentarily, the history Satan gives of himself is a temptation to the Son's interpretative and merciful faculties. In the case of the Son, the autobiographical passage of a hundred lines in the first book is nothing less than integral to the temptations that are sequential to it. The poem as a whole rests on the understanding Satan has of the Son; for although it has been argued that the poem is indeed an exercise of Satan's abilities to recognize the Son's "Son-ship," the premise that underlies such a suggestion has gone unheeded. The possibility of recognizing the status of Jesus presupposes both some knowledge of the Son's history—which Satan does have—and a knack of interpreting his career, which Satan has only to a degree. Louis L. Martz has made an interesting case for the poem being a "contest of styles."[4] To go further, it seems to me that we may see the poem as a contest of interpretative skills, a contest of discriminations. Who indeed is the better critic: Satan or the Son? While the answer is ultimately obvious, to see the poem in these terms is illuminating, shedding light perhaps on both the poem and the critical task—or, to employ pleasant terms, on both text and context.[5]

I

Now, to the poem. There are various "lives" of Jesus that play an important role in the poem. No less than six of these are offered: by God, Mary, Andrew and Simon, Jesus himself, and Satan (twice). Of these, Mary's and that of Andrew and Simon are of peripheral interest. God and Jesus' autobiography are of utmost interest, and Satan's initial and revised versions are integral to the story. There are also two biographies of Satan offered in the poem, one by himself and one by Jesus. It is the interpretation of each of the two combatants in this contest of critics that interests this study. For in the interpretation of the antagonist by the hero and of the hero by the adversary is both the basis of the future temptations and the development of character. To interpret is to demonstrate, by an exposition of a text within an open context, the mind of the character. In narrative poetics, when a local situation, or in narratological terms a "focalized," is defined by various "focalizers" within the narrative, the perspectival mood is accommodated through an "internal multiple focalization."[6] Neologisms aside, the character who does the interpreting of the situation is himself to be interpreted by the reader, and to be interpreted, moreover, by the quality of his (the character's) interpretative skills — his ability to assent to and to describe verities. The resolution of the relativism to which this scheme leaves us open — to whom do we grant central authority if even the narrator (our old "auctoritee") is under trial? — is important, but must be delayed until some of the terms of the interpretative dialectic are examined.

The elements of biographical interpretation, then, are those that define the characters of both the biographer *and* his subject. Let us see an example of this type of strategy at work. The scene at the temple is one upon which three minds come to bear. Jesus himself describes it initially. In his version, he does not mention the important statement that he was going about his Father's business (I, 209–14).[7] The humility is one of an educated human mind; he went hoping to learn, perhaps teach, and was, as a matter of fact, "admir'd at by all." Mary describes the scene emphasizing wholly different elements. She is trying to resolve what exactly it means to be the mother of the Son of God. She is incited to speak, of course, becasue her "Motherly cares and fears got head, and rais'd / Some troubl'd thoughts" (II, 64–65). And the reason for these maternal anxieties is the fact that her son is missing. The speech is hopeful in its attempt to resolve these fears into patience. It is natural then for Mary to remind herself of an episode in which her son has gone missing before this. She turns to the temple scene:

> But where delays he now? some great intent
> Conceals him: when twelve years he scarce had seen,
> I lost him, but so found, as well I saw
> He could not lose himself; but went about
> His Father's business; what he meant I mus'd,
> Since understand.   (II, 95–99)

To comfort herself Mary recalls this crucial moment in her son's life and emphasizes the element of divinity in it. The Son, on the other hand, was especially interested, at that point in his autobiography, to emphasize the educational element of his life.

The third person who interprets this scene is Satan. He prefaces the offer of the kingdom of Athenian learning by referring to the Son's precocity in wisdom. You were, he reminds him,

> addicted more
> To contemplation and profound dispute,
> As by that early action may be judg'd,
> When slipping from thy Mother's eye thou went'st
> Alone into the Temple; there wast found
> Among the gravest Rabbis disputant
> On points and questions fitting *Moses'* Chair,
> Teaching not taught.   (IV, 213–20)

Here we see Satan's interpretation of the event. He is wisely reticent about Jesus going about his Father's business; no need to remind him of that fact! And he is far more confident in assessing the Son's performance at the temple than the Son had been. Jesus claimed he had gone in order that he might learn or teach, hopeful of possible mutual benefit. Satan will have none of this false modesty: "Teaching not taught." What is important is the interpretative emphasis. Whereas the Son had examined the possible benefits of his early erudition in *context* of his ultimate career, as he worked out the implications of establishing a neverending kingdom, Satan simply clarifies one issue, the Son's skill at pedagogy, a *text*, out of the whole. Such is the strategy of the poet, placing the same situation in three mouths, and allowing each interpretation to define the interpreter. And the event was biographical, a historic moment revised according to the mind at work on it. Let us then look at the larger examinations of the biographical in the poem.

II

Let us first examine Satan's autobiography, told subsequent to the first temptation of bread. He is, he claims, that "Spirit unfortunate" who was one of those who fell from heaven. But he is not excluded from heaven, he asserts. He was present, he reminds Jesus, during the episode of Job. He goes on to define his relationship with God:

> I came among the Sons of God when he
> Gave up into my hands *Uzzean Job*

> To prove him, and illustrate his high worth;
> And when to all his Angels he propos'd
> To draw the proud King *Ahab* into fraud
> That he might fall in *Ramoth*, they demurring,
> I undertook that office, and the tongues
> Of all his flattering Prophets glibb'd with lies
> To his destruction, as I had then in charge;
> For what he bids I do.   (I, 368–77)

This is the way Satan offers his personal history. Let us see, then, how the Son responds to this:

> But thou art serviceable to Heaven's King.
> Wilt thou impute to obedience what thy fear
> Extorts, or pleasure to do ill excites?
> What but thy malice mov'd thee to misdeem
> Of righteous *Job*, then cruelly to afflict him
> With all inflictions? But his patience won.
> The other service was thy chosen task.   (I, 421–27)

Jesus will have none of this false historiography of self. Satan pretends to a rather amicable relationship with God, even suggesting that he takes on tasks at which the other angels demur. Thus does Satan offer his autobiography, his version of the self. This must be, in turn, interpreted and retold by Jesus. He demonstrates to Satan that this self-image is quite false—"compos'd of lies"—and then offers him the true biography: "As a poor miserable captive thrall" (I, 406, 411). Satan has also offered a history of his relationship with mankind. He has been charitable to humanity and has, he notes, offered them oracular aid. Jesus interprets this again, and answers:

> Who ever by consulting at thy shrine
> Return'd the wiser, or the more instruct
> To fly or follow what concern'd him most,
> And run not sooner to his fatal snare?   (II, 438–41)

Thus does the Son interpret and rewrite Satan's autobiography. He takes Satan's text and places it in a context more amenable to truth, the context of Satan's motivations and status in heaven. The falseness of Satan's autobiography becomes apparent in the wider context not of actions, but of motives; not of location, but of purpose.

We have seen that Jesus is a good reader of history; he has defined, veraciously, Satan's true life by interpreting the one Satan presents. This is not a singular event in the poem, though. Especially in the presentation of his own history, Jesus is always the interpreter.

III

"Some days" after the Baptism the Son begins to muse and revolve within his breast the possible means of publishing his mission. He is led to the desert, "Thought following thought, and step by step." There, he begins the serious business of cogitation on those "Holy Meditations." The whole of the passage is undeniably important, and for that reason it is best examined as a movement through time, that is, like any other self-dialectic, a debate composed and resolved in temporal sequence. The initial passage is intriguing in its echo of what, in Milton, is generally the introduction of machinations of conscience:

> O what a multitude of thoughts at once
> Awak'n'd in me swarm, while I consider
> What from within I feel myself, and hear
> What from without comes often to my ears,
> Ill sorting with my present state compar'd.   (I, 196–200)

The great speech of Samson as he begins his self-revelation must come to mind ("restless thoughts, that like a deadly swarm / Of Hornets arm'd, no sooner found alone, / But rush upon me thronging" [*SA* 19–21]), and perhaps also the introduction to Satan's anguished address to the Sun as he surveys Eden for the first time ("Now conscience wakes despair" [*PL* IV, 23]). But the thoughts that swarm within the Son's mind are vastly different. He does not suffer, as Satan does, from ill thoughts in a pure environment, or, as Samson does, from ill thoughts reflecting on the precedent actions that have created the present evil environment. These are swarming thoughts provoked by an external jarring discord playing upon a serene internal concord; a state truly of *concordia discors*, "that suitable disagreement which is always necessary to intellectual harmony."[8] The tension of public demands — the news of distress and necessity — acts on the internal knowledge, the knowledge he has a few days ago received of his messianic vocation.

The immediate response to these swarming thoughts — the attempt to resolve the external flux with the interior calm — leads to an autobiographical exposition. The autobiography of the Son begins with his childhood love of learning:

> When I was yet a child, no childish play
> To me was pleasing, all my mind was set
> Serious to learn and know, and thence to do
> What might be public good; myself I thought
> Born to that end, born to promote all truth,
> All righteous things: therefore above my years,

> The Law of God I read, and found it sweet,
> Made it my whole delight, and in it grew
> To such perfection that, ere yet my age
> Had measur'd twice six years, at our great Feast
> I went into the Temple, there to hear
> The Teachers of our Law, and to propose
> What might improve my knowledge or their own;
> And was admir'd by all.　　　　　　　　　　(I, 201–14)

The third line of the this quotation deserves examination. It develops the thought from the line preceding, telling on what the mind was set. The tripartite structure of the sense is divided by the caesura, not surprisingly since the first two verbs are verbs of knowledge, and the third is of action. Knowledge must be accumulated, acquired, before action is undertaken: "and thence to do." And do what? The break at the end of the line, the hanging sense of action, all are quite fit. Knowledge leading to action, action seeking a port of call. Nor is the answer to the question one of resounding confidence: "What *might* be public good" (my italics). Not only is the sense of action muted by having to wait on the enjambment; it is made weaker by the sense of possibility involved. The rest of the passage bears this out; the Son only *thinks* that this is the end to which he was born. The visit to the temple is not undertaken by the scholar full of himself; the suggestions he plans to propose are what "might" improve either the general knowledge or his own. And the description of the response he receives is glorious in its simplicity: "And was admir'd by all." As noted before, we will not discover from him that he was pursuing his Father's business at the temple. It is only when Mary delivers another version of the Son's history that we learn of this. What has been accomplished in this stage of the dialectic is this: knowledge has been elevated, but not at the expense of revelation; the desire to know and promote truth is still the product of an earthly desire, a thought. Action toward the public good has been examined and, though not found wanting, has not been exalted as any end in itself; it is an ambiguous entity, this public good (one does not always know what it "might" be).

The quotation was cut off where it was to emphasize the movement of the dialectic. I quote again, repeating the first clause of the verse:

> And was admir'd by all: yet this not all
> To which my Spirit aspir'd; victorious deeds
> Flam'd in my heart, heroic acts; one while
> To rescue *Israel* from the *Roman* yoke,
> Thence to subdue and quell o'er all the earth
> Brute violence and proud Tyrannic pow'r,

> Till truth were freed, and equity restor'd:
> Yet held it more humane, more heavenly, first
> By winning words to conquer willing hearts,
> And make persuasion do the work of fear;
> At least to try, and teach the erring Soul
> Not wilfully misdoing, but unware
> Misled: the stubborn only to subdue.   (I, 214–26)

As learning was primary to the first "chapter" of Jesus's self-revelation, so the question of power and heroics is basic to this second. Readers, of course, will notice that the themes of the temptations Satan offers the Son are already in the Son's mind, "much revolving in his breast." And though the Son, as we shall see, does come to a resolution apropos the potentials of knowledge (the rejection of the kingdom of Athens ought not to surprise after one has seen the Son's early examination of the limits of knowledge) and of power (qua Parthia and Rome), it is nonetheless a stressful situation when Satan offers these potentials. Adam and Eve, we must remember, resolved not to eat of the interdicted tree.

We must not disregard the tension within the Son in his rejections; he is, after all, rejecting things which have, before this, appealed to him. The verbal components of what we have chosen to call the "second chapter" of Jesus' autobiography are those of a mind imbued with a type of physical heroism. He thinks of "heroic acts," whereas we know his destiny is "Above Heroic"; the verbs are those found in Homeric or Virgilian heroic dialogues or monologues: "rescue," "subdue," "quell." The antagonistic forces to be quelled are common antagonistic archetypes: "Brute violence and proud Tyrannic pow'r." The things imprisoned, requiring a heroic savior, are truth, needing its freedom, and equity, needing its restoration. Truth and freedom are, of course, things that ought to be free and reigning respectively; nor is this a point which jars with the ultimate mission of Jesus. But, nonetheless, both are entities which are liberated by actions and perhaps motives which must be rejected. Verbs of action must give way to verbs of mediation. Truth will be freed and equity restored not by one who subdues and quells, but by one who mediates by persuasion.

Then comes that volta, the pause of the thought on "Yet." The mind has developed from this concept of heroic acts to means "more humane, more heavenly." The sole verb of action is now sandwiched in a line that will not allow it, without damage to the metrics, to dominate. "Conquer" is in itself a word that would have fit with the heroic thoughts preceding the "Yet," merging comfortably with "subdue," "quell," and "rescue." But placed, as it is, between its sweet determining force—"win-

ning words" — and its sweet ductile subject — "willing hearts" — it cannot
but be redefined. The softness of the line, with its abundance of w's,
brings to prominence and softens the word and the concept; this is a conquest above heroic. The exception, of course, is the concern for the "stubborn," who will yet be subdued. Too hastily we might be tempted to
assert this proposition as a statement of sound Calvinism, or even Christian doctrine of grace. But the issue in the narrative is more profound
than that. The whole of the proposition is involved with possibility. Note
that the effort is positively asserted: "At least to try, and teach." Suasive
rhetoric joins heroic action, public good, and knowledge as things that
"might" be of value in the establishment of a new kingdom. There has
been no statement yet of guaranteed application, only an examination
of possible ones. This is the process of "growing thoughts." And the or-
ganic metaphor is very nice: thoughts yet not budded, thoughts that may,
for the benefit of the whole plant, yet be pruned.

The next chapter of the autobiography is significant in that it is held
at a further remove than those seen thus far. Jesus is now repeating things
his mother has told him. And with repetition comes interpretation:

> These growing thoughts my Mother soon perceiving
> By words at times cast forth, inly rejoic'd,
> And said to me apart: High are thy thoughts
> O Son, but nourish them and let them soar
> To what height sacred virtue and true worth
> Can raise them, though above example high;
> By matchless Deeds express thy matchless Sire.
> For know, thou art no Son of mortal man;
> Though men esteem thee low of Parentage,
> Thy Father is th'Eternal King, who rules
> All Heaven and Earth, Angels and Sons of men,
> A messenger from God foretold thy birth
> Conceiv'd in me a Virgin; he fore-told
> Thou shouldst be great and sit on *David's* Throne,
> And of thy Kingdom there should be no end.
> At thy Nativity a glorious Choir
> Of Angels in the fields of *Bethlehem* sung.   (I, 227–43)

The concern is with the divine ideas attending the birth of Jesus: the
angelic messenger, the wise men led by the "Star new-grav'n in Heaven,"
the angelic choir, the prophecies of Simeon and Anna, the foretold ascension to the throne of David, the kingdom *sine fine*, and, of course, Jesus'
divine paternity. There is a significant alertness in this retelling of Mary's
speech that heightens the miraculous elements involved in the story. It
should not seem implausible to assume Jesus' special interest in the sym-

bolic factors attending his birth, especially given his situation *now*, as he repeats Mary's words. He has just received the divine word pronouncing who he is; as he recasts his mind to things his mother told him his interest will presumably be on the evidence that supports the pronouncement lately heard.

If we look ahead to Mary's history in the second book, we may see an altered perspective. Her speech is raised by motherly concerns, and is based justly on the terrestrial travails that have occurred since the fateful annunciation: "Hail highly favour'd." She spends a good portion of her narrative describing the night of the birth and its concomitant pains:

> While I to sorrows am no less advanc't,
> And fears as eminent, above the lot
> Of other women, by the birth I bore,
> In such a season born when scarce a Shed
> Could be obtain'd to shelter him or me
> From the bleak air; a Stable was our warmth,
> A Manger his.
>
> (II, 69–75)

This might nicely be compared with Jesus' remembrance of the story his mother told him. As the wise men come following the star, they are directed to "the Manger, where thou lay'st, / For in the Inn was left no better room" (I, 247–48). The simplicity of the declaration, with absolutely no concern for the quality of pain commensurate, shows how the interpreter foregrounds other aspects; this simple description of the place of birth is preceded by the rich description of the angelic choir, and proceeds to the ornate reference to the novel star in heaven, two symbols pertaining to the divine meanings in the birth. The beautifully pathetic description with which Mary's narrative is informed, the pain of the season, the unavailability of abode, the insistence on the poor quality of their lodgings, is simply encapsulated by Jesus in one reductive verse: "For in the Inn was left no better room."

Having attended both to his internal impulses, those leading him to consider his role in the pursuit of public good, and to the external, the information his mother gives him of his high "Parentage," Jesus returns to the "Law of God"—significantly, this is his second reading of it—and discovers himself to be indeed the Messiah. The resolution accepted, he goes on to interpret recent history, an event to which we, Andrew and Simon, and Satan, have been privy: the Baptism (I, 268–93).

We have here the second crux in the development of the hero. Immediately preceding this passage the Son has voiced knowledge of his ultimate destiny: "many a hard assay even to the death" (I, 264). He has just related Mary's revelation to him of his true parentage, after which he revolved the Old Testament to verify his vocation, "and soon found of whom they spake / I am" (I, 262–63). And so the assurance that begins this passage is not superficial; he is neither disheartened nor dismayed at this novel knowledge of the burden of the world's sin. And he awaits the "time prefixt" to receive the pronouncement, and irrefutable evidence, of his status from heaven.

His knowledge now is complete. He has heard from his mother of his "matchless Sire"; he has felt within him, even as a child, the desire to promote "public good"; he has had his aspirations for "heroic acts" transformed to another resolution of the "more humane, more heavenly" role of mediator; and he has searched out the scriptural evidence of his messianic status. Yet he still approaches the Baptism waiting for the pre-fixed time. The baptist recognizes him, but it is the ultimate revelation, both spiritual and auditory, the descending Spirit from heaven, and "last the sum of all," the voice of the Father, that gives the Son knowledge that the "time prefixt" has now arrived: "I knew the time / Now full." Even approaching the Baptism, having maternal, scriptural, and pro-phetic knowledge of himself, the Son must still wait on the spirit and word of God. The sentiment of the final verse of this passage, then, is both a recapitulation of the process of his self-discovery and a statement of the complete reliance on God that shall attend his future "exercise": "For what concerns my knowledge God reveals." Led by "some strong motions," the Son has assayed within himself the qualification of the mes-sianic calling, examining, at times muting, possible means of fulfilling his great calling. The most important aspect of the whole passage is the unrelenting reliance on God that its speaker demonstrates. Everything is examined in context of God; nothing in itself is good; all are "things indifferent." It is the potential, not the entelechy—the modal, not the substantial—that occupies the Son; for realization is always unerringly directed by God the Father. Thus, no means is too base to be unworthy of consideration, and by the same token no means is in itself worthy to be considered outside of the theocentric vision.[9]

This is the autobiography of Jesus, and its significance to his later exercise should not be understated. A great part of the temptations Satan offers depends on the subtlety with which he manipulates desires the Son has himself examined, and likewise a great part of our consciousness of the failings of these tempting offers has been heightened beyond Satan's because we have been privy to the Son's examination of their basis.

IV

Thus far, then, we have seen how Jesus has interpreted Satan's autobiography and his own autobiography. We arrive now at the final interpretative element of the poem, Satan's attempt to explicate Jesus's biography. How Satan understands Jesus is a measure of how effective the temptations he forms correspondingly will be. Satan, fitly, gives both the first life of Jesus and the last. It is his persistent concern to analyze a force he cannot comprehend, and, like many students of many things, he resorts to repetition. The first biography is briefly given in the first book.

Satan attends the Baptism and "with envy fraught and rage" summons a council of his infernal crew. Part of Satan's strategy in this council is this brief biography of Jesus:

> His birth to our just fear gave no small cause,
> But his growth now to youth's full flow'r, displaying
> All virtue, grace and wisdom to achieve
> Things highest, greatest, multiplies my fear.   (I, 66–69)

It is important that Satan has been cognizant of Jesus from his birth to his "youth's full flowr." As far as Satan knows, from the last time he has examined Jesus' thoughts and *understood* them, Jesus is still set to achieve "Things highest, greatest." And as Satan says elsewhere, offering his own credo of historical interpretation, "the childhood shows the man, / As morning shows the day" (IV, 220–21). As far as Satan knows Jesus' mind, as it was in the flower of youth, it is set on heroic greatness. But Jesus has already gone beyond this heroic stance; his rejection of "heroic acts," his theocentric attitude toward mediation over physical revolution, has made his mind set on things "Above Heroic." How Satan has misunderstood this concept of magnanimity will be examined after we look at the second biography. Satan's insistent use of superlatives — "highest, greatest" — indicates, as do his offers of means of heroism, that he himself is attuned to the heroic mind. But Jesus' mind is sublimated beyond that. He has seen a more heavenly, more humane, heroism: a superheroism of sacrifice and meekness, of utter devotion to the will of God.

Having assayed him through all earthly temptations, and found him adamant in his obedience, Satan reviews his previous biography of Jesus. This "second edition," as it were, lets us understand how close a study Satan has conducted on Jesus' early life.

> Then hear, O Son of *David*, Virgin-born;
> For Son of God to me is yet in doubt:
> Of the Messiah I have heard foretold
> By all the Prophets; of thy birth at length
> Announc't by *Gabriel*, with the first I knew,
> And of the Angelic Song in *Bethlehem* field,
> On thy birth-night, that sung thee Savior born.

From that time seldom have I ceas'd to eye
Thy infancy, thy childhood, and thy youth,
Thy manhood last, though yet in private bred;
Till at the Ford of *Jordan* whither all
Flock'd to the Baptist, I among the rest,
Though not to be Baptiz'd, by voice from Heav'n
Heard thee pronounc'd the Son of God belov'd.
Thenceforth I thought thee worth my nearer view
And narrower Scrutiny, that I might learn
In what degree or meaning thou art call'd
The Son of God, which bears no single sense;
The Son of God I also am, or was,
And if I was, I am; relation stands;
All men are Sons of God; yet thee I thought
In some respect far higher so declar'd.
Therefore I watch'd thy footsteps from that hour,
And follow'd thee still on to this waste wild;
Where by all best conjectures I collect
Thou art to be my fatal enemy.
Good reason then, if I beforehand seek
To understand my Adversary, who
And what he is; his wisdom, power, intent,
By parle, or composition, truce, or league
To win him, or win from him what I can.
And opportunity I here have had
To try thee, sift thee, and confess to have found thee
Proof against all temptation as a rock
Of Adamant, and as a Center, firm;
To th'utmost of meer man both wise and good,
Not more; for Honors, Riches, Kingdoms, Glory
Have been before contemn'd, and may again:
Therefore to know what more thou art than man,
Worth naming Son of God by voice from Heav'n,
Another method I must now begin.   (IV, 500–40)

Satan has conducted the temptations based on his knowledge of Jesus'
early aspirations: the child shows the man as morning the day. He was
not privy to the meditations, the musings on these themes, that have elevated the concept of heroism to superheroism. If he had indeed seen the
process of interpretation the Son undertook, he might, given Satan's ability to deceive himself, still have persisted in the same tack. In the terminology of biography, then, Satan has not been able to construe the
inner life of his subject. He has had a Boswellian presence — with the attendant impertinence that goes with that adjective — but he has under-

stood only the superficial fabric of his subject. And, like many biographers, he has composed the history of his subject from a knowledge of his own inner life. The subject is a Son of God. Well, so am I, says Satan the puzzled biographer; "relation stands." He confronts a phrase which "bears no single sense" (to him), and attempts to make bear on it his own sensibility. But this opaque subject will not be easily perceived. "All best conjecture" is the resort, and the weapon, of a frustrated historian.

In the interpretation of careers, then, Jesus has been able to comprehend Satan's, but the case may not be reversed. Satan has given his autobiography, and Jesus has taken the text and placed it in its veracious context. Satan, on the other hand, has attempted to supplant the context of Jesus' life by offering to emphasize, by elevating, certain texts from the whole. As a historian — that is, an interpreter of events — Jesus has been the more successful.

Satan has, of course, been recalcitrantly unwilling to interpret certain signs, even from the beginning. The dove that descended during the Baptism was clear to most observers; Satan, however, is not able or wills an inability to understand this: "what e'er it meant" (I, 83). He has shown a willingness to misinterpret his own life, and he is exerting that same self-deception here. This is a point of utmost importance. To what degree does Satan understand the process of his deposition; does he actually know who the Son is? The final temptation, the one immediately proceeding from Satan's second biography of Jesus, is the crux in the possible answers to these questions.

V

Satan carries Jesus to the "highest Pinnacle" and declares:

> There stand, if thou wilt stand; to stand upright
> Will ask thee skill; I to thy Father's house
> Have brought thee, and highest plac't, highest is best,
> Now shew thy Progeny; if not to stand,
> Cast thyself down; safely if Son of God:
> For it is written, He will give command
> Concerning thee to his Angels, in thir hands
> They shall up lift thee, lest at any time
> Thou chance to dash thy foot against a stone.   (IV, 551–59)

Satan is still persistently pursuing the concept of heroic measures that attend classical standards — and whose vocabulary Jesus has renounced in his examination of "heroic acts." "Highest is best," the words echo the superlative articulations Satan has made consistently throughout the

poem. Never, it seems, will he understand humility or meekness, degradation or servitude, or lowliness.[10]

Never, that is, will he understand the career of Jesus. And it is in
the final temptation that every sense of career will be involved. The temptation of the pinnacle has provoked much critical inquiry, but most if
not all of it, I believe, is based on the false premise that Satan falls with
full knowledge of the Son's status, physical and moral. But Satan's mori-
bund literalism has inhered itself into his being so that he does not understand that the stationary Jesus is the Son of God who had before this
and will after this quell him. Before I attempt to assert this point, let
us examine the scene at the pinnacle.

Satan "sets" Jesus on the pinnacle. The verb is magnificently apropos;
it possesses just the right ambiguity. Of the sixty-six significations Dr.
Johnson lists, both "stationed" and "situated" are found. There is the
possibility of arguing that Jesus is placed in a crouching posture or standing. But the movement of the verse suggests that indeed Jesus is always
standing, nor is there any evidence that standing on the pinnacle is not
humanly possible.[11]

Satan wishes to confuse the issue as much as possible. He tells Jesus
to stand there, and then modifies this by adding the conditional "if thou
wilt stand." Standing, he further states, will ask "skill." The key word,
however, is "Now." That is the point at which the temptation commences,
although Satan would like to blur this point. The theme of time has played
an important part in the poem, as the Son awaits its fullness and Satan
tempts him with its anticipation. And the temptation is for Jesus to show
his "Progeny." The whole of the episode is complex, but it is not beyond
interpretation. It would indeed be Satan's victory if we do become be-
sotted by besetting ambiguity. Having just asserted that all the temptations which Jesus overcame were overcome by men before and would
be overcome again, Satan wishes to insinuate that this is not enough:
that Jesus is still a mere man. But the point is certainly that Jesus is a
man, an exalted man but a man nonetheless. Satan takes him to his
"Father's house"; Jesus' proper abode is his "Mothers house." It would
be nothing less than Satan's victory if Jesus does *show* his "Progeny." But
Jesus perceives the essence of the temptation through the shroud of ambiguity, and acts exactly in accordance with God's will—he remains
standing: "To whom thus Jesus: also it is written, / Tempt not the Lord
thy God, he said and stood. / But Satan smitten with amazement fell
(IV, 560–62). Jesus undergoes no change of station and he retains his
status: Son of God.

Satan, moreover, falls deluded of any of this knowledge. Critics may be unwilling to allow Satan to depart in ignorance and for this reason contrive the miracle of a *deus ex machina,* visible and comprehensible to all; but Satan has already had one *deus ex machina* in this poem — the dove — and all he could see was the literal *machina.*[12] God is no longer accessible, in idea or symbol, to the myopic and autocentric Satan. He is deluded, blind to spirit, and a thrall to his own satanic perspective. The state of "amazement" in which he falls is nothing less than a state of "confused apprehension as does not leave reason its full force."[13] Satan, through ages of perversity and depravity, has had his understanding usurped, or, perhaps better, literally supplanted.

The point Milton wished to make, I think, is that this moment is the direct confrontation of the interpreters. It is worth noting that in this final temptation Milton does not use Luke's account, although he has followed the order of Luke's gospel. In Luke Jesus answers, "It is said, Thou shalt not tempt the Lord thy God." Luke shows, here as elsewhere, an abiding concern for the vocal narrative, the audition not the lection. But the use of "said" does not suit Milton's emphasis on the textuality of interpretation. Thus he accepts Matthew's account, in which Jesus answers, "It is written again, thou shalt not tempt the Lord thy God." The repetition of "it is written," then, by Satan and Jesus is important (*scriptum est* over *dictum est*). It allows for each to work upon, to interpret, the same text. And the text upon which they work, although literally Psalm xci and Deuteronomy chapter vi, is the life of Jesus. The combat of biographers, whether Satan or Jesus will write this life, is one that has been fought throughout the poem. The interpretative contest of facts, of temptations, of history, is now manifest in the ultimate text, Scripture. Satan quotes a passage that offers one possible conclusion to this biographical chapter. Jesus quotes another. In *context,* Jesus quotes the true one. For it is doubtless true that, as Psalm xci asserts, had Jesus cast himself off he would have been borne aloft by angels. That Satan quotes this text does not deny its truth (this might be kept in mind with many of Satan's temptations). But Jesus had quoted the most apposite text. Jesus has written his own life; Satan "with amazement fell."

My argument, then, is that Satan does not understand any more at this final temptation than he has at any other point in the poem who the Son of God is. If Satan has understood, he has willingly confounded the issue in his mind; if he has not understood, he does not acquire any pertinent knowledge at this point in the narrative. It strikes me that Satan has always had the facts in his mind, but is unwilling to arrange them into comprehension. When he encounters a crux that strikes him in the face, he pretends ignorance of hermeneutics: "whate'ere it meant."

Satan offers the temptation in ambiguous words, a text that he hopes will confuse the context. But to stand is not part of the temptation. To make it *seem* part of the temptation is one of the triumphs of the creator of the satanic character. And to judge its triumph one need only look at the commentary it has provoked. Surely this must attest to Satan's subtlety. From double delusive sense, Jesus has interpreted yet once more the offered text within the proper context, and replies with his own appropriate text.

As for Satan, he does not comprehend how the kingdom of God will be established, because he has not understood its foundation. The life of Jesus, the subject of the Gospels, is the basis of the kingdom *sine fine*. To interpret that sacred text is to assign the motivation and the effect of the kingdom of God. And it is a text that must be understood, properly. Satan has attempted to confound that text, has attempted to place it in contexts which would alter its hierarchical significance. One is tempted to say that Satan is the first to practice deconstruction. If, as in the words of one Miltonist, deconstruction is the bringing to the surface "the negative elements, so as to contradict the affirmation the poem seems to make," then Satan has anticipated, "prevented" in its Miltonic sense, deconstruction.[14] He places the text under the stress of an appropriated, though inappropriate, context and attempts to wring out the implicit meanings which, to the depths of the text, are simply not there. Satan wishes the text to have "no single sence." But unhappily for Satan, there is one: the theocentric vision. "What concerns my knowledge God reveals." There are a variety of knowledges, but there is one single source, and in the source is the sense.

Satan has claimed earlier in the poem that to lose the ability to admire excellence or virtue is to "have lost all sense" (I, 382). But he has wished to separate the love of God from the love of virtue. He proceeds from this distinction and claims his benevolence toward man. He has given man oracular aid, advice, and "answers." Jesus responds to this that, without the love of God, without a devoted theocentricity, all such oracular aid is "but dark / Ambiguous and with double sense deluding" (I, 434–35). Satan wishes no "single sence," wishes indeed for a delusive and deluding "double sense." But the ultimate context, Jesus asseverates, is and must be God. In Him the unity of senses *is*. And because Jesus has interpreted his life according to this context his interpretation is right. Satan falls "amazed" because he has failed in his attempt at extradition, that is, the localizing of sense at a distance from the center of sensation. In God is sense, singular and sufficient. All else is "vain deluding joy" of textual play. Authorial intention is essentially valid when the author is the undisputed creator of the text. Satan might find Gadamerian subjectivity or Derridean playfulness suitable to his purpose. One can see him in his gloomy consistory debating with Moloch the idea of the "hermeneutic circle," or posing to Belial the idea of supplementarity in a world without a center or origin of sense, a world in which the author is dead — an atheistic world. But Milton's world does have a center of seriousness: God. And both epistemology and ontology depend upon the concentric, though infinite, deity. Because interpretation is founded upon a perspectival focalization there is danger of a senseless relativity, but there does, in Milton's universe, exist a central authority against whose decrees validity is assessed. Those unable or unwilling to understand the focus of sense in the author of a creation are, to use Hirsch's term, "cognitive atheists."[15]

VI

The language in which this study has been conducted may be seen as unnecessarily grammatical and literary. But this captures, I believe, a point implicit in the very account of creation, destruction, revelation, and regeneration. The world was created by God's voice. Adam's nomination of the animals in Eden was done under the guidance of a "sudden apprehension." And the New Testament, with its vision of a kingdom *sine fine*, is based on an understanding of the life of its subject, the base upon which the pile of eternity is built. The Gospels are each a life of Christ. And it is truly upon them — those biographies — that regaining of Paradise is based.

Jesus has understood his own life through the temptations. In the interpretation of career he has defined himself, the *logos*. But to the temptation he has brought a mind replete with intelligence, the wisdom of reliance on God. To the temptations he had brought what is necessary in any reading task, the mind through which the text is refined into the self:

> who reads
> Incessantly, and to his reading brings not
> A spirit and judgment equal or superior,
> (And what he brings, what needs he elsewhere seek)
> Uncertain and unsettl'd still remains,
> Deep verst in books and shallow in himself.   (IV, 322–27)

This is a call, even more demanding than the original of it, for the "fit audience," that rare auditor who will apprehend and consider, and yet distinguish, and yet prefer, and finally understand. And it comes near the end of a poem that has offered alternatives, for Milton's poetry, as was recognized long ago, is ultimately the poetry of choice.

The relation of the War in Heaven gives Adam the "terrible Example" of disobedience, the falling away from God into destruction. The succeeding book of Creation gives Adam the example of essential goodness, the example of obedience expressed in creativity. It is up to Adam to choose, and it is up to the reader to gauge his response in relation to Adam's choice. In *Paradise Regained* Milton offers the same dialectic.

Satan, whatever else he was in the hands of Milton, and has become in those of his subsequent critics, was always an example of delusive self-interpretation. The painful consciousness of being athwart of goodness, the overwhelming and perpetual cognizance of self as an anomalous text in an otherwise unified context, is the role he holds from our first sight of him in *Paradise Lost,* as he lies on the burning lake following his pernicious fall, to our final glimpse of him in *Paradise Regained* as he falls, still smitten with amazement, still unable to comprehend himself or goodness. There is something almost pathetic about one who fails in writing both his autobiography and the biography of what, to the end, he persists in thinking was once his sibling: "relation stands."

Career can mean both motion and vocation; and each of these terms can again mean, in the case of the first, either the process of recognizing grace or the flux and reflux of human activity, and, in the case of the second, either the form of the process of grace or the form of human activity. But in each case, God is the ultimate reality. One can career toward or away from, for or against, but always, in Milton's universe, in relation to Him. He is, in other words, the center of sense — cognitive and emotive.

Christ's College, Cambridge

NOTES

1. E. D. Hirsch, *Validity in Interpretation* (New Haven, 1967) and *The Aims of Interpretation* (Chicago, 1976); Jacques Derrida, "Structure, Sign, and Play in the Discourse of the Human Sciences," in *Writing and Difference,* trans. Alan Bass (London, 1978), pp. 278–93; Hans-Georg Gadamer, *Philosophical Hermeneutics,* trans. David E. Linge (Berkeley and Los Angeles, 1976); Samuel Johnson, *A Dictionary of the English Language in which the Words are deduced from their Originals, Illustrated in their Different Significations by Examples from the best Writers* (London, 1755). Jonathan Culler, *The Pursuit of Signs: Semiotics, Literature, Deconstruction* (London, 1981), p. 5. Culler's

statement, that to "engage in the study of literature is not to produce yet another interpretation of *King Lear* but to advance one's understanding of the conventions and operations of an institution, a mode of discourse," has in it the otherworldly tone typically associated with conversion, the sincere but impractical call for everyone to arrest his or her motion and follow this chosen way. The "study of literature" is achieved in diverse ways, diversely tenable. The operations of the institution of understanding may be a "higher" mode of discourse than the modest study of individual poems (the quotation marks around the word indicate a spatial configuration without moral connotations), but it is neither novel nor need be omnipresent. Consciousness of any task, its modes, its operational status, is helpful, normative, and seemingly the precious consummation of human cognitive activity. Literary theory is just such a structure, sketching the boundaries and workings of critical praxis. But the study of theory—that is, of the consciousness of the processes of critical practice—need not deflect us from interpreting individual works. It is, after all, individual works that make up the body of "literature," that entity that Culler distresses between semiotics and deconstruction, least of all in his title.

I cite the three positions, Derrida, Hirsch, and Gadamer, because they have become familiar through the characterizations and caricatures they have suffered; and because each holds a strong theory of epistemology, covering a wide, though not exhaustive, purview of the possible theories of the locus of meaning. Each holds a respectable position, as attested by his writings and followers, and it is no part of my intention to offer an explicit critique of any of their positions. If ideology is as inhered in language as recent scholarship has taught us, then nothing but redundancy or irony is possible by explicit statement of one's critical position.

2. There are numerous examples of this type of criticism, e.g. Richard D. Jordan, "*Paradise Regained* and the Second Adam," in *Milton Studies*, vol. IX, ed. James D. Simmonds (Pittsburgh, 1976), pp. 261–75; Don Cameron Allen, *The Harmonious Vision: Studies in Milton's Poetry* (Baltimore, 1954); Lawrence W. Hyman, *The Quarrel Within: Art and Morality in Milton's Poetry* (New York, 1972). Dissenters from this viewpoint include Barbara Kiefer Lewalski, *Milton's Brief Epic: The Genre, Meaning, and Art of "Paradise Regained"* (Providence, 1966), pp. 133–63; Arnold Stein, *Heroic Knowledge: An Interpretation of "Paradise Regained" and "Samson Agonistes"* (Minneapolis, 1957); Irene Samuel, "The Regaining of Paradise," in *The Prison and the Pinnacle: Essays to Commemorate the Tercentenary of "Paradise Regained" and "Samson Agonistes,"* ed. Balachandra Rajan (Toronto, 1973), pp. 111–34, who makes a nice distinction between "biographic-particular" and "ethical universal" ways of reading the poem, making a good case for the greater validity of the latter (p. 133).

Other studies that emphasize the hermeneutic element in the poem are Mary Nyquist, "The Father's Word/Satan's Wrath," *PMLA* C, ii (1985), 187–202; Mary Ann Radzinowicz, "*Paradise Regained* as Hermeneutic Combat," *University of Hartford Studies in Literature* XVI, i (1984), 99–107; and Roger H. Sundell, "The Narrator as Interpreter in *Paradise Regained*," in *Milton Studies*, vol. II, ed. James D. Simmonds (Pittsburgh, 1970), pp. 83–101.

3. Cf. Stanley E. Fish, "Things and Actions Indifferent: The Temptation of Plot in *Paradise Regained*," in *Milton Studies*, vol. XVII, ed. Richard S. Ide and Joseph Wittreich (Pittsburgh, 1983), pp. 163–85, esp. p. 176. To understand Fish's impetus to establish a less schematic reading of the poem, one need only contemplate the numerous studies that have elevated the "triple-equation" above any other concern in the poem, e.g., Patrick Cullen, *Infernal Triad: The Flesh, the World, and the Devil in Spenser and Milton* (Princeton, 1974), who sees in the poem a structure of "recurring triads" (p. 172).

4. Louis L. Martz, *The Paradise Within: Studies in Vaughan, Traherne, and Milton* (New Haven, 1964), p. 183. Christopher Ricks, "Over-Emphasis in *Paradise Regained*," *MLN* LXXVI (1961), 701–04, while finding overindulgent elaboration in Jesus' and the narrator's speeches, also checks Martz's desire for clear and easy distinctions of style.

5. These are notoriously difficult terms to employ, but necessary. Hirsch, for example, points out the possible meanings of "context" and the density of the term in *Validity in Interpretation*, pp. 86–88; cf. his later usages in "Critical Response: The Politics of Interpretation," *Critical Inquiry* IX (1982–83), 235–47, esp. 246. What I mean by "context," in this instance, is obviously the host realm of critical discourse as it bounds and is parasitic on "texts" like *Paradise Regained*, which in an earlier day were called poems. More to my purpose, though, "context" is used throughout this paper to signify, in particular, the sum of events of a career, and, in general, the quality of faith in God that manifests itself in cognitive acquiescence.

6. Gérard Genette, *Narrative Discourse*, trans. Jane E. Lewin (Oxford, 1980), pp. 189–90. Cf. Shlomith Rimmon-Kenan, *Narrative Fiction: Contemporary Poetics* (London, 1983) pp. 71–85.

7. Quotations from Milton's poetry follow *John Milton: Complete Poems and Major Prose*, ed. Merritt Y. Hughes (Indianapolis, 1957), hereafter cited parenthetically in the text.

8. Samuel Johnson, "Rambler," no. 167, in *The Yale Edition of the Works of Samuel Johnson*, ed. W. J. Bate and Albrecht B. Strauss, vol. V, (New Haven, 1969), pp. 123–24.

9. Stein, *Heroic Knowledge*, to whom we owe the most thorough study of Jesus' autobiography, discerns four distinguishable stages of "heroic knowledge" in the passage: (1) intuitive, (2) discursive and disciplined, (3) aspiring, through "knowing-doing-promoting" to specific ends, and (4) redefinition of public good in terms of knowledge. Stein further notes the circularity of the stages, the fourth being a return to original intuition (pp. 38–40). I disagree with Stein's decision to stop the analysis after Book I, line 226, claiming that "what follows is not a further stage." I believe that Jesus further refines his thoughts by repeating Mary's history and the story of the Baptism. The final stage, moreover, is not merely the redefinition of public good in terms of knowledge, but rather in terms of acquiescence. Jesus' most complete knowledge, as he himself says, is acquiescence to God. Stein's "intuitive" may mean "divine," which is my interpretation of Jesus' ultimate knowledge, but seems to connote a proportionally significant human intelligence (cf. pp. 41–42).

10. Cf. George Herbert, "Redemption," in *The English Poems of George Herbert*, ed. C. A. Patrides (London, 1974) p. 60. The persona of that poem searches for Christ first in "heaven at his manour," then knowing "his great birth" he searches for him at "great resorts."

11. See *A Variorum Commentary on the Poems of John Milton*, ed. Walter MacKellar (London, 1975), vol. IV, p. 239. For other readings on the "pinnacle scene," see Karl J. Franson, "'By His Own Independent Power': Christ on the Pinnacle in *Paradise Regained*," *MQ* XIV, ii (May 1980), 55–60; Lewalski, *Milton's Brief Epic*, pp. 307, 317; Elizabeth Marie Pope, *"Paradise Regained": The Tradition and the Poem* (Baltimore, 1947), pp. 103–07; Stein, *Heroic Knowledge*, pp. 127–29; Cullen, *Infernal Triad*, p. 169; Stanley Fish, "Inaction and Silence: The Reader in *Paradise Regained*," in *Calm of Mind: Tercentenary Essays on "Paradise Regained" and "Samson Agonistes" in Honor of John S. Diekhoff*, ed. Joseph Anthony Wittreich, Jr. (London, 1971), p. 42; Jack W. Herring, "Christ on the Pinnacle in *Paradise Regained*," *MQ* XV, iii (October 1980), 98, and Samuel, "The Regaining of Paradise," pp. 111–15, 121–23. All these critics, except Fish, Herring, and Samuel, argue that Jesus is manifestly God by the pinnacle scene, and that it was humanly impossible to stand upon the pinnacle. Cf. Thomas Langford, "The Nature of The Christ

of *Paradise Regained*," *MQ* XVI, iii (October 1982), 63–67; W. A. McClung, "The Pinnacle of the Temple," *MQ* XV, i (1981), 13. Nyquist, "The Fater's Word," 199–200, presents an admirable but unconvincing case for the irreducible ambiguity of the pinnacle scene.

12. Pope, *The Tradition and the Poem*, p. 40. "Milton . . . had no intention of permitting the devil to go away unsatisfied and dubious . . . Satan obviously ought to be made aware of the Lord's true identity at the last, though not in any manner which he has foreseen, or which gratifies him in the least." Compare Mr. Calton's and Thomas Newton's notes in Newton's edition, *Paradise Regain'd: A Poem in Four Books. To Which is added Samson Agonistes: and Poems upon Several Occasions. . . . The Author JOHN MILTON. A New Edition, With Notes of various Authors* (London, 1752), pp. 181–82. Newton's note argues that Jesus' "*standing* properly makes the discovery, and is the principal proof of his progeny that the Tempter requir'd." Calton also argues that "Christ declares himself to be the God and Lord of the Tempter; and to prove it, stands upon the pinnacle." My argument is that Satan is denied this proof.

13. Johnson, *Dictionary*. One could, to gain an appreciation of what "amazement" might mean, compare *Troilus and Cressida*: "Behold, distraction, frenzy, and amazement, / Like witless antics, one another meet" (V, iii, 86–87).

14. Lawrence W. Hyman, "Christ on The Pinnacle: A New Reading of the Conclusion to *Paradise Regained*," *MQ* XVIII, i (March 1984), p. 21. It might be noted that Hyman's deconstruction is based on a misquotation and a dubious elision. He quotes "uneasy situation" instead of "uneasy station," and elides the very important "Now" from Satan's speech. Interestingly, another deconstruction of *Paradise Lost*, by Raman Selden, *A Reader's Guide to Contemporary Literary Theory* (Sussex, 1985) pp. 86–87, enjoys the benefit of eliding from the famous passage in *Aeropagitica* its most important clause, "As the state of man now is," and goes on to argue how Milton's text transgresses the laws it appears to set for itself. Elision is the prerogative of critics, but it is nothing less than churlish to condemn to senselessness that which we have already annihilated of meaning by our own carelessness. Meaning is begotten with difficulty for both author and reader, and Selden's and Hyman's cases are pregnant with warning for others desiring to be abortifacients of meaning.

15. Hirsch, *Aims of Interpretation*, p. 3.

THE THEOLOGY OF REPRESENTATION: THE META-ARGUMENT OF *PARADISE REGAINED*

James M. Pearce

T HE *ILIAD*, Longinus maintains, was written at the height of Homer's powers and was, as a consequence "dramatic and exciting." Of its sequel he writes, "Homer in the *Odyssey* may be compared to the setting sun; the size remains without the force."[1] A similar comparison is implicit in a number of modern critical discussions of *Paradise Lost* and *Paradise Regained*. Milton, however, seems to surpass Homer, albeit negatively, in that both the size and force of his later work suffer diminution. A.S.P. Woodhouse was among the first to note the restricted possibility of action in the poem, while Northrop Frye, commenting on Satan's exuberant mobility, thought it necessary to remind us that "the real source of life and freedom and energy is the frigid figure at the center of the poem." Douglas Bush explains the unfavorable critical responses by adverting to a shift in the sensibilities of Milton's audience, suggesting that the modern reader is "indifferent to the exalted didacticism [and] the heroic ideal of Christian 'magnanimity' developed by Renaissance criticism and poetry."[2]

Although *Paradise Regained* has outlived some, perhaps the most important, aspects of the religious culture from which it emerged, the poem's central interpretive challenge, understanding Christ's nature, depends at least as much on grasping the constraints and possibilities of poetic representation that Milton inherited, as it does on understanding seventeenth-century theology. Such, in fact, was the complexity of the canon which governed the literary discourse of the Renaissance that it could be likened to a theology, older than Christianity, and complete with epistemological, ethical, and metaphysical tenets. It is quite revealing to place the poem in this context, for, despite its affinities with the Platonic dialogue, the Boethian colloquy, the book of Job, and perhaps even the Georgics, *Paradise Regained* is *sui generis*. As Thomas Sloane has observed, "it is the formally most unique and isolated example of Milton's creativity." While readers of *Paradise Lost* may question "the literary success of Milton's anthropomorphic presentation of God as epic character,"[3] readers of *Paradise Regained,* in which the enigmatic figure of Christ is absolutely central, tend to question the literary success of the whole undertaking. *Paradise Regained* is indeed a profoundly problematical poem, representing simultaneously, as Sloane says, the culmination and the disintegration of the humanist rhetorical enterprise. The antithetical nature of the adversaries themselves almost provides a paradigm for the system of irreconcilable oppositions, insistent paradoxes, and incommensurate perspectives embodied in Milton's brief epic. To vary an observation Stephen Booth made about *King Lear,* if *Paradise Regained* has anything to teach us, it may be that what does not make sense may nevertheless be true.[4] Reading Milton's penultimate poem in a way that brings out this order of meaning, however, requires a critical strategy which provides us with some sort of access to the poem as a formal whole. Of all Milton's poems, *Paradise Regained* is the most difficult to interpret by zealously attending to discrete details; and, if we miss the forest in this poem, we are not likely to see the trees.

Broadly speaking, this essay attempts to bring the forest back into view by investigating the influence of the discipline of rhetoric on the execution of *Paradise Regained.* I argue that the humanist rhetorical tradition furnished Milton with the set of assumptions which, assimilated to his own slightly eccentric christology, governed the way in which he depicted Christ, providing, as it were, a theology of representation. Milton's rhetorical milieu also afforded him a specific technique for structuring his presentation. Central to rhetorical *controversia,* it was that mode of thinking which Cicero describes in *De Oratore* as "in utramque sententiam."[5] In *Paradise Regained* Milton artfully adapts it to the exigencies of poetic representation. Milton's penchant for transmuting controversial thinking into poetry displays itself in *L'Allegro* and *Il Penseroso* which, if not as dissimilar as their initial lines suggest, nevertheless owe their contrasting themes and ludic spirit to the academic disputation. What in these early poems was little more than a poetic exercise in elucidating both sides of a given issue became in the later poem a mode of thought which expresses itself on many levels. *Controversia* shapes the meta-argument of *Paradise Regained,* providing the vehicle through which the complex nature of Christ is artistically realized. By meta-argument I mean a set of governing assumptions which, though independent of the plot or fictional hypothesis, are realized sequentially in the work of literature. Meta-hypothesis might be another way of getting at the same notion. The meta-argument is a structural element which may be more or less visible in a complex work. Only such a procedure was capable of presenting Christ's nature in its unique contrariety. If

Milton's thinking was essentially unrhetorical, his mastery of the persuasive resources of rhetoric was consummate. Though, in general, *controversia* acknowledges the imperfection and uncertainty of human knowledge, Milton makes of it a two-edged sword, capable of acknowledging simultaneously the mystery of the hypostasis and the comprehensibility of the Savior.

I

The criteria which the discipline of rhetoric contributes to Renaissance literary theory primarily concern the importance of style to persuasion; it also contributes, though somewhat less directly, criteria for evaluating, in the strictest sense of the word, the content of literary discourse. For a clear formulation of the first set of criteria we need look no further than Aristotle who, summing up common wisdom, averred that distinct rhetorical styles are appropriate to different occasions, audiences, and circumstances, and that they "are capable of being used in season or out of season." One of the most important distinctions Aristotle makes is between the written style which "is the more finished," and the spoken style which "better admits of dramatic delivery," observing, in addition, that it is the "aptness of language," the appropriateness of style, which "makes people believe in the truth of your story."[6] Making people believe in the truth of a particular story is the purpose of rhetoric.

The able rhetorician is one who in most situations is able to discover the most likely means of persuasion, that is, the most likely way to enable an audience to *see* the truth, for believing is inextricably tied to seeing in Aristotle's rhetorical universe. As spatial distance is to the eye, so linguistic sophistication is to the mind:

Now the style of oratory addressed to public assemblies is really just like scene-painting. The bigger the throng, the more distant is the point of view: so that, *in the one* and *the other*, high finish in detail is superfluous and seems better away. The forensic style is more highly finished; still more so is the style of language addressed to a single judge, with whom there is very little room for rhetorical artifices, since he can take the whole thing in better, and judge of what is to the point and what is not.[7]

The analogy between scene painting and rhetorical style not only enforces the need for increasing the stylistic refinement as the work of art — be it lines, colors, or words — moves closer to the perceiver, but it also implies that accuracy and certitude, the ability to "take the whole thing in," depend on being the correct distance from the object of knowledge. Aristotle inherited this epistemological assumption from Plato, who also uses a spatial analogy in his discussion of persuasion in the *Critias*. Unlike Aristotle, Plato uses spatial distance as the equivalent of both intellectual and ontological distance, thus adding an element of value to certitude. The excellence of knowledge, for Plato, precludes exactitude of representation:

upon an audience of human beings *it is easier to produce the impression of adequate treatment in speaking of gods than in discoursing of mortals like ourselves.* The combination of unfamiliarity and sheer ignorance in an audience makes the task of one who is to treat a subject toward which they are in this state easy in the extreme, and in this matter of gods, we know, of course, how the case stands with us. But to make my meaning still clearer, kindly follow an illustration. All statements made by any of us are, of course, bound to be an affair of imagery and picturing. Now, suppose we consider the ease or difficulty with which an artist's portraiture of figures divine and human, respectively, produces the impression of satisfactory reproduction on the spectator. We shall observe that in the case of earth, mountains, rivers, woodland, the sky as a whole, and the several revolving bodies located in it, for one thing, the artist is always well content if he can reproduce them with some faint degree of resemblance, and, for another, that since our knowledge of such objects is never exact, we submit his design to no criticism or scrutiny, but acquiesce, in these cases, in a dim and deceptive outline. But when it is our own human form that the artist undertakes to depict, daily familiar observation makes us quick to detect shortcomings and we show ourselves severe critics of one who does not present us with full and perfect resemblance. Well, we *should recognize that the same is true of discourses. Where the subjects of them are celestial and divine, we are satisfied by mere faint verisimilitudes; where mortal and human, we are exacting critics.*[8]

Accuracy or "full and perfect" verisimilar representation can be achieved only in relation to familiar "human" objects, whereas "celestial" or "divine" objects can neither be reproduced with a high degree of exactitude nor are they susceptible to the same degree of criticism or scrutiny; it is sufficient if celestial objects are presented in merely a "dim and deceptive outline." Hence, the most excellent or divine knowledge is associated with distant objects such as "the sky as a whole, and the several revolving bodies located in it," while the less excellent or human knowledge is associated with the object near at hand such as "our own human form." In this manner a scale of diminishing accuracy proportionate to the increase in the epistemological distance of the perceiver from the object of knowledge is established. The "dim and deceptive outline" of divine knowledge is analogous to the oration addressed to public assemblies and, therefore, to the painting created by means of "shadows and shading" to be viewed from afar; at the other end of the

scale there is human knowledge, which is analogous to written ceremo-
nial oratory and thus to a highly detailed painting meant to be scrutinized closely. The former are accorded a degree of immunity from criticism and scrutiny characteristic of the skiagraphic representation, while
of the latter "we are exacting critics." This set of distinctions, then, blurs
the boundary between rhetorical and philosophical discourse in that it
both posits a universal and calculable response to a given category of
knowledge and places a valuation on that category. Though all knowledge is valuable, Aristotle asserts that we value "one kind more . . . than
another, either in virtue of its accuracy or because it relates to higher
and more wonderful things."[9] Just as orations are evaluated by their appropriateness, so knowledge itself can be valorized in relation to its accuracy or in relation to its inherent excellence. If, as Sloane persuasively
argues (*Humanist Rhetoric*, p. 87), rhetoric functioned as an alternative
to philosophy in the Renaissance, it was not simply because it "could
not avoid having philosophical implications," but also because, in their
least specialized forms, the two discourses were from antiquity capable
of addressing many of the same issues.

The practical import of these formulations for Milton was that, in
his presentation of deity—which, considered abstractly, clearly belongs
to the order of celestial knowledge—he knew that a dim and deceptive
outline would satisfy his audience because of their "sheer ignorance" of
the subject. In the most successful passages in which Milton depicts divinity in *Paradise Lost* he exploits to a remarkable degree the immunity
from exacting criticism which his subject admits. His description of Christ
coming to the aid of the loyal angels, for example, is very persuasive:

> Attended with ten thousand thousand Saints,
> He onward came, far off his coming shone,
> And twenty thousand (I thir number heard)
> Chariots of God, half on each hand were seen:
> Hee on the wings of Cherub rode sublime
> On the Chrystalline Sky, in Sapphire Thron'd.
> Illustrious far and wide, but by his own
> First seen, them unexpected joy surpris'd,
> When the great Ensign of Messiah blaz'd
> Aloft by Angels borne, his Sign in Heav'n:
> Under whose Conduct Michael soon reduc'd
> His Army, circumfus'd on either Wing,
> Under thir Head imbodied all in one.
> Before him Power Divine his way prepar'd;
> At his command the uprooted Hills retir'd

> Each to his place, they heard his voice and went
> Obsequious, Heav'n his wonted face renew'd.
> And with fresh Flow'rets Hill and Valley smil'd.[10]

This passage is a highly successful essay in the art of depicting celestial things because, as a whole, the probability of this series of events is not, perhaps cannot be, questioned by the "audience."

The artistic task, however, of presenting pure deity is incomparably easier than representing an amalgamation of the human and the divine, for, in the latter instance, the artist must provide in his work the clues which will guide the audience to the proper evaluation of a complex entity. In Milton's case, his definition of Christ as God and man or *theanthropos*, and his insistence upon the reality of this formulation, locates Christ, conceived as an abstract subject, somewhere on the ontological continuum between the celestial realm and the human realm. Implicit in Frye's censure of Christ is the assumption that he is a human subject and must be evaluated as such. He makes this assumption explicit when he comments: "one might almost say that the point at which the reader loses sympathy with Jesus in *Paradise Regained* is the point at which he himself would have collapsed under the temptation."[11] It might well be true then that, if Christ were simply a man, he would be "a pusillanimous quietist in the temptation of Parthia, an inhuman snob in the temptation of Rome, a peevish obscurantist in the temptation of Athens" (Frye, p. 439). But we know, at least theoretically, that Christ is more than man. When we succumb, however, to the temptation to interpret him as mere man, we move as far from Milton's universe as Byron did when he designated Satan the hero of *Paradise Lost*. The question, of course, arises that, given Christ's dual nature — the human and the divine — how is he to be evaluated or to what extent is he immune from exacting criticism? It is in answering this question that the visual analogy demonstrates its usefulness. Milton would no doubt, as we do, have located Christ at a hypothetical midpoint between near or human knowledge and distant or celestial knowledge. Whether the distance between the human and the divine is imagined as finite or infinite, such placement necessarily involves Christ's removal from the realm of closely observable objects; thus, Christ as an object of knowledge would, if Milton adhered to the modes of analysis outlined above, not be subject to the same kind of rigorous scrutiny as the human form. He must, as literary content, be assigned to the category of celestial knowledge and be granted the skiagraphic immunity to which the "dim and deceptive outline" is entitled. The Christ of *Paradise Regained* is no more susceptible to interpretation in strictly human terms — that is, he cannot be expected to represent *ac-*

curately anything with which the audience is truly familiar—than the Christ of *Paradise Lost* described above in the war in heaven. This is a fact which most of the invidious criticism of Christ does not take into account. Christ must be interpreted but he must also be accorded the immunity that Milton would have expected from an audience steeped in classical rhetoric. If he is not given this immunity, then those criteria by which Milton proposes he be judged become completely inverted: his obedience, mere obsequiousness; his ability to endure humiliation, mere pusillanimity; his ability to suffer, mere masochism.

II

Because Milton's poetics are essentially visionary, they are not what Yvor Winters, writing about poets for whom rhetorical process was an approach to truth, termed forms of discovery.[12] They are rather forms of embodiment. Vision, whether intuitive or revealed, is prior to form, which can only express, never reveal, prelinguistic insight. The poem, then, is formal statement, the realization in time and words of a truth which, for Milton, frequently transcends both time and the iron gates of discursive reason. Multivocality, ambiguity, and irony, which were process and purpose for those humanist poets who swam in the mainstream of the Renaissance rhetorical tradition, if not altogether missing in Milton's late poems, were not part of a pattern of intended effect. The notion that *Samson Agonistes* "is a recapitulation of Milton's own progress as a wayfaring Christian"[13] may be in disrepute, yet it may not be so far wide of the mark to see the Christ in *Paradise Regained* as the wayfaring Christian that Milton would have liked to be; in his brief epic Milton's "instinctive emphasis seems to be, like that of the Cambridge Platonists, on the imitation of Christ."[14] *Paradise Regained* embodies in poetic form the same vision which, more or less systematically, informs *De doctrina Christiana*.

Milton's christological model cannot be supposed to be in perfect accord with the hero of *Paradise Regained* because of the difficulty involved in converting a complex abstraction into a plausible character. But several passages from *De doctrina* are germane to the problem of representation. That Milton was convinced that the two elements of Christ's nature formed a unitary being is illustrated by the following:

Hence the union of two natures in Christ must be considered as the mutual hypostatic union of two essences; for where there is a perfect substantial essence, there must also be an hypostasis or subsistence, inasmuch as they are the same thing; so that one Christ, one ens, one person, is formed of this mutual hypostatic union of two natures or essences.[15]

A philosophical monist, Milton maintains that neither of these elements is obliterated by the union and that both are, presumably, capable of separate expression. He extends this idea by observing:

Inasmuch, however, as the two natures constitute one Christ, certain particulars appear to be predicated of him absolutely, which properly apply to one of his natures. This is what is called *communicatio idiomatum* or *proprietatum*, where by the customary forms of language what is peculiar to one of two natures is attributed to both jointly. (YP VI, p. 279)

And he concludes this part of his discussion by remarking on the converse situation: "It sometimes happens, on the other hand, that what properly belongs to the compound nature of Christ, is attributed to one of his natures only I Tim. 11.5. 'One Mediator between God and man, the man Christ Jesus.' Now he is not mediator inasmuch as he is man, but inasmuch as he is *Theanthropos*" (YP VI, p. 279).

Could Christ be presented strictly according to the preceding formulas, he would, at all times, be depicted as *theanthropos*, that is, a unified creature both qualitatively superior to man and qualitatively different from his own divinity, as this divinity is conceived as prior to and separate from his incarnated form. Certain of his actions, however, could be attributed to either one or the other aspect of his nature, or, less artificially, to his nature conceived as a whole. The actions that could be ascribed to his divine element would be those which exceeded human powers, whereas his human element would seem implicated in those actions which were characteristically manlike.

Using this hypothesis, we would almost be able to resolve the problem of Christ's nature quantitatively; we would simply tally the divine actions, tally the human actions, subtract the lesser from the greater sum, and state our conclusions, preferably in the form of an equation. But there is another variable, a variable which causes *theanthropos* to assume more human characteristics, and that is the concept of *kenosis*. "For after having 'emptied himself' he might," observes Milton, "'increase in wisdom,' Luke ii.52 by means of the understanding which he previously possessed, and might 'know all things,' John xxi.17 namely, through the teaching of the Father, as he himself acknowledged" (YP VI, p. 275). This implies that Christ can increase his knowledge and understanding to a certain theoretical maximum, commensurate with his identity as *theanthropos*, through the tutelage of the Father, which can be, we may assume, either internal or external.

This very human state of not knowing, combined with an ability to know more, obscures the distinction between the two elements of his nature. Indeed, the fact that Christ does not know how best to "publish his Godlike office," the details of his future life, or why he is in the "waste Wilderness," has been the cornerstone of interpretations in which the Christ of *Paradise Regained* is viewed primarily as a man. The assumption implicit in these interpretations is that in order for Christ to be divine he must be virtually omniscient, but this reasoning makes Christ's status as *theanthropos* depend upon the quantity of information he possesses, a very modern notion and a very un-Miltonic one. As the poem makes clear, it is the quality of the will that defines a being's status in the great scheme of things. Christ's antagonist would, no doubt, have been a magnificent scholar, but Milton meant us to decry the corruption of his will, not to admire his intellectual inventiveness. For *Paradise Regained*, if it celebrates anything, celebrates the perfected will.

Some sense of Milton's christology is a useful propaedeutic to reading both of his epics. But what is especially significant for this study is the consonance between Milton's theology and the canons of representation discussed above; Christ is representationally precisely the same being he is theologically. Commenting on the hypostasis, Milton declares, "the mode of union is unknown to us; and it is best to be ignorant of what God wills should remain unknown" (YP VI, p. 271). Similarly, as aesthetic object, Christ must not be scrutinized too closely, that is, from a vantage point which is too near. The irreducible residuum of mystery adhering to Christ requires that his audience "stand back," grasping his character in its broad outlines. There is, of course, an element of paradox here, for the doctrine of the hypostasis mandates one audience perspective, while the concept of *kenosis* demands quite another.

III

Milton was the heir and last example of the Platonic strain of humanist rhetorical culture. That he believed that the *doxa* of Christianity, particularly the *paradoxa* of Christ's nature, could be convincingly expressed through literary discourse was but a minor optimism in comparison to his deeply held faith in the efficacy of poetic form. For Milton, form, in which thought and speech stood in the perfect equipoise that Cicero posits in the *Orator*, could embody truth in such a way as to reform the wills of his audience, repairing "the ruins of our first parents."[16] Renaissance rhetorical culture, of course, was not monolithic, and Milton had a lifelong instinct for avoiding centrist positions. Almost from its inception rhetorical discourse, never wholly dissociated from its parent discipline, philosophy, developed, or more probably conserved, a set of dichotomous terms through which its practitioners viewed the world:

practical, speculative; *vita activa, vita contemplativa* — antitheses we might distinguish as Isocratean and Platonic. Although Cicero, the rhetorician Renaissance humanists most admired, was able to balance these oppositions in his work, Milton was not. In actualizing the contemplative possibilities of form, he negated the competing view of form as action; in seeing the conceptual potentials of form, he overlooked its verbal potentials. Rhetoric for Milton was an instrument of persuasion rather than an instrument of inquiry.[17] It is ironic, then, that Milton, whose poetry is, in one sense, so unrhetorical, should appropriate the mode of thought which was at the heart of humanist rhetoric, the argument *in utramque partem*, to solve the artistic problem of depicting Christ. Joel Altman has argued that Renaissance plays "literally were questions or rather the fictional realizations of questions."[18] Though this cannot reasonably be said of *Paradise Regained*, it can be said of its protagonist. To revert to Aristotle's analogy, Milton required a technique which would allow him to move his audience farther from or closer to the scene he was painting and to balance these perspectival shifts in such a way as to produce the illusion of *theanthropos*. Arguing both sides of a question implies two capacities: to change perspectives and to look in two directions at once. Thus the technique of arguing *in utramque partem* allowed Milton to keep the audience's eyes on two ontologically distinct realms, while he brought these realms into just the right focus to persuade them of the truth of his story.

Clearly not all matters can be argued *in utramque partem*, at least not with equal success. This particular treatment is appropriate for a certain type of matter which in the context of philosophical discourse was called the indefinite question (*quaestio indefinita*). It "may be argued from either side (*in utramque partem*) without reference to specific persons or circumstances."[19] Viewed in this context, D. C. Allen's theory that Christ "crosses and recrosses the boundary between the two persons," although it is finally misleading, provides a suggestive description of a larger movement in the poem, which corresponds to the argument *in utramque partem* translated into a form suitable to literary discourse.[20] The resources of rhetorical *controversia*, then, provided Milton with the ability to "argue" on both sides of the question of Christ's nature and to guide the argument to the conclusion of his choosing, while the unique characteristics of literary discourse enabled him to maintain a viable interaction between the generic proposition and the specific circumstances of the poem.[21] Considered solely as subject matter, Christ's nature is susceptible to discussion using such terms as *hypostatic union* and *God-man*, but when this concept is subjected to the exigencies of verisimilar representation and is plunged into "circumstances of place and time, motives, means, incidents, acts, instruments, [and] speeches,"[22] this idea, transformed into character, can only be realized by some form of alternating presentation.

It is precisely this, a mode of alternating presentation, that the argument *in utramque partem* supplied to Milton. But, before he could use it, he had to translate it into a form appropriate to the specific requirements of his poetic context, for the standard argumentative process, regardless of whether the subject matter belongs to the province of rhetoric or philosophy, requires a simple proposition, such as A equals B, and admits the possibility that the converse of the first proposition, A does not equal B, may be the truer statement; these two propositions comprise the two sides to a given question. The question of Christ's nature could be simply phrased, "Is Christ *theanthropos?*" Even if we exclude Satan, whose fondness for eristic disputation makes him an unreliable source, each of the two possible answers is supported by one of the characters in the rich multiplicity of perspectives the poem vouchsafes us. However, the most interesting and important function of the argument *in utramque partem*, although obviously related to the propositions implicit in the aforementioned question, occurs at the level of what I would call the poem's meta-argument. Milton resolves the concept *theanthropos*—a paradox to logical thinking—into two simpler propositions: Christ is a man or A equals B and Christ is God or A equals C. Unlike the propositions which form the basis of the standard argumentative process, these two statements, having been adapted to the requirements of the poem, lack their logical opposites. A equals B, then, becomes the obverse of A equals C, forming, as it were, the two poles of a single entity or the two sides of the question. It would have been ideal if literary discourse had contained within itself the possibility for A to equal B and C simultaneously but, since this was neither a logical nor a representational possibility, Milton was obliged to shift the argument from the proposition that Christ is God to the proposition that Christ is man and back again; in this manner a composite picture is created in which A equals B and C. Christ does not "cross and recross" anything; rather he is depicted, often in rapid succession, from shifting points of view.

The function, then, of the argument *in utramque partem* in *Paradise Regained* seems to be to articulate in sequence the celestial and human components of the nature of Christ, for although Christ is at all times a unitary being, it is obvious that different scenes emphasize different aspects of his constitution. Hence, Christ is depicted in the poem by an

argumentative pendulum, so to speak, which swings through the regions
of the divine, the human, the divine, a movement which also occurs on
the level of poetic detail.

Two approximately parallel passages, which illustrate this movement at the structural level of the poem and form parentheses, so to speak,
around the presentation of Christ, are the Father's speech ending in the
celestial measures of the angelic choir early in Book I, and the angelic
song which closes the action near the end of Book IV. Notice how their
larger function is also maintained on the smaller scale of their own interior movement:

> Gabriel, this day by proof thou shalt behold,
> Thou and all Angels conversant on Earth
> With man or men's affairs, how I begin
> To verify that solemn message late,
> On which I sent thee to the Virgin pure
> In *Galilee*, that she should bear a Son
> Great in Renown, and call'd the Son of God;
> Then told'st her doubting how these things could be
> To her a Virgin, that on her should come
> The Holy Ghost, and the power of the highest
> O'er-shadow her: this man born and now upgrown,
> To show him worthy of his birth divine
> And high prediction, henceforth I expose
> To Satan; let him tempt and now assay
> His utmost subtlety, because he boasts
> And vaunts of his great cunning to the throng
> Of his Apostasy; he might have learnt
> Less overweening, since he fail'd in *Job*,
> Whose constant perseverance overcame
> Whate'er his cruel malice could invent.
> He now shall know I can produce a man
> Of female Seed, far abler to resist
> All his solicitations, and at length
> All his vast force, and drive him back to Hell,
> Winning by Conquest what the first man lost
> By fallacy surpris'd. But first I mean
> To exercise him in the Wilderness;
> There he shall first lay down the rudiments
> Of his great warfare, ere I send him forth
> To conquer Sin and Death the two grand foes,
> By Humiliation and strong Sufferance:
> His weakness shall o'ercome Satanic strength
> And all the world, and mass of sinful flesh;

> That all the Angels and Ethereal Powers,
> They now, and men hereafter, may discern
> From what consummate virtue I have chose
> This perfect Man, by merit call'd my Son,
> To earn Salvation for the Sons of men.   (I, 130–67)

In this passage the Father presents Christ first as a divinely conceived being, a "Son of God," then simply as a man "far abler to resist" Satan's "solicitations" than Job, uniting the two by closing with "perfect man." The angels, in the lines which conclude the quoted passage, continue this theme, chanting their praises to the "Son of God," which returns our focus to the point from which the speech began. The pendulum of the argument swings from Christ's humanity, "this man born" (140) to the next line in which "his birth divine" is emphasized; thus one aspect, then the other aspect of Christ's nature is brought into relief; he is alternately "a man of female Seed" (150–51) and the conqueror designate of sin, death, and the devil. This passage indicates that Christ has a dual nature, but ends on a note which places him in a heavenly context and underscores his divinity. If we look more closely at the second half of the Father's speech, lines 150 to 167, we will notice that, though the Father emphasizes man, it is a man so extraordinary that he transcends every dimension of manliness that human audiences are likely to be familiar with. Job, we recall, was an upright and innocent man, a man who overcame Satan and of whom God said, "there is none like him in the earth." What the Father is asserting, then, is his ability to create a "man" greater than the greatest of earthly men. We would be left to confront the unintelligible had not Milton deftly shifted back to a more familiar definition of man. The Father, in reaffirming his intention to expose this man, implies that this "man of female Seed" still needs some experience before his agon with sin and death. "Exercise," no doubt, for Milton's audience would still have carried a strong secondary sense of "to practice." Despite the subtle internal oscillations in this passage, we are left squarely in the realm of the divine.

The second passage proceeds in the opposite direction in that it begins with an affirmation of Christ's divinity, "True Image of the Father, whether thron'd / In the bosom of bliss, and light of light / Conceiving," and then addresses his humanity:

> or remote from Heaven, enshrin'd
> In *fleshly Tabernacle*, and *human form*,
> *Wand'ring the Wilderness*, whatever place,
> Habit, or state, or motion, still expressing

The Son of God, with Godlike force endu'd
Against th'Attempter of thy Father's Throne,
And Thief of Paradise; him long of old
Thou didst debel, and down from Heav'n cast
With all his Army; now thou hast aveng'd
Supplanted *Adam*, and by vanquishing
Temptation, hast regain'd lost Paradise,
And Frustrated the conquest fraudulent:
He never more henceforth will dare set foot
In Paradise to tempt; his snares are broke:
For though that seat of earthly bliss he fail'd,
A fairer Paradise is founded now
For *Adam* and his chosen Sons, whom thou
A Savior art come down to reinstall,
Where they shall dwell secure, when time shall be
Of Tempter and Temptation without fear.
But thou, Infernal Serpent, shalt not long
Rule in the Clouds; like an Autumnal Star
Or Lightning thou shalt fall from Heav'n trod down
Under his feet: for proof, ere this thou feel'st
Thy wound, yet not thy last and deadliest wound
By this repulse receiv'd, and hold'st in Hell
No triumph; in all her gates *Abaddon* rues
Thy bold attempt; hereafter learn with awe
To dread the Son of God: hee all unarm'd
Shall chase thee with the terror of his voice
From thy demoniac holds, possession foul,
Thee and thy legions; yelling they shall fly,
And beg to hide them in a herd of Swine,
Lest he command them down into the deep,
Bound, and to torment sent before thir time.
Hail Son of the most High, heir of both worlds,
Queller of Satan, on thy glorious work
Now enter, and begin to save mankind. (IV, 598–635; my italics)

After his humanity is mentioned, the angels return to his divinity, calling Christ "The Son of God, with Godlike force endu'd." In respect to
the poem as a whole, these two speeches form the boundaries which limit
the pendulum of the poetic argument; both emphasize Christ's dual nature and his relation to the Father, although the second speech, unlike
the first, relocated Christ in a sublunary rather than celestial realm.
Structurally, these two passages form the brackets within which the
poem's meta-argument is deployed. Previous to the Father's oration, we
are given reliable information without reliable interpretations. His speech

not only defines what the poem will dramatize, divinity proved (130), and verified (133), but how it will be dramatized. In contrast, Satan's first speech initiates the pattern of willful obtuseness, equivocation, and unilateral debate which, by retarding the narrative, gives Milton ample scope to dramatize both aspects of Christ's nature. It is hardly fortuitous that the real movement in the poem is released and closed by the speeches of divine agents, who look alternately at heaven and earth.

An equally important component of Milton's meta-argument is Christ's soliloquy. *Theanthropos* himself replaces the celestial interlocutors of the previously mentioned speeches; the movement, like that of the Father's speech, is clearly from the human to the divine. Christ's review of his past primarily concerns his progress conceived in human terms:

> When I was yet a child, no childish play
> To me was pleasing, all my mind was set
> Serious to learn and know, and thence to do
> What might be public good; myself I thought
> Born to that end, born to promote all truth,
> All righteous things: therefore above my years,
> The Law of God I read, and found it sweet,
> Made it my whole delight, and in it grew
> To such perfection that, ere yet my age
> Had measur'd twice six years, at our Great Feast
> I went into the Temple, there to hear
> The Teachers of our Law, and to propose
> What might improve my knowledge or their own;
> And was admir'd by all: yet this not all
> To which my Spirit aspir'd; victorious deeds
> Flam'd in my heart, heroic acts; one while
> To rescue *Israel* from the *Roman* yoke,
> Then to subdue and quell o'er all the earth
> Brute violence and proud Tyrannic pow'r,
> Till truth were freed, and equity restor'd:
> Yet held it more humane, more heavenly, first
> By winning words to conquer willing hearts,
> And make persuasion do the work of fear;
> At least to try, and teach the erring Soul
> Not wilfully misdoing, but unaware
> Misled: the stubborn only to subdue.   (I, 201–26)

The next section of the soliloquy is not easily categorized because we cannot be certain of the precise relation between the divine and the human elements in the understandings at which Christ arrives. To become deeply engaged by Christ's uncertainty, however, is almost impossible for us because every element, from the star of Bethlehem to the adumbration of the crucifixion, is entirely unambiguous:

> A Star, not seen before in Heaven appearing
> Guided the Wise Men thither from the East,
> To honor thee with Incense, Myrrh, and Gold,
> By whose bright course led on they found the place,
> Affirming it thy Star new-grav'n in Heaven,
> By which they knew thee King of *Israel* born.
> Just *Simeon* and Prophetic *Anna*, warn'd
> By Vision, found thee in the Temple, and spake,
> Before the Altar and the vested Priest,
> Like things of thee to all that present stood.
> This having heard, straight I again revolv'd
> The Law and Prophets, searching what was writ
> Concerning the Messiah, to our Scribes
> Known partly, and soon found of whom they spake
> I am; this chiefly, that my way must lie
> Through many a hard assay even to the death,
> Ere I the promis'd Kingdom can attain,
> Or work Redemption for mankind, whose sins
> Full weight must be transferr'd upon my head.   (I, 249–67)

The conclusion of the soliloquy, unlike the middle passage, affirms both Christ's divine origin and his awareness of it:

> Yet neither thus dishearten'd or dismay'd,
> The time prefixt I waited, when behold
> The Baptist (of whose birth I oft had heard,
> Not knew by sight) now come, who was to come
> Before Messiah and his way prepare.
> I as all others to his Baptism came,
> Which I believ'd was from above; but hee
> Straight knew me, and with loudest voice proclaim'd
> Mee him (for it was shown him so from Heaven)
> Mee him whose Harbinger he was; and first
> Refus'd on me his Baptism to confer,
> As much his greater, and was hardly won.
> But as I rose out of the laving stream,
> Heaven open'd her eternal doors, from whence
> The Spirit descended on me like a Dove;
> And last the sum of all, my Father's voice,
> Audibly heard from Heav'n, pronounc'd me his.
> Mee his beloved Son, in whom alone

He was well pleas'd; by which I knew the time
Now full, that I no more should live obscure,
But openly begin, as best becomes
The Authority which I deriv'd from Heaven.
And now by some strong motion I am led
Into this Wilderness, to what intent
I learn not yet; perhaps I need not know;
For what concerns my knowledge God reveals.   (I, 268–93)

The three divisions of the soliloquy cited establish an interpretative norm; other passages may be understood by ascertaining the degree to which they approach or deviate from this norm. For example, the disciples, in the interlude which begins Book II, convey by their expectation that "Now, now, for sure, deliverance is at hand, / The Kingdom shall to *Israel* be restor'd" (35–36), a conception of Christ which is entirely human and which reiterates the first section of Christ's soliloquy, in which he too sees himself in human terms. This sort of repetition is important, for each side of the question must be well argued in order for the fictional realization of the argument *in utramque partem* to appear realistic. Mary's thoughts provide an even more personal commentary on Christ's history and humanity, thereby reinforcing the musings of the disciples. Even the narrator enters the debate by focusing on circumstances which emphasize Christ's human dimension:

Our Savior meek and with untroubl'd mind
After his airy jaunt, though hurried sore,
Hungry and cold betook him to his rest,
Wherever, under some concourse of shades
Whose branching arms thick intertwin'd might shield
From dews and damps of night his shelter'd head.   (IV, 401–06)

This is assuredly a contrast to Christ's assertion of his divinity in his declaration, "henceforth the oracles are ceast." These are the types of balanced contrasts by which the meta-argument progresses and, when viewed in conjunction with each other, they recapitulate the interpretative norm which the soliloquy establishes.

The meta-argument of *Paradise Regained* operates at a conceptual level roughly equivalent to the poem's fictional hypothesis and is realized more or less simultaneously. However, the rapid perspectival shifts characteristic of the poem's general movement also occur at the level of individual speeches, where they tend to reinforce the norms and expectations established by the speeches discussed above. Such a speech occurs immediately before the banquet scene:

Where will this end? four times ten days I have pass'd,
Wand'ring this woody maze, and human food
Nor tasted, nor had appetite: that Fast
To Virtue I impute not, or count part
Of what I suffer here; if Nature need not,
Or God support Nature without repast
Though needing, what praise is it to endure?
But now I feel hunger, which declares
Nature hath need of what she asks; yet God
Can satisfy that need some other way,
Though hunger still remain: so it remain
Without this body's wasting, I content me,
And from the sting of Famine fear no harm,
Nor mind it, fed with better thoughts that feed
Mee hung'ring more to do my Father's will. (II, 245–59)

The first nine lines emphasize Christ's human component, while the concluding lines, which depict Christ as "hung'ring more" to serve his divine progenitor, connect the passage as a whole to the divine context from which all of Christ's actions proceed. Only one line longer than the Petrarchan sonnet, this passage has a strong affinity with Milton's *Sonnet XIX* — a sonnet which itself argues both sides of what for Milton was an important question. Yet we sense here that something is lacking, and it is precisely what a number of critics have suggested: dramatic possibility. For in eschewing a concept of form as verbal action, action through which the poet can arrive at — or, more accurately, create — some provisional truths, Milton also limits the degree to which his audience can become engaged. Visionary poetics do not attempt to keep up with the flux but rather to fix the flux in timeless form, an island in "an unpredictable succession of novel, often contradictory and ambiguous experiences."[23] While Satan rushes about madly in the world of flux, Christ remains "unmoved," never really engaging the sublunary world. What works in *Sonnet XIX* is not as effective in the context of *Paradise Regained;* the "yet" at the caesura is a bit too easy, too confident. Instructing his audience in the nature of true heroism, Milton, as visionary poet, plunges his reader into a curious paradox: as Christ says,

who reads
Incessantly, and to his reading brings not
A spirit and judgement equal or superior
(And what he brings, what needs he elsewhere seek)
Uncertain and unsettl'd still remains,
Deep verst in books and shallow in himself. (IV, 322–27)

If we do not bring with us vision equal to that embodied in the poem, we will not find it. But if we have equal vision, we do not need to read.

Although Milton's unrhetorical approach to truth lessens the drama of inquiry in *Paradise Regained,* he has created a drama of contemplation through which we are permitted a view of what Milton held to be the highest image of human possibility. As D. C. Allen remarks, "the figure of Christ surpasses all traditions of artistic imitation, and it becomes Milton's almost impossible task to illustrate the unillustratable."[24]

University of California, Berkeley

NOTES

1. Longinus, *On Sublimity,* trans. D. A. Russel (Oxford, 1965), p. 13.

2. A.S.P. Woodhouse, "Theme and Pattern in *Paradise Lost*," *UTQ* XXV (July 1956), p. 180; Northrup Frye, "The Typology of Paradise Regained," in *Milton: Modern Essays in Criticism,* ed. Arthur E. Barker (New York, 1965), pp. 439–40; Douglas Bush, *English Literature in the Earlier Seventeenth Century, 1600–1660* (Oxford, 1945), p. 391.

3. Thomas Sloane, *Donne, Milton, and the End of Humanist Rhetoric* (Berkeley and Los Angeles, 1985), p. 269; Barbara Lewalski, *"Paradise Lost" and the Rhetoric of Literary Forms* (Princeton, 1985), p. 110.

4. Stephen Booth, *King Lear, Macbeth, Indefinition and Tragedy* (New Haven, 1983), p. 6.

5. Cicero, *De Oratore, Book III* (London, 1942), p. 64. For an excellent discussion of Milton's christology, see C. A. Patrides, *Milton and the Christian Tradition* (Oxford, Clarendon Press, 1966). Note particularly the table on page 17 in which Milton's view of the godhead is juxtaposed to a range of other formulations.

6. Aristotle, *Rhetoric,* trans. W. Rhys Roberts (New York, 1954), pp. 178, 179, 196.

7. Aristotle, *Rhetoric,* p. 160. Wesley Trimpi maintains that "scene-painting" should be translated "painting with shadows and shading." See "The Meaning of Horace's Ut Pictura Poesis," *Journal of the Warburg and Courtauld Institutes* XXXVI (1973), 5.

8. Plato, *Collected Dialogues,* ed. Edith Hamilton and Huntington Cairns, *Critias,* 107–108, trans. A. E. Taylor (Princeton, 1961), pp. 1213–14 (my italics).

9. Aristotle, *On the Soul,* trans. W. S. Hett (London, 1935), p. 3.

10. John Milton, *Complete Poems and Major Prose,* ed. Merritt Y. Hughes (New York, 1957).

11. Frye, "The Typology," p. 439.

12. Yvor Winters, *Forms of Discovery,* (1967), pp. 1–120.

13. Joseph Wittreich, *Interpreting "Samson Agonistes"* (Princeton, 1986), p. xi.

14. Bush, *English Literature,* p. 380.

15. *Complete Prose Works of John Milton,* ed. Don M. Wolfe et al. (New Haven, 1953–82), vol. VI, p. 269. Cited hereafter as YP.

16. John Milton, *Of Education,* in *Complete Poems and Major Prose,* ed. Merritt Y. Hughes (New York, 1957), p. 631.

17. In making a distinction between verbal and conceptual form I am following

Thomas Sloane, who articulates the difference between the two throughout his book, *Donne, Milton, and the End of Humanistic Rhetoric*. See especially pages 279–83. Sloane's book also introduced me to the idea that Milton represented a decline in the practice of humanistic rhetoric.

18. Joel Altman, *The Tudor Play of Mind* (Berkeley and Los Angeles, 1978), p. 3.

19. Wesley Trimpi, "The Ancient Hypothesis of Fiction: An Essay on the Origins of Literary Theory," *Traditio* XXVII (January 1972), p. 21.

20. Don Cameron Allen, *The Harmonious Vision: Studies in Milton's Poetry* (Baltimore, 1954), p. 118.

21. According to Wesley Trimpi, "Ancient Hypothesis," the "argument" (in the sense of plot or fictional *hypothesis*) of literary discourse developed through the partial assimilation of the "forms of hypothesis" peculiar to the disciplines of rhetoric and philosophy. In this way literary discourse "realized possibilities of analyzing human experience not present in" the other two varieties of discourse (22). The variation in the technical usage of the term hypothesis reflects the fact that rhetoric in its most liberal form addresses questions of right and wrong "in an ethical sense" whereas philosophy is concerned "with right and wrong in an *ontological* sense of true and false" (60). The process by which philosophical and rhetorical discourse amalgamate to produce literary discourse can be likened to what in chemistry is called a synthesis reaction. Thus, philosophy and rhetoric, the reacting elements, unite to form a unique but rather unstable compound — a compound which, moreover, displays a pronounced tendency to decompose into its more basic elements. Further, one element may preponderate in the initial mixture, in which case one element will remain in the environment of the reaction after it has proceeded to completion: if the philosophical element preponderates in this hypothetical mixture, the didactic intentions will be more apparent in the resultant literary production; if the rhetorical element preponderates, the formal or expressive intentions may be more in evidence. This analogy can be related quite specifically to *Paradise Regained* because informing the concrete particularization of the character, Christ, is the proposition: "the Son of God . . . was made flesh and . . . he is called and is in fact both God and Man" (YP VI, p. 424). Since this proposition concerns truth and falsity — ontological distinctions — it is the discipline of philosophy which, returning to the analogy, remains in the poetic "environment" and provides the paradigm (and even delimits the possibilities) for presenting the complex nature of Christ. Finally, it is the inability to ascertain the manner in which and degree to which the generic proposition functions in the presentation of Christ (which must be seen at the level of the argument as a whole) that renders the character and identity of Christ in the poem so problematical.

22. Trimpi, "Ancient Hypothesis," p. 26.

23. William Bouwsma, "The Culture of Renaissance Humanism," *American Historical Association Pamphlets* CDI (Richmond, Va., 1959), p. 11.

24. Allen, *Harmonious Vision*, p. 117.